A REPUBLIC OF EQUALS

JONATHAN ROTHWELL

A REPUBLIC OF EQUALS

A MANIFESTO FOR A JUST SOCIETY

PRINCETON UNIVERSITY PRESS
PRINCETON AND OXFORD

Published by Princeton University Press

41 William Street, Princeton, New Jersey 08540

6 Oxford Street, Woodstock, Oxfordshire OX20 1TR

press.princeton.edu
Library of Congress Control Number: 2019944499

ISBN 978-0-691-18376-3

ISBN (e-book) 978-0-691-18998-7

British Library Cataloging-in-Publication Data is available

Editorial: Sarah Caro, Charlie Allen, and Hannah Paul

Production Editorial: Jenny Wolkowicki

Jacket design: Emily Weigel

Production: Erin Suydam

Publicity: James Schneider and Kate Farquhar-Thomson

This book has been composed in Garamond

Printed on acid-free paper. ∞

Printed in the United States of America

10 9 8 7 6 5 4 3 2 1

CONTENTS

ACKNOWLEDGMENTS

As my father likes to say: "Everyone and anyone can escape the prison of their birth." That's one of his favorite syllogisms. His life was proof enough for him, and he maintains that it would have been impossible without the opportunities afforded by education. After a modest upbringing in an Irish-Swedish family in Boston, he enlisted in the military, played professional hockey, earned a bachelor's degree from a hockey scholarship, received benefits from the GI Bill, and went on to earn a doctorate and have a successful career in the administration of higher education; along the way, he met my mother, who became a preschool teacher and devoted convert to Roman Catholicism. She grew up in suburban Philadelphia in an English-American family who traces their American ancestors back to the 1600s. Despite very different family backgrounds and personalities, they've had nearly 50 years of happy marriage. I dedicate this book to them. Their love and careful investment in my development and education made this book possible.

I'd also like to thank the many other teachers—at all levels of education—scholars, professors, colleagues, friends, and family who have invested in me throughout my life and tolerated and encouraged my devotion to justice.

There are too many to thank, but I want to mention gratitude for the opportunity to study with a few who were particularly influential: Vincent Colapietro, Judith Van Herik, Ken Hirth, Leswin Laubscher, Roger Brooke, Duncan Foley, Anwar Shaikh, Lance Taylor, Carles Boix, Anne Case, Esteban Rossi-Hansberg, Paul Krugman, Atul Kohli, Katherine Newman, and Jesse Rothstein, among other excellent and generous professors and scholars. My mentor, advisor, and co-author Douglas S. Massey has been particularly influential.

I am also extremely grateful to Mark Muro as well as Alan Berube, Amy Liu, and Bruce Katz at The Brookings Institution for hiring me straight out of graduate school, recognizing something in my potential and fostering it over seven years. Fellow Brookings colleagues Richard Reeves, Carol Graham, Neil Ruiz, and Isabelle Sawhill were also encouraging and helpful.

I owe a great debt to Andrew Reamer and others at the George Washington University Institute of Public Policy for their willingness to welcome me as a visiting scholar and give me access to their library resources.

My Gallup colleagues, especially Patrick Bogart and Ilana Ron-Levy, and our leader, Jim Clifton, deserve special thanks for giving me the time and resources to work on this book and enrich the analysis with Gallup's wealth of data and expertise. It would have been impossible to write this book without their support.

A handful of scholars and friends generously reviewed earlier drafts or presentations and helped me make this book better than it would otherwise have been, including Carol Graham, Ashley Jardina, Carles Boix, Scott Winship, Richard Florida, Andre Perry, Richard V. Reeves, Eric Turkheimer, Dalton Conley, Piotr Paradowski, Jim Harter, Julie Ray, Xavier Harris, and Naftali Bean Rutter. Finally, I am grateful and fortunate to have benefited from the support and wise editorial guidance of Sarah Caro at Princeton University Press, the excellent editing of Erin Davis, and the anonymous referees who reviewed early drafts of the manuscript and helped me improve it.

A REPUBLIC OF EQUALS

1

Behind the Discontent

"OUR COUNTRY IS IN SERIOUS TROUBLE," began Donald Trump as he formally announced his candidacy for president of the United States in June 2016. He listed China, Japan, and Mexico as aggressors who are "beating us" and "killing us economically" via bad trade agreements. Mexico, meanwhile, is further harming the United States through immigration, he claimed: "The U.S. has become a dumping ground for everybody else's problems."[1]

In remarks that would be much quoted and criticized, he said:

> When Mexico sends its people, they're not sending their best. They're not sending you. They're not sending you. They're sending people that have lots of problems, and they're bringing those problems with us. They're bringing drugs. They're bringing crime. They're rapists. And some, I assume, are good people.

Trump eventually won 46 percent of the vote in the 2016 U.S. presidential election. His victory followed significant gains by nationalist parties in the European Union's 2014 parliamentary elections, and a shocking vote by the United Kingdom to leave the European Union.[2] In 2017, Marine Le Pen, representing France's National Front party, won 21.4 percent of the vote in the first round of France's presidential election before eventually losing in the second round.[3]

The nationalists seem to have two things in common: An insistence that their countries are declining, economically and culturally, and the identification of external forces as the reason—with trade and immigration being primary suspects. These views are badly mistaken, but the nationalists have a point about the ill-functioning of the economy, and much of the public shares their sense that something important is wrong with their country's political leadership.

This chapter lays out what is wrong and why. Rising income inequality and slow economic growth have been two of the most striking patterns in rich countries during the last 35 years. The explanation is not trade or technological innovation; nor is it mass migration or the rise of global superstars. Rather, countries are becoming more inefficient and unequal because services—which are regulated and controlled by elite associations to the benefit of their members—are taking over the economy, and a small group of elite service providers has managed to secure much of the gains for itself via the gradual accumulation of rights and privileges that elevate this group above markets.

VOTES OF NO CONFIDENCE

In most of the world's richest countries, political discontent reigns. Confidence in government is low and has fallen steadily in recent years. In 2006, 43 percent of residents living in Organisation for Economic Co-Operation and Development (OECD) member countries—the world's 35 richest democracies—expressed confidence in their national government, when asked by the Gallup World Poll.[4] By 2016, that already low share had fallen to just 37 percent of residents. Shockingly, that's lower than the global average of 54 percent.

Confidence has plummeted in a number of countries that have seen a rise in support for nationalist parties or politicians, including Greece, Finland, the United States, Denmark, the United Kingdom, and Austria (figure 1.1).[5] Confidence, which was already low, also fell in France ahead of a strong second place finish by the far-right National Front in the presidential election. Just 28 percent of French residents expressed confidence in 2016. As of this writing (early 2019), a "yellow jacket" populist movement has upended French politics with massive street protests in response to rising taxes on diesel, and according to reports, rising housing and living expenses.[6] In the United States, confidence is only slightly higher at 30 percent.

On the other hand, low or declining confidence in national government is not inevitable in rich countries. In the Netherlands, confidence increased from 43 percent to 57 percent. In Switzerland, confidence went from 63 percent to 80 percent. It is also up and relatively high in Canada and Germany. Extreme political parties have not been as successful in these coun-

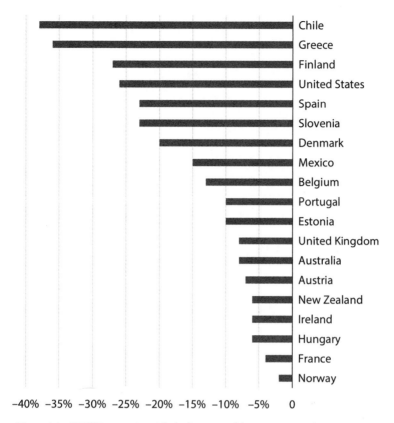

Figure 1.1. OECD countries with declining confidence in national government, 2006–2016

Source: Gallup World Poll, via Gallup Analytics. Chart shows change in the percentage of residents who expressed confidence in their government in 2016 compared to 2006.

tries, with the exception of Germany, where the far-right Alternative for Germany Party (AfD) has gained traction, reportedly, in response to the governing party's acceptance of a large number of refugees.[7]

SLOW ECONOMIC GROWTH, SPREAD LESS EVENLY

Lurking behind the rising discontent has been a major international slowdown in economic growth, or the rate at which living standards increase. The financial crisis that originated in a U.S. housing market bubble certainly

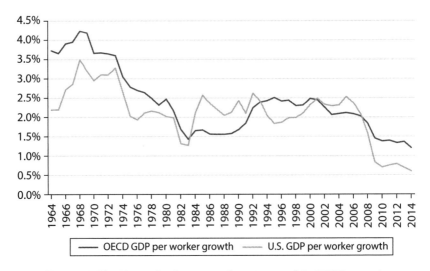

Figure 1.2. The 50-year slowdown in productivity growth in OECD countries
compared to the United States, 1964–2014

Source: Penn World Tables 9.0, Real GDP divided by employment,
annualized growth over ten-year periods.

had a large negative effect, but the growth slowdown preceded that, and in
many ways, the housing bubble can be understood as a desperate attempt to
find profitable investments in a low-growth world.

In 28 of the 30 OECD countries with available data, the rate of growth
has been slower from 1980 to 2014 than from 1960 to 1980. New Zealand
and Sweden were the only rich democracies to avoid this fate. For the average resident of an OECD country, the annual growth rate in gross domestic product (GDP) per capita slowed from 3.8 percent between 1960
and 1980 to 2.1 percent between 1980 and 2014. This can't be attributed to
the aging baby boomers dropping out of the labor force. Growth has also
slowed on a per worker basis, from 3.5 percent to 1.9 percent (figure 1.2).[8]
From 2008 to 2014, annual growth has been particularly weak, just above
1 percent in either per capita or per worker terms. Productivity growth—the
fundamental source of long-run living standards—has slowed.

This means an entire generation has now come of age in a less dynamic society than the one experienced by its parent's generation. Partly because of
the Great Recession, growth since 2008 has been particularly weak, but the
slowdown started even before then.

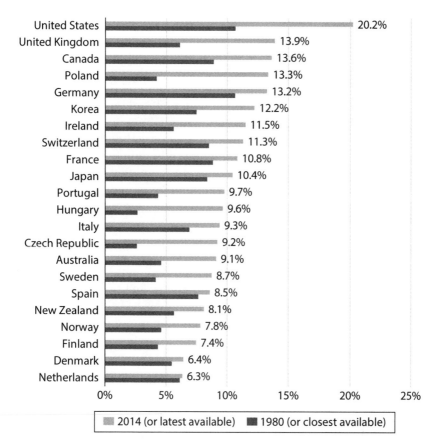

Figure 1.3. Share of national income going to richest one percent in 2014 and 1980
Source: World Inequality Database, accessed October 2018 via STATA program WID.

Slow growth, it must be said, is not a disaster. It is much better than no increase in living standards or, even worse, a decline. For most rich countries, living standards have continued to improve.

Yet, this minimal progress has been undermined by a disturbing trend, famously documented by the French economist Thomas Piketty and his collaborators. The earlier robust round of growth—after World War II—occurred under conditions of falling income inequality, while the latest round has coincided with rising income inequality. From 1980 to 2014, the richest 1 percent of taxpayers took home a larger share of national income in every rich country with comparable data (figure 1.3).

Modest growth, combined with high inequality, results in little to no gains for substantial portions of the population. This can be seen for the United States, which, by all accounts, stands out as one of the most unequal developed countries in the world and has become more unequal over the last 40 years.

The economists Piketty, Saez, and Zucman have used tax records and other public sources to trace where income growth has gone in the United States. From 1980 to 2014, the share of income going to the top one percent doubled from 10 to 20 percent, while the bottom 50 percent of taxpayers (those with taxable income at or below the median) saw their share fall from 20 percent to 13 percent. Average pretax real income for this group increased by only 1 percent from 1980 to 2014.[9] The middle distribution (those between the 50th and 90th percentiles) saw a 42 percent increase, but most of the gains went to the top 10 percent of income earners.[10]

Overall, the weak growth in income for those outside the very top made it difficult to accumulate wealth, according to the data from Piketty and collaborators. In 1980, the bottom half of the distribution had a meager $3,405 in average wealth (in 2014 USD).[11] Wealth for this group peaked in 1992 around $7,000 and declined thereafter—even turning negative during the Great Recession. As of 2014, average wealth was just $349 for this group. More recent data from the Survey of Consumer Finances—analyzed by economist Edward Wolff—shows the same pattern: zero increase in wealth for households in the middle of the wealth distribution. For the median U.S. household, wealth was $78,000 in 2016 compared to $80,000 in 1983, in inflation-adjusted dollars.[12]

Even as overall income growth stagnated for the bottom half of earners, there were notable changes across income sources. The weak positive growth didn't come from taxable labor income—which is the kind of income that shows up in bank accounts and can be readily used for spending. That fell by nearly 10 percent from 1980 to 2014 for the bottom 50 percent of U.S. adults. These losses were offset by gains in tax-exempt labor income—from healthcare and retirement benefits—with modest growth from capital gains associated with home ownership.[13] Thomas Piketty, Emanuel Saez, and Gabriel Zucman put it directly: "The bottom half of the adult population has thus been shut off from economic growth for over 40 years, and the modest increase in their post-tax income has been absorbed by increased health spending."[14]

The falling share of income going to this group has important implications for living standards. If their 1980 income share and economic growth had both been unchanged—a big assumption, no doubt—then the bottom 50 percent of Americans would have earned $26,000 on average in 2014, instead of only $16,000.[15]

Here's another way to think about the scale of the change in inequality: Divide the U.S. adult population in half. Tell the poorest half that they all need to pay $10,000 every year to the richest 1 percent of Americans, those with annual taxable incomes of roughly $300,000 or more. For many reasons, the same people won't be on the top or bottom every year (e.g., income typically rises with age until just before retirement). Still, regardless of who they are in any given year, the rich and poor used to be much closer together, and economic growth used to raise living standards more evenly across income groups. Indeed, Piketty, Saez, and Zucman's data show that income growth was higher for lower income groups than it was for the rich in the decades preceding 1980.

The basic point is simple: Economic growth is less effective at raising the living standards of the masses, when income inequality is high—and a small slice of elites reaps a huge chunk of the gains. That is likely to strike many people as unfair.

Accordingly, levels of confidence in national government could be explained in large part by looking at both growth and income inequality. Between 2006 and 2016, confidence did not increase in any of the 16 OECD countries that score below average on recent growth (figure 1.4). The places with low growth and high inequality saw the largest drop in confidence (15 percentage points on average). The United Kingdom's Brexit vote occurred under slow-growth/high-inequality conditions. However, it was also the case that poor performance on either inequality or growth was generally associated with flagging confidence in government. Thus, confidence fell in France during a period of low growth and low inequality, whereas Donald Trump was elected president of the United States with above average growth and inequality. Meanwhile, confidence in government rose in countries with high growth and low inequality by 5 percentage points. This describes Sweden and Germany.

At the individual level, there is also a very strong correlation between income, financial security, and feelings toward government within OECD countries. When it comes to predicting their confidence in government or approval of national leaders, people's feelings about their income are far more important than their actual income or even rank within society. Gallup World Poll has several items that capture financial anxiety, including whether economic conditions in the respondent's local area are getting better or worse and

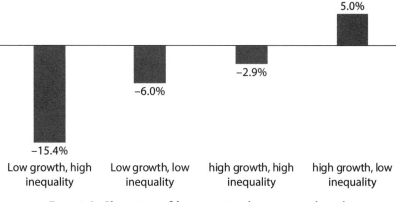

Figure 1.4. Change in confidence in national government, shown by
groups of countries defined by levels of economic growth and inequality,
2006–2016

Note: Growth is measured using GDP per capita from 2008 to 2015; inequality uses
the most recent measure of income inequality.

Source: Gallup World Poll, via Gallup Analytics, World Bank, and All the Ginis (ATG).

whether or not the respondent is living comfortably off his or her household income or having difficulty making ends meet.

The relative income of an individual's household has a small effect in the expected direction. Lower-income individuals are a bit less satisfied with the national government and its specific leader: top-quintile households hold confidence or approval ratings roughly four percentage points higher than bottom-quintile households. Those with lower education also tend to be somewhat less confident in their governments.

Yet, income and education are incomplete measures of financial security. Subjective judgments pick up nuances that are specific to an individual's life circumstances, including wealth, debts, the strength of supportive family ties, expectations for the near future, and political views that may bias their interpretation of the economy. More-anxious individuals are much less satisfied with government. A standard deviation increase in financial anxiety predicts a 16 and 18 percentage point drop in approval and confidence, respectively.[16]

The upshot is that even middle-class and affluent households are likely to turn against a government when they feel their financial conditions are becoming difficult, particularly if others seem to be gaining at their expense and they are dissatisfied with their living standard. Rising inequality and slow growth make that dissatisfaction more likely.

I agree with a number of scholars who have argued that slow growth in an unequal society is corrosive to politics, but the details of the argument are important.[17] Rising inequality in a growing society might come from superstar innovators, entrepreneurs, and performers, and one might argue they deserve to be rich, because their skills generate value for everyone. Yet, while that has happened, it does not accurately describe the last several decades, which have been characterized by low growth. The actual circumstances of weak growth and rising disparity indicate that something is fundamentally out of sorts. It may be that the process that leads to slow growth is making a small elite rich and hindering opportunities for a wide swath of the population.

Thus, figuring out the causes of both slow growth and rising inequality has enormous implications for what, if anything, can be done about them.

THE NATIONALIST EXPLANATIONS: BLAME THE FOREIGNERS

Nationalists on the Right, like Donald Trump, blame trade and immigration for impoverishing the middle class. By nationalists, I mean those who view the world as a conflict between citizens of a national community—usually thought of as those who have ancestral roots going back at least several generations in a country—and everyone else. Trump and some of his allies are also populists in the sense that they view elites—whether in business, culture, or academia—as hostile to common citizens. By contrast, left-wing populists, like U.S. senator Bernie Sanders, evince similar skepticism toward trade and immigration and likewise view elites (capitalists) as acting against the interests of common citizens (workers), but do not suggest the conflict is rooted in ethnic or national identity, and so are not nationalists. I have some sympathy with populist complaints about elite influence on the economy, as the book will discuss, but I believe that both of these perspectives fundamentally misidentify the core problems.

Start with the populists and trade.

Across rich countries, the share of workers employed in the manufacturing sector has declined for two reasons: automation/machines do much of the work once performed by human hands, and much of the work that still is more efficiently done by humans can be done far more cheaply in developing or middle-income countries like China, Poland, Mexico, and Turkey.

Trade is certainly an important contributor to industrial decline in developed countries. By comparing employment changes across counties and networked groups of counties (commuting zones), economists have estimated that trade with China is responsible for roughly one-quarter of the five million net job losses in the U.S. manufacturing sector from 1991 to 2011.[18] These losses also appear to have led to a decline in the incomes of manufacturing workers, as they took pay cuts or worked fewer hours. For the average American manufacturing worker, the best available estimate of the impact of trade competition on individual wages for workers in highly exposed industries is a reduction of just over $1,000 per year over the period from 1992 to 2007.[19]

Yet, the news isn't all bad. Chinese imports, which ramped up dramatically in the 2000s, did not coincide with a reduced risk of unemployment for manufacturing sector workers relative to workers in other industries that were not exposed to import competition but did face intense domestic competition. By some measures—like risk of layoff or short job tenure—it was actually safer to be a manufacturing worker over the last 15 years than a worker in retail, construction, or even professional services.[20]

More importantly, only about one in 20 Americans work in manufacturing and even fewer in the industries that compete directly with China. The vast majority of working- and middle-class Americans have benefited from cheaper imports, often disproportionately, because Chinese imports tend to compete on the mass market—think Wal-Mart—rather than on the market for luxury goods. On balance, it's likely that imports from China have lowered income inequality by disproportionately boosting the spending power of lower-income Americans, as Christian Brodis and John Romalis concluded after a careful study of consumption data, which proves that trade with China raised the spending power of the U.S. working class—and, to a great extent, all U.S. residents.[21]

The same point can be made by looking at consumption data by income group from the Bureau of Labor Statistics. Families in the middle of the income distribution spent more than their after-tax income, which implies they borrowed money to meet expenses. Meanwhile, families in the 90th percentile saved 24 percent of their after-tax income and so benefited proportionately less than lower-income families from falling prices for goods. It is easy to see how this connects to trade. Middle-income families spend 25 percent of their after-tax income on food, clothing, and automobiles.[22] Families in the top 90th percentile spend just 15 percent of their income on these things.

These goods—along with computers and cell phones, which have seen massive price declines—are precisely the industries most exposed to import competition. In this way, mass imports have resulted in a progressive redistribution of purchasing power. Without imports, inequality would be worse.

The economic effects of immigration are more complicated, but there are no logical or empirical grounds for linking immigration to the rising share of income going to the rich.

In general, immigrant labor has probably resulted in lower incomes for people working in the occupations most exposed to immigrant competition—such as construction workers, restaurant workers, cleaners, and childcare workers—though even this finding is disputed with strong empirical evidence from specific cases assembled by Michael Clemens and Jennifer Hunt, for example.[23] In any case, economists tend to agree that most Americans—including most of the middle and working classes—have seen net benefits, and that is the view of a recent comprehensive analysis from a committee of experts at the National Academies.[24] The benefits of immigration come primarily from two channels: greater spending from immigrants, which stimulates local demand for goods and services, and lower prices for services provided by immigrant entrepreneurs and workers. Immigrants, of course, also frequently start businesses and contribute to innovation, culture, and scientific advances; there the benefits are harder to quantify but are nonetheless important. In these ways, all but a small segment of America's middle and working classes have been enriched, at least somewhat, through mass immigration. The selective immigration of highly educated workers and entrepreneurs—through student or skills visas, for example—has been an even more obvious benefit to the average American.

The downsides of mass migration are not trivial but are not likely to have led to the rise in top income shares. George Borjas, an economist at Harvard, has assembled evidence over decades of research showing that mass immigration has lowered wages of other immigrants and U.S.-born workers with less than a high school diploma—a small share of the population. That finding has been disputed, but it, at least, has clear logic behind it in that employers can reduce wages when many new workers enter the labor market.[25] Even so, the estimated effects are small.[26] The large wage gap between elite professional workers or business owners and those with less than a high school diploma cannot be explained by immigration, and most estimates suggest that U.S. workers with moderate levels of education saw long-run wage benefits from mass immigration.

Aside from creating wage pressure on other less educated workers, many immigrant workers with low levels of education consume more in government benefits than they pay in taxes over their lifetimes, creating fiscal budgetary challenges.[27] Yet, one could say the same about U.S.-born Americans with low levels of education, as the National Academies report shows.[28] The fact is that undereducated immigrants are a lower fiscal burden than undereducated U.S.-born residents. For both populations, the net effect reflects, in part, the fact that the U.S. government typically runs a large budget deficit for political reasons entirely unrelated to immigration. If one makes the reasonable assumption that an additional immigrant does not increase the costs of pure public goods like national defense, then the average immigrant—especially those with higher educational levels—has had a net positive effect on government finances.

The favorable long-term effects of immigration are consistent with the most comprehensive analysis ever of intergenerational mobility. Using data from millions of tax records and the Census, economists from Harvard and the Census Bureau found that Hispanics living in the United States have high rates of relative intergenerational income mobility, such that incomes are converging with non-Hispanic white people.[29] The children of Asian immigrants, meanwhile, are earning more as adults than non-Hispanic white children raised with similar family incomes.

Neither an increase in immigrants from Latin America nor an increase in imports from China can explain the rise of incomes at the top. As we will see, people in the manufacturing sector—including the executives who would have benefited the most from offshoring production—make up a tiny fraction of the one percent. Likewise, immigrants lacking college degrees rarely comprise a substantial share of workers at the international corporations that pay top executives, nor at hedge funds, law firms, and physicians' offices.

Data across rich democracies tell the same story: OECD countries that are more exposed to immigration or trade are no more unequal and no more likely to have become more unequal since 1980. Whether one measures exposure to immigration as the foreign-born share of population in 2015 or the change in the foreign-born share from 1990 to 2015, neither is significantly correlated with the level and change in the top one percent's income shares. Trade exposure can be measured in a variety of ways (e.g., average tariff rates, the trade balance as a share of GDP, changes in the trade balance, or a "trade freedom index"), but none of them is even moderately correlated with the level or change in the top one percent's income shares, except that countries with higher tariff rates—and hence less exposure to globalization—have significantly higher inequality.[30]

THE CONVENTIONAL LEFT-LEANING VIEW: IT'S CORPORATE GREED

U.S. senator Bernie Sanders ran for president in 2016 and nearly won the Democratic Party primary. As a self-described democratic socialist, Sanders is concerned about income inequality and documents the rise of inequality in the United States on his campaign website.[31] It's the top issue on his list, and on his list of policy solutions, the first starts as follows: "Demanding that the wealthy and large corporations pay their fair share in taxes." In fact, other than changing trade deals, his primary solutions for reducing inequality seem to focus on three ideas: higher taxes on corporate profits, an increased minimum wage, and encouraging workers to join unions.

At bottom, this view has one explanation in mind for the rise of the top one percent in the United States and other countries: increasing corporate power.

Sanders and his aides are far from alone in embracing this view and these solutions to combating inequality. The argument goes that working people lost considerable bargaining power as unions declined in influence over the last several decades—a decline that coincided with large losses in manufacturing jobs, a fall in income tax rates for the rich and for corporations, and an increasing shift in U.S. income to corporate profits and capital. It follows that unions and the federal government are needed to forcefully combat rising corporate power through taxation, minimum wage requirements, and perhaps other regulations.

In academic circles, the lawyer and former U.S. labor secretary Robert Reich has been influential in embracing this view, and he and others have emphasized what is known as the *labor share of income*.

All rich countries keep national accounts. Using a combination of mandatory surveys and tax records, statistical offices keep track of where the nation's money comes from. GDP can be measured as the sum of the nation's income. Take every resident's salary, wage, business, and investment income and you essentially have GDP.

Since the beginning of the field, economists have been almost obsessed with what share of income is going to labor—by which they mean wage and salary income—versus capital—the income earned from asset ownership. Across most countries, the share of national income coming from wages and salaries has declined, and this has led many economists—such as those mentioned above—to conclude that workers are being exploited by corporations.[32] A search of Google Scholar for "labor share of income" finds that there have been 1,480 academic articles discussing the topic since 2000. Writing in the *New York Times*, Jared Bernstein, the left-leaning economist and former aide to Vice President Joe Biden, argues that the underlying cause is a fall in the bargaining power of workers.[33] The International Labor Organization lists technology, globalization, and union power, and, more plausibly, increasing reliance on finance.[34]

There is a logical and factual basis to this perspective, but there are crucial flaws in the corporate power analyses.

First, the capital share of income is nothing like an index of corporate power and worker exploitation. It can change for many reasons. Older people, for example, rely much more heavily on capital income, because many are no longer working, and most rich countries are seeing an aging population. An increase in the capital share of income follows necessarily from an increase in the share of the population that has retired and now lives, at least partly, off savings accrued during their career. The share of U.S. residents aged 65 and older increased from 9 percent to 11 percent from 1960 to 1980 and reached 13 percent in 2010.[35]

Many of these retired workers, who often spent their careers in blue-collar jobs, would be baffled to learn that their union pension income qualifies them as "capitalists" by left-wing writers or politicians. The OECD compiled data on the world's largest pension funds. Many of them were U.S.-based unions. CalPERs manages the retirement accounts of the California state and local government workers. As of 2014, it had $296 billion in assets under management, because California is a very large state with many retired public employees. The New York State Combined Retirement System had another $177 billion under management.[36] Private sector pension funds can be almost as large. The General Motors pension fund has roughly $100 billion in assets.[37] It would be ironic to conflate the value of union retirement funds with "corporate power."

Housing is another big source of capital income. Economist Matthew Rognlie has done painstaking work reassessing the claims that the capital share of income has increased. He concludes: "The long-term increase in capital's net share of income in large developed countries has consisted entirely of housing. Outside of housing, capital's rise in recent decades has merely reversed a substantial earlier fall."[38] In every OECD country except Switzerland and Germany, there are more homeowners than renters.[39] The rise of housing income is not equally distributed, and rising housing prices are a major problem for the middle class and poor, but this is very different from a rise in capital income resulting from business ownership.

Thoughtful analysis by economists Josh Bivens and Larry Mishel at the left-leaning Economic Policy Institute makes a similar point: "An analysis of income shares tells us little about the bargaining position of labor vis-à-vis owners of capital."[40]

A second flaw in the corporate power analyses has to do with the fact that the overall contribution of corporations to the U.S. economy has unambiguously declined during the era of rising inequality. Income from corporations was over 60 percent of national income in the 1980s and 1990s. In the twenty-first century, corporate income has accounted for just 56 percent of national income. At the same time, corporate profits went from 9.2 percent of national income in 1980 to 12.5 percent in 2017 (figure 1.5). Roughly one-third of this increase was driven by profits earned by foreign establishments of U.S. corporations.[41] The domestic operations of U.S. corporations increased their share of national income by only two percentage points from 1980 to 2017, and that share is well below the contribution of corporate profits in the 1960s and 1970s, when unionization rates were much higher and the income distribution more equal. Considering that the top 1 percent of income earners increased their share of income by 10 percentage points since 1980, corporate profits—whether foreign or domestic in origin—could not have accounted for more than a third of the increase, even if all the profits went to the top one percent. In fact, 64 percent of income from stocks goes to the top one percent.[42]

Third, as we will see, the sectors that generate the vast majority of top earners—including finance, healthcare, and professional services—were never meaningfully unionized, so the decline in unionization—largely a manufacturing phenomenon—could not have any direct effect on the incomes of most top earners.

Fourth, while capital income disproportionately goes to the rich and very rich, during the most important period of rising income inequality in the United States—1980 to 2000, when 80 percent of the top one percent's gains

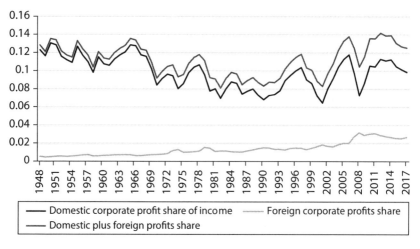

Figure 1.5. Corporate profits by domestic and foreign status as a share of national income, 1948–2017

Source: Author analysis of U.S. Bureau of Economic Analysis, "Table 1.13. National Income by Sector, Legal Form of Organization, and Type of Income," https://www.bea.gov/ (accessed June 20, 2019).

occurred—most of the gains to the top one percent (70 percent) came from labor compensation, not capital income, according to evidence compiled by Piketty, Saez, and Zucman.[43] While capital income has contributed to rising income shares of the top one percent during the early twenty-first century, it increasingly goes to homeowners and noncorporate businesses, which include entities such as hedge funds, law firms, physician's offices, and hospitals. While capital income accounts for 56 percent of the income going to the top one percent, just 25 percent of total top one-percent income comes from stocks as of 2014, which is down slightly from 1980.[44]

Fifth, tax policies won't solve the inequality problem. I agree with Senator Sanders that the rich have seen a decrease in tax rates in recent decades, and I agree with him that increasing the progressivity of tax rates would benefit lower-income groups and be a reasonable way to rebalance federal budget obligations, but it is difficult to find empirical evidence that pretax income inequality rose principally as a result of declining tax rates. Top marginal tax rates on personal income were very high after World War II, but started declining in the 1960s, long before the rise in inequality. It's true that tax rates fell still further in the 1980s, but they went up again in the 1990s, even as labor income became more unequally distributed. A progressive income tax is, I believe, a fair way to distribute the burden of paying for government services, but it won't solve the more fundamental issues of differences in economic opportunity and access to markets.[45]

Finally, the corporate power story also risks exaggerating the importance of the mega-rich. To be at the 90th percentile of U.S. income earners in 2014, you needed $124,000 in total pretax income (taxable plus tax exempt) or $88,600 to be in the top 10 percent in labor income. To be in the top one percent, you needed $477,500 in total income or $268,937 in labor income. To be in the top 0.1 percent, you needed $2 million in total income or $0.95 million in labor income. The top ten percent gained 12.8 percentage points of total income from 1980 to 2014. Of all that money 25 percent went to those in the top 90 to 99 percent (so not even the top one percent), 30 percent went to those in the top 99 to 99.9 percent, and 45 percent went to the top 99.9 percent. A large number of elite professionals have salaries that fall in between $88,600 and $950,000, and many of them own publicly traded stocks and noncorporate businesses. Most of U.S. income growth since 1980 went to this group.[46]

Don't get me wrong—the mega-rich have contributed greatly to rising income inequality, but so did the upper middle class, as my friend Richard Reeves of The Brookings Institution has argued, and at least some of the mega-rich, like the superstar entrepreneurs, have generated value for large numbers of people.[47]

THE CONVENTIONAL RIGHT-LEANING VIEW: TO EVERYONE WHO HAS, MORE WILL BE GIVEN

A widely accepted view among academic economists is that the top one percent's growing share of income is largely a result of the way skills interact with technology. In one version of the theory, people with high skills have always been paid more because they are more productive, but information technology has magnified the value of complex cognitive skills (meaning job tasks that involve specialized knowledge, creativity, and abstract thinking) and lowered the value of performing routine physical or clerical work. The reason is that workers who perform complex tasks use technology in ways that increase their productivity and make them more attractive to businesses, whereas some subset of workers who perform routine tasks have had to compete against automated software programs, industrial machines, and user-friendly internet platforms. David Autor has contributed many influential papers to this theory, and in a recent summary of literature, he suggests that the theory is particularly relevant for explaining income differences among the bottom 99 percent of income earners. The evidence for this view includes the well-established fact that the earnings advantage of holding a tertiary degree (at the bachelor's level in the United States) relative to having only a high school diploma grew sharply from 1980 to the present, reaching around 80 percent in 2010 from just over 40 percent in 1980.[48]

A related line of scholarship argues that superstar companies and individuals benefit disproportionately from expanded access to global markets. Information technology has lowered the costs of transmitting information—including ideas and intellectual property—which, in turn, has expanded the market for ideas and enlarged the rewards. A blockbuster book, movie, or architectural design is worth more now than it used to be because content producers can sell around the world to a much greater extent than in earlier decades. This helps explain why certain businesses and individuals can become enormously rich by gaining just a fraction of global market share.[49]

At the heart of this research is the notion that inequality is largely about who does and does not possess valuable skills—or "human capital." As to where human capital comes from, a large literature in economics holds that human capital comes about through investments in education and is not preordained by one's DNA.[50] Yet, Harvard economist Greg Mankiw argues that the earnings going to the top one percent are largely a result of their genetic endowment, and thus, he suggests that the large earnings of the rich may be justified by their contribution to society.[51]

Yet, what this theory misses is that people with not only identical credentials but also identical traits associated with earning power—such as cognitive and noncognitive skills—often earn wildly different salaries, and not as a result of luck, but as a result of working in a specific industry or occupation that over-rewards or under-rewards pay for what are ultimately political reasons related to how institutions affect competition and rewards in specific markets. For example, the average earnings advantage people get from working in the financial or legal industry compared to working in the restaurant industry is almost as large as the college premium, even after accounting for individual talent.[52] If pay differences resulting from skill was the only source of earnings differences, then the United States would be far more egalitarian, as I argue in chapter 3 in detail. For now, I simply want to lay out what evidence we would expect to see if talent alone explained the rise of the one percent and the cross-country and U.S. patterns.

If the theory linking talent to inequality is right, the richest one percent should be largely and increasingly comprised of people who would most benefit from technological change and globalization.

Some of the obvious examples include the founders of massively successful tech start-ups. Certainly, Bill Gates (Microsoft), Steve Jobs (Apple), Marc Andreessen (founder of Netscape and the venture capital firm Andreessen-Horowitz), Mark Zuckerberg (Facebook), Jeff Bezos (Amazon), and Sergey Brin and Larry Page (both Google) are among the richest people in the world, and their companies would not have been possible but for recent scientific and business innovations related to communications technologies. I have no doubt that these founders possess a great deal of skill and talent, and yet there are roughly 1.7 million individuals in the top one percent of the U.S. income distribution. There are less than 4,000 domestic publicly traded companies, a number that has been declining in recent decades, along with the number of start-ups.[53]

Likewise, globalization has vastly expanded markets for professional entertainers such as superstar actors, actresses, movie directors, models, musicians, writers, and athletes. Beyoncé and Bono sell music around the world and are paid a lot of money to perform internationally. No doubt, they are super-talented. The same could be said about global tennis and soccer stars such as Serena Williams, Roger Federer, and Cristiano Ronaldo.

The implication is that if you add global *individual* superstars to executives, high-level managers, and employees of superstar multinational *companies*, you get the one percent. The theory seems to suggest a merit-based view of income inequality—one that may lead some people to feel better about the situation, or if not, to strongly support policies that create a more egalitarian distribution of skills, which I discuss in later chapters.[54]

The merit-based interpretation that Greg Mankiw drifts toward reminds me of Voltaire's character Dr. Pangloss, who was a spoof of leading intellectuals of his day: "All is for the best in the best of all possible worlds."

Those outside the top one percent don't have to accept this story. The superstar theory is relevant for explaining a small number of people in the one percent, but it fails even to come close to explaining the level of inequality in the United States or the trend toward greater inequality. Trade, technology, and talent play relatively minor roles in accounting for the extraordinary income inequality observed in the United States. If the rich consisted only of successful entrepreneurs and entertainers, there would be far less inequality.

THE WORK OF THE ONE PERCENT

One simple way to understand why the one percent earn so much is to observe how they earn their money. Work can be classified into either an occupation—what you do—or an industry—what the business (or entity) you work for produces. Both are important for testing the global superstar theory of the one percent.

Let's start with the actual superstars in the United States.

In 2015, just 0.2 percent of U.S. adults (1.9 percent of top earners) worked as athletes, artists, writers, actors, directors, coaches of professional sports teams, news anchors, fashion designers, or any other occupation broadly classified under arts, design, entertainment, sports, and media (table 1.1). Since 1980, there has been very little increase in the share of people in the top one percent who come from these occupations. This analysis is based on the American Community Survey, which surveys 1 percent of the U.S. population, but the figures match administrative tax records analyzed by economists, one of whom works at the Internal Revenue Service.[55] Accordingly, in 1979 and 2005, people in this broad occupational category comprised 1.4 percent and 1.7 percent, respectively, a trivial increase. This group of people may be super-famous and super-rich, but that is in part because there are very few of them. A key prediction of superstar theory thus fails right out of the gate.

These results are for the United States, but international data suggest that other countries have even fewer entertainment stars among their top earners. Sufficiently detailed data were not available for most OECD countries, but using the Luxembourg Income Study, I found comparable figures for Denmark, Estonia, Germany, France, and Israel.[56] Of these, Denmark has the highest share of top one-percent earners in arts, entertainment, journalism, and sports-related occupations, and that share is just 0.8 percent. Thus, none of the top earners in these superstar entertainment occupations is in the top one percent in any of these countries.

Table 1.1. Share of employed U.S. residents in the top one percent and probability of being in the top one percent by occupation or occupation and sector, 1980 and 2015

	Share of all workers in 1%		Probability of being in 1%	
	1980	2015	1980	2015
Most likely to be superstars				
Actors, directors, and producers	0.3%	0.4%	5.1%	2.4%
Athletes, sports instructors and officials	0.1%	0.2%	2.7%	1.2%
Writers and authors	0.2%	0.3%	4.1%	1.5%
Chief executives and legislators		12%		14%
Most likely to benefit from globalization (trade agreements and falling transportation costs of goods)				
Executives and managers working in manufacturing, energy, and agriculture	12%	9%	6%	4%
Executives and managers working in communications, transportation, and utilities	2%	3%	3%	3%
Medical scientists	0.3%	0.3%	12.4%	2.1%
Most likely to benefit from information technology				
Computer software developers	0.1%	1.5%	0.2%	1.1%
Computer systems analysts and computer scientists	0.1%	1.1%	0.4%	0.6%
Electrical engineers	0.2%	0.2%	0.7%	0.8%
Chemical engineers	0.1%	0.2%	1.2%	3.0%
Industrial engineers	0.1%	0.1%	0.3%	0.4%
Managers and specialists in marketing, advertising, and public relations	2.8%	2.8%	3.4%	3.0%

Source: IPUMS-USA, using data from the U.S. 1980 Decennial Census and 2015 American Community Survey.

THE UNIMPORTANCE OF TRADABLE SECTORS

The other core prediction of the superstar theory of income inequality is that most is generated by technology-enabled globalization.[57] For superstar firms in manufacturing and technology—including Apple, Volkswagen, Royal Dutch Shell, British Petroleum, Toyota, and Microsoft—the international market just keeps getting bigger, and global integration has resulted in lower tariffs and greater ease of doing business across borders. There have been substantial reductions in tariffs over the last 20 years, according to the World Trade Organization, all of which should have created more opportunities for global manufacturing and technology firms.[58]

And yet, if you add up all the executives, managers, scientists, software developers, and other employees in export-oriented sectors such as communications and manufacturing, they amount to a surprisingly small share of the one percent in OECD countries, just 21.6 percent.[59] All of mining, and manufacturing, yields just 16.8 percent, whereas the sector that includes transportation, warehousing, and communications comprises 4.8 percent of OECD countries' top income earners. Agriculture, which is often export-oriented, employs just 2 percent of top earners.

Stated otherwise, nearly 80 percent of top income earners in rich countries are in sectors that do almost no trading across international borders. Nor, as we saw, are they entertainers, media stars, writers, or athletes.

For those thinking that the rise of the one percent is linked to the small but rich portion of top earners tied to global export markets, the country-specific results put that idea to rest. There is a negative correlation between the share of a country's top one percent in these export and technology-oriented sectors and income inequality. In fact, some of the countries with the largest increases in inequality have a very low percentage of top earners in these sectors. These include the United States and Canada, where just 16 percent and 14 percent of top earners, respectively, are in mining, manufacturing, and communications (plus transportation and storage) (figure 1.6). In the Scandinavian countries, the share is above 25 percent, with a high of 31 percent in egalitarian Finland. Denmark is one of the few countries to experience almost no increase in the share of income going to the top one percent, but a relatively high share of its top earners work in export and tech-oriented sectors.

BIG FISH IN DOMESTIC PONDS

The fact is that the majority of the one percent in rich countries work primarily in domestic industries. These individuals are rarely famous and globalization and information technology have had relatively little effect on their business model or daily activities.

Across OECD countries, just three broad domestic sectors account for the majority—52 percent—of the one percent (table 1.2). These are (1) public administration, education, health, and social work; (2) real estate, renting, and

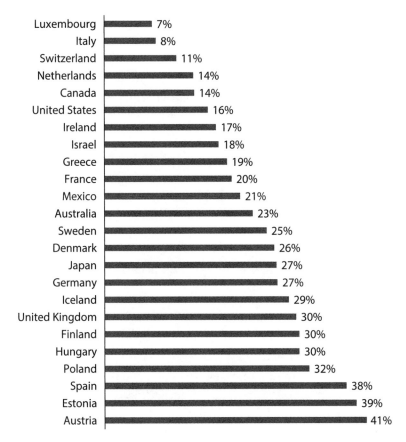

Figure 1.6. Share of top earners in trade-oriented sectors, 2013 or latest available year
Source: Analysis of Luxembourg Income Study. The sectors included are mining, quarrying, manufacturing, transportation, storage, and communications.

business activities—including legal services, and financial intermediation; and (3) finance. Some may argue that financial services are global—and big investment banks certainly have international clients—but exports account for just 8 percent of the U.S. financial sector's value added—compared with 51 percent for manufacturing.[60]

At the national level, Luxembourg, Ireland, the United States, and Switzerland have the highest percentages of one percenters from these sectors, with over two-thirds of the one percent coming from these industries. Finance is particularly important in Switzerland, Luxembourg, and Ireland, but not as much in the United States and the United Kingdom, despite the internationally famous banking centers in New York and London.

Table 1.2. Share of national top one percent in OECD by sector

Domestic sectors

Public administration; education; health and social work	23%
Real estate, renting, and business activities	18%
Wholesale and retail trade, repair; hotels and restaurants	12%
Financial intermediation	11%
Construction	6%
Other services	5%

Tradable sectors

Mining and quarrying; manufacturing; utilities	17%
Transport, storage, and communications	5%
Agriculture, forestry, and fishing	2%

Source: Luxembourg Income Study; 24 countries with data for each sector, covering 85% of the OECD's population. Population data are from Penn World Tables 9.0.

Across OECD countries, but especially in those that are English-speaking, healthcare, education, and public administration are the major occupations for top earners (figure 1.7). In the United States and the United Kingdom, 26 percent of the top one percent come from healthcare, education, and public administration. In Ireland, it's 23 percent, in Canada, 21 percent, and in Australia, 19 percent. So there is a very high correlation between income inequality and the share of the top one percent from these sectors.[61]

Denmark, Finland, Iceland, Austria, and Japan are among the countries with relatively low shares of top earners working in these sectors.[62]

These professional and human services can also account for the extraordinary rise of the one percent in the United States. In 1970, just 47 percent of the nation's top one percent came from these domestic service industries. By 2015, the share had risen to 66 percent. Most of the increase came from finance, real estate, and healthcare, but legal and other professional services also contributed substantially to the rise.[63]

WHAT TALENT, TECHNOLOGY, AND TRADE GET YOU

Having established that the one percent work primarily in domestic sectors that are relatively sheltered from global competition, I turn now to what they do.

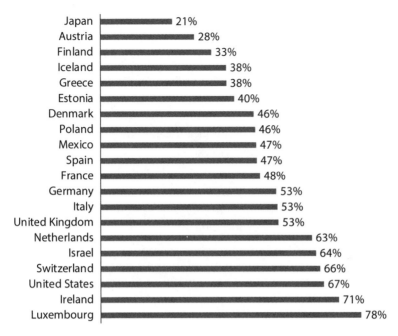

Figure 1.7. Share of country's top 1 percent income earners working in healthcare, education, public administration, finance, real estate, or business services

Source: Analysis of Luxembourg Income Study.

Analysts on the political Left assume that the top one percent are largely executives from publicly traded corporations.[64] In fact, executives are but a small share of the one percent.

In the United States, executives and legislators comprise just 12 percent of the top 1 percent of income earners, according to data from 2015, the latest available at time of writing.[65] In other OECD countries, the figures are similar, even higher. In Denmark, 25 percent of the one percent are classified as managing directors and chief executives. In Austria, 17 percent are classified as CEOs, senior officials, and legislators, and 13 percent are in Switzerland and Israel. In Ireland and Finland, 16 percent qualify; in the Netherlands, 11 percent; in France, 6 percent; in Germany, 4 percent; and in Luxembourg, just 3 percent.[66]

The point is that executives are a small minority of top earners in every rich country. The emphasis on executives of publicly traded companies is understandable in that they are highly visible representatives of the elite, but this focus has perpetuated the theory that capitalism itself naturally leads to massive income inequality, whereas we will see there is nothing natural about it.

To be sure, the share is considerably larger if middle- and lower-level managers—not just executives—are included, as they are very large in number, but this total still amounts to just over one-third of top earners (37 percent) across the OECD countries.[67] The United States is roughly at the OECD country average on this measure in that 36 percent of its top one percent are legislators, managers, or executives.[68] In Canada, the comparable figure is on the high end at 48 percent.[69] Overall, the share of top earners who are managers is negatively correlated with income inequality.

As stated before, most economists and analysts on the political Right assume that talent, technology, and globalization explain the one percent, but that too is contradicted by the occupational data.

In the United States, detailed data on earnings by occupation show that the largest occupational category for top earners is physicians and surgeons, who comprise 14.5 percent of the top one percent. The probability of being in the one percent is also highest for this group. Slightly over one out of every five physicians or surgeons is in the top one percent (21.6 percent) compared with one out of seven for CEOs (13.9 percent).

Under the techno-talent theory of the top one percent, this shouldn't be possible. It would be difficult to think of a professional occupational group less affected by technological change and globalization than physicians. Physicians do not export their services and are so behind in their use of information technology that the U.S. government passed legislation in 2009 to fund and encourage more widespread IT adoption among doctors.[70]

Altogether, health professionals account for 17.7 percent of top earners. Lawyers—who also rarely export their services and make less use of technology than many professionals and blue-collar workers—represent another 8 percent. Another 10 percent work in one of several financial occupations. Combined, one out of every three top earners is either a health, finance, or legal professional.

Workers in STEM occupations—those in science, engineering, and computer programming professions—exhibit higher cognitive scores and are more likely to use sophisticated software technologies compared with health, finance, and legal professionals.[71] Yet, contrary to the predictions of conventional economic theory, only 3 percent of top earners work in computer or mathematical occupations, 2 percent in engineering or architecture, and

Table 1.3. Occupations that represent at least 1 percent of the top one percent, United States, 2015

	Share of total one percent	Probability of being in top one percent
Physicians and surgeons	14.5%	21.6%
Chief executives and legislators	12.0%	13.9%
Miscellaneous managers	9.0%	2.7%
Lawyers, judges, magistrates, and other judicial workers	7.7%	9.5%
Financial managers	4.2%	4.5%
First-line supervisors of nonretail sales workers	2.7%	2.9%
Marketing and sales managers	2.5%	3.3%
Personal financial advisors	2.4%	8.5%
Accountants and auditors	2.2%	1.5%
Securities, commodities, and financial services sales agents	2.1%	11.1%
Sales representatives, wholesale and manufacturing	1.8%	1.7%
Management analysts	1.8%	2.9%
General and operations managers	1.5%	2.1%
Miscellaneous sales representatives	1.5%	2.9%
First-line supervisors of retail sales workers	1.4%	0.6%
Software developers, applications and systems software	1.3%	1.3%
Dentists	1.2%	10.7%
Real estate brokers and sales agents	1.1%	2.0%
Medical and health services managers	1.1%	2.1%
Financial analysts	1.0%	5.2%

Source: Analysis of IPUMS-USA, 2015 American Community Survey.

1 percent in science and social science occupations. So the probability of being in the top one percent is also much lower for STEM professionals than for health, legal, and finance professionals.

Take software development. It is arguably the most in-demand career in the United States, as measured by job vacancy rates, hiring difficulty, and the market value of its skills.[72] Yet, just 1.3 percent of software developers are in the one percent (table 1.3). A number of unglamorous professions have a higher percentage of workers in the top one percent than software developers: financial clerks (2 percent), financial specialists (4.1 percent), veterinarians (3.2 percent), and insurance agents (1.8 percent).

In fact, there were 1.1 million software developers working in the United States in 2015 and 140,000 dentists, but there were approximately the same number of dentists in the one percent as there were software developers (15,000 dentists versus 15,750 software developers). Tech may be glamorous, but you are 10 times more likely to get rich going into dentistry than software development, and over 20 times more likely to be in the top one percent if you become a physician.

This level of detail is difficult to get for countries outside the United States, but available data from the Luxembourg Income Study suggest that medical and legal professionals comprise an important share of top earners around the world, though usually not to the same extent as in the United States.

In Israel, medical doctors comprise 17 percent of top earners, which is close to the 15 percent figure in the United States, but in more egalitarian countries the total is usually less. In Denmark, specialized and general medical practitioners represent 9 percent of top earners. In Germany, medical doctors comprise 6 percent of top earners. In Luxembourg, it's 6 percent.

Legal, social, and cultural professions—which include lawyers, librarians, and entertainers—comprise 18 percent of top earners in Luxembourg, 14 percent in Spain, roughly 10 percent in the United States, 9 percent in Ireland, 7 percent in Germany, and 5 percent in Finland, the Netherlands, and Switzerland.[73] In Denmark and Estonia, lawyers comprise just 2 percent of top earners, versus 5 percent in Russia and 8 percent in the United States and Israel.

Meanwhile, STEM workers represent a somewhat larger share of top earners outside the United States but are still just a small fraction of top earners. Science and engineering professionals comprise 10 percent of top earners in Ireland, 8 percent in Finland and Austria, 5 percent in Switzerland, and 4 percent in the Netherlands, but just 3 percent in Spain and the United States. Engineers comprise 9 percent of top earners in France, and architects and engineers represent 9 percent in Israel, but just 2 percent in the United States.[74]

For those living in rich countries, talent, technology, and trade, as measured by cognitive ability, sophisticated computer use, and work for an export-oriented company, usually lead to well-paying jobs, but rarely get you to the top of the income distribution. For that you need political power, as we shall see.

WHY PRODUCTIVITY GROWTH SLOWED

A conventional explanation for income inequality is that the world's most productive companies in highly competitive industries are generating enormous profits for the "winners" of globalization, while everyone else loses out.[75]

The opposite is closer to the truth. The sectors that contribute the most to the one percent contribute the least to innovation and global productivity growth. Great inventors, innovators, and cultural stars who often become rich while contributing to human prosperity and happiness are rare. Most top earners work in industries that are not objectively innovative.

Over the last 35 years, the least productive sectors of the economy have absorbed an increasing share of productive resources while delivering fewer benefits. That explains the low productivity growth. The most important example is healthcare. In the OECD countries, healthcare spending accounted for 6.1 percent of total national spending in 1980, but 35 years later, it had grown to 10 percent (figure 1.8). In the United States, the healthcare share of national spending doubled from 9 percent to 18 percent over the same period. In other words, residents of the United States, through a combination of tax dollars, business spending on insurance, and personal spending, now allocate 18 out every 100 dollars to healthcare.

This pattern also explains the rise in income inequality. The majority of top income earners work in financial services, real estate, legal services, or healthcare, and these sectors display slow productivity growth. Meanwhile, the highly productive sectors such as information and manufacturing have relatively few top income earners. Even advanced services—such as computer services, software, and engineering—constitute only a small share of top earners.

What Is Productivity Growth?

Conceptually, there are two ways to measure productivity growth. One, which is how most economists think about it, is to compare output to inputs. Output is usually measured as gross value added, which can be thought of as revenue from sales once expenses paid to outside vendors are subtracted. Take a car manufacturer, for example. Its gross value added could be calculated as total vehicle sales less the amount it paid suppliers for metal, glass, tires, and

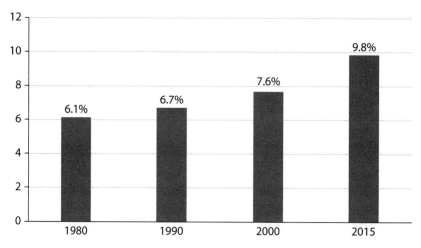

Figure 1.8. Share of national income spent on healthcare in OECD countries, 1980–2015

Source: OECD.STATS. "Health Care Resources: Remuneration of Health Professionals." https://stats.oecd.org (accessed April 3, 2018).

other inputs. The easiest way to calculate productivity is to divide gross value added by the number of workers.[76]

While conceptually simple, this approach depends upon accurate price data. For example, consider a hypothetical scenario in which a new law forbids the construction of new homes in a country with growing demand for housing because of immigration and demographics. House prices would soar, as would hourly incomes of real estate agents who are paid a percentage of the sales price. It would look as if real estate agents had become far more productive, when in fact they had not changed the quality of their services, so the apparent productivity growth would be a mirage. This sort of artificial increase in productivity is generally corrected when government statisticians calculate a price index for the real estate sector that takes this trend into account and adjusts the sector's gross value added accordingly.

Thus, price changes are fundamental to productivity growth, but any changes to quality need to be included too. If the ratio of quality to price increases, either because prices fall or quality increases, there is productivity growth. Another example from the auto industry is the not-yet-released Tesla Model 3, which is being advertised with a price of $35,000. Its features—its quality—are only slightly worse than the Model S, which costs $69,500.[77] Thus, if every consumer who would have purchased a Model S switched to the lower-cost Model 3, the result would be a rise in living standards and economic growth. This has been happening with computer equipment. The cost of processors and other inputs has plummeted in recent decades, reducing the cost of computer devices relative to their computing power. Those who buy computer devices are richer as a result. Productivity growth, therefore, can be measured by growth in the ratio of quality to price.[78]

Inequity and Inefficiency

Both productivity measures—growth in GDP per worker and changes in prices—show declines in productivity growth in those sectors with the most top income earners. The inescapable conclusion is that top income earners are benefiting less from innovation than from inefficiency.

Take value added per worker. As a starting point, consider that from 2000 to 2015, inflation-adjusted GDP per worker grew slightly faster in the United States—22 percent over the entire period—relative to the 15 original members of the European Union (EU 15), where it grew by 15 percent.[79]

In both regions, the growth was driven by advanced industries—including those in manufacturing, computer services, information—which are seeing fantastic productivity increases. In the United States, the information sector registered 151 percent productivity growth over the period. In the EU 15, it was 52 percent. Manufacturing saw 67 percent growth in the United States, and 33 percent growth in the EU 15. As we saw, roughly 20 percent of top income earners work in these sectors across the OECD countries and slightly less in the United States.

Now, consider the sectors employing most top earners. GDP per worker in healthcare and social assistance increased by a meager 6 percent in the EU 15 and just 4 percent in the United States, far below aggregate productivity growth (figure 1.9). In both the EU 15 and the United States, the education sector registered negative productivity growth, −9 percent and −5 percent, respectively, and so did legal services (−3 percent and −13 percent, respectively). Computer services saw rapid growth, but all other professional services brought negative growth to the EU 15 (−4 percent) and modest growth to the United States (5 percent). Meanwhile, finance saw relatively strong productivity growth from 2000 to 2015, especially in the United States, but it is unlikely that this is the result of innovation in financial services; rather, it appears to have more to do with the rising return to capital incomes discussed above, as

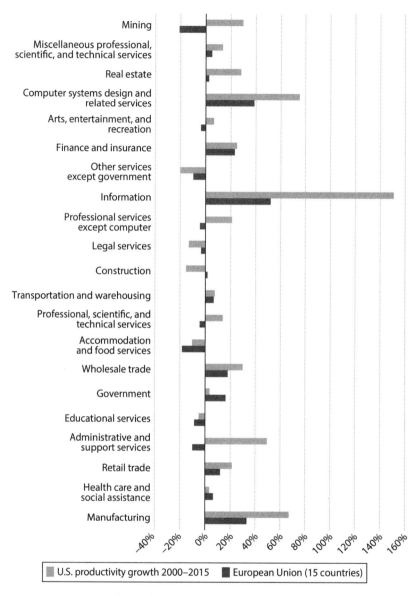

Figure 1.9. Growth in real GDP per worker by sector in 15 European countries and the United States, 2000–2015

Source: Eurostat, Bureau of Economic Analysis.

Table 1.4. Sector-specific price changes relative to total national price changes, in selected OECD countries and the Euro Area

	Germany	Italy	France	UK	Euro Area	United States
Education	0.22	0.05	0.23	1.96	0.20	0.76
Health	0.11	0.16	−0.02	0.20	0.08	0.33
Housing services	−0.01	0.16	0.14	0.22	0.07	0.05
Food	0.02	−0.01	0.02	0.01	0.01	0.06
Clothing and footwear	−0.15	−0.05	−0.17	−0.65	−0.14	−0.39
Motor cars	−0.11	−0.09	−0.15	−0.42	−0.16	−0.37
Communications	−0.55	−0.62	−0.56	−0.36	−0.56	−0.25

Source: European Central Bank, Statistical Data Warehouse, May 1996 to May 2017 price index; values divide item growth rate by overall growth rate. U.S. data is from the Bureau of Labor Statistics for the same period except Communications starts in 1998.

well as factors I discuss in chapter 9.[80] Comparable data for Canada show the same pattern of slow productivity growth in the sectors of the one percent.[81]

Price data show the same pattern. Throughout the EU as well as the United States and the largest individual European economies, prices for education, health, and housing have exceeded total price growth. This means that these sectors are driving inflation and eroding the spending power of consumers and businesses. These sectors are becoming relatively less efficient compared with other sectors, such as clothing, motor vehicles, and communications. Clothing, motor vehicles, and communications services and equipment provide better value to consumers than they used to (table 1.4). The price data suggest that the same can't be said for education, healthcare, and housing.

The only serious objection to the conclusions offered above is that the price indexes don't consider advances in quality. That is not a concern with housing, where quality is easy to measure (by, for example, looking at price changes of the same unit over time), and statistical offices include quality changes. For education, there is no evidence to suggest that quality has improved in the United States and some grounds for concluding the opposite, as the administrative costs associated with higher and lower levels of education have grown sharply.[82] It is possible that there have been modest gains in other OECD countries, but it is unclear if they would be enough to justify the price increases. On the surface, you might think it would be impossible to make education more efficient—to raise the quality relative to the price, but consider online low-cost education services such as Coursera and Udacity, in which highly qualified instructors provide clear technical lessons at a fraction of the traditional cost.

Healthcare is more complicated. The productivity metrics described above arguably miss what really matters—healthcare's benefits to society. Indeed, the benefits of healthcare may be increasing as medical technologies and procedures improve. There is some evidence for this claim, particularly in Europe, where mortality rates, adjusted for age, continue to fall. Certainly, there have been many improvements in treating the diseases of old age through prescription drugs that lower blood pressure, for example, or surgical procedures. Infants are also considered viable at much earlier ages than they used to be.

In the United States, however, the added benefits of healthcare have been very modest relative to the added costs. Mortality rates have not fallen for most age groups, only the elderly and the very young. Subjective health status worsened between 1990 and 2015 for U.S. residents between the ages of 25 and 59, and the share of the population who report being unable to work as a result of disability increased from 4.4 percent to 6.8 percent between 1980 and 2015, after adjusting for age.[83]

Indeed, the best available evidence suggests that most new treatments and procedures introduced since 1976 are actually worse than the standard ones in terms of the ratio between quality and costs, according to a comprehensive analysis by the economist Tomas Philipson and his co-authors Kristopher Hult and Sonia Jaffe.[84] New procedures are usually slightly better than those they are replacing at extending life, but they typically cost several times more per quality-adjusted life year, which is the standard metric for evaluating costs relative to benefits. In other words while patients may live slightly longer, most new treatments are less economically efficient.

Thus, the most likely interpretation of the data described above is that healthcare and other domestic sectors have dragged down economic growth, even as they have been the principal source of income for the very rich.

Economic growth and changes in the income distribution are extremely complex phenomena, which likely have many causes. Some scholars, such as Robert Gordon, have argued that the productivity growth slowdown is a consequence of the fact the Industrial Revolution—with its marvelous inventions—can happen only once in history.[85] Subsequent technological advances simply have not been as powerful. He may be right, and labor economists are likely correct that recent technological change has favored skilled workers, thereby exacerbating income inequality.

Still, these are at best incomplete explanations for slow growth and the extreme inequality found in the United States and, to a lesser degree, other advanced countries. A more complete analysis must consider how political forces shape the economy, including the historic and contemporary institutions that govern markets. As later chapters will discuss in detail, the institutions that govern the domestic service industries are controlled by them—a situation that allows elites to charge extraordinary and uncompetitive prices. Elite professions and some domestic industries operate as if they were cartels. This allows individuals to get rich, while at the same time blocking innovations that would benefit society. As prices rise in these sectors, the purchasing power of consumers is slowly reduced and even undermined.

SLOWING PRODUCTIVITY GROWTH, RISING INEQUALITY, AND POISONED POLITICS

Trends within the United States illustrate how slow productivity growth combined with high and rapidly rising income inequality can undermine democratic institutions. Confidence in elected officials, big business, and the media has plummeted since the 1970s, according to Gallup surveys, which have asked the same questions using the same basic methods for decades.[86]

The percentage of U.S. adults who are confident in Congress was over 40 percent in the early to mid-1970s (figure 1.10). After a brief fall, it climbed back up to 41 percent in 1986, but since 1989, confidence in Congress has never risen above 30 percent, and in recent years it has hovered near just 10 percent. This is extraordinary considering that people responding to Gallup surveys are themselves responsible for selecting members of Congress. The trend reflects an increasingly polarized population. Similar declines in confidence have been observed for other important institutions, such as the press, large businesses, and even public schools. Confidence in the "medical system" has also plummeted from 80 percent in the 1970s to 36 percent today, as healthcare costs have soared.

It would be tempting to dismiss this as a psychological change in attitudes to confidence or trust, but other institutions have remained popular. Confidence in the military has actually increased from 58 percent in the tumultuous 1970s to 74 percent in 2018, and confidence in the police has remained just above 50 percent since the early 1990s—despite recent

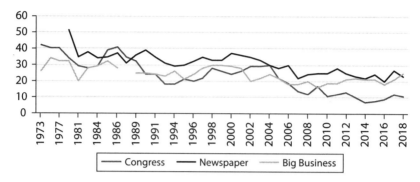

Figure 1.10. Confidence in Congress, big business, and newspapers, among U.S. residents, 1973–2018

Source: Gallup, "Confidence in Institutions," https://news.gallup.com/poll/1597/confidence-institutions.aspx.

controversies. Small businesses are also widely popular (confidence in 2018 is 67 percent) and more so now than in the early 1990s, perhaps because they are often engaged in intense competition with other businesses—including large ones—and often operate on relatively low profit margins.

The fact that falling confidence in politics has coincided with rising inequality in the United States and other developed democracies does not mean that one has caused the other. Yet, I will present some facts that are consistent with the theory that inequality has sapped confidence and, more importantly, undermined civic health.

For instance, there is direct evidence that extreme income inequality distorts politics by giving undue influence to the rich, who can readily outspend the vast majority of ordinary people. There are two reasons to be worried about this: The rich are more politically engaged than the middle and working classes, and they have different policy preferences.

People in the richest income group in the Current Population Survey were 15 percentage points more likely to vote than those in lower groups, according to my analysis of the 2016 Voter Supplement.[87] The situation is even worse, as the political scientists Benjamin Page, Larry Bartles, and Jason Seawright uncovered in a revealing study of the super-wealthy. Not only do the top one percent vote at much higher percentages, they are also extremely engaged in making campaign contributions and coordinating such contributions, as well as contacting their elected officials and attending political events.[88]

As for policy preferences, Page and his co-authors find that the very rich are distinctly and almost unanimously concerned about the federal government's national deficit—which they may view as merely delaying future tax increases—and less committed than the middle class to supporting the welfare state, including public spending on Social Security, healthcare, and education. It is interesting to note, though, that the majority of the super-rich (62 percent) agrees that income differences in the United States are too large.

The differences run deeper, as Gallup data shows by asking people to state the most important financial concern facing their family in their own words. Gallup has done this each year from 2006 to 2018 and received 33,000 responses. The data were recoded into categories afterward by listening to the verbatim recordings.

Stark differences emerge between the rich and the middle- and lower-income classes. The rich, who are much less likely to have any financial problems, are overwhelmingly preoccupied with the future, while the middle and lower classes struggle with current expenditures on things like housing, healthcare, and paying off debts (table 1.5). Among lower-income families, 51 percent of their top financial concerns fell into these categories, but for the rich, these amounted to only 19 percent. These rates were almost reversed for future concerns, including retirement savings, tax obligations, and saving for college, which were cited by 52 percent of rich families but only 31 percent of lower-income families.

Here the connection between lackluster productivity growth and political concerns is clear. Rapid inflation in healthcare, starting around 1980, has resulted in skyrocketing prices, which are born by consumers, businesses, and the government. Healthcare went from 8 percent of GDP in 1976 to 18 percent 40 years later.[89]

What the U.S. dollar is spent on is very different now compared with what it was spent on in the past. Spending has shifted away from cars and appliances, food and clothing and toward insurance, healthcare, education, and shelter. These changes are felt by the middle classes, most of whom rate their personal financial situation rather poorly when asked by Gallup.

Economic inequality played a complex role in the 2016 U.S. presidential election. Republican Party primary voters rejected the proposals supported by the party's upper-middle-class leadership—such as reducing the budget deficit, expanding trade agreements, and making reforms to immigration that would increase legal channels to work and provide a path to citizenship for

Table 1.5. The financial health and most important financial problems facing different income groups in the United States, 2006–2018

	All	High income (income of $250,000 or higher)	Middle to upper-middle income ($50,000 to $249,000)	Low income (below $50,000)
Personal financial situation is good or excellent	47%	84%	65%	28%
No financial problems	15%	25%	15%	12%
Problems meeting current expenses				
Cumulative current expenses	43%	19%	36%	51%
Healthcare	12%	7%	11%	13%
Lack of money	9%	2%	5%	13%
Debt	9%	4%	8%	11%
Housing	7%	4%	7%	8%
High cost of living	5%	3%	5%	6%
Problems meeting future expenses				
Cumulative future expenses	36%	52%	40%	31%
Retirement, lack of savings, interest rates, state of the economy, or stock market	26%	30%	26%	26%
Saving for college	6%	12%	10%	3%
Taxes	3%	10%	4%	2%

Source: Gallup Poll Social Series, 2006–2018. The items are "How would you rate your financial situation today–as excellent, good, only fair, or poor?" and "What is the most important financial problem facing your family today?" Open-ended responses were subsequently recoded by Gallup into various categories. Sample size is 33,464 respondents interviewed by phone via random-digit dialing.

the nation's undocumented residents. Instead, the party's middle- and lower-income base embraced Trump's aggressively nationalist rhetoric about reducing the flow of immigrants by building a wall on the Mexican border, deporting them, and enacting tariffs on imports. They also strongly supported Trump's proposals to eliminate the existing healthcare system and to invest heavily in both the military and in public infrastructure. Republicans with modest and low incomes were much more likely to tell Gallup that these Trump proposals were very important to them, relative to the Republicans with over $250,000 in household income.[90]

Trump was the only candidate except Ted Cruz—the other Republican Party front-runner—to see larger support in low- and middle-income households than in rich households among core party supporters. For every other candidate, rich members of his or her party were more favorable about the candidate than less affluent party members (figure 1.11).

As for the general election, Trump won largely because of success with middle-income voters. I analyzed candidate favorability ratings from Gallup surveys conducted between October and November 2016 and weighted the approximately 33,000 responses by the probability of voting in the general election. Hillary Clinton had much higher favorability ratings from rich voters ($250,000 and above) and low-income voters (less than $36,000). Her margins were 10 and 6 percentage points, respectively, for those groups, but she tied Trump votes in the middle of the income distribution. Moreover, in swing states, Trump had a three-percentage point advantage among middle-income voters, even as Clinton won narrowly among the rich and tied Trump among low-income swing state voters.

THE POLITICAL CONSEQUENCES OF RACIAL INEQUALITY

I believe the multi-decade slowdown in economic growth and the related rise in income inequality spurred mass political dissatisfaction, while draining confidence and trust in national governments, the media, and other once-respected institutions, as conventional political parties, party leaders, and thought leaders failed to devise and implement solutions that would enhance economic growth and allow the gains to be more broadly shared across the population.

Yet, dissatisfaction with conventional political platforms need not have led to a surge in far-right nationalist party popularity—as it has in a number of European countries—or allowed a nationalist Republican Party candidate like Donald Trump to win his party's nomination and the general election.

The deeper political context of votes for the far Right in Europe and for Donald Trump in the United States is that European people and their descendants comprise the demographic majority in most of the world's rich countries and all but a handful of the world's rich democracies. Thus, when citizens in European-majority democracies consider policies such as openness to trade and immigration, minority rights, or access to markets and benefits,

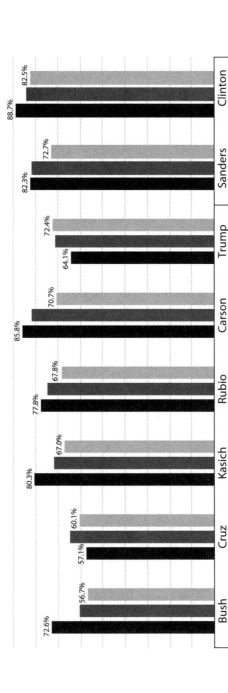

Figure 1.11. Favorability of 2016 presidential candidates in their own party by income group

Source: 2016 Gallup Daily Tracker. Sample size is approximately 113,000 for Clinton and Trump favorability scores and varies for the other candidates relative to their perceived viability at various points in the primary election. Income is defined for the household as low if under $36,000 and very high if in the highest category of $240,000 or more. Everyone else is in the middle- to high-income group. The favorability item response was weighted using both the Gallup weight and in the reported data above using the probability of voting in the 2016 election. To calculate this, I matched data from the Current Population Survey's 2016 voter supplement to Gallup data using race and Hispanic status, educational attainment, age in ten-year bands (after 18–25), and income in three groups that roughly correspond to the groups above.

it is generally from a perspective of relative power and privilege compared with people from other groups.

For a subset of people of European ancestry, many of whom are struggling to pay their bills, the thought of people from poor countries moving into theirs provokes fear of the economic consequences, including whether their governments can continue to meet the obligations of the welfare state, or, in the United States, Medicare and Social Security. There is also strong evidence that issues tied to ethnic differences and attitudes are important in shaping political preferences for nationalism and are largely independent of economic concerns. Here, I will quickly review the evidence.

First, there is virtually no relationship between the probability of voting for Trump or a far-right candidate in Europe and working in the one sector that has been the source of the most upheaval in Europe and the United States: manufacturing.[91] Working in manufacturing is among the least predictive factors of voting preferences measured in large-scale surveys. To emphasize the point further, consider that only 3.5 percent of American adults who hold a favorable view of Trump report to Gallup that they work in manufacturing or production compared with 2.8 percent of those who hold an unfavorable view. Moreover, living in regions of the country that have experienced larger job losses in manufacturing or increased import competition from China does not predict greater support for Trump, as I found in a large-scale analysis of 125,000 U.S. adults using Gallup data.[92] Geography is likewise often seen as an important factor, but county population density is weakly predictive of lower support for Trump.

Second, the relationship between income and nationalist support does not suggest deprivation or poverty is a strong motivating factor for most supporters of nationalist or far-right parties, but those voters are more likely than moderate voters to have missed out on the gains from economic growth. In Europe, 6.5 percent of far-right voters are in the top 10th percentile of the national income distribution, according to my analysis of the European Social Survey, which suggests that they are much less likely to have benefited from rising income inequality than other voters.[93] Likewise, only 27 percent report living comfortably on present income (versus 33 percent of non-far-right voters). Yet, controlling for education and age removes any significant relationship between voting preferences and these variables.

Likewise for Trump, subjective assessments of personal financial conditions don't explain support for him. Republicans—and Trump supporters in particular—rated their personal financial situation very poorly while Obama was president, but that assessment rose immediately after Trump won and remained high thereafter, despite no actual change in prosperity relative to Democratic Party supporters. As the Gallup Poll's former Editor in Chief Frank Newport put it, "[Americans] view their own *personal* finances through the lens of partisanship, becoming more positive when the president is from their party and more negative when he is not."[94] Using more objective data, I find that personal income has a modestly positive effect on the probability of holding a favorable view of Trump, mostly because Trump supporters are much less likely to have low incomes than those who don't support him. Importantly, however, they are less likely to have very high incomes ($240,000 or above) and tend to live in zip codes with lower average incomes, as reported by the Internal Revenue Service.

Finally, objective measures related to racial isolation and subjective responses to survey items about race are important predictors of nationalist support and much more important than income. One of the variables that most strongly predicts support for Trump overall among white people and even for white Republicans is the share of white people living in the neighborhood of the respondent. For every standard deviation increase in the zip code white population share (25 percent), the probability of favoring Trump increases by 12 percentage points among non-Hispanic white respondents. This effect controls for every observable demographic characteristic and several other geographic ones.[95]

In Europe, those who voted for right-wing party candidates in the last election are 14 percentage points more likely to say that European ancestry is an important criterion for immigration policy compared with those who voted for other parties. They are also significantly more likely to say that races differ by work ethic and intelligence.[96]

Many U.S. adults of European ancestry who identify with the Republican Party—which contains both those on the moderate and far right on the political spectrum—report that black people are lazier than other groups (42 percent) or lack the will power to move out of poverty (55 percent).[97] A substantial fraction rate black people as less intelligent than white people (26 percent).[98]

Republicans who supported the candidacy of Donald Trump were even more likely than others in their party to express racial bias or lack of sympathy toward black people. For example, white Americans who reported a favorable opinion of Donald Trump during his campaign for president were 13 percentage points more likely to say that black children have the same opportunities to receive a good education as white children compared with other white people affiliated with the Republican Party, and they were 37 percentage points more likely to hold this view compared with white people who supported the Democratic Party.[99] An excellent book on the U.S. 2016 presidential campaign by John Sides, Michael Tesler, and Lynn Vavreck assembles still more compelling evidence along these lines across a large number of surveys and sources.[100]

For further evidence that racial and cultural differences are important to nationalist politics generally, consider the actual party platforms, speeches, and manifestos of nationalist leaders. Researchers at the Wissenschaftszentrum Berlin für Sozialforschung (WZB, or Berlin Social Science Center) created Project Manifesto, which codes the public documents and speeches of political parties from around the world. The parties they classify as "nationalist," based on these materials, received 9 percent of votes in the most recent elections in 19 OECD countries. The database breaks down political documents by sentence-like fragments and uses country-level experts to code these statements by theme. I used these data to compare the content of nationalist party materials with those of other parities. Strikingly, I found that nationalist parties in the OECD countries are 12.6 times more likely than nonnationalist parties to make statements that immigration is harmful to the national way of life. Such statements comprised approximately 4 percent of all political sentences among nationalist parties (figure 1.12). Other distinctive themes raised by nationalist party materials include a high percentage of statements against multiculturalism and internationalism, as well as statements in favor of protectionism (and so against trade); the nationalist parties were far less likely than other parties to make statements favorable to minority groups or statements in favor of welfare, equality, or education.

There can be no doubt that views regarding cultural, ethnic, and racial differences have a large effect on policy attitudes. Not many generations have passed since European countries occupied much of the world and exerted nondemocratic influence over many non-European people. Likewise, many African Americans living today remember the overt formal and informal prejudice of the Jim Crow era, which waned in the 1960s but lingers in various forms today.

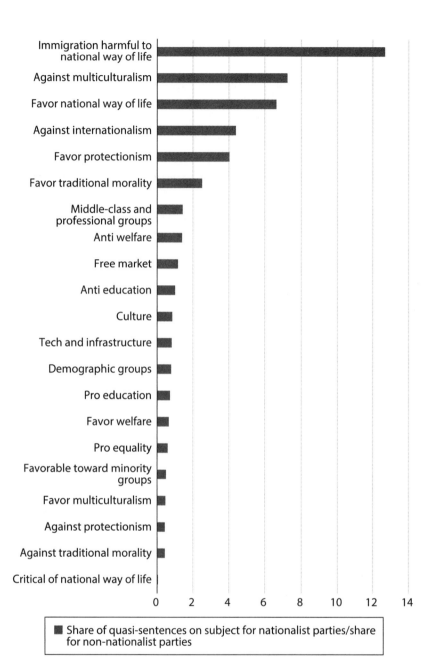

Immigration harmful to national way of life	
Against multiculturalism	
Favor national way of life	
Against internationalism	
Favor protectionism	
Favor traditional morality	
Middle-class and professional groups	
Anti welfare	
Free market	
Anti education	
Culture	
Tech and infrastructure	
Demographic groups	
Pro education	
Favor welfare	
Pro equality	
Favorable toward minority groups	
Favor multiculturalism	
Against protectionism	
Against traditional morality	
Critical of national way of life	

0   2   4   6   8   10   12   14

■ Share of quasi-sentences on subject for nationalist parties/share for non-nationalist parties

Figure 1.12. Share of OECD nationalist party public speeches and documents devoted to various positions relative to share from all OECD parties, 2000–2017

Source: Data from Andrea Volkens et al., "Manifesto Project Main Dataset (Party Preferences)," Manifesto Project Dataset (version 2018b) (Berlin: Wissenschaftszentrum, 2018), https://doi.org/10.25522/manifesto.mpds.2018b.

The inequality in income and social status analyzed in this chapter is inextricably tied to racial and ethnic differences both across and within countries. Across countries, there are massive gaps between the richest regions of the planet—North America, East Asia, and Northwestern Europe—and the rest, and within countries there remain large gaps in social status between those of European or East Asian descent and other groups. Brown University economists Louis Putterman and David Weil have constructed measures of racial diversity across global countries and find that racial diversity strongly predicts income inequality and that people with ancestry from poorer regions of the world tend to occupy lower social status in the countries where they now live.[101] That pattern is evident in Europe, using data from the European Social Survey (table 1.6), and with some exceptions, to be discussed later, it holds for the United States, where African Americans and Hispanic Americans generally have lower incomes and levels of education than European Americans and East and South Asians. In Europe, people with ancestry from a Sub-Saharan African country or region are much less likely to be in the top 10th percentile of the earnings distribution relative to those of West European or Northern European ancestry.

In the United States, the United Kingdom, and Europe, people descended from West African slaves—who were forcibly brought to British colonies and the Americas—still suffer from discriminatory attitudes that affect public policy, the provision of public goods, and access to markets, as later chapters will discuss

Fully 81 percent of African Americans living in the United States say that racism is widespread, according to Gallup survey data.[102] Discrimination appears to be less overt in Europe, but people of African descent are disproportionately victims of it, according to data from the European Social Survey.[103] European residents descended from Sub-Saharan Africans—and especially those who were likely to have been enslaved—are far more likely to report being victims of discrimination based on their race, ethnicity, or nationality (figure 1.13). Roughly half (54 percent) of black people from the United States, Canada, and the Caribbean—as well as those of general West African or Sub-Saharan regional ancestry—report being discriminated against in their country of residence. The figure is high but much lower for Sub-Saharan Africans who name a specific country as their ancestral origin (30 percent), lower still for East and South Asians (24 percent and 21 percent, respectively) and other groups, and negligible for those of European ancestry.

Table 1.6. Household income status and immigration status of European residents by ancestral region, 2016

	Percent in top 10th percentile of national income distribution	Born in country of residence
East Asian	13	12
North European	13	96
West European	10	95
East European	9	92
South Asian	8	32
South European	7	89
Likely African slave ancestry	7	53
Latin American	5	25
Sub-Saharan African	5	17
West Asian or North African	5	48

Source: European Social Survey 7. Sample consists of 20 European countries plus Israel. African slave ancestry determined for respondents who say their ancestry is "African American," "Black Canadian," or from a predominantly black Caribbean country (e.g., Bahamas, Barbados, Jamaica, Trinidad, Haiti), or from the region of Sub-Saharan Africa or West Africa. The post-stratification weight was combined with the population size weight to produce these estimates. Estimates shown only for groups with at least 50 observations.

This is not to suggest that discrimination applies only to those with Sub-Saharan African ancestry. Data from the Pew Research Center show that other groups confront unfavorable views across Europe.[104] These include the Roma, who are thought to have originated in India, as well as Muslims and Jews, both of whom have ancestral or at least cultural origins largely from North Africa and West Asia. When Europeans were asked by Pew about what immigrants want in 2014, the majority of Italians, Germans, and French selected "be distinct from our society" rather than "adopt our customs and way of life." In the UK, 47 percent chose "distinct" and 34 percent chose "adopt."[105]

Detailed evidence from Italy shows real-world consequences of these attitudes. Harvard economist Alberto Alesina and his collaborators gave implicit association tests to school teachers in Northern Italy, which are meant to measure partially unconscious automatic responses to stimuli. They found that 67 percent of teachers exhibited severe bias against immigrants, meaning they were highly likely to associate immigrants with bad things. Teachers with greater implicit bias also gave out lower math grades, even after

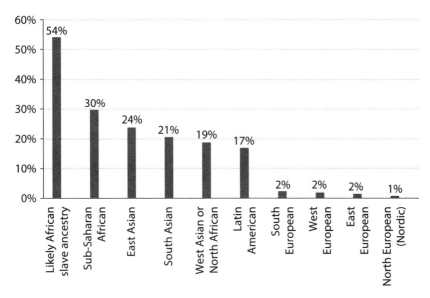

Figure 1.13. Percentage of population living in Europe or Israel who believe they are discriminated against based on their race, ethnicity, or nationality, 2014

Source: European Social Survey 7. Discrimination is based on the following question: "Would you describe yourself as being a member of a group that is discriminated against in this country?" The respondent must answer yes and indicate that the basis for this discrimination is their nationality, ethnicity, race, or color.

controlling for test scores on standardized math exams.[106] In a separate study with Stephanie Stancheva and Armando Miano, Alesina surveyed adults in the United States, the United Kingdom, Sweden, Germany, Italy, and France, asking them to estimate the characteristics of immigrants, including their education, employment status, reliance on welfare, and percentage who are Muslim and Christian. In every country, native residents tended to exaggerate the economic weaknesses of immigrants and their religious differences from the white population. Right-wing respondents were especially likely to make these mistakes, and they made larger mistakes than other respondents, suggesting biased political attitudes distort their perceptions of reality at the expense of immigrants or potential immigrants.[107]

Along these lines, racial chauvinism—if not outright racism—is closely linked to right-wing politics both in the United States and in Europe. Transparent support for notions of white superiority and nationalism can be found among a subset of Trump supporters who identify with a far-right movement known as the "Alt-Right." The movement was described and summarized in the far-right publication *Breitbart*, which is owned and developed by one of Trump's closest political advisors, Steve Bannon, who is no longer working in the Trump administration.[108] Though there is diversity in its approaches and influences, the following are among the principles associated with the alt-right movement: (1) Racial and ethnic hierarchies are natural and related to genetic diversity; (2) it is far more natural to care about your own demographic in-group, rather than a human being as such; (3) free markets should be subordinate to in-group cultural concerns and preferences for ethnic isolation; (4) race determines culture, and thus white people who want to preserve their culture should not mix with or integrate with other races.

According to a 2017 online survey conducted by psychologists P. S. Forscher and N. Kteily, who collected data from approximately 500 people who identified as Alt-Right, 89 percent were white and roughly 63 percent were male.[109] Among those who voted in 2016, 84 percent of the Alt-Right voted for Donald Trump; 40 percent rated "genetic inferiority" as a trait that better describes black people than white people on a scale of 1 to 7; and 60 percent rated black people as less "rational and logical" than white people.

When asked to rate groups on a scale of 0 to 100, with 0 being something like a chimpanzee and 100 being a modern *Homo sapiens*, alt-right supporters expressed a clear racial hierarchy, with white people and Europeans at the top and Muslims, Arabs, Nigerians, black people, Mexicans, and Jews at the bottom (figure 1.14).

Among alt-right supporters, 64 percent rated white people as more evolved than black people. Those results can be compared with a separate survey of white Americans conducted by Ashley Jardina of Duke University and Spencer Piston of Boston University. They found that 52 percent of white Trump supporters rate black people as less evolved than white people. This share was smaller but still very high among white Republicans (39 percent) and white Democrats (33 percent). Jardina and Piston, writing with Sean McElwee, conclude that dehumanizing views are "pervasive across white social groups." In open-ended responses, those who indicated that white people ranked higher mentioned such notions as black people lack intelligence or morals, according to the authors.[110]

Data from the previous decade show a similar and substantial number of white people harbored racist views of some kind. When asked in 2003 and 2004 why black people have lower incomes and worse housing than white

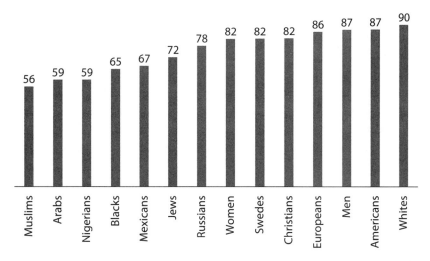

Figure 1.14. How the average alt-right supporter ranks human groups on 0–100
scale where 0 is a chimpanzee and 100 is a human

Source: Forscher, P. S., and N. Kteily. "A Psychological Profile
of the Alt-Right." August 10, 2017. Retrieved from osf.io/preprints.

people, roughly one-third (38 percent) of white respondents agreed that "fundamental genetic differences between the races" explained at least a little of the gap, according to survey data collected by political scientists Leonie Huddy and Stanley Feldman. A similar share (35 percent) attributed at least a little of the black-white gaps in test scores to fundamental differences, with 2.9 percent saying fundamental differences explain "a great deal" of the gap and 17.5 percent choosing "some."[111] The same authors report evidence that these overtly racist attitudes predicted opposition to policies that would increase economic opportunities for black people—such as integrated housing and more spending on schools.

Interestingly, most alt-right adherents don't consider themselves racist, because they claim to avoid discrimination in their personal lives, even as they hold views that are the textbook definition of racism. They thus distinguish themselves from a neo-Nazi subset of the Alt-Right, who are actively hostile toward those who are not white. The Forscher and Kteily survey suggests that principled nonprejudice in individual interactions with black people is not as important as the article implies, although this attitude is common among roughly half of those in the Alt-Right. Just under half of alt-right supporters (45 percent) expressed some level of agreement with the statement "Being non-prejudiced toward Black people is important to my self-concept," even as 38 percent rejected it, and the rest gave a neutral response (17 percent).[112]

Whether these responses are described as racist, ethnocentric, or otherwise, they have important policy implications with respect to immigration, education and training programs, and welfare. White Trump supporters are 11 percentage points more likely than other white Republicans and 27 percentage points more likely than white Democrats to say that the government has "no role" to play "in trying to improve the social and economic position of blacks and other minority groups in this country."[113]

In short, after decades of slow growth and rising inequality, and a recent and large financial recession, nationalist voters in the United States and Europe are broadly unhappy about their financial conditions and have benefited less from economic growth than rich voters but are fairly typical economically. More distinctively, issues tied to race, culture, and immigration loom large in explaining nationalist attitudes. In this way, nationalist voters tend to be victims of elite-driven inequality and beneficiaries and defenders of race and nation-based inequality. Politics is likely to remain unhealthy unless both types of inequalities are combatted.

2

The Natural Foundations of a Just Society

REFLECTING ON THE REALITIES OF Jim Crow America and the psychological tension it created, the author James Baldwin wrote: "Injustice is a commonplace." And yet, "one must never, in one's own life, accept . . . injustices as commonplace."[1]

Amid the political turmoil gripping contemporary democracies, along with stagnant economic conditions, rising inequality, and dissatisfaction with government institutions, I believe there is a need to move beyond superficial policy discussions and revisit what it is we hope to achieve through our lives and political institutions and how to do so justly. As I develop later, the problems outlined in the previous chapter are, in large part, grounded in commonplace injustices that are repairable.

In both ancient and modern writing, justice is regarded as a principal virtue of individuals and political entities. Yet, in this age of irony, skepticism, and post-modern sensibility, it seems embarrassingly antiquarian to even pretend it exists. But, at the risk of embarrassment, I say it does. A sense of justice can be found in every corner of the world in every era of history. It can even be found in our ancestral DNA and in our neurons. Justice has a material reality like health. Much as ill-health weakens the body, deprives it of normal functioning, and exposes its vulnerabilities, so injustice weakens social ties, dissuades people from investing in the future, prevents its victims from optimal functioning, and endangers groups of people.

Even if you believe my interpretation of justice goes too far, I hope you will at least agree that a robust sense of justice is found across human populations. Whether justice be thought of as natural or metaphysical, or as an emergent concept dependent on specific historical circumstances, it is rooted in principles and convictions that are widely shared across humanity and fundamental to the basic organization of a healthy society. It is this sense of justice that I believe leads to an egalitarian but not strictly equal economy.

UNIVERSAL MORALITY

If justice is an inherent quality of human life, as I maintain, an understanding or sensitivity to justice should be ubiquitous across cultures and societies, even as the unique history and circumstances of a society shape views about how justice should be understood and implemented.

Aristotle wrote extensively about justice, and his work offers one of the earliest and lengthiest meditations on the subject for which written records exist. Modern scholars find two key aspects of justice in his work: One concerns conformity with laws that serve the common good; the other, proportionality or fairness, especially with respect to the rewards of merit.[2] The King James translation of Jewish religious texts provides clear illustrations of justice as conformity with law and proportionality in market exchanges.[3]

Reciprocity in this broader sense, and in the narrower sense of exchange and trade of valuable commodities or services, has been deemed a human universal. Reciprocating behavioral norms are found across every society studied by anthropologists.[4] A related ethical norm is the "golden rule," which implies some measure of selflessness, in that it stipulates that one should treat others as one would oneself. This is more advanced than straightforward reciprocal exchanges of things that are of equal value and requires an ability to empathize with others.

The golden rule is a well-known teaching of Jesus of Nazareth, who urged his followers to "love thy neighbor as thyself," but variants of the rule have been found in almost every religious and social tradition, such that it too is likely a universal aspect of human culture.[5] Well-documented examples of the golden rule have been found in the writings of the ancient Chinese philosopher Confucius, ancient Syrian, Persian, Indian (Hindu and Buddhist), and Greek texts, as well as in the oral tradition of West Africa.[6] Since it is prominent in Christianity, it should not be surprising that both Jewish and Muslim texts include the idea.

The golden rule also emerged in secular republican Rome, independently of Judeo-Christianity. The classical Roman senator, politician, and philosopher Cicero developed his own reciprocal ethical aphorisms. In an essay known as "On Duties," which was nominally a letter addressed to his son in 44 BCE, Cicero wrote, "No one do harm to another, unless provoked by injury," "Those who have the same virtuous desires and purposes love one another as they love themselves," and "There is no more essential duty than that of returning kindness received."[7] Likewise, he told his son, "One must not injure anyone else for one's own profit," adding that this idea was a natural law with international validity.[8]

Further, Cicero emphasized a nonreciprocal element of magnanimity, also found in many religious traditions, which is to treat the poor with generosity: "But alike in bestowing benefit and in returning kindness, other things being equal, it is the highest degree incumbent upon us to do the most for those who need the most."[9] Moreover, he wrote, "Justice is to be maintained even toward those of the lowest condition." Mentioning slaves in particular, he said that they ought to be paid for their labor and assigned daily tasks in advance as if they were "hired servants."[10] These statements together point to a core element of the golden rule that distinguishes it from fair exchange: empathy for the plight of the weak.

Though Cicero wrote just before the birth of Christ, this is similar to the Catholic ethical teaching known as the *preference option for the poor*, which instructs Catholics to give greater weight to the preferences of the poor.[11] The option for the poor can be thought of as rebalancing the scales to their benefit, especially in the marketplace, where their poverty is a clear constraint. It is quite likely to have been widespread throughout human cultures, as Cicero claimed, but because literacy was rare until recently, it is difficult to establish documentary evidence. Still, we know it has deep ancient roots. An inscription attributed to the Egyptian king Amenemhat I, who died roughly 2,000 years before Christ (in 1976 BCE), boasted: "I gave to the destitute, and raised up the orphan. I promoted the man with nothing as much as the man of means."[12]

NATURAL JUSTICE

The ubiquity of the golden rule and related precepts suggests that this notion of justice is an important and universal characteristic of human existence. Consequently, altruism should be a natural aspect of human moral perception, as Cicero thought. That is, perhaps human minds grasp gradations of justice along a spectrum of reciprocating behavior, just as the human eye naturally distinguishes color along gradations of the electromagnetic spectrum. If so, we could expect to observe the recognition of something like fairness among nonhuman animals and across all human societies.

In a remarkable experiment, primatologists Sarah Brosnan and Franz de Waal trained female capuchin monkeys to exchange tokens for cucumbers, which they readily did in 95 percent of cases.[13] Brosnan and de Waal then changed the price of the token for the capuchin's neighbor but not for her. Specifically, they allowed the neighbor to receive a grape—which these monkeys prefer over cucumbers—in exchange for the token. Video evidence presented by de Waal shows that this new deal did not go down very well.[14] The capuchin stuck with the bad deal became visibly upset upon receiving the cucumber instead of the grape. Despite having enjoyed the cucumber seconds ago, she now flung it out of the cage. Her gestures made it clear that she wanted the grape instead. When made the same offer, she did the same thing again, strenuously rejecting the trade. This rejection of the trade was observed far more frequently when the payout for the token was lower for the subject. Brosnan and de Waal interpret this experiment as evidence that the monkey recognized when it was being treated unfairly or at least not in the same way as the other monkeys.

By switching the payoff from cucumbers to grapes, the experiment increased the value of the tokens, which is analogous to economic growth, but the gains of growth had gone only to the monkeys that received grapes and that did nothing to deserve those gains relative to those in the other group. Despite no material reduction in their living standards, the monkeys that received only cucumbers were less happy.

Primates also exhibit behaviors that are closer to the golden rule—namely, generosity toward others. In one experiment, capuchins were given a choice between one of two tokens. One of the tokens resulted in a reward for that monkey but not the monkey next to it, visible but in another cage. The other token resulted in both monkeys being rewarded. Thus, there was a 50–50 chance of prosocial behavior and selfish behavior. In the course of 30 rounds of this game, the monkey chose prosocial behavior much more frequently than random chance would have allowed and nearly 70 percent of the time by the last ten trials. The greatest amount of sharing was with kin, followed by non-kin monkeys within the same group. There was no prosocial behavior with strangers. Likewise, when the rewards were unequal, prosocial behavior also declined to the point that it could be attributed to random chance. The results imply that capuchins have preferences to bestow benefits to those in their group but not outsiders, provided the rewards are equitable.[15]

In another experiment, marmoset monkeys displayed even more generosity. They were frequently willing to pull a tray that gave food to a partner but nothing for themselves, and they were far more likely to do this when it actually benefited another monkey than in the control condition in which the adjacent cage was empty and no monkey benefited.[16] Thus, these monkeys displayed a willingness to contribute to the welfare of others, even when doing so resulted in no immediate benefit to themselves.

The extent to which primates recognize and respond to fairness is unresolved in the scientific literature, but there is clear evidence of some recognition. In addition, behavior that helps others at one's own expense is commonly observed.[17]

HUMAN FAIRNESS IN EXPERIMENTAL AND CULTURAL SETTINGS

Humans also show a clear and consistent awareness of unfairness.

An innovative experiment conducted by the Swiss economists Ernst Fehr and Simon Gächter recruited 112 Swiss students to play a game for two hours and earn a modest amount of money.[18] In the game, four players were given 20 francs each. They were told to decide how much they wanted to contribute to the group, knowing they would get only 40 percent back from what they contributed, while everyone else in the group would also get 40 percent but without giving anything up. In this sense, the group contribution is akin to taxation in support of a "public good," such as infrastructure, security, and education, but it is valuable only if many people chip in, and in this setup, doing so is voluntary.

This game was played ten times in a row, and the players could keep their money at the end. Table 2.1 shows the hypothetical payoffs for individuals who chose to be completely selfish or generous under the extreme scenarios in which the group was either entirely selfish or generous. It's clear that average income was highest when everyone donated (32), while the individual best-case-scenario (44) involved that person donating nothing, even though that harmed the group. Thus, for those motivated by self-interest alone there are strong incentives to donate nothing.

Table 2.1. Hypothetical income of public goods game for extreme cases

	Everyone else donates all their money	No one else donates
Your income		
Donate all your money	32	0
Donate nothing	44	20
Average group income		
Donate all your money	32	17
Donate nothing	11	20

Source: Based on parameters from Fehr, Ernst, and Simon Gächter. "Altruistic Punishment in Humans." *Nature* 415.6868 (2002): 137–140; Fehr, Ernst, and Simon Gächter. "Cooperation and Punishment in Public Goods Experiments." *The American Economic Review* 90.4 (2000): 980–994.

People who started the game acting generously learned the strength of these incentives and quickly stopped donating. The average contribution in the first round was just under half of total wealth (nine francs) but fell to around 10 percent of total wealth (two francs) by the tenth round.

In modern states, as well as less formally structured tribal societies, humans have mechanisms that range from criticism and shaming to ostracism, fines, prison time, and even execution to force compliance to support public goods and induce sharing.[19] So, Fehr and Gächter tested an alternative game that was exactly like the first but allowed the players to punish one another. A donor in the first round could decide to punish a nondonor by taking away three of his or her francs, but as in real life, punishment was itself costly: a punisher had to forgo one franc.

In contrast to a standard economic theory that people are selfish, many people were willing to punish nondonors. The results were spectacular, and it did not matter which version of the game people played first. The average donations rose from just over 50 percent in the first round to nearly 100 percent by the final round. In short, people were willing to pool almost all of their resources when they were assured of two things: (1) Doing so would make everyone better off, including themselves, and (2) cheaters wouldn't get away with it. Follow-up research by the same authors found that cheating elicited strong expressions of anger in the subjects, which may have contributed to their willingness to altruistically punish. (I draw on the scientific literature's definition of altruism as behavior that benefits others, such as the group, while imposing a cost on the helper).[20]

This and similar experiments have been tested many times and across many cultures, including in relatively poor and nonindustrialized societies.[21] Consistent evidence emerges that humans reject unequal distributions when they are not based on merit and that they cooperate to enhance the strength of their group and help others in need.[22]

In experimental settings, seeing another person in pain elicited a distinctive blood-flow pattern in the brain, which researchers distinguished from cases in which the subject's own pain was taken away by generous behavior.[23] Both reciprocating gratitude and empathetic generosity were correlated with similar neural activity across individuals.

Further evidence that there is a biological basis for altruism comes from studies of extraordinarily generous people. Their brains show distinctive patterns of activity. The difference is found specifically in the amygdala, a region of the brain that processes emotions. A study of kidney donors—an act of extraordinary altruism—found that their amygdala was activated more than that of ordinary people when shown pictures of frightened people, and much more so than that of psychopaths, who actually show impairment in this region of the brain.[24] In other words, altruists have a heightened empathic sensitivity.[25]

As for its origins, an older theory of altruism argued that helping others was beneficial to oneself because those one was likely to help were also likely to share one's DNA, but this theory is no longer accepted by most scholars. The cooperative behaviors described above cannot be explained by direct genetic relations since they occur among those who are not kin. Other forms of cooperation have a similar pattern. A detailed study of chimpanzee males in the wild, for example, found that they cooperate—by sharing meat, grooming, forming coalitions, guarding territory—mostly with unrelated individuals, rather than with brothers or close relatives.[26]

Samuel Bowles and Herbert Gintis, who have done extensive research in the field of evolutionary social science, recently reviewed the latest theoretical issues. Based on extensive evidence and compelling logic, they conclude that humans evolved to care about others and cooperate with them because groups that did so were more successful at protecting fellow group members from neighboring tribes during violent intergroup conflict.[27] Other theorists have proposed that preferences for fairness may have evolved among apes and then humans as a means to sustain cooperation among group members.[28]

And yet, it would be easy to exaggerate the extent to which humans are altruistic. The religious codes that evolved independently across so many human societies would not have been needed if the dominant and default human instinct was to submit oneself to the desires and benefits of the group. Despite the frequency of altruism, selfish behavior—sometimes extremely selfish behavior—is also found across experimental settings in evolutionary social science. In a competitive environment with limited resources—an empire of scarcity—individuals, family units, and groups are more likely to exhibit selfish behavior.

The biologist E. O. Wilson has written about the evolutionary tension between selfishness and altruism and believes it has profound consequences for human morality and our sense of justice:

> Selection at the individual level tends to create competitiveness and selfish behavior. . . . In opposition, selection between groups tends to create selfless behavior, expressed in greater generosity and altruism, which in turn promote stronger cohesion and strength of the group as a whole.[29]

In fact, some degree of selfishness at the group level—"parochialism," in the scientific literature—may increase the advantage of within-group altruism by increasing the fertility and survival rates of groups with members characterized by strong loyalty to one another and a willingness to fight outsiders, according to one prominent theory.[30]

Still, two crucial issues related to the viability of groups are: How are outside groups regarded, and how easily can the boundaries between groups be bridged? Early human tribes that created unbridgeable divides between groups would have perished. Unwavering hostility toward outsiders or a refusal to see them as equals would have made tribes vulnerable to an alliance of competing tribes. It would also have prevented trade between groups, without which many groups would have perished in the wake of disease, drought, or natural disaster. Almost every hunter-gatherer society ever observed was recorded to engage in trade across groups.[31] Indeed, if humans were incapable of including diverse people in their communities, then ancient and modern cities, and their intellectual, cultural, and technological achievements, would never have been possible. There is clear evidence from wars that humans form alliances across ethnic and religious lines, even in spite of former or existing antagonisms.[32] At a more mundane level, hundreds of studies have demonstrated that cooperative contact and geographic integration enhance trust and lower prejudice across racial and ethnic lines.[33]

Cicero dwelled on these considerations explicitly in his treatise "On Duties." Starting from his view of a common humanity, he laid out principles for when to go to war—to avoid injury and maintain peace, never to profit at the expense of others—and how to treat the vanquished after war: "Those whom you conquer are to be treated kindly, those who, laying down their arms in good faith," should receive food and shelter. He praised Romans from centuries past for admitting people from conquered foreign tribes as citizens in the aftermath of war, provided that they were not "cruel and inhuman in war."[34]

The task of just institutions is to set up rules to balance the complex, competing interests within and between individuals, families, and groups.

FROM ALTRUISTIC GROUP MEMBERS TO JUST SOCIETIES

With this background in mind, let's explore what the fundamental conditions of a just society should be.

Writing in the thriving Republic of Athens around 380 BCE, Plato set out to describe a just society. His starting point was to imagine what humans need at the most basic level, such as food, shelter, and clothing, and what system best meets these needs.

Plato argues that human needs can be met only through cooperation, which benefits everyone through mutually beneficial exchange and occupational specialization. People who have come together for these exchanges set up rules among themselves, forming a state. Anticipating modern economic theory, Plato observes that people are more productive—can create higher quality goods and services per hour of effort—when they specialize in one occupation rather than trying to supply all of their needs by themselves. The efficiency gains from cooperation result from learning and practice and the natural diversity of human talents. "There are diversities of natures among us which are adapted to different occupations," Plato writes.[35] Beyond meeting basic needs by facilitating exchange, the state should also provide public goods such as wise leadership, security, protection of property, and education. For Plato, it is clear that the best way to provide this diverse array of goods and services is that "each individual should be put to the use for which nature intended him." Drawing on the justice-as-proportionality principle, Plato has Socrates suggest that "justice is the giving to each man what is proper to him."[36] What is due corresponds to what is needed, which is highly varied—a fair interpretation of the law, food, shelter, shoes, medical care, and so on—and providing the precise thing that is due is best accomplished by expert specialists. For Plato, it follows that justice is doing one's own business, a job that suits one, and a just state is one in which people do the occupation that best suits them. This is how people in a community get what is due to them.

In order to bring everyone up to his or her optimal level of productivity, Plato emphasizes the importance of education from an early age. While *The Republic* discusses the strengths and weaknesses of a hypothetical curriculum and a few other details, *Laws*, a later and less famous work, elaborates on much more ambitious educational ideas. There, Plato endorses compulsory public education "open to all"—that is, including both boys and girls, both of whom would receive military and academic training at the public's expense. One passage suggests that he would start public education at around age three and continue until adulthood. "The most important part of education is training in the nursery," he wrote.[37] This policy makes him more progressive than many U.S. politicians who erroneously oppose public "preK," as it is called, as an extravagant waste of money.

Moreover, in *The Republic* and *Laws*, Plato explicitly argues that women's "original nature is the same" as men's. Women should be warriors, he claims, when they prove capable after preliminary training. "Many women are in many things superior to many men," Plato posits, through the character of Socrates, whom he uses to convey his vision.[38] To forbid naturally talented women from pursuing the occupations of men is a "violation of nature" and unjust.

Consistent with his views on education, Plato considers that merit is not determined by social class and that pathways to leadership positions must be available to people of every social rank. In these respects, Plato advocates for a society in which ability and merit, forged out of common access to public goods such as education and security, determine occupational status and positions of leadership.

These are compelling principles worth preserving that follow logically from his unstated goal of maximizing the happiness of his ideal city-state. Yet, Plato proves too willing to subordinate the individual to the state. In *The Republic*, he places a great deal of faith in the wisdom of rulers, even if chosen meritoriously, and gives them too much power to dictate the lives of people, including what they learn in school, whom they are allowed to reproduce with and marry, and even their access to property of any kind. In this sense, the citizens of Plato's Republic, and even more so the slaves, are not respected as individuals who are capable of making even basic decisions about their own lives.

These flaws are less extreme in *Laws* than in *The Republic*. In *Laws*, he is more respectful of republican institutions and more concerned about the concentration of power and wealth.[39] For example, he praises three constitutional policies in Sparta that curbed the executive power of rulers.[40] In the ideal city presented in *Laws*, Plato proposes a complex system of elections to ensure that all classes are politically represented. He also proposes rather dramatic reforms to property in order to make wealth more equally distributed and curb what he regards as unfair advantages that flow to the rich.[41]

In the end, Plato's vision of a just society should not be accepted in its entirety by any means. He argues that we should not look to enhance individual happiness but rather to aim for happiness that "resides in the state as a whole."[42] Perhaps, this view explains why *The Republic* has many bad ideas about suppressing free speech and artistic activity, eliminating property ownership among soldiers, using false propaganda to motivate public service and acquiescence, and forcing soldiers to share common wives and not know who their children are. Still, Plato's ideas offer important principles worth preserving: checks on political power, gender equality, the need for representative government, equality of access to occupations, and public universal education. These ideas support his fundamental vision, which is worth defending: A just society is one in which people do what they do best.

John Rawls is arguably the Plato of modern philosophy, in that no single scholar has influenced academic views of justice more than he, at least in wealthy Western countries. His arguments are worth studying in detail.

Unlike Plato, who begins by asking how society's needs should be met, Rawls begins with an individual's concerns and asks readers to engage in an imaginary exercise. It's a bit like the following scenario: Pretend you are in a room with ten people you regard as your equals. All of you know that you are going to compete and potentially cooperate with one another in a game, whose basic rules you have to work out together. The things you care most about—life, health, dignity, income, happiness—all depend on your relative performance in this game. None of you can know before you make the rules how your individual strengths and weaknesses will matter in this game, and so there is no way to design the rules to take advantage of your specific abilities. What principles would you work out to govern this game after rational deliberation?

These background conditions are fair in the senses described above, as proportional, equal, and unbiased. Hence, the principles that follow from this deliberative exercise are just.

Of course, Rawls's actual argument is not about a game. Rather, it concerns the "fundamental terms of association" among people and the institutions that govern behavior in a group of people. But it is similar to the exercise above in that he asks readers to set aside any knowledge about their own social status at birth or their natural abilities.

From this "original position," Rawls makes a strong analytic case that a logical person would want a society characterized by two basic principles (the second of which has two distinct parts):

First Principle: Each person has the same indefeasible claim to a fully adequate scheme of equal basic liberties, which scheme is compatible with the same scheme of liberties for all;

Second Principle: Social and economic inequalities are to satisfy two conditions:

a. They are to be attached to offices and positions open to all under conditions of fair equality of opportunity;
b. They are to be to the greatest benefit of the least advantaged members of society (the difference principle).[43]

The radical equality of the original position—where advantages of social status are wiped out—encourages respect of others as oneself. That means giving them the freedom to learn, develop, and choose the occupation that suits their interests, ambitions, and natural and acquired talents. It means allowing them to foster the familial and social relationships that enrich their lives and to engage in work that is meaningful to them. It means letting them keep much of the value of their work and use it as they see fit and cooperate and exchange with others when they believe it is in their benefit to do so. It also means empowering them to choose their political representatives, evaluate them, and hold them accountable not only to their own distinct priorities—informed through experience, education, and citizenship—but also to the public good.

For Rawls, the first principle includes these things. He explicitly refers to the U.S. Constitution's Bill of Rights and subsequent amendments as examples of basic liberties: freedom of expression, assembly, and religion; freedom from unreasonable government claims on property; freedom from slavery; and equality and due process before the law. Part "a" of the second principle evokes equality of opportunity in a way that is consistent with Plato's *Republic* and *Laws*. Both Rawls and Plato imagined a society in which people pursue the occupations that engage their talents, without restrictions placed upon them based on their gender or parents' social status.

The most controversial element to these principles is the difference principle, but I think the controversy is rooted in a misinterpretation. Some have taken it to mean that the rich should be forced to redistribute their income until the income of the poor has reached its upper limit, given total national resources. That is profoundly mistaken. Rawls did not take a position as to what policies should be implemented to raise the welfare of the least off. Instead, he suggested that the well-being of the poor might be maximized under a free market economy. After all, in a poor and unproductive society, the least advantaged will live in truly deplorable conditions.

The optimal level of taxation, public goods spending, and redistribution that would maximize the well-being of the poor is an open question. Historically, the government ownership of the means of production (communism) has not served the least advantaged members of a society well, and yet, the legitimacy of some positive economic role for the state is indisputable. To take just one sphere of economic activity as an example, evidence from the United States suggests that access to public goods, income transfers, and related programs do effectively raise the welfare of the poor and the children born into disadvantageous conditions.[44] This does not, however, imply that increasing the value and use rate of income transfers is always the most just policy. Depending on the specific circumstances of the individuals involved, there may be more effective ways to raise the welfare of the least off, such as training programs or mental health services.

Without minimizing the richness and sophistication of his analytic argument, I would suggest that Rawls's difference principle is really no different at its core than the Catholic preferential option for the poor or even Cicero's secular republican maxim: "Do the most for those who need the most."[45] Rawls himself had once thought he would become a priest, so it is hardly surprising that his views would be consistent with Catholic social teaching.[46] The late French philosopher Paul Ricoeur has argued that Rawls's difference principle and the background conditions of equality in his original position are "equivalent to the Golden Rule applied to institutions."[47]

Rawls explicitly rejects the common competing utilitarian ethical idea of "the greatest good for the greatest number" on grounds that "each person possesses an inviolability founded on justice that even the welfare of society as a whole cannot override. For this reason, justice denies that the loss of freedom for some is made right by a greater good shared by others."[48] Rawls is debating modern scholars, but he might as well have been debating Plato. Because Rawls is not willing to sacrifice individuals to a collective, his difference principle "2a" is the only one that is perfectly consistent with the principles of Plato's Republic.

It is instructive to compare these views of justice with other widely held doctrines.

Both Rawls's and Plato's theories of justice are at odds with essential communist principles of justice. One, famously articulated by Karl Marx, is "From each according to his ability, to each according to his need."[49] For many reasons, it is unrealistic to expect that the value of everyone's work will be identical. Not only does value differ by job, but even people with the same job vary in their performance. Hence, this principle requires equal compensation for unequal work, which is fundamentally unfair from a reciprocal perspective. Experimental evidence from economists at Brigham Young University suggests that people accept some levels of inequality when the distribution is based on merit but reject it otherwise.[50]

Another Marxist idea that is problematic for justice is the public ownership of the means of production. This is difficult to reconcile with occupational choice, insofar as entrepreneurship, small-business ownership, and even self-proprietorship are explicitly foreclosed. If the means of production were truly nationalized in every way, which did not happen even in Soviet Russia, website designers, consultants, plumbers, electricians, hairdressers, taxi drivers, and other independent workers would be forced to apply for employment with the state. These independent work arrangements were generally against the law in Soviet Russia, as was the hiring of private employees, though there were many informal and formal exceptions.[51] In general, most people were forced to be employees of the state, regardless of whatever talent they might have for entrepreneurship or innovation or whatever desire they might have to work independently and set their own work schedule and fees.

The communist vision of society also fails to maximize the welfare of the least off in at least one vital way: Through the elimination of merit-based compensation, it fails to provide the means and incentives to discover and implement innovative ideas through entrepreneurship or other means. The worst off have benefited greatly from advances in science, technology, and business that have raised the quality of goods and services—including healthcare—relative to their costs.[52] Recognizing this, the Soviet Union did include merit-based compensation schemes, but given the prohibitions on private business ownership, there were nonetheless very strong incentives against risking one's savings (or capital) through research and development and business development. In noncommunist societies, this risk-taking has led to many new technologies and business ventures that have benefited the least off.

At the same time, a strength of the communist vision is its commitment to comprehensive public support for the least off, who have often suffered unnecessarily in affluent noncommunist societies, including the United States, where low or even moderate income severely restricts access to quality housing and important services such as healthcare, transportation, and post-secondary training, despite a patchwork of both public and private sources of charity.

Rawls did endorse both liberal socialism and property-owning democracy as potentially consistent with his principles, so long as occupations are freely chosen, political power is distributed equally among citizens, economic power is not concentrated to the point of blocking competition, and public goods are provided in such a way as to equalize opportunity at the start of life.[53] Social democracies in Northern Europe have managed to reject public ownership of the means of production, preserve entrepreneurship and innovation, and provide comprehensive support to those with the least resources, creating societies that realize greater justice than either communist societies or those, like the United States, with relatively weak safety nets.

Basic libertarian conceptions of justice are also problematic in that they ignore whether or not people start their lives on an equal basis or have equal access to public goods. This indifference violates Plato's goal of maximizing social welfare by allowing people to do what they do best, and it violates Rawls's sense of fairness by allowing inequality to be strongly founded on unfair advantages, such as parental social status and economic power. Finally, libertarianism is also inconsistent with the difference principle insofar as leading libertarian thinkers such as Robert Nozick and Frederick Hayek oppose publicly funded endeavors that give priority to the well-being of the poor and thereby support unnecessarily depriving the least off of welfare.[54]

Libertarian society would leave any efforts to provide for education, poverty relief, and upward mobility to private collective action, where the incentives to do so are weak, volatile, and subject to arbitrary decisions. Fundamentally, it would put the least off in a position of subservience to the rich. One can imagine what this would look like by studying conditions in ancient Rome's patronage networks, in which the poor and middle classes provided various services to the super-rich in exchange for regular payments. These services could as readily be criminal as military in nature. They also included educational services, which meant that teachers were viewed as something like a private charity; thus, they could be easily exploited, as well as being subject to any losses suffered by their patrons.[55] It's worth mentioning in this context that no society has ever achieved mass literacy without publicly funded education.[56] The philosophers Amartya Sen and Martha Nussbaum have extended Rawls's vision by considering what conditions true equality of opportunity require.[57] The core idea developed by Sen is that individuals should be given the capacity to create the conditions of a flourishing life. The practical implication of this is that equality of opportunity means more than just equal eligibility for occupations and income generation. As Nussbaum argues, for a society to be just, it must provide its people the capabilities to pursue a life of dignity, including health, education, and some degree of control over their political and material conditions.[58] These strike me as logical extensions of the core ideas developed by Rawls and Plato.

Another test of theories of justice is to see how they are regarded by extreme political groups. Other than committed libertarians, perhaps, it would be hard to identify a political group in the United States more likely to be hostile toward Rawlsian principles than the Alt-Right, and yet, when surveyed, a majority of people identifying as "alt-right" express support for the basic principle of equal opportunity, and just as many agree with the princi-

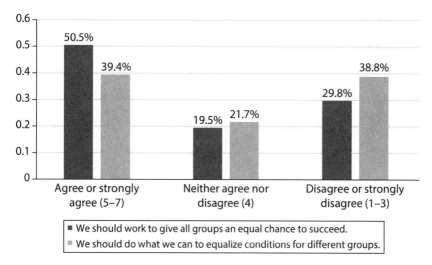

Figure 2.1. Agreement with basic principles of justice on a 1–7 scale among those who identify with the alt-right movement

Source: Forscher, P. S., and N. Kteily. "A Psychological Profile of the Alt-Right." August 10, 2017. Retrieved from osf.io/preprints.

ple of redistribution in favor of greater equality as oppose it (figure 2.1). This makes it hard to imagine how the libertarian rejection of equal opportunity could ever become a widely supported view.

In summary, the Rawlsian vision of a just society is remarkably consistent with universally held cultural conceptions of reciprocity and justice and experimental evidence regarding altruistic behavior among primates and humans. It balances individual liberty with egalitarian concerns about fairness in opportunity, and it provides opportunities for merit to influence welfare, while stripping away arbitrary advantages and alleviating disadvantages. These attributes stand in contrast to competing visions of justice from Platonic utilitarianism, communism, and libertarianism.

Having established what I believe the most basic rules of a just society consist of, I offer a glimpse in the next chapter of what would happen if an equal-opportunity society were allowed to unfold.

3

Merit-Based Egalitarianism

A CENTRAL CLAIM OF THIS BOOK is that well-functioning markets—characterized by mutually beneficial exchange among political equals—lead to egalitarian outcomes with respect to income and well-being. This is possible because the skills and traits that lead to productive work are broadly distributed. The extreme inequality that exists in the contemporary United States and other countries is not the result of well-functioning markets or vast differences in natural ability. Rather, it results from political inequality and corrupted markets.

In an egalitarian market society, differences in market-based compensation would largely be the result of differences in productivity among individuals. Productivity would vary less than the current distribution of income in many countries because the rich are presently compensated well above their productive contributions, and in an egalitarian market society opportunities would be equal in basic ways: Poor children would be given adequate shelter and nutrition, educated from a young age in schools of similar quality to those attended by rich children, and geographically and culturally integrated with their more affluent peers, so that neither rich nor poor children would view the other as alien or develop idiomatic values and beliefs based on ignorance of the other. Adults, moreover, would have access to education and training opportunities so that they could foster the dispositions and skills that arise from their specific genetic and environmental makeup. This background would give nearly all people the ability to be productive at something that is valued in society.

I want to emphasize that government institutions, combined with private charity, would complement and partially rectify market outcomes so as to further promote egalitarian conditions. Such redistributive arrangements are consistent with our natural inclinations to show altruism toward those in need and treat others with reciprocal concern. Still, the claim here is that nonmarket redistribution will be less necessary in a politically egalitarian market-based society than in one characterized by ubiquitous restrictions on mutually beneficial exchange.

This is the opposite claim of most people on the political Left in the twenty-first century, who assume that free markets are the source of inequality and that government institutions—including state-supported worker institutions such as unions and the collective ownership of companies—are the only means available to counteract market injustice. My claim is also contrary to arguments on the political Right that income inequality is the result of a competitive but fair market process.

This chapter sketches some of the conceptual issues that arise when thinking about how people could distinguish themselves in a just society and provides evidence that the traits people need for success are broadly available, even under current conditions in the United States, where social advantages in upbringing differ widely across groups.

COMPENSATION AND PRODUCTIVITY

In this context, productivity means the value created by someone's work. Value, in this sense, is complex and highly dependent on the work being done, but humans have learned to define, recognize, and appreciate value when they see it in the course of their interactions with others.

Consumers have proven to be very good at identifying the valuable traits of highly complex goods and services, ranging from artistic works, repair services, meals at restaurants, higher education, vacations, and automobiles. Companies such as Yelp, Rotten Tomatoes, Amazon, and Consumer Reports systematically collect and report ratings and reviews of a wide range of products, and in many cases, scholars have found that when assessed against other standards, these measures are valid predictors of product quality.[1] Even for a service as intangible as higher education, recent evidence shows that consumers of higher education provide subjective evaluations of their experience that strongly predict better outcomes for other students, such as their probability of graduation, obtaining an advanced degree, or earning higher incomes after graduation.[2]

Subjective evaluations of worker performance are also extremely common, particularly in large companies.[3] But there is strong evidence to suggest that in this context there are often serious issues associated with reviewer bias. Employee evaluations that rely on objective performance metrics are associated with better management practices and firm performance. Firms are more likely to adopt performance-based pay where labor markets are relatively unregulated—and payment is based on market mechanisms.[4]

Where employee pay and pay growth are tied to performance within firms,[5] managers are not simply trading on political power, except insofar as their political advantages affect their productivity. These advantages might include greater learning opportunities, or, for many men, not facing the cultural expectations and burden of childcare and other domestic responsibilities, which so often derail the careers of many women.

Compensation based on performance will not lead to perfect equality. Rather, it will lead to greater fairness in compensation than currently exists because it diminishes the impact of political power, and links pay closer to productivity. In a politically egalitarian society, people will be given nearly equal opportunities to become productive.

Of course, there are limits to the extent to which compensation can be linked to productivity, especially when it comes to services that are partially or fully paid for by governments. Within a given public organization, whether a school district, hospital system, or military branch, it is straightforward to design a system linking relative pay to productivity, but the amount of revenue available to distribute to workers will depend on political factors, such as how the voters in a society and their political representatives value the services being performed and how much they can afford to allocate to those services.

Nonetheless, even in socially democratic countries, most goods and services are privately produced, and there is a great deal of room for labor markets to function well, if they are allowed to. Moreover, even when goods and services are publicly produced, political egalitarianism demands that compensation be fair, which necessitates that performance be considered. The current practice in the United States of paying teachers based on their education credentials and experience may seem like an egalitarian policy, but it is unfair in a fundamental sense: It grants power to older and more experienced teachers regardless of whether or not they are actually deserving. There is very strong evidence that subjective teacher ratings—based on research-based rubrics—predict a teacher's ability to promote learning, and yet ratings of any kind are rarely used to influence compensation because of the bizarre politics of education.[6]

WHEN MARKETS GENERATE LOW WAGES

One important concern that may be raised against linking pay to markets relates to workers who provide what are typically poorly compensated but socially valuable services, such as early childcare, elementary education, elder care, home healthcare, and social services. These services are recognized as socially valuable because they embody widely shared social and ethical obligations to children, the poor, the weak, and other groups who need the support of their fellow citizens. Other services that are essential to the smooth running of society but are not deemed socially valuable in the same sense, such as cleaning services, food preparation, delivery services, and retail sales jobs, also pay consistently low wages. In addition to their social value, the provision of these services frees others to do more specialized work of greater market value.

Yet, consistently low pay suggests that markets bestow little value on these basic services. The providers face extreme competition, which surely holds compensation down. Most of the population could perform these tasks if they had to, and the providers of the services are competing against the buyers of the services themselves.

For instance, the parents of young children and the adult children of elderly parents can provide educational or caretaking services to their family members, but may decide that it is more efficient or satisfying for them to do something else with at least a large portion of their time—like hold a full-time job—than devote most of their waking life to taking care of others for no pay. As a result, early childhood caretakers and educators have to compete against parents. If the price becomes too high, parents will find it impractical or unaffordable and elect to quit their job and provide their own childcare. Similar competition holds down prices for cleaning services and restaurants. Most people are capable of preparing their own meals or cleaning their own living space, but if they are affluent enough, they may decide to hire other people to provide these services. As a result, there will always be a subset of occupations that pay a small percentage of the average worker's wage. The economist Alan Manning has developed a formal analysis of these dynamics showing that demand for low-wage work will grow alongside the local income growth of the affluent.[7]

Other labor markets do not face this kind of pressure. Most people would find it impractical if not impossible to manufacture things they buy—like a pencil, clothing, home, or new technology. Unless they live on a farm, it is highly unlikely that they could produce even a modicum of the food they need to consume. Likewise, for professional services: In law, finance, medicine, engineering, architecture, computers, and higher education the product is complex and specialized enough such that competition between providers sets prices, rather than competition between buyers and sellers. The same would be true for entertainment services. People don't pay to watch amateurs play backyard football games or sing karaoke at bars, but they do pay to see elite athletes and musicians perform.

Within low-paying occupations, there is considerable variation in pay, and more productive workers may be rewarded, but even highly effective early childhood educators, nannies, and home healthcare workers often get saddled with pay rates that would fall below the levels of the worst-performing professional workers. They are also underpaid relative to their cognitive and noncognitive skill set, as I discuss later. Redistributive policies—such as income supplementation and the provision of benefits from the public—are an appropriate response to this problem for several reasons. Such forms of redistribution are inherently fair relative to market distribution, because they come closer to accurately compensating people for the application of their skills and abilities as well as their real contribution to society.

PRODUCTIVE TRAITS, INCOME, AND HEALTH

In practice, performance is based on a set of skills and traits that are widely distributed now and would be even more broadly available under egalitarian political regimes.

For example, in 1979, the U.S. Bureau of Labor Statistics (BLS) started collecting data from a random sample of 12,682 Americans born between 1957 and 1964 and continued to do so until 2012. In 1981, it measured cognitive ability with the Armed Forces Qualification Test (AFQT), an achievement test similar to college admission exams. Researchers at the BLS also collected results of traditional IQ measures, such as the Stanford-Binet, as well as a simple battery of five questions meant to capture the "Big 5" personality traits: extroversion, openness to new experiences, anxiety, self-discipline, and agreeableness. Additionally, the survey measured life outcomes such as family income and health status.

An important research question is: To what extent do cognitive ability and personality traits predict income and health? The answer is quite a lot. But the answers would surprise those who believe that IQ is the only thing that matters in earnings or life success.

To study this I calculated average income in middle adulthood and compared it to cognitive and personality traits measures in late adolescence. First of all, in terms of earnings, the achievement test of the AFQT is a notably better predictor of income than classic measures of IQ.[8] If both are in the same model predicting income or health using the 1979 National Longitudinal Survey of Youth (NLSY), only the AFQT is significant. This is not surprising. IQ tests are more abstract and less relevant to real-world problems than the AFQT and other measures of cognitive achievement. A one standard deviation in cognitive ability, as measured by the AFQT, predicts 22 percent higher family income, after controlling for other demographic factors, education, and personality, whereas more traditional IQ measures predict only a 9 percent increase. The AFQT is also more predictive of educational attainment than traditional IQ measures. To put it bluntly, achievement tests are a better measure of cognitive ability than conventional IQ tests, even though they are highly correlated with one another.[9]

Second, educational attainment is a stronger predictor of family income and health status than cognitive ability. In other words, when both factors are used as independent variables, educational attainment has stronger statistical power (a higher t-statistic). If you take two people with the same cognitive ability, the first person earns 10 percent higher family income for every additional year of study and reports significantly higher levels of general health.

Third, personality traits—as measured by responses to just three questions—are as important or almost as important as cognitive ability in explaining income and more important than cognitive ability in explaining health status. The questions that have the most predictive power are those that ask how people would rate themselves on three characteristic traits: extroverted/enthusiastic, dependable/self-disciplined, and anxious/easily upset,

Table 3.1. Statistical relationship between cognitive ability, personality, and other factors in predicting income and health in the United States

	People born 1957–1964		People born 1980–1984	
	Family income, 2000–2012	Health	Personal income, 2013	Health
Educational attainment in years	20.6	9.2	11.2	6.3
Cognitive ability	15.4	5.4	6.6	2.5
Personality (3 out of "Big 5" traits)	10.9	10.4	6.7	12.9
Parental education (mean of both parents)	5	1.4	1.2	3.6
Perception of self-control	−3.3	−4.2		

Notes: The first two columns are from the author's analysis of NLSY 1979. The third and fourth columns analyze the NLSY 1997. All values are t-statistics from regression of age and whether the respondent is Jewish, Catholic, another non-Christian religion, black, or Hispanic on either the log of family income, personal income, or health status, on a 1–5 scale, with 5 being excellent and 1 being poor. Cognitive ability is measured by the Armed Forces Qualification Test for the 1979 cohort and the Computer-Adaptive Armed Services Vocational Aptitude Battery for the 1997 cohort, using mathematical knowledge (MK), arithmetic reasoning (AR), word knowledge (WK), and Paragraph Comprehension (PC) subtests. Personality is measured by responses to three questions about the extent to which the individual agrees on a 1–7 scale with descriptions of him- or herself as extroverted/enthusiastic, dependable/self-disciplined, and anxious/easily upset. The personality score adds extroverted with dependable and subtracts anxious. Personality and cognitive ability are measured in 1979 and 1997 for the respective surveys. Health status is asked around age 50 for the NLS 1979 cohort and age 30 for the NLS 1997 cohort.

with the last trait negatively predicting income and health and the other two being positively related. Likewise, when people report feeling that fate and luck control their lives, they tend to earn less income and be less healthy than those who feel a greater sense of agency. Personality is far more important than even parental education.

Fourth, the main analysis presented here assumes that income and cognitive ability move up in a linear relationship, such that a little bit higher IQ matters as much at the top as it does at the bottom. The more complex reality is that changes in IQ matter less at the top than at the bottom. Cognitive performance maximizes income at about the 88th percentile. After that, there is no income benefit of having a higher IQ for the average person. The super-rich are no more intelligent than the merely affluent.[10]

In sum, cognitive ability is not as important as educational attainment to income and health, and very rough personality measures are equally important for income and even more so for health. In other words, self-discipline, enthusiasm, and the ability to avoid getting anxious and upset in the face of stress matter about as much as intelligence in terms of predicting success in life.

Merit Pay

What are the implications of these findings in terms of access to the good things in life—such as income and health? The argument here is that IQ, personality traits, and education are far more evenly distributed than the current distribution of income and health status would suggest. In a politically egalitarian world, roughly equal access to a healthy family life and good schooling would even out IQ, personality differences, and educational attainment, but even in the unequal world we live in, paying people based on these characteristics—instead of these characteristics plus political power and market distortions—would reduce income inequality dramatically.

To illustrate the point, one can compute existing inequality in health status and income inequality using the U.S. Bureau of Labor Statistics' NLSY 1979 sample. What would income and health look like if they were based only on IQ and personality traits?

People on the political Right might assume that payment based on IQ and personality would generate greater inequality, because social and political pressures—such as regulation, unions, and affirmative action—overcompensate unproductive workers. Meanwhile, people on the political Left might assume that IQ and personality traits are like luxury goods that are purchased via a privileged upbringing and that paying people based on these traits would exacerbate inequalities that start in childhood.

Both expectations would be wrong. Inequality in health status and income would be 34 percent and 56 percent, respectively, of the current distribution if based on "merit," as measured by cognitive ability and personality. In other words, inequality in health would fall by two-thirds and inequality in income would fall by half. The United States would become one of the most egalitarian countries in the world if the only things that mattered to income were age, personality, and cognitive ability.

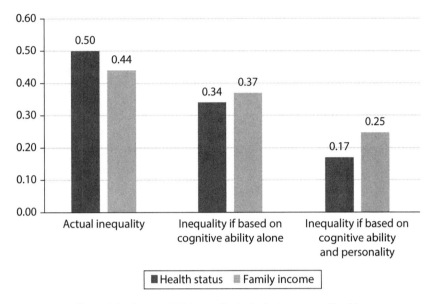

Figure 3.1. Current U.S. inequality index by income and health
and an alternative estimate if income and health were based on the
distribution of cognitive ability and personality

Notes: National Longitudinal Survey of Youth 1979 sample. Cognitive ability is measured by the
Armed Forces Qualification Test. Personality is measured by responses to three questions about the
extent to which the individual agrees on a 1–7 scale with descriptions of him- or herself as extro-
verted/enthusiastic, dependable/self-disciplined, and anxious/easily upset. The personality score adds
extroverted to dependable and subtracts anxious. The analysis regresses AFQT score and then AFQT
score and personality on health status at or near age 50 (measured on a 1–5 scale) and family income
(averaged from 2000–2012 and adjusted for inflation). The regression also controls for year of birth.
The predicted values from this regression are used to calculate the Gini coefficient of inequality,
which is compared to the unadjusted Gini coefficient shown on the far-left bars. The sample size is
approximately 6,000 to 8,000 adults born between 1957 and 1964.

Beyond the United States

The important but limited relationship between cognitive ability and earnings
applies to developed countries beyond the United States. In 2011, the Organisation for Economic Co-Operation and Development (OECD) implemented
the Programme for the International Assessment of Adult Competencies
(PIAAC) to measure cognitive ability of adults aged 16 to 65 around the world
and better learn how those skills relate to labor market and health outcomes.

Detailed income data and cognitive test scores are available for 78,000 individuals in 23 countries, including the United States, in the main public

data files.[11] I measure cognitive ability by combining standardized scores on math, literacy, and technology exams. A standard deviation in cognitive ability predicts a 13 percent increase in earnings. That is a substantial effect, and it is highly significant (meaning the margin of error is low), but just as with the U.S. data discussed above, it is comparable to the effect of educational attainment, work experience, and gender. In fact, work experience measured by age has slightly more predictive power for earnings than cognitive ability.[12] Education and gender are also slightly stronger predictors of income than cognitive ability, while health status is slightly weaker. The PIAAC does not ask about personality directly, but it does ask whether the respondent likes learning new things, is able to relate new ideas to real life, and whether he or she trusts other people. Positive answers to these questions are roughly as predictive of earnings as cognitive ability and remain highly predictive when controlling for cognitive ability. Likewise, higher cognitive ability is a strong predictor of health status across countries, but these factors—education, trust of others—are just as good at predicting health.

As in the U.S. case, if pay were strictly tied to cognitive ability, as well as education, gender, and age, income distribution would become far more egalitarian. Health status would also be more egalitarian. Inequality in health status, as measured by the Gini coefficient, would fall from 0.52 to 0.21. Inequality in income would fall from 0.47 to 0.17.[13]

The reason is that in nearly every rich country elite professionals and managers are paid the highest salaries, but those salaries exceed what would be predicted based on the cognitive ability and other measured attributes of the workers—such as age, education, gender, and the education of their parents. This earnings advantage of working in a managerial or professional occupation is 28 percent for the average developed country in the PIAAC database, but it is especially pronounced in highly unequal countries such as Chile, Israel, the United Kingdom, and the United States (exceeding 37 percent), while it is much lower in more egalitarian Scandinavian countries and the Netherlands. Paying people based on cognitive ability would be redistributive.

To put the relatively egalitarian nature of education in perspective, consider that the richest 1 percent of Americans account for roughly 20 percent of income but just over 1 percent of years of education because the average rich person is only slightly more educated than the average nonrich person.[14] A millionaire (in U.S. dollars) earns somewhere around 20 times the typical OECD worker's income (roughly $50,000), but it is not because the

Table 3.2. The earnings advantage (%) of working in a professional occupation above cognitive ability, education, and other characteristics, by country, 2011–2015

	All professionals	Managers	Professionals excluding managers and technicians	Technicians and associate professionals
Chile	0.59	0.86	0.72	0.45
Japan	0.43	0.73	0.39	0.36
New Zealand	0.43	0.58	0.39	0.32
United Kingdom	0.39	0.54	0.24	0.33
United States	0.37	0.56	0.38	0.28
Ireland	0.36	0.56	0.35	0.26
France	0.34	0.68	0.37	0.27
Israel	0.32	0.52	0.28	0.24
Netherlands	0.32	0.44	0.26	0.29
Poland	0.30	0.56	0.26	0.22
Norway	0.24	0.44	0.16	0.20
Czech Republic	0.22	0.52	0.22	0.14
Slovenia	0.21	0.39	0.23	0.16
Lithuania	0.19	0.27	0.22	0.14
Spain	0.19	0.35	0.17	0.15
Korea	0.18	0.49	0.16	0.13
Italy	0.18	0.27	0.12	0.19
Denmark	0.18	0.46	0.12	0.18
Belgium	0.17	0.26	0.14	0.16
Slovak Republic	0.14	0.04	0.07	0.23
Greece	0.08	0.36	0.00	0.11
Russian Federation	−0.07	0.17	−0.22	0.02

Note: Author anlaysis of data from OECD PIAAC. Professional premium is the average percentage difference in adjusted earnings for those working in a professional occupation compared to nonprofessional workers. The second column ("All professionals") is the coefficient or slope of a linear regression of the log of earnings on cognitive ability—measured as the international standardized values of mean scores on math, literacy, and technology; indicators for education (including primary, associates, bachelor's degree, and graduate degree); age measured in quartic values (age, age^2, age^3, age^4); a binary variable for male; whether respondent is born in the country; whether respondent is a native language speaker; country fixed effects; and a measure of social advantage. The social advantage indicator is the predicted value from a regression of mean cognitive ability on the number of books in home as child; parental education; gender; age; whether born in country or not; and whether a native language speaker. The results in column 2 are from one regression. Results in columns 3–5 are from a separate regression where the three professional groups are analyzed independently, with the omitted category being nonprofessionals.

To interpret one line, in Denmark, professional workers earn just 18 percent more than nonprofessional workers—compared to 59 percent in Chile—after adjusting for cognitive ability, education, parental background, and other factors. Elias, P. (1997), "Occupational Classification (ISCO-88): Concepts, Methods, Reliability, Validity and Cross-National Comparability," OECD Labour Market and Social Policy Occasional Papers, No. 20, OECD Publishing, Paris. http://dx.doi.org/10.1787/304441717388.

millionaire's IQ is 20 times higher. An IQ score at the top 99.9th percentile (149, or 3.3 standard deviations above the mean) would translate into predicted earnings of $76,000.[15] Indeed, the very small number of people who took the PIAAC exam and scored two standard deviations above the mean (which would mean an IQ over 130) exhibited the same average earnings and health status as those who score between 115 and 130.

The richest 1 percent of income earners globally in the PIAAC database have a mean IQ score of roughly 108.8, which is high but not extraordinary. It is below that of the average person with a postgraduate degree (109.5). The United States scores somewhat low compared to other countries in the PIAAC database, so it should not be surprising that the top 1 percent of income earners in the United States score below top earners globally, exhibiting a mean IQ of 103.6, despite being richer.

The PIAAC database reports cognitive ability results for 540 managing directors and chief executives and 339 other occupations with at least 20 observations globally. CEOs are among the highest paid occupations, as you would guess. To account for country differences in compensation, I use the average decile rank for income within each country. The median CEO in the database is at the 9th decile (meaning that he or she is paid more than 80 percent of the population of that country).

There are 195 occupational categories that score above managing directors and CEOs on cognitive performance. The average CEO scores about 0.3 standard deviations above the mean adult, which corresponds to an IQ of 104.7. By comparison, the average African American with a postgraduate degree in the PIAAC database has an IQ of 103. Stated otherwise, the average African American who has gone to graduate school has roughly the same cognitive ability as the average CEO living in 29 developed countries. The average CEO is overpaid by roughly 23 percent relative to his or her cognitive ability, education, age, and other skills measured in the database. It is likely that CEOs have personality traits, intangible skills, and personal connections that are valuable to companies, but their cognitive ability does not appear to be among their main assets.

Likewise, lawyers and legal professionals are overpaid relative to their cognitive ability. In Norway and the UK, PIAAC classifies lawyers as "Legal professionals." Their mean cognitive ability score is extraordinarily high (119.4 or 1.3 standard deviations above the global mean for all 29 rich countries in the database), but they are still overpaid by 62 percent compared with people with identical cognitive scores, levels of education, and other characteristics. In the United States, legal professionals have a cognitive score of 115 (on a global basis—so slightly lower than lawyers in the UK and Norway) and excess compensation of 23 percent. Elsewhere in rich countries, those classified as "Lawyers" score much closer to the average worker (109.6), slightly below a draftsperson (someone who makes detailed technical drawings), and well below many other professional occupations. This group is overpaid by 17 percent on average, while the average draftsperson, who typically does not have a four-year college degree, earns a premium of only 7 percent.

Medical doctors and specialist medical practitioners score at roughly the same level as lawyers across countries (108.4 or 110.4 in the United States), but are not overpaid on average in the 20 countries outside of the United States (mean premium is −.02 percent), likely because of the central role of governments in setting doctor pay in those countries. In the United States, medical students and residents in training may not be overpaid, but medical doctors over the age of 40 bring in a salary premium of 48 percent. Incidentally, dentists score slightly below doctors (107.2), but are paid a premium of 38 percent across all countries in the database.

In general, the highest-scoring professional groups on cognitive exams are overpaid relative to their objective scores and characteristics, while low-scoring workers in jobs that require little training are underpaid. Moreover, life science professionals, software application developers, university and higher-education teachers, and social and religious professionals all exhibit high cognitive scores (111 or higher across 29 countries), but they are not paid nearly as well as most managers, financial analysts, or lawyers. Sociologists and anthropologists, for example, score the same on cognitive tests as financial analysts (112), but their salaries are 77 percent below the average worker who has similar skills, whereas financial analysts have salaries 46 percent above comparable workers.

More broadly, workers in the lowest-skilled jobs—food preparation, cleaners, and helpers—are underpaid rather substantially, taking into account cognitive ability and other traits, whereas professional managers tend to be the most overpaid. Information and communications technology professionals are an exception in that they have high cognitive scores but are paid in line with those skills (table 3.3).

Any way you slice the data, paying people based solely on cognitive ability would vastly reduce income inequality compared to the current distribution.

And cognitive ability is more unevenly distributed than the personality traits conducive to higher pay. Likewise, training and experience are likely to be more evenly distributed than cognitive ability, and all of these factors could be spread more evenly with policy changes, as I will discuss in later chapters.

RACIAL AND GENDER DIFFERENCES IN VALUABLE SKILLS ARE SMALL, AND MALLEABLE ENVIRONMENTAL MECHANISMS ARE READILY IDENTIFIED

As demonstrated above, IQ and valuable personality traits are distributed more equally than income and health status in the United States, as measured by the Gini coefficient of inequality.[16] Moreover, the importance of IQ for income and health is not nearly as dominant as some scholars have implied. Factors such as age, participation in labor markets, and personality are more important when combined.

Cognitive Skills

With respect to racial and ethnic differences on standard cognitive performance measures, contemporary data show that the average scores for black people and Hispanics are lower than for non-Hispanic white people and Asians. This is the case for adolescents who were born in the United States between 1980 and 1984 and tested with the Armed Services Vocational Aptitude Battery (ASVAB), according to my analysis of the 1997 NLSY. It also applies to data in the OECD's PIAAC examination of adults.[17]

The black-white gap in the NLSY 1997 cohort is roughly 0.86 standard deviations, which is slightly lower than the gap reported by Charles Murray and Richard Herrnstein in *The Bell Curve*, their influential and controversial book about intelligence.[18] The gap between Hispanics and non-Hispanic white people is 0.63 standard deviations in the NLSY 1997 and slightly more in the PIAAC.

In the NLSY, Jews and Asians score higher than white Christians or white people on overall cognitive performance, but the sample sizes are small and the differences are not significant after adjusting for parental education. White Christians from highly educated families score just as highly on IQ tests as their Jewish and Asian peers from similar backgrounds in these data.

Table 3.3. Cognitive performance, rank in income distribution, and income premium by occupation across 29 developed countries, 2011–2015

Occupation group	Mean cognitive score	Median income decile	Mean income premium
Information and communications technology professionals	114.5	9	−3%
Business and administration professionals	111.3	9	29%
Administrative and commercial managers	110.8	9	49%
Science and engineering professionals	110.6	8	14%
Technicians and associate professionals	109.5	6	17%
Information and communications technicians	109.4	7	7%
Legal, social, and cultural professionals	108.8	6	−4%
Production and specialized services managers	108.0	9	37%
Teaching professionals	107.4	7	−10%
Health professionals	107.4	7	4%
Chief executives, senior officials, and legislators	107.3	9	25%
Business and administration associate professionals	105.7	7	20%
Armed forces occupations	105.6	6	14%
General and keyboard clerks	105.4	5	−4%
Electrical and electronic trades workers	104.3	6	11%
Science and engineering associate professionals	104.2	8	15%
Customer-services clerks	103.1	4	−6%
Numerical and material recording clerks	102.9	6	7%
Hospitality, retail, and other services managers	102.4	7	32%
Health associate professionals	102.3	5	4%
Legal, social, cultural, and related associate professionals	102.3	5	−11%
Other clerical-support workers	102.2	5	6%

(continued)

Handicraft and printing workers	101.4	6	-7%
Sales workers	100.1	3	-14%
Protective-services workers	99.7	5	2%
Metal, machinery, and related trades workers	99.2	6	12%
Assemblers	96.5	5	6%
Personal-service workers	96.5	3	-13%
Personal-care workers	96.0	3	-19%
Food processing, woodworking, garment, and other craft and related trades workers	95.8	4	-6%
Stationary plant and machine operators	95.8	5	8%
Refuse workers and other elementary workers	95.6	3	-27%
Drivers and mobile plant operators	94.9	6	-5%
No paid work for past five years	94.9		
Building and related trades workers, excluding electricians	94.7	6	5%
Laborers in mining, construction, manufacturing, and transport	93.9	4	-4%
Market-oriented skilled agricultural workers	93.1	4	-51%
Agricultural, forestry, and fishery laborers	90.4	3	-19%
Food-preparation assistants	90.2	2	-31%
Cleaners and helpers	87.5	2	-31%

Source: PIAAC database for 29 countries and 188,168 adults aged 16–65. Median decile of income is shown, using within-country income rank. Income premium is calculated by regressing the log of actual income (available for seven countries in main data files) on cognitive ability—measured as the international standardized values of mean scores on math, literacy, and technology, indicators for education (including primary, associates degree, bachelor's degree, and graduate degree), age measured in quartic values (age, age^2, age^3, age^4), a binary variable for male, whether respondent is born in the country, whether respondent is a native-language speaker, country fixed effects, and a measure of social advantage. The social advantage indicator is the predicted value from a regression of mean cognitive ability on the number of books in home as child, parental education, gender, age, whether born in country or not, and native-language speaker.

The PIAAC sample is much larger but does not collect data on religion. It shows that U.S.-based Asian and Pacific Islanders score lower than non-Hispanic white people by roughly one-third of a standard deviation, despite higher levels of education. This is based on an overall score, but white people also score higher on each of the three test sections—math, literacy, and technology.

Upcoming chapters will discuss the nongenetic origins for these gaps and how they have changed—or even reversed—over short periods of time.

Despite the gaps between racial and ethnic groups, there is enough overlap such that substantial fractions of the black, Hispanic, and working-class white population already score high enough to enter and succeed in every profession. For example, in the United States, 25 percent of information and communications technology professionals score below 105 on the PIAAC (using U.S.-based means and standard deviations). That is the highest-scoring broad occupational group in terms of educational attainments (83 percent have at least a bachelor's degree). Yet, more than one in five African Americans with a bachelor's degree score above that entry-level threshold in cognitive ability. Likewise, a sizeable percentage of information and communications technology professionals in the United States are black (7 percent in the PIAAC database).

For now, the important point to take away is that black people, women, and people born to less educated mothers are all currently paid below what their cognitive scores alone would predict, as suggested by data from the NLSY 1997 and the PIAAC.[19] In other words, pay would be more egalitarian by race, class, and gender, if people were compensated based purely on formal measures of cognitive ability. A later chapter of this book will discuss one reason why this is the case: Elite professionals, who are often white males from educated backgrounds, create policies and cultural norms that prop up their incomes.

There are other ways to think about cognitive ability that go beyond the abstract reasoning and literacy skills that IQ and achievement tests are designed to measure. These include musical, artistic, or performance ability, though I know of no systematic data collection effort to measure those skills and how they are distributed.

There have been efforts to measure cognitive skills related to skilled blue-collar work. The military vocational exam tests nonacademic technical knowledge about automotives, shop or craft work, electronics, and mechanics, and these data are also available in the NLSY 1997. Black people score no lower than white people on automotive or shop knowledge, and Asians, white Christians, and Jews all score the same on all four measures. Mastering this body of technical knowledge can be helpful for a variety of skilled trades in construction, repair, and production. While the vocational test is not intended to measure IQ, the fact that black people perform the same as Jews, Asians, and white people on at least two of the four subtests illustrates the power of environmental exposure and influence to affect test scores. So-called hereditarians argue that IQ measures genetically determine a general intelligence that is applicable to any intellectual problem, but repairing machines is a major intellectual challenge, and these data suggest that people with somewhat low IQs—as typically measured—may be just as good as people with higher IQs at solving this type of problem.

In fact, racial gaps in knowledge are much narrower when it comes to the technical and scientific knowledge that people commonly use in real-world jobs. The U.S. Bureau of Labor Statistics surveys workers in every detailed occupational category (roughly 900 of them) about the level and use of science, technology, engineering, and math (STEM) knowledge in various domains through its O*NET program. These domains include science (biology, chemistry, physics), engineering, computers, math, design, mechanics, construction, production, economics, and telecommunications.

Expanding an analysis that I conducted for the National Academies of Science using these data, I find that black people work in occupations that are just .24 standard deviations less demanding of STEM knowledge or technical knowledge than white workers. The average Hispanic worker is in a job that requires .20 standard deviations less STEM knowledge and a similar amount of more general technical knowledge.[20]

The broad occupational groups with the highest scores on STEM knowledge are engineers, healthcare practitioners, scientists, computer workers, managers, installation, maintenance and repair workers, and construction workers. The cognitive skills needed to perform these jobs are clearly valuable in that workers with the same level of education and experience earn higher incomes if they report higher knowledge in these domains. The magnitude is such that a one standard deviation in technical knowledge (or STEM knowledge) predicts 13 percent (or 15 percent) higher incomes. And yet, knowledge in these technical domains is commonly held across all groups of people even in a highly unequal country such as the United States.

The Unnatural Gaps in Scores by Gender

One might also be concerned about gender differences in cognitive skills. In 2005, the economist Larry Summers, who also served as the president of Harvard University and U.S. Treasury secretary, infamously claimed that the overrepresentation of men among top scientists was at least partly the result of the "different availability of aptitude at the high end," by which he meant that there are simply not enough women with very high IQs to be top scientists and that biological factors explain this. In response to a question after his speech, he clarified his remarks:

> My point was simply that the field of behavioral genetics had a revolution in the last fifteen years, and the principal thrust of that revolution was the discovery that a large number of things that people thought were due to socialization weren't, and were in fact due to more intrinsic human nature.[21]

The phenomenon that Summers was trying to explain is why only 19 percent of U.S. PhDs in physics are awarded to women; shares for computer science (21 percent), engineering (23 percent), and mathematics (29 percent) are only slightly higher.[22]

It is not difficult to test and reject Summers's hypothesis, which harkens back to the erroneous assumptions about women made by male intellectuals throughout recorded history.[23]

One of the largest-ever studies of IQ scores among high school students in the United States—called Project Talent—was undertaken in the 1960s, when gender norms were particularly unfavorable to women. Young women born in the 1940s had the same mean IQ as young men but comprised only 35 percent of top-scoring students, defined as those scoring at least two standard deviations above the mean (IQ of 130 or more).[24] Only 33 percent of top-scoring students were female for math and only 13 percent for science.

Yet, much has changed culturally since the mid-twentieth century. International data on adolescents born at the start of the twenty-first century show that young women have made great progress in catching up to the highest-scoring young men. On the OECD's Programme for International Student Assessment (PISA) exam of 15-year-olds, 44 percent of top-scoring test-takers—those at least two standard deviations above the mean—are currently women, for overall scores across all subjects.[25] This is true for both the international average and the United States. By subject, women comprise 37 percent of top scorers for math, 39 percent for science, and 60 percent for reading. The breakdown is similar in the United States.[26] Cultural issues clearly come into play. Girls, but not boys, score lower on science and math when their mothers have lower levels of schooling than their fathers.[27] In 25 of the 73 geographic units (a mix of countries and regions within countries) with test score data, the average girl outscores the average boy on math. It is difficult to imagine a biological explanation for the variation observed across countries or the emergence of more females among top scorers over the span of a few decades within the United States, from 13 percent to 41 percent in science.

Noncognitive Skills

While cognitive skill gaps between racial, gender, and ethnic groups are well documented, there are no black-white differences overall or Hispanic-white differences in personality assessments; moreover, on the personality traits that predict health and income status described above on the NLSY 1997, Jewish-Americans have the same scores as Christian-Americans, and Asian-Americans score only slightly lower than white people. Black people are significantly more likely than white people to report being enthusiastic and self-disciplined, both traits that predict higher income and health, but black people are more likely to report being anxious, which predicts lower income and health. Asians rate themselves the same as white people on self-discipline and anxiety, but lower on enthusiasm.

Environmental Predictors of Cognitive and Noncognitive Skills

The absence of racial gaps on personality assessments is striking because children growing up in more privileged home settings tend to have more robust personality traits. The family environment—including exposure to poverty—and parental education are significant predictors of positive personality traits. The NLSY 1997 researchers created a Family/Home Risk Index to measure exposure to unfavorable living and family conditions. The index includes data on the following concepts:

- Cleanliness of home exterior and interior, as reported by interviewer
- Neighborhood safety
- Access to quiet space for study, dictionary, and computer
- Religious engagement
- Family routines
- Parental disability
- Parenting style (neither permissive, nor authoritarian), warmth, and level of monitoring

Black people and Hispanics are strongly disadvantaged according to this index, whereas Jews, Mormons, and Asians are strongly advantaged. White Baptists score close to average but considerably below white Catholics. Roughly one full standard deviation separates the home environment of Jews from black people and roughly 0.60 standard deviations from non-Jewish white people and black people.

These conditions are strongly predictive of personality characteristics. Children raised in the least-risky quintile (top 20 percent) on the family risk index score half a standard deviation better on the personality traits conducive to higher income and health than children raised in the bottom quintile. This means the children raised in a predictable, safe, and supportive home environment are more disciplined, enthusiastic, and less anxious. This translates into better health and higher incomes later in life.

This same environmental variable also strongly predicts variation in cognitive ability and IQ. Children raised in the top-quintile environment score over one standard deviation higher on cognitive performance than children raised in the higher-risk home environment. Even when parents are equally educated, those who create a more supportive, safer, and warmer home environment raise children who score higher on cognitive tests.

None of the above evidence offers definitive estimates of the causal effect of parenting on cognitive performance or personality development, since children are not randomly assigned to families. Yet, such evidence does exist.

Adoption studies have found very large effects on IQ when low-income children are placed in the homes of affluent parents.[28] A study in France found that adoption into a high socioeconomic status family—with a manager or professional parent—raised the IQ of children aged four to six years old with low IQ by 1.3 standard deviations (19.5 IQ points) by the time they reached the age of 13, which is much larger than the U.S. black-white IQ gap. Children

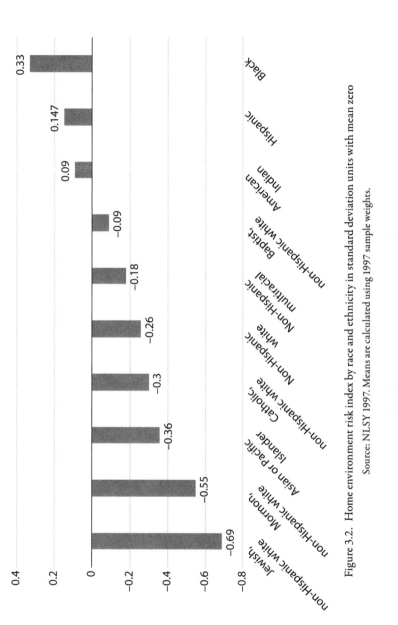

Figure 3.2. Home environment risk index by race and ethnicity in standard deviation units with mean zero

Source: NLSY 1997. Means are calculated using 1997 sample weights.

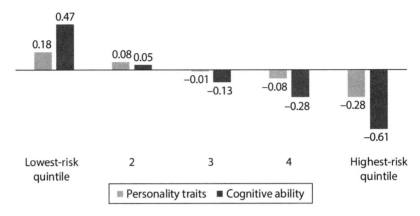

Figure 3.3. Cognitive ability and personality by riskiness of home and family environment

Note: Expressed in standard deviations with mean of zero.

Source: NLSY 1997. Means are calculated using 1997 sample weights.

adopted into a working-class family also benefited, but by much less (0.5 standard deviations).

Likewise, both IQ scores and personality measures improve when children are randomly assigned to high-quality preschools.[29] These studies often find that the IQ effects do not last long after the programs end but the personality effects do; since personality is no less genetic than IQ in standard twin estimates, one implication is that cognitive achievement requires sustained exposure to enriching environments during childhood, whereas long-term benefits to personality may come from the confidence gained from even temporary cognitive benefits and the supportive environment that created those benefits.[30]

All of this evidence demonstrates that exposure to less risky family environments and access to high-quality schooling would dramatically boost the earnings potential and health status of many black people, Hispanics, Native Americans, and working-class white people. Moreover, even some children from rich families would be better off if their parents created warmer, more routine home environments.

Differences in Actual Performance and Productivity

So far, the discussion of merit-based pay has focused on individual traits that predict income and good health, such as educational attainment, cognitive ability, and self-reported personality profiles. Even if one accepts that payment based on these traits alone would narrow the income distribution, one could argue that payment based on actual performance would not generate the same egalitarian result.

For example, the founder and owner of a start-up business is compensated directly based on the performance of his or her company. If profits grow because of successful innovation and expansion, the owner gains at least a share of those profits. Likewise, employees in many large corporations are paid according to actual measures of performance, whatever they might be.[31]

A body of psychology research investigates the factors that predict better performance. Both personality traits—especially conscientiousness—and cognitive ability are strong predictors.[32] Cognitive ability seems especially relevant for the performance of complex tasks, but less so for other types of work.

Psychologist and Gallup senior scientist Frank Schmidt and co-authors In-Sue Oh and Jonathan Shaffer recently analyzed 100 years of academic research on job performance and its relations to employee selection metrics.[33] A number of fascinating findings comes out of this work

First, job performance varies significantly but not nearly as much as the income distribution would suggest. The standard deviation in the value of output produced is roughly 40 percent of the average employee's salary, so if the mean salary for an occupation is $100,000, then a worker in the 84th percentile produces $140,000 in value compared to $60,000 in value for a worker in the 16th percentile. The implication is that some inequality in earnings could certainly be based on performance, but this in no way justifies the extreme disparities in payment observed in the United States, among CEOs for example.

Second, cognitive ability (IQ essentially) is the best single predictor of job performance identified in the literature for applicants to a new role. Its error-adjusted correlation with job performance is 0.65 in the selection-science literature (i.e., the body of research on how to predict employee performance). It works much better for professional and managerial roles (error-adjusted correlation of 0.74) than for blue-collar jobs (error-adjusted correlation of 0.39).

Yet, other measures that have zero or even negative correlations with IQ are also highly predictive of job performance. These include measures from tests of integrity (0.46), conscientiousness (0.22), and emotional stability (0.12).[34] Assessments from structured interviews are only weakly correlated with IQ but almost as predictive of job performance (.58 versus .65) and add 18 percent to the validity of the assessment when combined with IQ.[35] Thus, a conscientious candidate who interviews well but has below-average IQ is likely to outperform a candidate with high IQ whose interview is unimpressive and rates low on integrity or conscientiousness.

A body of literature in psychology has reported on race and gender gaps in performance evaluations—both subjective and objective—of actual workers. The main finding from the most recent and comprehensive meta-analysis from Patrick McKay and Michael McDaniel is that black-white gaps in work-based evaluations exist but are small and constitute only about one-quarter of the size of gaps in cognitive performance.[36] Notably, the most recent meta-analysis from McKay and McDaniel finds substantially smaller black-white gaps in performance than older studies, suggesting that the performance of black people has converged or that discriminatory effects of ratings have declined. Other scholars have found essentially no Hispanic-white gaps in performance across a smaller number of studies.[37] The literature includes various performance criteria, such as task performance, absenteeism, service complaints, commendations, and personality-related factors. There are reasons to worry about racial bias in at least some of these measures, but even with that caveat, the black-white gap is small overall, and there is no gap at all on things like social skills and involvement in workplace accidents.

After decades of research and refinement, Gallup's management consulting scientists developed a survey instrument called the Q12, which measures employee engagement. It asks workers to rate their level of agreement with 12 statements on a 1–5 scale. Here are some examples:

- At work, I have the opportunity to do what I do best every day.
- There is someone at work who encourages my development.
- At work, my opinions seem to count.
- I know what is expected of me at work.
- In the last seven days, I have received recognition or praise for doing good work.

When combined, the answers to these and the other seven items have extraordinary predictive power when it comes to performance. If you rank work units—individuals or small teams within organizations—by employee engagement using Q12, those units in the top quartile (top 25 percent) score dramatically better than those in the bottom quartile on absenteeism, turn-over rates, shrinkage (the dollar amount of lost merchandise), personal safety incidents, and product or service quality defects. The more engaged business units also performed better in terms of profitability, productivity, sales, and customer satisfaction.[38] These results come from an analysis of 1.8 million employees across 82,000 business units over 230 organizations spanning 73 countries. There is further evidence that increases in business unit engagement leads to better outcomes in the future, whereas better outcomes are only weakly predictive of an increase in engagement.[39]

To investigate racial and gender differences in engagement, I analyzed two Gallup surveys.[40] One includes all 12 items from the Q12 but is limited to a small sample (3,500 U.S. working adults) collected from a random sample of respondents from the Gallup Panel and weighted to be nationally representative. The Gallup Panel consists of people who have previously taken Gallup surveys—through random selection—and said they would be willing to be re-contacted for an online survey. The second dataset is from the Gallup-Sharecare Well-Being Index and includes a much larger number of respondents (85,000 U.S. working adults), but it only includes the three Q12 items that tend to be most predictive of engagement (the first three listed above).

In both databases, engagement is correlated with higher levels of educational attainment. In the larger database, people with graduate degrees are the most engaged and show a 0.12 standard deviation difference from those with a high school diploma, controlling for age, race, and gender; people with bachelor's degrees are only slightly more engaged than those with a high school diploma (.05 standard deviations).

Despite these educational differences, the results show very small differences between races and between men and women in both databases. In general, Hispanics, white people, and Asians had essentially equal engagement levels, whereas black people scored just one-tenth of a standard deviation (0.11) lower than white people. In the panel, the differences between black people and other groups were driven by responses to a small number of items: Black people were significantly less likely to say they know what is expected of them at work, that they receive recognition or praise for good work, and that their opinions seem to count. In the larger database, black people were also less likely to say that they have an opportunity to do their best work and that someone encourages their development. Overall, on both databases, the difference between black people and white people was equal to the difference between men and women, with women expressing higher engagement scores by 0.10 of a standard deviation.[41]

If one classifies workers as engaged when their average answer to the 12 questions is a 4 or higher (on a 5-point scale), then 36 percent of black workers are engaged compared to 40 percent of white workers, 37 percent of all male workers, and 42 percent of all female workers. These are obviously small gaps. Moreover, the gender engagement gap goes in the opposite direction from the gender pay gap—despite there being a strong correlation between engagement and pay.

In the larger database, I can also see how religion related to engagement. Again, the differences are very small. Controlling for demographic characteristics and whether the respondent's company is growing, Protestants and Catholics tend to score slightly higher than other groups. Protestants score 0.10 standard deviations higher on engagement than Jews, 0.09 standard deviations higher than Mormons, 0.10 higher than those with no religion, and 0.15 higher than those who report other non-Christian religions. Differences with Muslims are insignificant.[42]

Although these are not direct measures of performance, their strong connection with performance and the quality of work suggests small differences in actual work performance between groups.[43] This reinforces my claim that payment based on merit would not lead to significant differences between groups.

There is some evidence to suggest that good management practices may be enough to eliminate the small racial gaps in performance. Recent evidence from one large company shows that establishment-specific gaps in black-white performance can be entirely explained by the climate of the store. This result comes from an impressive study by Patrick McKay, Derek Avery, and Mark Morris, who obtained data from 6,130 workers across 743 retail stores.[44] They found no black-white differences in sales performance but did find that relative performance by store varied according to how employees rated the climate of the store on four questions using a 1–5 scale, where 5 means strongly agree.

1. I trust the company to treat me fairly.
2. Top leaders demonstrate a visible commitment to diversity.
3. The company maintains a diversity-friendly work environment.
4. The company respects the views of people like me.

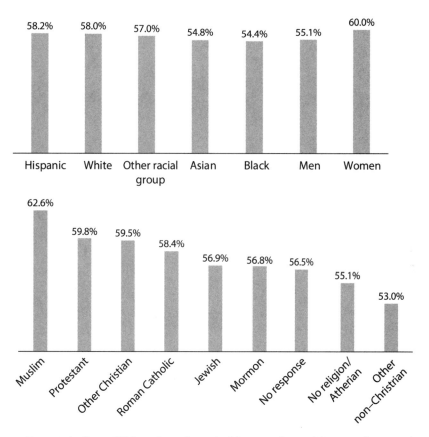

Figure 3.4. Share of U.S. workers who are highly engaged at work by race, ethnicity, and gender, 2009–2015. Share of workers who are highly engaged by religious preference, among white respondents only

Source: Gallup-Sharecare Well-Being Index. The sample consists of 84,749 U.S. adults surveyed in 2016. Respondents were asked to rate their agreement on a 1–5 scale to questions about their primary job. High engagement means an average score of 4.3 or higher on each of the following three items, which are taken from Gallup's longer Q12 battery: At work, I have the opportunity to do what I do best every day; There is someone at work who encourages my development; At work, my opinions seem to count. To be considered highly engaged, respondents must have at least one answer that reflects strong agreement (5) and none below agreement (4).

The research team calculated sales per hour of work for each employee using electronic data maintained by the company and tied to each employee identification number. Black sales workers performed equally as well as white people on average, but there were important differences across stores. Black people performed worse in stores with a poor climate rating and better in stores with a favorable climate rating. It stands to reason that residual black-white gaps in performance could be reduced more broadly by promoting respectful workplace cultures.

Entrepreneurship

Another important measure of a person's productivity capacity and performance relates to her or his inclination and ability to start and run a successful business. Entrepreneurial activity is important for maintaining or increasing living standards because unchallenged incumbent businesses would have little incentive to launch new and better products or lower prices with respect to quality unless they were challenged by potential or actual competitors. Likewise, some entrepreneurs launch entirely new and important goods or services in their own right.

In the United States, there are very large gaps by race and gender in business ownership rates. In 2014, black people and Hispanics comprised 29 percent of the U.S. population but only 7.2 percent of business owners. The underrepresentation of Hispanics and black people is even worse in prominent venture capital funds and at tech companies.[45] Women are also heavily underrepresented. Yet, there is compelling evidence that this is the result of differences in economic opportunity, not entrepreneurial talent.

Gallup scientists developed a "Builder Profile" to identify the people most likely to start and succeed as entrepreneurs, based on their personality characteristics and thought processes—including their confidence, tolerance for risk, creativity, and other factors.[46] The index predicts business performance in several ways—whether the owner meets revenues and profit goals, the number of employees, the level of revenue, and revenue growth. People with higher builder profile scores also live in richer zip codes.

Yet, Gallup data reveal no racial or gender gaps in entrepreneurial potential. Black people and non-Hispanics score no differently than white people. White business owners score significantly higher than nonowners, but so do black and Hispanic business owners and there are no racial differences between them. Among non–business owners, there are also no differences between non-Hispanic white people and Hispanics and black people. The implication is that an equal opportunity society would generate egalitarian rates of entrepreneurship between racial and ethnic groups and even similar success rates among business owners.[47]

In sum, the research described above provides even stronger evidence that merit-based pay would reduce income inequality overall and between groups, even in the absence of efforts to make education and family environment opportunities more egalitarian. When combined with efforts to enhance the equality of opportunity, merit-based pay would most likely eliminate race and ethnic gaps in income and health status.

BEYOND SKILLS

The chief problem with labor market inequality is not the market per se. Rather, it is the way political power operates to control and affect markets. This power is sometimes acute, such as when Wall Street banks and shareholders are "bailed out" by taxpayers, saving them from bad decisions and irresponsible behavior. Yet, more often, the power that shapes markets works gradually and cumulatively through decades of lobbying, cultural persuasion, and minor changes here and there to state licensing laws, tax laws, or other means of affecting how much people are paid.

The notion that skills—both cognitive and noncognitive—determine pay is the basis for the "human capital" theory. It has a lot of theoretical strength, as the above discussion illustrates, but it is also limited. The problem, for the theory, is that social rules are a key determinant of pay for many occupations. This explains why there is such variation in pay across industries and occupations, even after taking into account cognitive and noncognitive skills. Later chapters will discuss specific rules that shape some of these differences in pay across professional occupations. The importance of nonmarket factors is fairly obvious when considering compensation for public employees, which depends on the willingness of state and federal legislatures—and their constituents—to pay for the services provided, including policing, fire prevention, education, and, in many countries, healthcare. The vagaries of politics, not productivity, explain why teachers are paid different salaries in different cities, after adjusting for the local costs of living.[48] Likewise, there is no reason to expect the "market" to determine prices in which the government is one of the largest buyers. That includes healthcare. It is political power—not the market—that leads to nurse practitioners being paid only half as much as family physicians, even though they are qualified to perform the same services.

The bottom line is that if political equality prevailed, markets would produce far more fair and egalitarian outcomes. The traits that predict performance and performance itself vary far less than actual income, and under conditions approximating equal opportunity, these differences would shrink further.

4

The Importance of Equal Access
to Public Goods and Markets

IN THE SPIRIT OF RAWLS AND PLATO, I define a just society as one that grants and defends the basic liberties of individuals, while it maximizes the welfare of the least advantaged members under conditions of political equality and provides equitable opportunities for everyone to do the work that naturally suits them.

By basic liberties I mean the right of individuals to engage in mutually beneficial transactions with other parties and live as they see fit, provided their actions injure no one else. These stipulations follow from a basic principle of reciprocal fairness.

By the least advantaged, I mean something like those people who are at the bottom of various overlapping distributions for the good things in life: emotional and loving family and friendship networks; psychological and physical good health; the capacity to learn, understand, and influence the world; purchasing power; a sense of accomplishment; and respect from others. In principle, the least well off would score in the bottom quintile on an index that measures all of these things, if one existed. Maximizing their welfare ensures that everyone's welfare is at least as high.

By political equality, I mean several things:

1. Citizenship is available to all born in the territory and open to foreign-born immigrants under certain conditions, which I outline later in this chapter.
2. Each citizen holds equal power in choosing his or her leaders and equal protection under the law. Access to power is not based on hereditary ties, gender, tribe, ethnicity, race, nationality, or parental social status.

3. Public goods are provided to all through public funding and on an equitable basis. The most important of these are security, education, and the infrastructure of commerce and production (e.g., roads, bridges, ports, environmental resources, telecommunications).

   a. The education curriculum is universal and encourages youth at an appropriate age to specialize in and master occupations that suit their interests and, presumably, their natural ability.[1]

   b. Security applies to physical protection (e.g., police and military), protection of property (e.g., firefighting services), protection from injury or disease through healthcare, and relief from poverty, job displacement, and disability.

4. Each citizen is entitled to the basic liberties, including equal access to markets and the right to engage in mutually beneficial exchange as a customer or seller.

FREE EXCHANGE AND POLITICAL EQUALITY

Among the basic liberties, I follow Rawls in including those enumerated in most modern republican constitutions, including that of the U.S. Bill of Rights. However, I would also include one that is rarely mentioned, at least outside of libertarian philosophy: the right to engage in mutually beneficial exchange with others. The right to free exchange is as important as other fundamental liberties, such as freedom of expression, due process, and equality under the law. Without it, governments can block vitally important economic activity, thereby suppressing individuals or groups of people and preventing them from achieving health and political influence.

In medieval Europe, commerce was dominated by politics at the expense of free exchange. The largest economic organizations had to win favor and monopoly status from the ruler.[2] At a more basic level, and therefore more significant for individuals, commercial activity within and across cities was dominated by guilds. As economic historian Sheilagh Ogilvie shows, guilds suppressed competition both by limiting rights to trade or transport products to members and by limiting membership to a thin slice of the male population, often those with hereditary privileges of ownership and deep community ties, as well as the right ethnic affiliation, who qualified as citizens.[3]

These practices eviscerated opportunities for upward mobility and directly lowered the living standards of most medieval Europeans.

From the end of slavery in 1865 until the mid-twentieth century, African Americans were forced to live in a society that forbade them access to markets and to engaging in mutually beneficial exchange with others in fundamental ways. In the labor market, African Americans could not become professionals in many states because state licensing boards and professional associations would not allow it. Until the late 1960s, the American Medical Association's state and local affiliates frequently prohibited African American doctors from membership, depriving them of licenses, hospital affiliations, patients, and income.[4] The American Bar Association (ABA) was even worse in that even the national organization—not just local or state affiliates—officially barred black would-be lawyers until 1943, and the first black member was not admitted until 1950.[5] This was not for want of candidates. In 1911, the ABA's executive committee formally rescinded the membership of William H. Lewis, who was born to newly freed slaves after the Civil War and was appointed assistant attorney general of the United States by President Howard Taft.[6] The ABA stated that it was settled practice to admit only white men.

Education in general has also commonly been distorted to disfavor politically oppressed groups. Most northern colleges and almost all southern colleges—except those deemed historically black—refused to admit African Americans well into the twentieth century. Despite its location in New Jersey—not a former confederate state—Princeton University did not admit its first black student until 1935.[7]

Similarly, access to housing markets through mortgage financing was also systematically stifled for African Americans. African Americans were forced—in many cases by formal law and, in the rare cases when that failed, informal violence—to live in segregated communities throughout the United States. Deed restrictions that forbade sales to African Americans, zoning laws, and real estate industry policies all prohibited black people from buying or renting homes in desirable neighborhoods, which, in turn, limited access to desirable schools and neighborhood amenities.[8]

Segregated black communities, moreover, were deprived of great wealth and the benefits of investment and home ownership. In the 1930s, the federal government created tiered neighborhood-based evaluations of credit worthiness, which were quickly adopted by private lenders and the federal housing agencies that subsidized and secured mortgages. These standards systemically deemed black neighborhoods or even white neighborhoods with black population growth as unworthy of credit, thereby locking out a huge portion of the black population from access to financial markets.[9] These standards prevailed during the massive post–World War II housing boom, which otherwise dramatically improved living standards for many white working-class families.

FREE MARKETS AND THEIR LIMITATIONS

Any full accounting of liberties must consider access to markets to be fundamental. By equal access to market, I mean that markets are open or "free" in the sense that all exchanges are permitted that are voluntary and mutually beneficial between parties, with some important caveats and exceptions. Exchanges that are coercive or made under fraudulent or false pretenses are prohibited. Hence, basic regulations on the quality of goods and services will likely be required for many products, and in some cases, this would justify licensing requirements, clinical trials, or inspection from public officials. The same rule also applies to exchanges between workers and employers, which should be entirely voluntary, recognized as mutually desirable, and never conducted in an exploitative or misleading fashion. Likewise, exchange that harms the public—such as exchange that results in pollution—would also be subject to regulation, such as a pollution tax or prohibition, depending on the seriousness of the harm. Such exchanges violate the principle that the exercise of basic liberties should injure no one.

Exchanges between citizens and noncitizens are permitted under the same conditions, resulting in free trade of goods and services. In this context, it should be clear that I do not mean "free trade" to refer to the absence of tariffs on imports. As I mean it, free trade would not permit exchanges for goods produced by slave laborers or workers who are coerced into oppressive working conditions. In practice, people with different political views and standards may disagree about whether a specific factory or workplace should be designated as oppressive, but in principle, such disputes could be effectively resolved by independent third-party agencies, nonprofit organizations, and courts. In practice, at least since Karl Marx, political pressure from activists and student groups has often been able to hold corporations accountable for reforming and improving conditions in factories, thus making trade more mutually beneficial than it would otherwise be.

Assuming the exchanges qualify as mutually beneficial as described above, prohibitions and even tariffs on imports should generally be regarded as unjust when they go beyond minimal sales taxes on imports, which may be needed for government revenue, to penalties meant to deter the consumption of foreign products or protect domestic companies from competition.

The reason restrictions on trade are generally unjust is that they prevent mutually beneficial transactions. If you, as an individual or business owner, can get a better deal (i.e., a higher quality-to-price ratio for the product), you should be able to make that deal, so long as it otherwise meets the conditions laid out. When buyers have access to the best available deal, welfare increases, as the quality of a product increases relative to its price. Such transactions also have dynamic effects in that they increase the number of competitors in a market, encouraging innovation and limiting profit margins. In this way, open markets do not benefit only the two parties who are exchanging goods; they also create broader benefits to all those who participate in the market as buyers—either directly (as customers) or indirectly (as buyers of products that use imports as components of a final product).

One argument against free trade is that the beneficiaries—even if large in number—should not be allowed to benefit at the expense of even a small number of local producers (e.g., factory owners) and their employees. My response is that the right to trade is a basic liberty, but there is no meaningful right to work in a specific industry, occupation, or company, nor could there be in any practical sense. There are countless reasons why a layoff may occur or a firm close down, including poor managerial choices, poor product quality, supply-chain problems, and competition from domestic companies. There is no ethical obligation for taxpayers to bail out a slumping clothing store or restaurant so that its employees do not have to seek out new work. There is, however, an important consideration in determining how producers are harmed by foreign imports. The issue is whether harm comes from cheating or fair competition. If it is through cheating—such as corporate espionage, intellectual property violations, or forced transfers of technology as a condition to market participation—then the domestic producers have a legitimate complaint, and the foreign producers should not be allowed to participate in the market. The National Bureau of Asian Research and scholars such as Robert Atkinson, the president of the Information Technology and Innovation

Foundation, have documented that Chinese companies routinely commit these abuses at the expense of U.S. and other companies.[10] These practices do not meet any authentic definition of free trade and should be rejected, even if short-term economic costs are large. At the same time, it must also be recognized that Chinese entrepreneurs have made genuine improvements in efficiency in many industries.[11] Chinese firms that invest in R&D and win intellectual property protections are much more likely to export than those that do not. This does not prove that the gains in Chinese market share are the result of fair competition, but it does suggest that successful Chinese companies are taking actions that create social value.[12]

If there is agreement on the enforcement of rules against cheating, the key question is: Should companies that offer products at a lower quality-to-price ratio be compensated when a domestic, or even a foreign, competitor beats them fairly? The answer must be no; otherwise anyone could open an inefficient and poorly managed business and cash in on incompetence. Reciprocity does not imply that those who lose under fair competition should be sheltered or compensated. In the context of a welfare state, with protections against poverty, entrepreneurs must be allowed to risk and experience failure. They also must be allowed to realize gains when they succeed; if their superior products will be taxed until the quality-price ratio is dragged down to their competitors' level, the entrepreneur's motivation to make sacrifices, take risks, and invest great effort into starting and growing a business will vanish, making many people worse off and depriving the market of innovation. Thus, tariffs cannot be justified as a means to protect domestic producers.

The logic of this position is clear when applied outside of international relationships to other economic relationships. If tariffs, taxes, or other restrictions on exchange made with the aim of sheltering lower-performing businesses could be justified, then local governments or state governments would have every right to protect their retail establishments, restaurants, theaters, entertainment complexes, hospitals, and other businesses from competitors in neighboring states or even local jurisdictions. Should Washington, DC, residents pay a 20 percent tax to protect hospitals or surgeons who work within the District of Columbia if they see a specialist surgeon at Johns Hopkins University in Baltimore? Should a cure for cancer that is developed by a pharmaceutical company in Minnesota be taxed by the New Jersey legislature until the price in cost per quality-adjusted life year is the same or higher than a New Jersey–based pharmaceutical company?

Such interventions would rightly be regarded as corruptions of the political process and economically self-defeating from a national perspective. The same logic applies to international relationships.

Some may argue that restrictions on international (or domestic) trade could be justified by concerns for the worst off, if one counts laid-off workers—or those in their communities—as being among the most vulnerable members of society. There are two reasons why this logic does not justify tariffs. First, neither manufacturing workers nor former manufacturing workers are among the worst off on any obvious measure. Manufacturing and even export-oriented service jobs tend to pay well, but available evidence suggests that workers laid off in manufacturing experience smaller wage decreases relative to workers in other sectors.[13] Manufacturing workers also enjoy higher levels of job security relative to workers in domestic-facing sectors, despite competition from China and other countries. Comprehensive government data show that the risk of layoff is considerably higher for the average nonmanufacturing worker relative to a manufacturing worker, especially construction, retail, and even professional services.[14] Laid-off workers from any sector deserve sympathy and compassion, and a republican state should create and maintain supportive programs to smooth the transitions to new jobs, and if needed, new career paths. It shouldn't matter if the source of competition that led to the layoff is foreign or domestic.

A second reason that restrictions on domestic or foreign trade cannot be justified as a means for protecting the worst off is that by protecting some workers, they harm others—and almost always a much larger number. Lower-income workers spend a larger percentage of their incomes than richer workers, because it is harder to afford savings when you have less money. Raising the price of things they buy is the same as lowering their purchasing power. Protecting a small number of manufacturing workers through tariffs takes money from a massive group of poor people—many of whom don't even have jobs—and gives it to people in manufacturing who do have relatively decent paying jobs and, since they are in the labor force, are unlikely to be suffering from ill health or disability.

A final justification for restrictions on trade is to make domestic companies stronger. It is dubious as to whether protecting businesses from competition actually makes them stronger. A comprehensive investigation by the World Bank of East Asian "infant industry" practices found that innovation—measured via productivity growth—was slowest in the most protected industries and strongest for companies that faced strong international competition.[15] Even if tariffs did make domestic companies stronger, they would be unfair to both foreign producers and domestic businesses and consumers who would prefer to buy the foreign product at its market price, rather than a heavily taxed price. In this framework, tariffs to support infant industries are no different from any other form of "corporate welfare" designed to tax consumers or businesses in order to support special interests. Such tariff policies should be rejected, regardless of their "strategic" benefits. This does not mean that supporting business or "competitiveness" is fundamentally problematic. There are many legitimate ways governments can make their domestic businesses more valuable: workforce development, subsidizing R&D, creating high-functioning national laboratories and encouraging business spin-offs, enforcing smart intellectual property laws, and ensuring a robust venture capital market, as well as through direct government grants. The economist Mariana Mazzucato has laid out best-practice principles and policies in this area, as has Robert Atkinson of the Information Technology and Innovation Foundation.[16]

IMMIGRATION AND THE RIGHTS OF NONCITIZENS

Immigration is generally highly beneficial for the receiving country because population density fosters occupational specialization and greater productivity, as Plato, Adam Smith, and contemporary urban economists all agree. In their roles as workers, entrepreneurs, and consumers, immigrants contribute to the affluence of society.

There are two important caveats. Immigration affects the distribution of income by redistributing from the groups who compete most closely with the immigrants in the labor market (or for public resources) to the groups who employ immigrant workers or work with them as employees or co-workers. Second, while immigrants benefit society as workers, they, like everyone else, absorb public resources such as antipoverty assistance, health, retirement, and other welfare payments. When immigrants disproportionately work in the lowest-paying occupations, their net effect on public resources is considerably greater than that of those who work in the highest-paying occupations.

In a recent book, the Harvard economist and immigration expert George Borjas makes these points with unusual clarity and care. He is one of the world's leading scholars on immigration and has published dozens of articles in top peer-reviewed journals.[17] Borjas is clear that if the only national goal were to maximize income, immigration policy would allow virtually any number of highly educated immigrants in but no "low-skilled" immigrants— meaning they lack a college degree. A massive influx of highly skilled immigrants would redistribute income from the affluent to the less affluent, boost economic growth, and lower the tax burden on native-born Americans.

Despite the seductive logic of favoring only highly educated immigrants, Borjas rejects the idea that immigration policy should be closed to those with low levels of education, and I agree. There are important moral and civic reasons to accept migrants, even when their economic contribution is predicted to be modest. Allowing less-educated workers entry and integration into society provides economic and social mobility for the workers and their descendants, thereby creating a slightly more prosperous world and elevating the disadvantaged. This process occurred for European and Asian immigrants to the United States, who were often poor and unskilled upon arrival, but in subsequent decades converged or even surpassed the Anglo-Saxon native population with respect to average income and education levels, as I discuss in chapter 6. Recent Asian and African immigrants have already converged, and Hispanics will soon reach parity with non-Hispanic white people, if current trends continue.[18] In this way, it would be an empirical error to categorize a group of immigrants as permanently "low-skilled."

A nontrivial number of less-educated migrants will also make large and direct contributions to their new society by starting valuable enterprises, assisting in the generation of innovative practical and cultural ideas, and becoming caretakers, security providers, partners, friends, companions, or spouses to the native-born population. It is impossible to precisely measure let alone predict the value that might come through these sorts of activities and relationships. The cultural exchange that migrants carry as they come and go across borders also ensures more harmonious relations between countries and allows good ideas and innovations to diffuse more widely and quickly than they otherwise would.

When migrants are a small proportion of the native workforce, the effects on labor markets will also be small, but mass immigration raises more troubling issues that warrant careful consideration, as I describe next. With respect to the worst off, immigration policy differs from free trade in that it puts the poor at greater risk. The four lowest-paid major occupational categories in the United States for workers aged 36 to 45 are food preparation and related occupations; personal care and service occupations; building and grounds cleaning and maintenance; and farming, fishing, and forestry. It probably isn't a coincidence that these occupations are heavily staffed by foreign workers: 23 percent of all workers aged 36 to 45 are foreign born, but they make up 39 percent of workers in those four low-paying occupations.

To investigate this further, I examined income data for 1.6 million workers born in the United States and calculated the relationship between incomes from 1994 to 2017 and the percentage of workers in their occupational field who are foreign born. I found that for every 10-percentage-point increase in the foreign-born share of workers in an occupation, native-born income was 2 percent less. If an occupation went from 10 percent foreign born to 60 percent foreign born in a given state, the model predicts native workers would see a 10 percent reduction in income. This effect is a bigger problem for less-educated workers because they are in occupations with higher rates of foreign-born workers and, as a result, are more likely to experience an influx in competition.[19]

These correlations do not necessarily indicate that immigration depressed wages. Few topics are more controversial in economic research, but a review of many economic studies on the subject does suggest that workers with low levels of education often see small but nontrivial reductions in wages as a result of the immigration of workers with similar skills.[20] These income reductions would be only partially offset by increased purchasing power that resulted from entrepreneurship and lower prices for services. My general conclusion after reviewing the data and academic literature is that large-scale immigration of workers with low levels of education has exacerbated income inequality by hindering growth below the median of the income distribution. Immigration has not made any important difference to the rise of the top one percent's share of income, as I mentioned in chapter 1, but it still raises important issues for how to organize a just society.

Likewise, immigrant labor must be regulated differently than trade because of how immigration interacts with citizenship and political power. In just societies, citizens are required to have equal access to public goods from birth to death and to power in adulthood. The education of citizens prepares them to maximize their productive capacity and freely choose the occupation that suits their ability. This arrangement is needed to meet reciprocal obligations to one another, but it also has the practical benefit of sustaining social and physical security systems, including antipoverty relief; a society with low labor-force participation or a high share of low-paid workers with unrealized potential will have difficulty meetings its obligations. A policy of open borders would thus risk collapsing the political and economic foundations of a just society.

For these reasons—political stability and the protection of the worst off—it is ethically important to impose limits on the influx of immigrant workers in order to fulfill obligations to fellow citizens, despite the fact that immigrant workers—even those with little formal education—contribute to economic growth and lower prices for consumers. What is the greatest good for the greatest number sometimes conflicts with the greatest good for the worst off.

A related ethical question pertains to whether or not we should give preference to fellow citizens over noncitizens, other things being equal. I believe the answer is yes due to reciprocal moral obligations. Living in the center of the vast cosmopolitan Roman Empire, Cicero nevertheless gave priority to local relationships. He writes: "It is still a more intimate bond to belong to the same city; for the inhabitants of a city have in common among themselves forum, temples, public walks, streets, laws, rights, courts, mode and places of voting, beside companionship and intimacies, engagements and contracts, of many with many."[21] In other words, the sharing of public goods, laws, and commitments, as well as commercial exchange, all create tighter bonds than between strangers, even between kin living in different cities. Likewise, security considerations speak to the importance of shared citizenship bonds. It is one's fellow citizens who fight in times of war to protect one's property and life or engage in protests to win rights or protect liberties, and even if these were the only bonds, it would warrant preferential treatment from the perspective of reciprocal altruism.

While Cicero valued shared local bonds, he was not indifferent to noncitizens or foreigners. He praises past Romans for generosity in war and allowing former enemy combatants to become citizens when they fought honorably. He also develops a compelling principle: "Whatever one can give without suffering detriment should be given even to an entire stranger," even as he emphasizes the limit is a necessary one "so that we may have the means of generosity to those peculiarly our own."[22] He finds people at fault who give to strangers "what ought to be employed for the needs of their own families or bequeathed for their future use."[23]

The implication for immigration policy is that foreigners should be freely admitted up until the point when their participation in labor markets begins to seriously harm the least advantaged domestic workers or when their requirements for aid—if many are disabled or too old to work, for example—impose a harmful burden on the nation.

In recent decades, I believe the United States may have exceeded this threshold. The foreign-born share of the U.S. population spiked from 4.7 percent in 1970 to 13.7 percent in 2017. The current figure is near the long-term average from 1850 to 1930, when immigration fueled the growth of a new country.[24] As other chapters describe, racial and ethnic conflict was extreme during that time, and economic historians conclude that mass immigration contributed to income inequality by lowering wages for blue-collar workers.[25] Since 1970, the annual net flow of immigrants has been roughly 743,000, which is 20 percent as many as the total number of annual births. If annual net flows were reduced to 400,000, the foreign-born share of population would stabilize at around 10 percent.[26]

Immigrants to the United States hold every level of education and skill but have been heavily represented among the poorly educated: 27.5 percent of the foreign-born population aged 25 and over has not completed high school compared to only 8.7 percent of U.S. natives.[27] Reducing the net inflow from this group—many of whom are not authorized—would go a long way to reducing harm to the U.S. economy and the disadvantages to current U.S. residents.

Reducing the net flow of migrants should not be considered a border security problem. In fact, the best available evidence on the effects of border security is that it has been counterproductive and exacerbated rather than reduced the negative consequences of immigration. Princeton sociologist Douglas Massey and his collaborators have been surveying Mexicans and Mexican residents living in the United States every year since 1982, collecting detailed information about migration and border crossings. The startling conclusion from this research is that border security has locked migrants in the United States, preventing the natural back-and-forth flow that otherwise would have taken place. From 1970 until the mid-1980s, more than half of Mexican immigrants—both those with legal documents and those without them—returned to Mexico within a year of working in the United States, but investments in border security caused the probability of returning to plummet to 20 percent in 2007 for undocumented workers, even as 92 percent of documented migrants returned to Mexico within a year.[28] Massey, writing with Jorge Durand and Karen Pren, finds that border security has no effect on the likelihood of migrating from Mexico to the United States, only on the likelihood of leaving the United States to return to Mexico. As a result, restricting legal work visas and increasing the risk of crossing the border did not reduce the number of undocumented workers in the United States; it increased it. The evidence strongly suggests that legalizing migrations from Mexico and easing border crossings would reduce the number of permanent Mexican-born residents in the United States. Border security and mass deportations are completely unnecessary. Paradoxically, empowering immigrants politically by granting them legal work and residential status will reduce the net flow of migrants dramatically.

While mass migration can harm the poor, there are several other important caveats to be kept in mind when considering the justice of immigration policy. One is that rich countries can afford to take on thousands of even the poorest refugees, and doing so, bring benefits that go beyond simple economic considerations. The harm imposed on noncitizens by prohibiting their entry should be compared to the harm imposed on the least well-off citizens by allowing their entry. Noncitizen migrants fleeing extreme political persecution and high risk of death should arguably be given priority over the threat of small wage reductions, even for disadvantaged members of society.

Another point more closely tied to economics is that there will be job vacancies that simply cannot be efficiently filled using domestic labor because of local shortages or the undesirability of the work in relation to other opportunities. Thus, visas for less-educated immigrants should be inversely proportional to measures such as the local unemployment rate for workers in that occupational category and proportional to hiring difficulty or income growth. Such policies increase the chances that immigrants will complement rather than compete with the worst-off domestic workers. In recent years, jobs that require specialized technical skills are those most likely to show signs of hiring difficulty and also trigger a disproportionate number of visa requests from employers.[29]

For those who do enter, the more empowered immigrants are to pursue the occupation that best suits their abilities, the more positive will be their effect on society. A practical implication is that workers should not be closely tied to any one employer for legal status, so that they can pursue employment relationships that best use their talents. Likewise, those who enter with temporary work visas should be readily able to convert them to permanent work visas on a pathway to citizenship, if they choose to follow it, and the children of migrants should be given full access to public services when they qualify.

To summarize, equal access to markets in the context of immigration policy means two things. First, it means regulating and stabilizing the flow of migrants so as to protect native citizens from wild distortions in the labor market and preserve a close relationship between domestic residency and citizenship; part of those regulations should entail penalties to employers for violating labor laws. Second, it means granting legal access to a large but proportionally manageable population of migrants, so they can come and go freely, move up socially, gain access to public services, and be empowered to insist on mutually beneficial exchanges with employers. All authorized migrants, under reasonable conditions and requirements, should be allowed to become citizens and encouraged to do so.

THE BASIC CONDITIONS AND INEQUALITIES IN SOCIAL STATUS

The above discussion is meant to clarify what I mean by access to public goods and markets in a just society through the lens of two especially controversial market topics—namely, trade and immigration. This is not meant to suggest in any way that these are the only relevant issues. Later, I discuss inequality in access to education (chapters 5 and 6), housing and neighborhoods (chapters 7 and 8), and professional services (chapter 9). Reforms spanning all of these spheres of economic inequality, as well as those not mentioned, would be needed to meet the general conditions of a just society described above. If implemented, I believe these changes would radically reduce income inequality, along with inequalities in subjective well-being, education, health, and other things that matter to a good life. And yet, it is worth pointing out that such a society would not be a communist utopia with everyone possessing the same spending power and living standard.

The vast gaps in welfare found in contemporary rich countries such as the United States are in many ways the result of differences in political power. However, political equality would still result in some inequality in income and welfare.

Modest differences in welfare, or income specifically, are an inevitable (one could say natural) quality of the world because economic relationships are highly complex and dynamic, path dependent, and affected by random chance. Moreover, not everyone has the same preferences or aptitude for work. Modest wealth inequality exists even in hunter-gatherer societies where occupational roles are virtually identical, members use the same technologies, and political equality prevails; anthropologists estimate wealth inequality in such societies to be comparable to income inequality in modern Scandinavia, but roughly one-half the level of income inequality observed in the United States (and roughly one-quarter of the level of U.S. wealth inequality).[30]

I would argue that some market-based inequality is inherently consistent with basic notions of fairness and a reasonable conception of equality of opportunity. There are several ways that merit or skill differences would emerge even in a just society.

One way is through innate differences, or their interaction with society. Individuals differ in terms of innate ability or attributes. I do not believe there are compelling moral grounds for refusing to reward those lucky enough to have certain genetic advantages, including personality and physical attributes. Though their gifts may be unrelated to effort (and effort itself likely has some genetic basis), it is entirely fair that more attractive models and actors should be paid more if they add greater value to a marketing campaign or artistic production, just as the best athletes should be paid more if their participation in a professional sports league attracts more viewers and fans, whether or not they had to train as hard as less-gifted athletes. Likewise, a sales worker with a more charming personality should be rewarded if she or he is able to close sales deals more effectively than someone who comes across as less charming. It would likewise be foolish and immoral to eliminate any economic advantages that may accrue to inventors and entrepreneurs, whether or not their genes gave them an edge in sparking the creativity, motivation, or insight that others lacked.

Differences would also emerge in compensation across occupational categories, because the labor market would play a role in setting the price of work. Yet, here a just society would look very different from the contemporary United States. In a just society, people would be educated in such a way that they would be capable of doing the work they found most valuable and fulfilling, which might oftentimes not be the work with the highest social status or income. The wages of people in many "low-skilled" occupations are presently far below those in professional occupations, but this is partly because inequality in educational opportunities has pushed too many people into low-skilled occupations. There would be more balance in a just society, such that the salaries of professionals would fall much closer in line with the salaries of house cleaners, day-care workers, and hair stylists as a result of supply and demand. As imbalances arise, more people will move into that line of work until balance is restored.

This is not to say that all occupations would have the same average income levels in a just society. I think not. It would still be the case that some careers would lend themselves to higher compensation because of higher levels of productivity, longer training requirements, the level of experience needed, or the demonstration of excellence at lower levels of work (i.e., managers, who work their way up from entry-level positions). Careers that combine those advantages with the development of innovative new technologies and entrepreneurship would likely garner the greatest financial rewards in a just society.

Individuals will also differ based on family circumstances, even in a just society, which can affect career outcomes and general well-being. Political equality and equal access to public goods could never eliminate every relationship risk, such as the death of a parent or being born to a parent with psychological problems. The best a just society could do, perhaps, would be to ensure that best-practice mental and physical health treatments are available to families who need them and to otherwise shore up the conditions and capacity of the worst off with respect to bad luck or genetic disadvantage.

A more difficult case involves the transition from an unjust to a just society. In such cases, family inequalities may be quite large and based on historical injustices, such as slavery, colonization, or some other form of political oppression, and there it would be appropriate for the government to purposefully elevate the conditions of the least well off. For example, I've already provided evidence that the average African American child grows up in a less privileged home environment; other chapters reinforce the point and describe the historic and current factors that produced and reproduce that disadvantage. Giving low-income African American families extra resources—such as health and family counseling, educational support, and tutoring for children—would be a fair way to address this historical injustice without placing excessive burdens on the rest of society. These interventions could also be justified as a means to enhance the well-being of the least well off.

Even if genetic and parenting conditions were identical—say, for identical twins raised together by their biological parents—inequalities could still emerge as a result of differences in the quality of training and education. It would be impossible to assign teachers of exactly the same quality to every child. Some teachers are better than others as a result of personality differences or other innate traits, or because they themselves had better training. What should matter is that the best teachers are not systematically assigned to children with greater political power, and society should take active steps to ensure that overall teaching quality is maintained at a high level. Parents should be free and encouraged to invest as much of their own resources—in terms of money or time—on private educational experiences that might give their child skills that distinguish him or her from peers. Distinguished excellence—even if derived from private familial circumstances—is a benefit to others in a just society, whereas nepotism obviously is not. Still, a high-quality baseline education—one that draws teachers and principals from a pool of highly competent professionals—should be universally available starting as early as practical, such as age three.

If the other criteria are met, any inequalities that arise under these conditions could be considered just, and in principle they would meet Rawls's criterion of benefiting the least well off, because unequal compensation would be based on the productive contributions of individuals, rather than political connections. Rewards based on productive contributions encourage innovation, investment, and productivity and lower the costs of goods and services, while enhancing their quality.

The discussion above is far from comprehensive in terms of the complex set of issues that arises when considering the justice of a society, even at the most foundational level. Yet, it is intended to provide enough details to move forward with more practical considerations of how contemporary democracies fail to meet the basic conditions sketched out here in several crucial ways.

5

Unequal Access to Education

THIS CHAPTER STARTS BY DISCUSSING how the United States has failed to deliver equal access to public education and how this failure creates inequality in the skills that are most predictive of income and health. It ends with a review of the latest scientific literature on the genetic basis of education and intelligence. The clear implication of this evidence is that environmental factors are the dominant explanation for why people vary in intelligence and education. Across individuals in the same birth year and growing up in the same country, 55 percent to 87 percent of variation in intelligence and education is explained by nongenetic factors, with twin studies showing higher genetic effects than analyses based on actual genes. Across generations and countries, individual variation is almost entirely explained by nongenetic factors, and group-level variation can be explained entirely by nongenetic factors.

Inequality in educational opportunity has a long history in the United States.

More than a decade before he escaped from slavery, Frederick Douglass, at the age of seven or eight, as far as he could remember, was transferred from a harsh plantation to serve a young couple, the Aulds, in Baltimore, who were related to his owner. Mrs. Auld, who had never owned a slave, soon began teaching him the alphabet and how to spell until, after a short time, her husband found out and forbade further instruction in no uncertain terms, telling her that literacy would spoil Frederick and make him unfit for slavery.

Overhearing his master state that educated people could not be slaves, the young Douglass was emboldened to take every opportunity to further his education in the hope that it would prove a path out of slavery. Whenever he had a moment, often at great risk of retribution from his masters, he would study a newspaper or book. To further his instruction, he took bread from the Aulds' house and, while performing various household errands, shared it with poor white boys who lived in his neighborhood in exchange for brief lessons. In this way, he taught himself to read well enough so that by age 12 Douglass could understand complex philosophical works. Eventually, he became internationally famous as one of the greatest orators, writers, editors, and public intellectuals in American history.[1]

Douglass's example shows how extraordinarily difficult and unlikely it was for American slaves to become literate. The mandatory illiteracy of an oppressed group went hand in hand with political domination. Political inequality was the cause of their enforced illiteracy. Accordingly, the obverse is true. Political equality requires universal investment in and encouragement of the skills needed to thrive in a given society.

SCHOOLING AND THE DISTRIBUTION OF VALUABLE SKILLS IN A MARKET SOCIETY

When the U.S. Congress passed the 1964 Civil Rights Act, it included a provision that mandated a survey and report "concerning the lack of availability of equal education opportunities by reason of race, color, religion, or national origin in public educational institutions at all levels in the United States."[2]

That study was led by a social scientist named James Coleman and became known as the "Coleman Report."[3] It was a massive undertaking, collecting data from over half a million U.S. students. The report confirmed perhaps not surprisingly that black students were extremely segregated, even in the North, and that they attended schools with significantly fewer resources in the South. But some of its findings were surprising and unlikely to motivate policy change. After controlling for the race of students, Coleman found that "schools are remarkably similar in the way they related to the achievement of their pupils when the socioeconomic background of the student is taken into account. Differences in schools account for only a small fraction of differences in pupil achievement."[4]

This finding—that families matter more than schools—has been echoed through the years by many liberal and conservative observers of education and inequality in the United States, often citing Coleman's work. For example, in his popular but scholarly book *Our Kids*, which makes the case for investing in the success of poor children, the social scientist Robert Putnam argues that opportunity gaps between children are largely the result of families, not schools: "The gap is created more by what happens to kids before they get to school, and by what kids bring (or don't bring) with them to school—some bring resources and others bring challenges—than by what schools do to them."[5]

Likewise, supporters of teachers' unions have used Coleman's work to challenge the "No Excuses" idea, which is prominent in certain charter schools and asserts that all children should be expected to learn, regardless of their family circumstances. Instead, these critics of charter schools emphasize the importance of improving the conditions of students outside of school.[6] Along these lines, education policy expert Diane Ravitch writes: "Children who grow up in economically secure homes are more likely to arrive in school ready to learn than those who lack the basic necessities of life. If we are serious about closing the achievement gap, we should make sure that every pregnant woman has good prenatal care and nutrition and that every child has high-quality early education."[7]

It is certainly true that parents affect the level of scholastic achievement of their children, and in a society with great inequality in income and political power, it should not be surprising that family life is also unequal. There are ways it can be made much less unequal—via better-functioning markets for housing and professional services, criminal justice reform, and public support for specific programs—but it would be unfortunate if liberals concluded that there is little that can be done through schools to reduce inequality in cognitive performance of children. Ironically, the view that schools are impotent in reducing cognitive inequality aligns rather closely with the hereditarian school of thought, even though that perspective holds radically different views about the fundamental origins of test score gaps. Hereditarians attribute social inequality to genetic differences. Here is what Richard Herrnstein and Charles Murray have to say about the Coleman report in their book, *The Bell Curve*:

> In affecting IQ, [schools] do not matter nearly as much as most people think. This conclusion was first and most famously reached by a study that was expected to demonstrate just the opposite. The report, issued in July 1966, announced that it had failed to find any benefit to the cognitive abilities of children in public primary or secondary schools that could be credited to better school quality. The usual ways in which

schools tried to improve their effectiveness were not likely to reduce the cognitive differences among individual children or those between ethnic groups. . . . The Coleman report did not prove that educational reform is always futile, but that, on the whole, America had already achieved enough objective equalization in its schools by 1964 so that it was hard to pick up any effects of unequal school quality. The Coleman report tells us that the cognitive ability differences among individuals and groups alike on a national scale cannot be reduced much by further attempts to equalize the kinds of bricks-and-mortar factors and teacher credentials that school boards and taxpayers most often concern themselves with.[8]

Murray repeated this basic argument 18 years later in his book *Coming Apart*, which at its heart, argues that the dysfunction he sees in the white American working class is largely a result of their weak genes for intelligence and social competence. "Education does not have much of an effect on IQ after the child enters elementary school," writes Murray. "The children of the well educated and affluent get most of the top scores because they constitute most of the smartest kids. They are smart in large part because their parents are smart."[9] After claiming that a child's IQ score at age 6 will not be affected by age 18, even after an expensive private education, he writes, "This finding goes back to the famous Coleman report in the 1960s. . . . No one contends that education routinely transforms average children into intellectually gifted children."[10]

Hereditarians argue that genes largely determine test scores. Teachers' unions argue that family environments largely determine test scores. Both groups are skeptical that the quality of schooling makes much of a difference.

Coleman was a leading social scientist and a good one, but that does not mean he did the analysis correctly or used the best possible methods, as the influential Stanford economist Caroline Hoxby has recently argued, and I draw on her argument in laying out my own concerns.[11]

The most important part of Coleman's analysis compares test scores within the same school to average test scores across schools separately for each race. For black sixth graders, he finds that 20 percent of the variation in test scores can be accounted for by variation across schools, and for white people, schools account for somewhat less (14 percent) of the variation.[12] Based on this, he concludes that school quality is a minor factor in test scores.

But as Hoxby points outs, this evidence does not warrant Coleman's conclusion and represents the biggest methodological flaw in his analysis. Unpacking the corollaries of test scores is not the same as identifying the causal factors. Moreover, Coleman's method aims to explain variation among black people separately from variation among white people and other students. Using Coleman's method, which analyzes races separately, it is possible that 100 percent of the gap between black people and white people is between schools, whereas 0 percent of the gap between high-scoring black people and low-scoring black people is between schools. Coleman himself concedes the point:

> Why are the racial and ethnic groups separated in the analysis? Let us suppose that all Negroes go to equally bad schools and all whites go to equally good schools, or vice versa. Then the analysis which keeps the groups separate will show no effectiveness of school characteristics, because for each racial or ethnic group, the schools are uniformly bad or good.[13]

Other data in his report do suggest that black people go to very different schools than white people. Only 16 percent of students are white in the average elementary school attended by black children, whereas 91 percent of fellow students are white for the average white elementary student.[14]

Coleman nonetheless justifies his analysis by stating that failing to control for race would bias the analysis of schools because race has an effect on test scores independent of any school effects. That conclusion, however, remains to be proven, and his methods do not allow him to prove it, because children are not randomly assigned to schools irrespective of their race.[15]

To see this from another perspective, consider an imaginary case. In a hypothetical world, there are high-quality heart surgeons, with very high patient success rates, and other people who perform heart surgery but lack the proper training and skills, with very low patient success rates. The success rates of surgeons, however, are not publicly disclosed—only their experience, measured in years, which does not predict success. Patients nonetheless infer quality based on price and reputation, which is highly correlated with quality. The rich buy high-quality surgery, whereas the poor pay as much as they can scrape together and hope for the best.

Now give these hypothetical data to James Coleman and tell him to run a regression the way he did in his famous report. He would use patient mortality as the dependent variable and family income and experience of the surgeon as the independent variables. The results would show that family income explains almost all of the variation in patient mortality after surgery. The media headline would be: "Go to Any Surgeon You Want, Because Your Income Is All That Matters." The "evidence-based" policy that would come from this would be exactly wrong and 100 percent ineffective: Give money to poor people but have them use the same surgeons they would have otherwise—telling them that money, not surgeon skill, matters for survival. They would still die at the same rate as before.

With education, we have done something similar. Since the Coleman report, the national teaching strategy has been based on the idea that poor kids won't learn until their family dynamics and socioeconomic status improve. The quality of teaching doesn't matter. That view is not universally held, of course, and many proponents of education reform (such as former Washington, DC, education chancellor Michelle Rhee) strongly disagree with that position, but it is arguably the dominant position of teachers' unions, Democratic Party leaders such as Hillary Clinton and Bernie Sanders, and far-right white nationalists, who would otherwise have little in common politically.

A second reason the conclusions of the Coleman report are wrong is that they are based on the wrong measures of quality. Coleman's measures of teacher quality included teacher verbal test scores and other administrative data—such as years of experience, race, and teacher education, none of which is consistently predictive of objective or subjective performance measures, which were not part of the study.

There is strong evidence that getting the measure of quality right matters. Modern education research employs several sophisticated and accurate measures of teacher quality. One is to calculate the test score gains by the teacher's average student. This is called the teacher's *value-added* to test scores. One large-scale study finds that being taught by a high-quality teacher for two years between ages 14 and 16 compared to a low-quality teacher predicts a large increase in subject-matter test scores, which are crucial to gaining acceptance for higher education levels.[16] Moreover, this value-added measure is unrelated to the types of administrative measures used in the Coleman report, such as teacher experience, education, and salary.

A third problem is that the Coleman report did not track learning—or changes in test scores over time. Even using his own methods—estimating the factors that are correlated with an outcome—would have shown two things: Student learning between 9th grade and 12th grade is substantial, and it varies systematically across schools. Those are the results of a major study, called "Project Talent," of 10,000 high school students that took place around the same time as the Coleman study.[17]

Finally, and importantly, Coleman made no effort to estimate the causal effect of school, teacher, or neighborhood quality on achievement, but still inferred that these things do not matter much. To estimate the causal effect of teacher quality, you need two things: a valid measure of teacher quality and a research strategy that uses some form of random assignment of students to teachers to account for the fact that family privilege or prior test scores are likely to be important predictors of access to high-quality teachers and schools. Modern research has done this.

THE EFFECTS OF HIGH-QUALITY PUBLIC EDUCATION ON COGNITIVE ABILITY

Many studies in the field of psychology have examined how education affects IQ. It is obviously not enough to simply observe that people with higher education have higher average IQs (they do), because natural ability is likely to provide extra encouragement and motivation to pursue higher levels of education. Psychologists and other social scientists have tried to get around this problem by observing how IQ changes over time for a given individual as he or she acquires more education and how IQ changes in response to government policy changes that encourage or mandate higher levels of education. A recent meta-analysis by Stuart J. Ritchie and Elliot Tucker-Drob examined 42 databases covering 600,000 people with IQ scores. They found that a year of education raises IQ between 1 and 5 points (which amounts to .07 to .33 standard deviations).[18] The average effect across studies was 3.5 IQ points.[19] To put that in perspective, the test score gap between non-Hispanic white people and black people is approximately 15 points, according to Department of Education data from the National Assessment of Education Progress; that amounts to four years of education, based on this analysis.

Results from the Project Talent database of 10,000 randomly selected U.S. high school students found similar effects of education on IQ measured in the 1960s. For example, boys gained 14.4 IQ points in math and 19.1 points in literature over three to four years of high school. Some IQ tests attempt to measure cognitive ability that is less tied to knowledge and more about pure reasoning and memory. Even these tests reveal huge gains resulting from education. Among boys, memory increased 6.3 IQ points, abstract reasoning increased 7.8 IQ points, and visualization in three dimensions increased 9.5 points.[20]

To really appreciate the relationship between education and IQ, however, one needs to consider the massive gains in IQ over the last century. During that time, in the United States and on every continent on earth, people have gotten steadily better at IQ exams—at a rate of around 0.3 points per year. The phenomenon is known as the *Flynn effect*, after the New Zealand–based scholar who, in painstaking detail, documented a half-century of gains in his groundbreaking 1984 article.[21]

Since then, the finding has been replicated around the world across every kind of intelligence test measure.[22] Indeed, for the Embu tribe in rural Kenya, IQ scores went up 11 IQ points from 1984 to 1998 for seven-year-old children of subsistence farmers on a measure of intelligence (Raven's matrices) that uses no words and is meant to measure raw capacity for abstract reasoning (fluid intelligence).[23] The Kenyan children also showed large gains in verbal intelligence. The authors investigated potential causes and showed that the 1988 group had greater access to calories, particularly protein, but was more likely to suffer from intestinal parasites, even though less likely to suffer from hookworm. More conclusively, the 1988 group was more likely to have attended preschool (15 percent versus 7 percent), and Sunday school attendance also increased from 90 percent to 99 percent. Fathers were less likely to be living with the family in the latter group, and mothers less likely to be married, but maternal literacy and education were much higher, suggesting an enriched home environment.

Altogether, the Flynn effect shows that the environment plays a massively important role in shaping intelligence, and IQ and cognitive exams should not be taken as measures of natural intellectual capacity. Rather, they measure intellectual performance that has been deeply shaped by environmental and social influences.

The other crucial insight of the Flynn effect is that intelligence is highly dynamic across cohorts. Population groups with relatively low IQ scores today would score the same as the average white American living in the 1960s and much higher than white people born at the beginning of the twentieth century.

Looking back at the massive surge in invention and innovation in the nineteenth and early twentieth centuries, it would be ridiculous to say that people were dramatically less capable than people living today. In the United States, the most inventive period in history began in roughly 1870 and lasted until roughly 1940, as measured by the number of patents granted to U.S.-based inventors per capita.[24] It is bizarre to think that intelligence measures would have suggested widespread stupidity. These people, most of whom had not attended college and would have done poorly on formal exams, nonetheless invented the modern world.

On many tasks not measured on IQ tests—such as mechanical and agricultural knowledge, skill at inventing and fixing tools and machines—I suspect that people today would score lower. Quite likely, even the purest IQ tests measure elements of formal learning, as well as exposure to language and culture. People adapt their learning and patterns of thought to the opportunities and demands of their environment. If parents and teachers emphasize the importance of literature, writing, and abstract reasoning, children respond by developing those skills, and if political circumstances devalue those skills or cut off their applicability, investment in education will be diminished.

In any case, the link between IQ gains and mass schooling is clear. Enrollment, literacy, and educational attainment have risen dramatically since the early twentieth century (figure 5.1). The IQ data suggest that these investments in education have had enormous benefits to the population in terms of cognitive capacity and performance. Of course, other factors not strictly tied to education have also likely played a role: improvements in healthcare, sanitation, water quality, and exposure to toxins, for example. I also believe that the rise of more cognitively demanding occupations that require sophisticated literacy and numeracy on a regular basis—especially in professional services—have led to more concerted efforts for teachers, parents, and individuals to invest in the skills and way of life, such as daily reading and writing, consistent with those work opportunities.

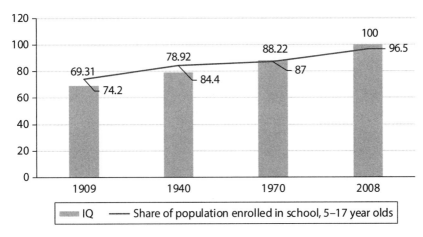

Figure 5.1. A century of IQ and education gains in the United States, 1909–2008

Sources: I simulated IQ scores using data from Jakob Pietschnig and Martin Voracek, "One Century of Global IQ Gains: A Formal Meta-Analysis of the Flynn Effect (1909–2013)," *Perspectives on Psychological Science* 10.3 (2015): 282–306, which show average annual gains of roughly 0.31 IQ points from 1909 to 2008 in the United States. This is consistent with research from James R. Flynn and Lawrence G. Weiss, "American IQ Gains from 1932 to 2002: The WISC Subtests and Educational Progress," *International Journal of Testing* 7.2 (2007): 209–24. Education data is from Table 8 in Thomas D. Snyder, "120 Years of American Education: A Statistical Portrait," https://nces .ed.gov/pubs93/93442.pdf. I calculated the 2008 data for educational attainment using enrollment data from the 2006–2010 Five-Year American Community Survey, using American Fact Finder and taking the mean enrollment values across ages 5–17.

THE CAUSES OF NEGATIVE-FLYNN EFFECTS

Recently, scholars of intelligence have pointed to some evidence for a reversal of the Flynn effect—a *negative-Flynn effect*, meaning a decline in intelligence between cohorts at the population scale. Thus far the evidence is thin, short in duration, and applicable to only a small number of countries.[25] The most recent large-scale literature review finds a continuation of IQ gains in every continent in recent decades, but these studies cobble together many very small samples, often from nonrepresentative populations.[26]

Data from large-scale international cognitive assessments provide the relevant evidence either way, with the most noteworthy being the OECD's Programme for International Student Assessment (PISA) for 15-year-olds. The PISA exam has been conducted from 2000 to 2015 with comparable scales for people of the same age in a large number of countries. The data show no significant change in math, science, or literacy scores over various years during this period for the average OECD student. In OECD publications, reported math trends cover the longest period (2003–2015), and only a handful of the 63 countries saw a significant decrease: Finland, Australia, Iceland, Netherlands, Belgium, Sweden, Canada, France, Hungary, the Slovak Republic, the Czech Republic, and Vietnam.[27] Many countries saw significant math test score gains over this period, including Italy, Brazil, Indonesia, Israel, Portugal, Peru, Costa Rica, Argentina, Russia, Poland, Romania, and Albania. The upshot is that for most rich countries, the Flynn effect appears to have leveled off over the last 15 years, but there is no evidence for decline outside of a small number of countries.

Norway and Finland are two countries where there is convincing evidence of a decline in cognitive performance. Large-scale data from Finland shows test scores having fallen, which is consistent with Finland's PISA data. The test scores of Finnish military conscripts grew over the late 1980s and early 1990s and peaked in 1997 (representing people born in 1977 or 1978); by 2009, scores were approximately 2 IQ points lower.[28]

A strikingly similar pattern emerged in Norway, where the test scores of Norwegian-born military conscripts rose by 3 IQ points for those born between 1962 and 1975 and then fell by roughly 2.5 IQ points for those born between 1989 and 1991.[29] Thereafter, IQ scores have apparently stabilized in Norway or even ticked back up. Children born in 2000 scored slightly better than those born in 1988—with differences falling within the margin of error—on the PISA math exam, and reading scores increased significantly for children born in 2000 compared to those born in 1994.

Some hereditarian IQ scholars attribute the decline to biological dysgenic effects (higher fertility rates among lower-IQ parents), but the data from PISA suggest that that is highly unlikely, and an analysis of the Norwegian data rules it out entirely. More-educated parents—with higher IQs, typically—have been having fewer children than less-educated parents in essentially every country, and yet the positive Flynn effect has dominated in all but a few, and the only declines have occurred for those born since 1980.[30] If dysgenic effects matter at all, they must be trivial compared to environmental forces such as access to education or better health. Moreover, I find that the negative trend in Finland and the positive trend in Norway for PISA results occur for both the native- and foreign-born student populations in those countries, which, again, makes dysgenic factors unlikely, since the fertility patterns of immigrants differ from those of native northern Europeans.[31]

The causes of the positive and negative Flynn effects were teased out more systematically by Bernt Bratsberg and Ole Rogeberg. They isolated test results from Norwegian-born males who had brothers who also took the test (355,438 individuals) and found that both the positive and the negative Flynn effect occurred in the same families, depending on when the brothers were born, and matched the Flynn effects that occurred across different families. The unavoidable implication is that the Flynn effect is caused neither by parenting characteristics that apply equally to brothers in the same family nor by genes, because each brother is equally likely to have more or less advantageous genes for intelligence. Instead, the Flynn effect observed in recent decades in Norway—and the more recent smaller decline—is explained by cohort-level environmental factors that work across families, such as the quality of neighborhoods or schooling.

THE EFFECTS OF QUALITY OF SCHOOLING ON IQ

The gains in IQ from education apply to the average student, with average-quality schooling. Since schooling matters, it stands to reason that higher-quality education—either formally in school or through after-school programs, tutoring, or parental efforts at home—would result in even larger IQ benefits. Indeed, there is now irrefutable evidence showing that higher-quality education results in greater cognitive gains.

One of the most impressive studies collected data on 2.5 million U.S. students from 1989 to 2009 and linked these data to teacher and administrative records in one the country's largest school districts. The researchers—Raj Chetty, John Freidman, and Jonah Rockoff—calculated a valid measure of teacher quality—effectiveness at raising test scores—and used quasi-experimental methods to link teachers to students by taking advantage of random changes in teacher staffing.[32] They find that a one standard deviation in teacher effectiveness raises student test scores by .14 and .10 standard deviations for students in grades three through eight (corresponding, roughly, to ages 9 to 14). In a follow-up paper that links students to income tax records, the same authors find that even one year of having a teacher that is one standard deviation above the mean raises lifetime earnings by approximately $39,000.[33] One can imagine that the cumulative effects of having consistently good or bad teachers would be dramatic.

Another approach to measuring teacher quality does not rely on test score data to measure quality. Instead, it relies on classroom observations from independent observers who are trained to use certain criteria. There are several different measures that have been studied in detail, and teachers tend to be ranked in very similar ways using any of the measures. Yet, these measures clearly capture something distinct from the test score gains of previous students, because they are only moderately correlated with them.

One such observational measure of teachers—called CLASS—seeks to measure the quality of student-teacher interactions. It measures emotional support, the quality of instruction, and the quality of classroom organization and management.[34] A teacher's CLASS rating strongly predicts gains in student math and language, as well as noncognitive skills related to student effort. When combined with student survey information about their teacher, these ratings are especially effective, yielding large increases in both learning and student effort between good and not-so-good teachers.[35] We know these effects are causal because students were randomly assigned to classrooms in this study.

Moreover, the findings have been replicated by other scholars in a different sample of 24,000 kindergarteners. They found that the result of assigning students to better teachers as rated by CLASS was significant improvement in math and reading, as well in as the children's executive functioning—including their ability to pay attention and regulate their emotions.[36]

Other data using CLASS at the prekindergarten level is publicly available for scholars from the Study of Statewide Early Education Programs, and I have analyzed it.[37] Using informal measures of knowledge, such as letter, number, and color recognition, as well as counting, I found that the black-white gap in test scores among pre-K to fourth-grade students is roughly nil. Black parents seem to do just as well as more-advantaged and higher-educated white parents at teaching their children these things (table 5.1). Asian children came in the most prepared, and Hispanic children the least prepared. On more formal IQ tests of math, vocabulary, and language, the results were rather different. Asian, Black, and Hispanic children scored significantly lower than white people and multiracial children. The mean IQ gap was 0.91 between white people and black people and 0.82 between white people and Asians. There were no significant IQ differences between Asians and black people. As expected, differences in parental education and income explain much of these gaps.

Table 5.1. Fall pre-Kindergarten 4 test scores by race and ethnicity, expressed as standardized scores with mean of zero and standard deviation of one

	Formal IQ tests	Knowledge tests
White	0.42	0.28
Multiracial	0.10	0.14
Asian	−0.39	0.95
Native American	−0.47	−0.37
African American	−0.48	0.17
Latino/a	−0.58	−0.50

Source: Data from Study of State-wide Early Education Programs (SWEEP) from The National Center for Early Development and Learning (NCEDL) at UNC Chapel Hill. Test scores were collected in fall and spring of pre-K-4. Sample size is 721 classrooms with 2,982 children across 11 states. Summary means presented here use fall test scores and fall sample weight. Formal IQ measures include the Peabody Picture Vocabulary, Woodcock to Johnson III, and the Oral and Written Language Scale. Knowledge tests use number counting, number recognition, letter recognition, and color recognition. For details see Diane Early et al. "Pre-Kindergarten in Eleven States: NCEDL's Multi-State Study of Pre-Kindergarten and Study of State-Wide Early Education Programs (SWEEP)." ICPSR34877-v1. Ann Arbor, MI: Inter-university Consortium for Political and Social Research [distributor], 2013-10-02. http://doi.org/10.3886/ICPSR34877.v1.

THE EFFECTS OF QUALITY OF TEACHING ON EARLY CHILDHOOD IQ GAPS

In examining CLASS data, I also found that students learn more when they are assigned to higher-quality classrooms, and this has important implications for cognitive gaps by race and class. Black and Hispanic pre-K–4 students demonstrated extraordinary gains in learning and IQ when placed in high-quality classrooms. Black children gained roughly one-third of a standard deviation in language and math over just a few months of instruction when they were placed in high-quality classrooms, but they experienced almost no relative gains in low-quality classes (table 5.2). Likewise, Hispanic children demonstrated very large learning gains in high- but only modest gains in low-quality classrooms. For the average white student, classroom quality did not seem to make much of a difference in how they scored relative to their peers. The reason may be that the white parents of children in lower-quality classrooms were more apt to engage in supplemental learning exercises at home, but the data do not provide any clues.

Table 5.2. Learning gains from fall to spring in high- versus low-quality classrooms among pre-kindergarten–4 students, measured in standard deviation units

	High-quality classrooms	Low-quality classrooms
Black students		
Change in language IQ	0.37	0.06
Change in math IQ	0.34	0.04
Change in overall cognitive scores	0.21	−0.04
Hispanic students		
Change in language IQ	0.39	0.16
Change in math IQ	0.13	0.17
Change in overall cognitive scores	0.12	0.03
White students		
Change in language IQ	0.15	0.15
Change in math IQ	0.00	0.08
Change in overall cognitive scores	0.02	−0.01

Source: My analysis of data from Study of State-wide Early Education Programs (SWEEP) from The National Center for Early Development and Learning (NCEDL) at UNC Chapel Hill. Asians were only 2.7% of the sample and so are omitted here for lack of reliable estimates. High-quality classrooms are in the top quartile, while low-quality are in the bottom quartile for the summary CLAS measure. Test scores were collected in fall and spring of pre-K–4. Sample size is 721 classrooms with 2,982 children across 11 states. Summary means presented here use Spring sample weight. Language IQ measures by the Peabody Picture Vocabulary; math uses Woodcock to Johnson III, and overall score combines the two above with the Oral and Written Language Scale and assessments of number counting, number recognition, letter recognition, and color recognition. For details see Diane Early et al. "Pre-Kindergarten in Eleven States: NCEDL's Multi-State Study of Pre-Kindergarten and Study of State-Wide Early Education Programs (SWEEP)." ICPSR34877-v1. Ann Arbor, MI: Inter-university Consortium for Political and Social Research [distributor], 2013-10-02. http://doi.org/10.3886/ICPSR34877.v1.

While these results are adjusted for the relative performance of same-age peers, students from all racial backgrounds progressed on raw measures of learning over the course of the school year. By spring, the average pre-K–4 student could recognize and name more letters and numbers, count higher, and identify more colors. All of these things were positively correlated with higher IQ, which also increased. Raw IQ scores went up by roughly .41 to .49 standard deviations (6.2 to 7.5 IQ points) relative to fall scores.[38] Thus, even average-quality classrooms raise IQ substantially for all races, but the best

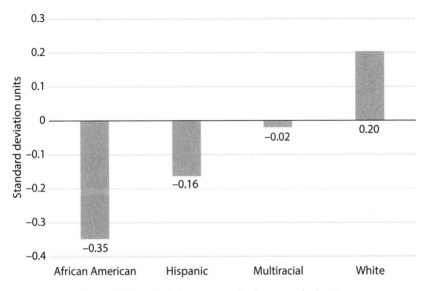

Figure 5.2. Pre-K–4 classroom quality by race and ethnicity
Source: My analysis of SWEEP database, using fall student weight.
See note in table 5.1 for details.

teachers are especially effective in raising scores for children from less-privileged backgrounds and thereby lowering the overall achievement gap between groups. This is exactly what you would expect if high-quality teaching compensates for limited family exposure to reading and literacy promotion for low-income children.[39]

High-quality teaching allows disadvantaged students to catch up with their more advantaged peers. These teacher quality effects go a long way to explaining longer-term gaps in cognitive performance in late adolescence and adulthood. Black children, especially, but also Hispanic children were much more likely than white children to be in low-quality classrooms (figure 5.2). The black-white pre-K gap in classroom quality is just over half a standard deviation, and that translates into missed learning opportunities for black people and divergence rather than convergence in IQ. Other research from Washington State also finds that black people, Hispanics, and low-income children are consistently assigned to lower-quality teachers, as measured in several ways.[40] Fortunately, there is strong evidence that teachers can be taught to manage their classrooms more effectively and literally become better teachers.[41]

THE POSITIVE EFFECTS OF SCHOOL-BASED
INTERVENTIONS ON BOOSTING IQ

Above, I mentioned just a few examples of recent studies using rigorous experimental designs that have proven that high-quality schooling raises cognitive ability and the personality traits associated with higher income and health, but these examples are hardly exhaustive.

One of the world's top education scholars, economist Roland Fryer, compiled evidence from 196 education experiments, in which children were randomly assigned to different treatment conditions, ranging from early childhood education, family-based interventions, and school-quality interventions. The home-based interventions in Fryer's study had small effects on reading and math scores, with some important exceptions. Reducing poverty and giving parents extra educational resources were rather ineffective. On the other hand, home visits to low-income mothers from a specialized nurse during and after pregnancy proved very effective at boosting maternal and child health outcomes, as well as cognitive ability. A random experiment showed that 12-year-olds who participated in the program as infants scored 0.20 standard deviations higher on IQ tests than their peers in the control group.[42] Aside from early childhood interventions, getting parents involved more in their child's school has also proven to be effective.

Overall, however, school-based interventions have been more consistently powerful. Among the most effective education treatments are intensive ("high-dosage") tutoring, which has huge effects on test scores; attendance at high-quality charter schools; and the professional development of teachers (table 5.3).

Attendance at high-quality pre-K classrooms has also proven to be highly effective at raising IQ according to the most rigorous social science research.[43] High-quality childcare at an early age emphasizes language learning through games and has been found to eliminate IQ gaps between very disadvantaged children and their average American peers. The Infant Health and Development Program had a similar effect on low-birth-weight, mostly minority children, and most of the IQ gains persisted for years after the program ended.[44] Similar positive long-term effects from the Chicago Child-Parent Center were found to persist in terms of education and the probability of arrest for the children who attended it, who were mostly black.[45]

Table 5.3. The experimental effects of educational interventions

	Math	Reading
Early childhood interventions	0.12	0.2
All home-based interventions	0.04	0.08
Parental involvement	0.12	0.14
Educational resources	−0.06	0.07
Poverty reduction	0.01	0.02
All school-based interventions	0.14	0.2
Student incentives	0.04	0.1
Tutoring (high-dosage)	0.4	0.41
Tutoring (low-dosage)	0.07	0.05
Teacher certification	0.03	0
Teacher incentives	0.05	0
General teacher professional development	0.17	0.15
Managed teacher professional development	0.06	0.49
Data-driven teacher evaluations	0.11	0.07
Extended time	−0.03	0.16
School choice/vouchers	0.08	0.07
Charters	0.12	0.07
"No Excuse" charters	0.17	0.1

Note: Average treatment effect is reported above in standard deviation units for 196 studies that use random assignment or experimental methods. High-dosage tutoring means small groups (six or fewer) for four days or more per week.

Source: Reproduced from Fryer, Roland G. "The Production of Human Capital in Developed Countries: Evidence From 196 Randomized Field Experiments." *Handbook of Economic Field Experiments* 2 (2017): 95–322.

In consistently demonstrating large effects on educational achievement, these interventions prove that public education has enormous potential to enhance the cognitive ability of children born in low-income households, especially when combined with family interventions that promote the adoption of routine healthy behaviors.

THE EFFECTS ON SKILL OF GROWING UP IN A RICH REPUBLIC: EVIDENCE FROM IMMIGRATION

Across Europe and the United States, far-right politicians and supporters view immigration as a threat to the prosperity of the country. They seem to believe that immigrants—who typically come from poorer countries with lower rates of educational attainment—are not capable of making productive contributions to the host country. In the most extreme cases, opponents of immigration argue that the cultural or genetic characteristics of immigrants make them and their children incapable of contributing. These commentators, encouraged by recent comments by President Trump, appear to regard the poverty of a country as an indicator of the natural capacity for its children to learn and develop.[46] They are wrong. Something almost incredible happens when children from poor countries with very low-quality education systems grow up in countries with strong and equitable educational systems.[47]

A comprehensive 2002 study of performance in English national exams taken by half a million children found that African immigrants to England born in 1991 scored only 2 IQ points behind white people at ages 7 and 11, and Indian children scored the same as white English children at age 7 and somewhat higher at age 11.[48] Both groups significantly outscored Pakistani and Bangladeshi immigrants, but they scored lower than Chinese immigrants. Black African immigrants scored higher than black Caribbean immigrants. But there is no natural law that group test scores are stable. For example, exam data from the London borough of Lambeth (a poor area of London with a high proportion of immigrant families) for 2011 show that the highest-scoring ethnic groups were black African speakers of Luganda (from Uganda) and Krio (from Sierra Leone), who had higher pass rates on the national exams than Chinese immigrants.[49] Nigerian Igbo and Yoruba speakers, as well as Ghanaians, outperformed Indian immigrants and white British natives (table 5.4).

The high achievement of these African ethnic groups—who come from the nations that supplied much of the Atlantic slave trade—cannot be attributed to high socioeconomic status. Many of the students are eligible for free school lunches because their families have low incomes, but, like East Asians and Indians, their parents are highly motivated for them to study and succeed in education, and they behave accordingly. And in Lambeth, at least, the qualitative evidence suggests that the teachers and staff provide a high-quality learning environment.[50]

While not all ethnic groups from Africa are so high achieving, by 2013, the average 16-year-old black African in England was scoring higher than the average white British student on the national exams.[51] Likewise, children with one black African parent and one white parent were also

Table 5.4. Percentage of 16-year-olds with passing grade (5+A*-C) or higher on all five of England's Key Stage 4 national exams, 2011

Black African, Luganda speakers	83%
Black African, Krio speakers	78%
Chinese	76%
Black African, Igbo speakers	76%
Black African, Yoruba speakers	75%
Black African, Ga speakers	75%
Indian	72%
White British	55%
Bangladeshi	54%
Black African	53%
Pakistani	50%
Black Caribbean	44%

Source: Feyisa Demie, "Raising the Achievement of Black African Pupils: Good Practice in Schools" (Lambeth Research and Statistics Unit, 2013), available at https://www.lambeth .gov.uk/rsu/sites/lambeth.gov.uk.rsu/files/Raising_the _Achievement_of_Black_African_Pupils-Good_Practice _in_Schools_2013.pdf, accessed June 18, 2019.

outscoring white people, achieving the same scores as those with two African parents. White British and black Africans both outscored black Caribbeans.

THE EFFECTS OF MOVING TO A BETTER COUNTRY

To further understand how immigration might affect IQ, I examined data from the Programme for the International Study of Adult Competencies (PIAAC). With this initiative, the OECD has created the most ambitious international database ever assembled for the study of adult cognitive performance across countries, examining a random sample of 250,000 people aged 16 to 65 living in 33 mostly rich countries.

The IQ of immigrants who arrive in developed countries before the age of ten is roughly 97, just one-fifth of a standard deviation below the international norm of 100. Scores are much lower—by as much as 10 IQ points—

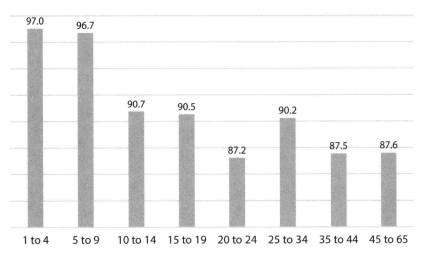

Figure 5.3. Mean IQ of immigrants to rich countries by age of arrival
when tested as adults

Source: Author analysis of OECD PIAAC data for 10,808 adults in 22 countries, which is everyone
in the database with nonmissing data for age of entry and immigrant status. IQ scores were first
adjusted by age using AGEG10LFS, which has five categories, before putting into standardized IQ
units of mean 100 and standard deviation of 15.

for those who enter the country as adults (figure 5.3). If selection bias
explained the high performance of immigrants (meaning that only highly
capable parents migrate), then it should not matter at what age their children
arrive, but if the environment matters, then the amount of time spent in the
poor country of origin compared to the rich destination country should
matter, and it does.

Other scholars have found the same effect, even for children within the
same family. For immigrants to Germany, arriving at age one compared with
doing so at age 15 raises educational attainment by two years. Similar results
have been found for immigrants to Sweden and Norway.[52] Arriving before
age ten seems to be particularly beneficial.[53] I believe the reasons for the age
pattern are twofold: First, rigorous classroom evaluations show that school
quality is dramatically better in rich countries, so arriving in a rich country
early means more cumulative years of higher-quality education; second, early
childhood education is especially powerful relative to adult education for
practical reasons—children aren't expected to work and take care of families—
and, likely, for biological reasons—brain development is more rapid among
children and levels off during puberty.[54]

Table 5.5. Education, entrepreneurship, and income of African immigrants growing up in the United States by age of arrival

	Percentage with at least a bachelor's degree	Percentage with a doctorate or professional degree	Percentage who own an incorporated business	Median income
Moved to United States at 10 or older	41.6	5.1	2.9	$26,134
Moved to United States before age 10	53.5	8.8	4.3	$39,000
Whites, born in United States (aged 30–50)	36.3	3.4	3.1	$36,588

Source: Data from the 2012–2016 American Community Survey. Analysis is limited to adults aged 30 to 50 between 2012 and 2016. There were 31,610 African immigrants surveyed, 1,532 of whom arrived before age 10.

Test scores from 15-year-olds who took the OECD's PISA exam show the same effect. Only a handful of highly developed countries reveal the country of birth of test-takers. Among them are New Zealand, Finland, Denmark, and Belgium. Children born in Africa who arrive in these countries after age ten score well below international norms (91.2), but those who arrive before age ten score above international norms (101.1). For a black African, being raised in northern Europe or New Zealand instead of Africa is akin to gaining 33 years from the Flynn effect.

This applies just as well to other measures of success. African immigrants who come to the United States from poor countries before the age of ten are far more likely to have a college degree, own a business, and earn higher incomes as middle-aged adults—aged 30 to 50—than those who arrive after the age of ten. In fact, the children of African immigrants earn higher incomes than U.S.-born white people and are more than twice as likely to earn a PhD or advanced professional degree (table 5.5).

Indeed, children born in poor countries with low national measures of educational attainment or cognitive performance routinely become more educated than U.S.-born white people and Asians. One out of every four children (25 percent) of Iranian immigrants who arrived in the United States before age ten had obtained a PhD or advanced professional degree between the ages of 30 and 50, making American-raised Iranian immigrants the highest-educated group of Americans. Immigrants from 16 other countries were more likely to obtain this level of education than native-born Asian Americans (10.3 percent), and immigrants from 51 countries surpassed native-born white people (3.4 percent). These high-performing countries cover much of the world's regions: India, Taiwan, Israel-Palestine (which are grouped together in the data), South Africa, Nigeria, Pakistan, the United Kingdom, Malaysia, Syria, Egypt, Australia, Korea, Lebanon, and Ireland. Even more countries would be represented, but I limited the analysis to countries with at least 100 respondents surveyed by the census to minimize sampling errors.

Taken together, the evidence is conclusive that educational opportunities in rich countries are far better than those in the home regions most migrants are leaving, and this exposure to high-quality education leads to massive gains in the skills and knowledge they acquire and their ability to be productive citizens.

REASSESSING THE HERITABILITY OF INTELLIGENCE: FROM TWIN STUDIES TO GENOMIC STUDIES

In 1994, a group of 52 scientists working in psychology and other areas on the measurement and inheritance of intelligence signed a letter in the *Wall Street Journal* stating that "individuals differ in intelligence due to differences in both their environments and genetic heritage. Heritability estimates range from 0.4 to 0.8 (on a scale from 0 to 1), most thereby indicating that genetics plays a bigger role than does environment in creating IQ differences among individuals."[55] Moreover, leading genetics scholar Robert Plomin has recently suggested on the basis of twin studies that the heritability of adult IQ is as high as 80 percent and that both schools and families make little difference in accounting for IQ.[56]

Yet there are good reasons to believe that these conclusions are badly overstated.

Very high heritability does not imply that environment has no impact. Nor does it indicate whether genes or environment has the strongest effects.[57] In fact the latest evidence suggests that it is the environment that is the dominant factor in accounting for differences between individuals, and as I will argue in the next chapter, the environment is almost certainly the only significant source of differences between groups of people. So why has heritability been considered so important?

The answer lies, in large part, in the dependence upon twin studies. Typically, twin studies estimate heritability of IQ and other traits by observing the difference in correlations between identical twins and nonidentical same-sex sibling twins. (It is also worth noting that using opposite-sex nonidentical twins biases the heritability estimate since gender has significant environmental consequences.) Early estimates, which were typically based on small samples, often produced highly variable results. The most compelling estimates are from meta-analysis. Recently, a team of genetics scholars led by Tinca Polderman analyzed the results of nearly every twin study ever published in a massive meta-analysis of hundreds of thousands of twin pairs across many countries. For male identical twins, they found that cognitive ability had a moderately high correlation of 0.56; this would seem to imply that 31 percent (or 0.56 squared) of the variation in cognitive ability is explained by having equivalent genes. For nonidentical male twins, the correlation was 0.34. There are a few methods to calculate heritability based on these data. Using Falconer's formula, scientists multiply the difference between these two correlations by two. The reason is that identical twins share all of their genes, whereas nonidentical twins (siblings) share only 50 percent of their genes, on average. Twice the difference yields a heritability estimate of 0.45 for IQ, which is somewhat higher than what the raw correlation between identical twins would suggest.[58]

Heritability estimates for cognitive ability fall somewhere in between those for health and height, when using the same database and methods used by Tinca Polderman and co-authors. Male identical-twin mortality is correlated at just 0.36, and male dizygotic twin mortality is correlated at 0.21. The Falconer's formula suggests that mortality is 29 percent heritable.[59] On the other end, male identical twins have very high correlations on height (0.92), compared to just 0.53 for dizygotic male twins. That suggests heritability of 78 percent for height.

The estimates based on the meta-analysis above use data from every country with published results, but the heritability estimates vary widely across countries. For male identical versus nonidentical twins, heritability is as low as 0.14 in Japan and 0.31 in Denmark. In the United States, estimates were 0.43; in Sweden, they were 0.56. Thus, one cannot say there is one "true" figure for the heritability of intelligence; it depends very much on the date of the study, the sample population, and most of all, on the environment.

This is also true for the heritability of educational attainment, according to another meta-analysis from Amelia Branigan and others.[60] Their estimates for educational heritability range from −5 percent to 77 percent. The grand mean across all studies they located is 40 percent. This raises serious concerns about the validity of twin methods. In contrast to older studies with smaller sample sizes, their study found large effects for both shared and nonshared environment. While it is on the low range of the old consensus, the 45 percent estimate of IQ heritability from twin studies is certainly too high. Beyond IQ, it is well known among genetics researchers that twin-based methods lead to higher estimates of heritability than methods that analyze actual genes.[61]

There are two main reasons why twin studies generate higher heritability estimates. One reason favors twin studies. Insofar as the assumptions are correct, twin estimates provide a complete analysis of all genetic effects—including gene-to-gene interactions and gene-environment interactions. Indeed, there has been considerable research on gene-environmental interactions as summarized in a recent review by Richard Nisbett and co-authors.[62] Eric Turkheimer and his collaborators have found evidence that genetic heritability—based on twin studies—tends to be lower in families with lower socioeconomic status and higher in more affluent families. This makes sense if one assumes that environmental variation is lower in affluent families.[63]

By contrast, studies of actual genes cannot take into account all of these complexities using existing methods. Since humans have over 99 percent of their genomes in common, genetic researchers focus on the locations where genes vary between individuals; they are called *single nucleotide polymorphisms*, or SNPs. Estimates of heritability from SNPs generally assume a simple relationship between a gene and a phenotype (e.g., cognitive performance), the idea being that having a nucleobase of adenine instead of guanine, for example, at a particular location is always better for intelligence, regardless of the environment or other genes present. In reality, whether it is good or not may depend on the presence of other complementary genes or environmental circumstances. Twin studies do not make this kind of assumption, but neither can they shed light on what genetic mechanisms are working.[64]

The other reason twin studies show higher heritability estimates than gene studies is that they impose strong assumptions that bias the results upward.

The heritability formula assumes that nonidentical twins share the same environment and to the same extent as identical twins. That simply isn't true. The fact is that identical twins share certain environmental experiences to a greater extent than nonidentical twins. As a recent review article concludes: "Identical twin pairs were more similar than fraternal pairs on bullying, sexual abuse, physical maltreatment, emotional abuse and neglect, and general negative life events or trauma."[65] The Polderman database likewise shows that negative life events in childhood are much more likely to be shared by identical than by dizygotic twins (the correlations are 0.55 versus 0.37).[66] Identical twins are also more likely to be assigned to the same classroom than nonidentical twins and to spend more time with each other.[67] In short, important life experiences are more closely linked among identical twins.

Alternative twin-based heritability methods, such as studying twins who were adopted, also have important flaws. The convention is to assume that any association between the IQ of identical twins reared apart must be entirely genetic, but that's not right. The homes provided by adoptive parents are often very similar, especially in terms of parental education.[68] Moreover, the womb is an environment with varying exposures to nutrition, toxins, and stress, and adopted children often spend significant time with their biological mother before adoption—sometimes years. The upshot is that even twins who are reared apart may share many important environmental circumstances in the womb and the first few months or years of life.

Another problematic assumption in twin studies is that siblings share 50 percent of their genetic material: This is correct only on average. In fact, siblings share between 37 percent and 62 percent of their genes, according to a study that examined the actual genomes of siblings.[69] This variation should be taken into account when calculating heritability from twin studies. Doing so, as scientists did recently, lowers the heritability estimates by about half. In the case of educational attainment, the heritability estimate falls from 43 percent to 17 percent.[70]

Given these limitations, the direct study of actual genes offers a compelling way to measure heritability, despite the difficulties mentioned above. This method was impossible until recent breakthroughs in the mapping of the human genome made the study of molecular genomics feasible on a large scale.

The three most ambitious scientific efforts to date have brought together teams of scientists from around the world. The first was published in 2013 by Cornelius Rietveld and a massive team of scholars at 129 different research institutions, who analyzed genomic data from 101,069 people.[71] They looked at the correlation between over one million genes and educational attainment, after controlling for gender and year of birth, among a sample of people with European ancestry. Using this method, Rietveld and his co-authors identified just three genes (SNPs) as having a statistically significant effect on education, and the strongest effect could explain only 0.02 percent of the variation in educational attainment, which is equal to about a month of schooling. When they added up each of the million tiny effects from the individual genes—to get a "polygenic score"—they were able to explain roughly 2 percent to 3 percent of the variation in educational attainment and IQ. They also suggested that with an extremely large sample size, the effect of each gene would become more accurate, and they would be able to explain 22 percent of the variation in educational attainment with fully mapped genomes from millions of people.[72]

The second study had access to a larger sample of people (293,723 instead of 101,069), and consistent with their prediction, the explanatory power increased. That effort, led by Aysu Okbay, Jonathan Beauchamp, and scholars from 185 research institutions, identified 74 genes that had significant associations with educational attainment.[73] Yet, even after adding up the effects of every gene (including those that aren't significant), their polygenic score could explain only 3.2 percent of the variation in educational attainment.[74]

Finally, in a third, still larger analysis, the same team of scholars—this time with James J. Lee, Robbee Wedow, and Aysu Okbay listed as the first of dozens of authors—obtained genomes for 1.1 million individuals. This much larger sample did give them the power to identify more genes that significantly predict educational attainment (1,271 compared to 74 in the previous study).[75]

It is worth noting that many of these genetic effects appear to be biased by family environment, since the predicted effect of 35 percent of genes points in the opposite direction when siblings are compared to one another. In other words, say that gene rs9859556 on the third chromosome predicts more education across 1.1 million people of European ancestry, but the results change when only siblings are compared. If two brothers are compared, the brother *without* the gene systematically has *more* education. This kind of switch in the predicted direction occurred for 35 percent of genes that were identified as significant. This type of reversal of a regression coefficient occurs commonly in social science when an omitted variable (such as family background) is added to a model that is fundamentally biased without it. This finding, in and of itself, directly contradicts Plomin's contention that nongenetic family effects do not matter to educational outcomes.

Additionally, the authors find important environmental effects on how genes are expressed. The genes identified as significant had different effects in different cohorts, which suggested to the authors that environmental circumstances—such as access to public education and college or opportunities to work in cognitively demanding professional jobs—interact significantly with genes.

Nevertheless, in this larger sample, the polygenic score (the combined effect of all the genes) was again used to predict educational attainment, controlling for sex, age, and multicollinearity with closely related genes. The amount of variation explained by the polygenic score (the model's R^2) was approximately 13 percent in the strongest model, which used complex statistical techniques to calculate both the polygenic score and its predictive power. The strength is somewhat lower if only genes with a significant individual relationship to educational attainment are included, and it falls to 4.6 percent if the authors control for parental education, which has a stronger effect than genes—presumably because it includes both genetic and nurture effects.

Finally, going beyond educational attainment, the authors were able to construct a polygenic score for IQ specifically (for 257,841 individuals), self-reported math ability (for 564,698 individuals), and the highest level of math taken in school (for 430,445). These polygenic scores explain 7 percent to 10 percent of the variance.

To summarize, the best state-of-the-art research on genetics with over one million people of European ancestry shows that genes directly explain 11 percent to 13 percent of the variation in educational attainment and a similar amount of variation in IQ.

The team of scientists conducting this research formed the Social Science Genetic Association Consortium and are utilizing best practices in science—data sharing, complete transparency in methods, replication studies—as they continue to publish results in the world's top science journals. Their website summarizes the results of their work:

Educational attainment is primarily determined by environmental factors, not genes.... The bottom line is that individual genetic variants have very little explanatory power for educational attainment, and even composite indexes of millions of genetic variants have too little explanatory power to usefully predict any individual's educational attainment.[76]

This is a scientific revolution, but not one that many psychologists expected.

Between 1994 and 2018, scientists have gone from suggesting that IQ and educational attainment are mostly genetic and that genes account for 40 percent to 80 percent of variation in a population to saying that genes have "little explanatory power." This is quite a reversal. To be fair, the Genome-Wide Association Studies methods don't capture all rare SNPs or complex interactions; future research will likely boost the amount of variation explained by polygenic scores. Still, even with twin studies, the best estimate for the heritability of education for a given cohort likely lies somewhere between 13 percent and 40 percent, but not 40 percent to 80 percent.

Furthermore, even these very rigorous genomic-based studies are biased in favor of finding genetic effects. As Augustine Kong and colleagues have found, genes that parents do not transmit to their children still appear to have causal effects on educational attainment. They dub this phenomenon "genetic nurture" and estimate that it explains 30 percent of observed heritability.[77] Other research also finds that a mother's polygenic score for education is significantly correlated with her child's educational attainment, even after controlling for her child's genes.[78] Thus, whatever the preferred estimate from the 13 percent to 40 percent range may be, it needs to be reduced to something like 9 percent to 28 percent.

At this point, there is no evidence that there are meaningful differences between ancestral groups (or races) with respect to the frequency of genes that predict education or intelligence. Thus far, most of the genetic samples analyzed—including in the largest studies described above—have come from people of European ancestry. Thus, the correlations between education and SNPs are limited to the environments of people from Europe. The most recent and robust analysis from James Lee and his collaborators found that their polygenic score did not work for a small sample (1,519) of African Americans in that it explained only 1.6 percent of the variation in their educational attainment. This suggests that genes commonly found in highly educated white populations may be just as likely to be found in African Americans with low levels of education.[79] Scientists still have far to go before understanding the genetics of education, particularly across cohorts and ancestral groups.

Meanwhile, even within people of European ancestry, there is little to suggest that social class has any genetic origins. One U.S. study finds that high-income fathers have children with slightly higher polygenic scores for education, but paternal income explains only 1.2 percent of the variation.[80] Using a larger number of samples—including data from the UK and New Zealand—and an improved method for estimating polygenic scores, another research team did find a more substantial link between parental socioeconomic status and the polygenic scores of their children.[81] Still, the correlations were weak to moderate. Almost all of the variation in genetic advantage (in terms of higher education)—over 90 percent—is *not* accounted for by parental socioeconomic status.[82] This suggests that if you think you can judge a child's genetic propensity to be intelligent or highly educated on the basis of the status of their family, you'd be wrong. As Plato wrote: "As all are of the same original stock, a golden parent will sometimes have a silver son, or a silver parent a golden son."[83]

The bottom line is that the latest genetics research supports the notion that highly intelligent people can come from any class or ethnic group. Having parents with genes advantageous to intelligence or education gives one a small advantage, not a big one, for two reasons: The environment matters a great deal, and the genes associated with intelligence are extremely common. Scientists have found no relationship between very high IQ and the presence of rare genetic alleles.[84] Likewise, none of the specific genes identified as significant predictors of IQ qualifies as rare in the latest genome-wide studies with 1.1 million people.[85] The average SNP that predicts intelligence is present in half of all people with European origins. The genes that were strongly associated with intelligence were no less common than genes that did not predict intelligence. Thus, the odds are that everyone has at least some of the genes that predict high IQ. Highly intelligent people may be somewhat more likely to have a beneficial combination of many common genes, but they score well and achieve higher levels of education largely based on environmental advantages.

To summarize, the most scientifically rigorous non-twin-based estimates suggest that as much as 13 percent of differences between individuals in educational attainment is the result of genes for a given population, and even twin studies—despite their upward bias in estimating heritability—also suggest that most of the variation in education (60 percent) is explained by the environment.

The key caveat is within a given population. From twin studies to genomic-based polygenic scores, all the estimates of heritability are limited to a specific population—that means people born at roughly the same time in the same place, typically of the same race. The large-scale genomic work described above used only people of European ancestry, for example, because the sample sizes are too small for people of recent African descent.

The implication is that heritability estimates do not apply between generations and groups of people.

It is a very different to ask: What percentage of the variation in IQ between all of humanity is the result of genes? Right now, no one can give a good answer, but we can say that it is much lower than the current estimate for heritability in IQ or educational attainment for several reasons.

First, even genomic-based heritability estimates are inflated because they ignore the purely environmental sources of variation between generations. If genomic scholars could include everyone born between 1880 and 1980 in their database, and if they did not control for cohort effects, they would find that the explanatory power of genes shrinks dramatically as a result of economic development (or the Flynn effect).

Second, as shown above, we know that IQ differences between countries are at least largely environmental and likely 100 percent environmental. Thus, when the same relatively uneducated parents raise their children in northern Europe before age ten instead of in a poor country until age ten, IQs go up by about 10 points. The subsequent generation of children born in northern Europe will no doubt benefit from the fact their parents will be raising them in a more literate household, with all the other advantages that go along with living in a rich country with high-quality public services, schools, healthcare, and well-functioning markets.

We know that sustained economic development has coincided with growth in IQ by roughly 0.3 points per year, so it stands to reason that economic development in currently poor countries would raise IQ by a similar magnitude and has already started to do so. As it happens, most poor countries today—those not classified by the World Bank as high-income—are even poorer than the United States was 50 year ago, when IQ scores for the United States were approximately 15 points lower.[86] So, if one considers all humans who ever lived, the genetic basis of intelligence—as measured by IQ tests—

would be infinitesimally small. The share of human variation explained by genetics is negligible, because environmental differences are absolutely dominant.

Thirty years ago, scientists thought IQ was dominated by genes. Contemporary social science shows that genes are important in explaining variation in education and other social outcomes, but the environment is more powerful, and the two interact in complex ways that scientists are only beginning to understand. The underlying capacity of individuals to perform cognitively demanding tasks is far more egalitarian than twentieth-century science led us to believe. The next chapter uses historical analysis to illustrate how group differences in intelligence—which have reversed rankings in very recent years—cannot be explained by genes. Instead, political power and culture—in the form of readily transferable family norms—explain the gaps.

6

The Historical Contingencies of Group Differences in Skills

WRITING IN THE FOURTH CENTURY BCE, at a time when slavery was widespread, Aristotle argued that some people are by nature slaves. He distinguished between people who become enslaved because they lose a war and people who are naturally servile and worthy only of being slaves. He argued that women and certain classes of people are fundamentally "inferior" and should justly be ruled by their superiors. After developing his concept of natural slavery, Aristotle later attributed the trait to different races, ascribing a tolerance for tyrannical rule to non-Hellenes (non-Greeks): "Barbarians, being more servile in character than Hellenes, and Asiatics than Europeans, do not rebel against a despotic government. Such royalties have the nature of tyrannies because the people are by nature slaves."[1] It is worth noting that this was not the prevailing opinion in his day. Indeed, his own teacher, Plato, rejected the notion of natural slavery and Aristotle's view of women. Aristotle acknowledged as much: "Others affirm that the rule of a master over slaves is contrary to nature, and that the distinction between slave and freeman exists by law only, and not by nature; and being an interference with nature is therefore unjust."[2]

The Aristotelian theory of the natural slave has endured a long time. White political leaders of the U.S. South were explicit in their view that black people were naturally inferior and thus deserving of slavery. Alexander H. Stevens, vice president of the Confederacy, criticized Thomas Jefferson for espousing the view that slavery violated the laws of nature. These ideas were wrong, according to Stevens, because

> they rested upon the assumption of the equality of races. This was an
> error. . . . Our new government is founded upon exactly the opposite

idea, its foundation are laid, its corner-stone rests upon the great truth that the Negro is not equal to the white man. That slavery—subordination to the superior race—is his natural and normal condition."[3]

The twentieth-century version of this theory gave it an air of spurious scientific legitimacy by linking it to genetic research, but as we saw in the last chapter and will explore further here, those assumptions are fundamentally flawed. While there have been many efforts throughout history to attribute social status to some essential group trait, the theories make implausible scientific and evolutionary assumptions and fail to acknowledge or account for the fact that the social status of actual groups fluctuates and reorders itself in ways that essential traits cannot explain.

WHEN RACISM BECAME AN EPIDEMIC

The processes of urbanization, development of local political autonomy, and then industrialization that lifted northern Europe from its long-standing global mediocrity to economic and military power coincided with a deeper understanding of the role of evolution in long-term human development. Many assumed that the factors at work in the transformation of primitive apes to *Homo sapiens* could also be seen in the differences between races, and like Aristotle, those of northern European stock often mistook their very recent success as being the result of essential traits that they believed distinguished them from other people, rather than the result of exogenous forces.

In the first few decades of the twentieth century, the near consensus among U.S. scholars and scientists—if not the general public—was that genetic endowments varied between races, that IQ was a broad measure of human competence and almost entirely genetic, that northern Europeans had the highest IQ, and that therefore northern European genes were at risk of dilution from other people—unless only those non–northern Europeans with the highest IQ were allowed into the United States. The history of these ideas has been documented extensively by the excellent work of historians like Nell Irvin Painter and Louis Menand, who point out that many scientists believed the races evolved from fundamentally distinct populations, if not species.[4] Modern genetic research has since proven that all humans share a common origin in Sub-Saharan Africa.

Flawed science—in combination with widespread racism—led to a vigorous eugenics movement, as well as immigration policies designed to discriminate against people who were not from northern or western Europe. The eugenics movement resulted in the forced sterilization of tens of thousands of Americans during the first six decades of the twentieth century; 63,678 sterilization cases were documented between 1907 and 1964.[5] Just over half of those sterilized were deemed mentally deficient, meaning they registered a low score on an IQ test. The other half were sterilized mostly because they were diagnosed as mentally ill.

Moreover, many children—disproportionately from immigrant and black families—were sent to institutions for the mentally deficient, where they were put to work doing routine jobs that required low levels of cognitive ability. An IQ score below 80, as tested by a local public school or physician, put a child at risk of forced institutionalization under the New York State Mental Deficiency Law, which was passed in 1919. In 1920, there were roughly 6,000 children—deemed "defectives" by the state of New York—who were removed from their families and placed in institutions.[6] The state estimated 40,000 "defectives" living outside of institutions. The most common cause listed for their admission was "hereditary." Conditions were such that 96 children died while living in these institutions from 1919 to 1920.[7] In other words, children raised in poor or uneducated families were at high risk of low test scores and being deemed genetically defective and denied basic freedoms, with no effort made to remediate gaps in their education.

THE CONTEMPORARY HEREDITARIAN VIEW OF INTELLIGENCE

The idea that people can be classified into distinct races and ordered as part of a hierarchy of races was the dominant intellectual view in the early twentieth century. White scholars of "Anglo-Saxon" or northern European ancestry openly wrote in leading academic journals that other groups were inferior intellectually and socially as a result of their genetic endowment, and they used this logic to motivate eugenics policies and regulations on immigration and wages.[8]

It should be said that IQ testing was not usually involved in these debates. The IQ literature from the period shows that the tests were conducted for immediate practical considerations—such as assigning soldiers to particular occupations or flagging children for educational remediation or access to advanced courses—and the authors often mentioned possible environmental explanations, even as they seemed to almost universally appeal to genetics in explaining group differences.

Starting in the second half of the twentieth century and into the twenty-first, this theory of racial hierarchy has been largely decimated by social science research and cultural and historic trends. Still, as I discussed in chapter 1, the racist views of a minority of citizens and politicians still carry political weight—and arguably affect important public policy positions on issues such as immigration and education. Prominent cultural and academic figures still maintain the basic tenets of racial hierarchy, which are openly espoused on social media, even if rarely in academic journals or books. The fact that these views are currently unpopular among Hollywood celebrities, athletes, and entertainers makes them attractive to a certain segment of the population, as I discussed in chapter 1, when describing the "Alt-Right." Those who defend the theory of racial hierarchy portray themselves as stalwart defenders of truth in the face of politically correct mobs.[9]

In psychology literature, the theory that there are important racial differences in the genes that determine success in life is now called *hereditarianism*. In its essence, it attributes differences in social status between groups of people—including educational attainment and cognitive performance in tests—to innate genetic differences. This belief that group differences between people whose ancestors came from different continents are innate is the textbook definition of racism whether or not any animosity is evinced toward lower-status groups.[10] These views are also stridently classist in that they attribute low educational attainment, low test scores, single-parent child-rearing, and crime, as well as other difficulties confronting the working poor, whether they are white or otherwise, to genetics, rather than social and political inequality.

It would be tempting to reject such views solely because they are racist or classist, but that would be a mistake politically and intellectually. Politically, rejecting unpopular views without considering their foundations creates a backlash and subjects well-meaning critics to charges of sentimentality or wishful thinking, while giving hereditarians the status of "realists." It's no way to win an argument. Hereditarian views should be subject to scrutiny and testing just as any other theory in science and should be treated on those terms. In fact, hereditarianism can be shown to fail using empirical analysis and logic.

Two of the intellectual leaders of the modern hereditarian movement were the late Arthur Jensen and Phillipe Rushton; both died in 2012. Jensen was a hugely influential but controversial figure in psychology, who had a long career as a professor at the University of California, Berkeley, and published many papers that seemingly had little to do with race. His colleague Rushton taught psychology at the University of Western Ontario.

Like scholars of the early twentieth century, Jensen and Rushton observed differences in social status between groups and concluded that these were due to "the natural order." Rushton devoted much of his career to measuring and discussing differences in cognitive performance between individuals and groups and arguing for their genetic origin, and Jensen seems to have held the view for decades at least. In 2005, they published a defense of hereditarianism, based on their review of the psychology literature. Similar themes came up in a widely cited and criticized 1969 article by Jensen claiming that IQ cannot be increased by postnatal environmental influences—an absurd and false claim, as chapter 5 in this book proves.[11]

The fundamental reasoning of hereditarians is quite simple. According to their interpretation of the psychology literature, genes explain roughly half of the variation in individual performance on cognitive exams—which include IQ tests. Group differences, Jensen, Rushton, and hereditarians reason, can be thought of similarly. They are enormously impressed by the observation that the mean test scores of African Americans—on various cognitive exams—are consistently lower than those of white Americans (by roughly one standard deviation, in statistical terms, or 15 IQ points). They also note that Asians and Jews of European descent (the Ashkenazi) living outside of Israel tend to score higher than non-Jewish white people. They note that studies have found that mixed-race black-white children score in between children with two white parents and children with two black parents. Further, they cite research showing that people living in Sub-Saharan Africa score even lower than African Americans and believe this provides further evidence that racial differences are genetic in origin, since many African Americans have white ancestors as a result of the raping of enslaved women.[12] The IQ tests are not biased, they argue, because in each of these groups, people who score better on cognitive exams exhibit greater success, as measured by educational attainment, income, or other outcomes.

Richard Herrnstein and Charles Murray made some of these points in their controversial 1994 book, *The Bell Curve*, which popularized the earlier research of Jensen, Rushton, and other hereditarians, while contributing their own novel analysis and interpretation of the literature.[13] *The Bell Curve* is well written, well organized, and extremely useful for understanding how a segment of academic psychologists and social scientists understand differences in social status across race and class. I don't think it would be fair to say that Murray and Herrnstein misunderstand or grossly distort the literature on IQ; rather, the book is fundamentally wrong, as I see it, because they accept so much of the scholarship uncritically and with insufficient attention to contradictory evidence and interpretations, especially from other disciplines.

In many ways, Herrnstein and Murray's interpretation of the evidence was typical, at least among older white scholars who specialize in intelligence research. They point to survey data of prominent academics, which suggest that just under half believe group differences in IQ are partly genetic in origin. After *The Bell Curve* came out, a group of 52 of the 100 most prominent researchers on intelligence published a letter in the *Wall Street Journal*, which endorsed many of Murray and Herrnstein's claims, such as the claim that IQ heritability is between 40 percent and 80 percent. This task force endorsed the following statement: "Most experts believe that environment is important in pushing the bell curves apart, but that genetics could be involved too." Murray and Herrnstein could be characterized as emphasizing the importance of genetics to a greater extent than the average expert in the field, but many were open to at least some role for genetics in explaining group differences.[14] Along these lines, a survey conducted in 2013 and 2014 of scholars who have published in journals specializing in intelligence research confirmed that many view genes as important in explaining group differences in IQ performance—between nations, races, and ethnic groups. The average respondent attributed one-sixth to one-fifth of differences to genes.[15]

Disproportionate Group Achievement

The hereditarian community has put a great deal of stock in the argument that Jewish and Asian intellectual achievements should be regarded as evidence that group differences are explained by genes, not the environment. While hereditarians concede that severe discrimination against African Americans is an environmental force that has lowered scholastic achievements, they suggest that white Christian Europeans are not discriminated against and so the higher performance of European Jews and Asians must not be caused by environmental factors. In fact, Jews and Asians have been subjected to intense discrimination in the United States. They reason that if genetic factors cause Asians and Jews to demonstrate high achievement, genetic factors likely explain most of the differences across all groups. Thus, these arguments have important implications, and for that reason, and because I believe the arguments to be entirely unsound, it is very important to understand the details.

The average American Jew and Asian American is considerably more educated and affluent than the average non-Hispanic, non-Jewish white person, black person, Native American, or Hispanic. Gallup data from 2015 to 2017 show that 43 percent of Jews and 35 percent of Asians aged 25 to 50 have earned a graduate degree, compared to 16 percent of non-Jewish white people. Jews and Asians are also far more likely than white people to be in a household with at least $240,000 in income (figure 6.1).

In 2015, Asian American 12th-grade students outscored their white peers on a national math assessment by 0.3 standard deviations, whereas scores on reading and science were roughly equal.[16] More significantly, from 1986 to 2015, Asian Americans outscored white people on the math section of the Standard Achievement Test (SAT) for college entrance by a comfortable margin, including by as much as 0.6 standard deviations in 2015. White people consistently outscored Asians over that period on reading, but on writing, Asians closed the gap and outscored white people after 2008.[17] The high academic performance of many Asian Americans during high school has increased their share of students at top American colleges even though Asian Americans need to score higher on average than other groups to gain admission, at least to Harvard.[18]

Likewise, Jewish Americans once faced similar discriminatory quotas at prestigious colleges, even as they made outstanding contributions to the nation's academic achievements. From 1901 to 2018, people with at least one Jewish parent or grandparent have won 22 percent of all Nobel Prizes, including 37 percent of the awards granted to Americans. Jews also have won 38 percent of U.S. Medals of Science. Most of the Jewish Nobel winners have been American and were awarded the prize in the second half of the twentieth century.[19] Of course, Jews have also made valuable and celebrated contributions across all fields, including the arts, with, for example, many commercially successful and Academy Award–winning directors including Steven Spielberg, Woody Allen, and Stanley Kubrick.

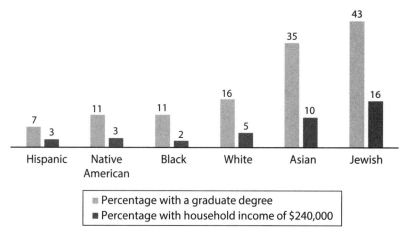

Figure 6.1. Percent of U.S. residents aged 25–50 with a post-bachelor's degree and household income of $240,000 or higher, 2015–2017

Source: Gallup Daily Tracker phone survey of 314,101 randomly selected U.S. residents aged 25 to 50.

A number of social scientists—Gregory Cochran, Jason Hardy, Henry Harpending, Richard Lynn, Charles Murray, Nicholas Wade, and Steven Pinker—have published academic or popular commentaries noting these achievements and embracing, with some reservations, the theory that genetic advantages explain this success.[20] In considering how extraordinary the contributions mentioned above are, some of these writers refer to the tiny proportion of Jews in the global population. That is a misleading comparison. The majority of the global population was illiterate for the first half of the twentieth century, and as late as 1975, only 3 percent of the global population had any postsecondary education.[21] In 2015, that share had increased, but only to 10 percent.[22]

Lynn reports that Jews are ten times more likely than non-Jews in the United States to have won the Nobel Prize, which is accurate considering that Jewish people comprised around 4 percent of the U.S. population around the middle of the twentieth century and have won 37 percent of Nobel Prizes.[23] Yet, Jews were so disproportionately educated that in 1970 Jews comprised 23.5 percent of the U.S. population with at least six years of higher education, including 30 percent of the population aged 25 to 29.[24] In 1970, 18.2 percent of the Jewish population had obtained at least a master's degree compared to 2.7 percent of the total American population. Since a graduate education is effectively a prerequisite for a scientific award, the disproportionate number of leading scientists is not so far out of proportion from the Jewish share of the population with the required level of education.

Still, this begs the question as to why Jews are so much more likely to obtain high levels of education. Hereditarians have advanced two theories.

The most comprehensive genetic theory was developed by Cochran, Hardy, and Harpending. Noting that ancient Jews did not distinguish themselves in any way that would indicate higher intelligence relative to other populations, they point to the unique occupational structure of Jews in professional and banking jobs in Europe, which they believe gave Jews a unique opportunity to profit from cognitive ability. Cochran and his co-authors argue that merely 500 years of selective breeding are necessary to transform a group with ordinary intelligence—ancient and medieval Jews—into a group with extreme intelligence (a standard deviation above the mean—an IQ 115). They get there by assuming that IQ is 80 percent hereditary within a given population and that Jewish overrepresentation in highly skilled occupations gave them unique opportunities to afford more children. In other words, intelligence was rewarded among Jews with extra children, but not among any other group to the same extent, and they speculate (with no factual basis) that as a result of this process, the average Jewish child could have been born to a family with one extra IQ point above the population. These two assumptions— heritability of .8 and selective breeding of one extra IQ point—allow them to estimate 500 years as necessary for Jews to go from average to extraordinary. Using the sample assumptions but changing IQ heritability to .25 (which would be a high-end estimate from molecular biology) requires 1,500 years. Without selective breeding, the theory does not work at all.

The second theory explaining Jewish achievement has been developed by the economists Maristella Botticini and Zvi Eckstein.[25] This is not a hereditarian theory at all, but it has subsequently been adapted by Wade and Murray, as I will discuss. Botticini and Eckstein point out that ancient Jews were nearly all illiterate farmers during the time of the Roman Empire and up through the birth of Christ. Breaking from previous scholars, Botticini and Eckstein document that there were no legal restrictions prohibiting Jews from owning land or working in any occupations, even in the Roman, Byzantine, Persian, and Islamic Empires, and yet Jews in the medieval era were disproportionately engaged in business ownership, trading, and banking. The simple explanation is that Jews were far more literate than every other large community, and so they found employment in jobs that benefited from literacy.

The reason for high rates of ancient Jewish literacy is no mystery. Around the year 63, a Jewish high priest named Joshua ben Gamla issued a law requiring every Jewish father to educate his son starting around age six. According to Botticini and Eckstein, this law was prompted by the traumatic destruction of the Second Jewish Temple in Jerusalem by the Roman Army after the Jews attempted to revolt against Roman colonization. By diffusing literacy, Jewish leaders hoped to safeguard and preserve their laws and teachings.[26]

As mentioned in chapter 2, universal childhood education was not a new idea: Plato had actively recommended it centuries before, even for girls, but evidence from the ancient world suggests that none of the large imperial powers invested in public primary education.[27] In Plato's Athens, there is some evidence for widespread but by no means universal literacy among craftsmen and others in high-paying occupations and jurists were expected to be literate. Schools were common, and even slaves were often taught by their masters. One source, Diodorus Siculus, claims that publicly funded education was the law in the Sicilian city of Catania.[28] But because these literacy-promoting norms were tied to city-states, they could be eliminated by raiders or larger powers waging successful wars with those city-states.

For Jews, by contrast, those norms were tied to their religious practice, not their status as citizens. Wherever Jews lived, they set up synagogues that acted as primary and even secondary schools. Local taxes funded the schooling, which allowed even lower-income fathers to educate their children. The Roman Jew Josephus wrote that "children's education is the principal care among the Jews."[29]

Shortly after the requirements for literacy were made, Botticini and Eckstein document a large decrease in the Jewish population that cannot be readily explained by death and seems to be the result of conversion. They argue that Jewish fathers who could not afford to educate their sons chose conversion over the social sanctions they faced as Jews for disobeying this important norm.

It is here that hereditarians such as Charles Murray pick up the argument as evidence that only the most naturally gifted Jews remained Jews and that the rest converted to Christianity or other religions. Hence, according to

Murray and Wade, they argue Jewish achievement is explained by the fact that Jewish legal requirements pushed out the Jews with low IQ genes.[30] To be clear, this argument is not made by Botticini and Eckstein.

Evaluating Hereditarian Theories for Jewish Achievement

There are three major flaws with the theories described above.

First, according to the sorts of measures used by hereditarians, Jewish intellectual achievements were similar to those of other groups until the nineteenth century and certainly nowhere near the level of the mid- and late twentieth century, as Michael Goldfarb has pointed out.[31] Jewish contributions to the Industrial Revolution also came rather late, with a few exceptions. This is hard to reconcile with any kind of genetic explanation for more recent achievement because genes are very slow to change even under the most aggressive assumptions.

Second, IQ has been extensively measured for the Jewish population living in the United States and more recently for Israeli Jews. There is strong evidence that Jewish Americans had no more than average and even lower intellectual abilities in the first half of the twentieth century than the native white population, but the data do suggest rapid growth in IQ between generations as Jews became more educated. Israeli Jews, meanwhile, perform at roughly the global average for developed countries and well below residents of high-scoring European and Asian countries.

Third, there is no evidence for selective breeding among American Jews that could explain the growth in achievement or IQ. The most elite American Jews—measured in several ways, including IQ—have fewer children than lower-status Jews, and this gap is even more pronounced among Jews than it is for non-Jews.

I will discuss each of these points in detail below. The focus on the Jewish population stems from the central role hereditarian theorists have given them. Some aspects of the discussion are applicable to explaining changes in the status of Asian and non-Jewish northern European populations as well, at various points in history. The overarching theme from the study of group status—measured by education, income, or IQ—is its fluidity and high rate of turnover. No group of people has persisted in maintaining sustained levels of high status for long enough periods for population genetics to explain their success. Likewise, between slavery and Jim Crow, African Americans living in northern states achieved at intellectually higher rates than European and Asian immigrant groups and possibly even native white Americans. The reason is that the genes that favor productivity, intelligence, and conscientiousness are common to humanity, and economic status depends on political history and cultural practices that can change rapidly for the better or worse.

European Jews before and during the Era of Mass Migration

These hereditarian theories for Jewish achievement posit sustained long-term advantages in cognitive ability going back hundreds of years. Cochran and his co-authors provide anecdotal evidence that European Jews were overrepresented in cognitively demanding professions such as finance. Richard Lynn, meanwhile, also claims that Jews are genetically advantaged with respect to intelligence but does not offer any explanation as to when or how this extra intelligence may have evolved in the Jewish population.[32] He does go to great lengths to assemble facts that he believes support his argument, and so I will address them. However, a point-by-point rebuttal would be extremely tedious, given that I found flaws with his analysis in almost every case, but I will attempt to summarize the crucial points.

One type of flaw in Lynn's analysis is that he often shows that a high percentage of European Jews worked in professions in a particular town or city, but ignores the fact that selective migration accounts for much or even all of this. For example, in the Russian Empire, only Jews in elite professions were allowed to leave the Pale of Settlement;[33] thus, Jews living outside the Pale of Settlement were by definition from elite families. It is nonsensical to then suggest, as Lynn does, that the high percentage of professional Jews in St. Petersburg is representative of the larger Jewish population in Russia. In fact, it was well documented by the Russian government that the Jewish population within Poland and the Pale of Settlement suffered from high rates of poverty and worked mostly in low-paying occupations.[34]

In 1913, two-thirds of European Jews—who themselves comprised most of the global Jewish population—lived in the Russian Empire or Romania, with another 21 percent in Austria-Hungary.[35] According to Bernard Wasserstein, a leading historian of the Ashkenazi, in the early twentieth century, "The great mass of Jews in east-central Europe were sunk in dire poverty—and sinking further into total immiseration."[36]

Outside of Russia, few Jews were farmers, but neither did they occupy highly skilled occupations in large numbers. In Prussia, in 1849, 48 percent of Jews worked in commerce—they were mostly retail merchants, peddlers, and dealers, as listed by the census. While more reliant on literacy, perhaps, it is not clear that these jobs are more cognitively demanding than farming, which is also a small business enterprise that requires knowledge of production techniques, agricultural science, supply chains, and distribution networks. Only 1 percent of Jews worked in banking and 2 percent as physicians or teachers. A large portion (20 percent) were also mechanics or handicraftsmen, while 10 percent were servants, and 10 percent were paupers. In 1861, again in Prussia, 57 percent worked in commerce, but still only 1 percent in banking and 3 percent as physicians or teachers. In both periods, only 1 percent were farmers. Statistics were similar for Italy and Budapest.[37]

Decades later, in Germany, the status of Jews appears to have been much better, and Jews were far more likely than the general population to be business leaders, scientists, and mathematicians, up until their expulsion and persecution by the Nazi government in the early 1930s.[38] Incredibly, German Jews comprised roughly 16 percent of corporate board members, despite constituting only 1 percent of the population.[39]

Still, German Jews were hardly representative of the global or even European Jewish population. They constituted 6 percent of European Jews.[40] Moreover, the extent to which this population can be considered to have unique genetic characteristics is highly questionable. In Berlin, in 1899, 18 percent of Jews married Christians, and it is reported that more prosperous Jews were more likely to do so.[41] Nazis later persecuted people as Jews if even one grandparent was Jewish.

American Asians, Jews, and Black People in the Late Nineteenth and Early Twentieth Centuries

Data from U.S. sources corroborate the un-extraordinary social status of American Jews and Asians in the early twentieth century.

My analysis of U.S. census data from 1920 shows that men aged 30 to 40 who listed Yiddish or Hebrew as their mother's tongue (which would have been the vast majority of Jews) were less likely than native white people to be working in professional occupations (2.7 percent compared to 3.6 percent). White people born in the northeastern United States were twice as likely as Jews to work in the professions. These included jobs such as engineers, academics, doctors, and lawyers. Only 1.3 percent of Asians worked as professionals at the time. The small share of Jews working in professional occupations is even more striking when one considers that only 1 percent of Jews worked as farmers at a time when 25 percent of native white people were farmers.

Home ownership rates were also low for Asians and Jews, even compared to other immigrants, perhaps because they lived in urban areas with higher home prices. Literacy in any language was much higher for Jews—and to some extent Asians—than it was for Hispanic and Italian immigrants, but both Jews and Asians had lower literacy rates than the native white population and lower rates than northern European immigrants.

Jews and Asians did stand out as being much more likely than other immigrant groups to be business owners and managers, but the share of owners who actually employed other people was roughly equal to the same share for native white people. Where Asians and particularly Jews were most distinctive was in their propensity to work as self-employed managers—such as independent proprietors (table 6.1).

Other data from the period suggests that Jews were disproportionately likely to be working in finance, but these jobs were still dominated by Anglo-Saxons throughout the early twentieth century, and the relationship appears to have been geographic. For example, 65 percent of traders on the New York Stock Exchange were Anglo-Saxon in 1910 and just 3 percent Jewish. By 1930, the number of Jews had risen to 8.6 percent, but Anglo-Saxons still comprised 60 percent.[42] But then 8.6 percent is not a large percentage considering that while Jews comprised roughly 4 percent of the U.S. population in 1929, they constituted 30 percent of the New York City population.[43] Thus, from the perspective of the local population base, Jews were underrepresented at the stock exchange.

Likewise, while Jews were disproportionately chief executives of the largest companies in Germany, the same was not true in the United States. Just 4.6 percent of CEOs of the 200 largest U.S. companies in 1917 were Jewish, which roughly equaled their share of the population.[44] Two-thirds were Episcopalian or Presbyterian, though they represented just 4 percent of the U.S. population.[45]

There is also no evidence to suggest that Jews or Asians were prominent in U.S. invention or science in the late nineteenth and early twentieth centuries—at least until the Nazis forced German Jewish scientists to leave in the 1930s.[46] The 1920 census data, for example, shows that compared with U.S. white people, as well as immigrants from England, Germany, and

Table 6.1. Men aged 30 to 40 living in the United States in 1920, by occupational category, literacy, home ownership status, and ethnic background

	Share in professional occupations	Share in managerial occupations	Share who are farmers	Share who are machinists	Share who own a business	Share who are laborers	Literacy	Home ownership rate
Northeastern white, U.S.-born	4.6%	7.1%	9.1%	4.1%	4.1%	29.9%	99.2%	37.4%
Born in England	4.2%	5.8%	5.3%	5.7%	2.8%	29.3%	99.6%	34.5%
White, U.S.-born	3.6%	6.7%	26.3%	2.6%	7.8%	25.4%	97.7%	44.6%
Yiddish-speaking mother	2.7%	20.8%	0.7%	1.0%	8.0%	24.8%	92.2%	19.4%
Born in Germany	2.5%	6.3%	15.5%	4.9%	6.4%	27.8%	98.1%	43.0%
Northeastern black	1.6%	1.4%	3.2%	0.8%	0.6%	49.1%	94.6%	12.6%
Born in Ireland	1.6%	3.9%	3.6%	3.2%	1.3%	39.3%	99.0%	28.0%
Born in Sweden	1.5%	3.7%	16.4%	5.6%	5.4%	30.3%	98.6%	45.4%
Asian	1.3%	9.7%	26.3%	0.4%	8.5%	28.0%	89.2%	10.0%
Black	1.2%	0.9%	35.7%	0.4%	5.4%	37.3%	77.9%	20.4%
Spanish-speaking mother	1.0%	2.5%	22.7%	0.7%	2.0%	46.2%	65.6%	15.5%
Italian-speaking mother	0.9%	5.7%	4.4%	1.5%	2.5%	44.0%	74.2%	28.2%

Source: 1920 complete count U.S. Census, with 9 million U.S. male residents aged 30–40. Steven Ruggles, Katie Genadek, Ronald Goeken, Josiah Grover, and Matthew Sobek. Integrated Public Use Microdata Series: Version 7.0 [dataset]. Minneapolis, MN: University of Minnesota, 2017.

Sweden, Jews and Asians were greatly underrepresented as scientists, machinists, and engineers, the occupations most likely to initiate a patent.[47]

This puzzle has been noted by social scientists who have delved deeply into Jewish social status and achievement. It is worth quoting Joel Mokyr, a noted Israeli American economic historian, at length:

> By 1850, technological innovation had become a central source of economic change. Yet despite their huge head start economically, Jews played an almost imperceptible role in the history of science and technology before and during the early Industrial Revolution. . . . Given the high investment in human capital by Jews, their obsession with learning and books, and their devotion to the education of their sons (many of whom mastered high-skill crafts), one might have predicted otherwise. . . . Yet in the annals of the Industrial Revolution, Jews are hard to find.[48]

Biographies of prominent inventors during the most prolific period of the Industrial Revolution show close to zero Jews or Asians—either in Europe or the United States. For example, the National Inventors Hall of Fame aims to recognize the greatest inventions ever patented at the U.S. Patent and Trademark Office (USPTO). Of the 104 inventors born between 1743 and 1850—which include renowned inventors such as Thomas Edison, Alexander Graham Bell, Cyrus McCormack, and Eli Whitney—I could not identify any who were of Jewish or Asian heritage. Thereafter, only a handful are apparently Jewish until the twentieth century; among the early inventors are Eli Berliner, who was born to German Jewish merchants in 1851 and contributed to the gramophone and microphone, and Willem Einthoven, who was born to a gentile mother and a Dutch Jewish father in 1860 and patented the electrocardiograph, which also won him the Nobel Prize for medicine in 1924.[49]

It is well known that northern European gentiles—particularly the British people—were the driving force of the Industrial Revolution. This is difficult to explain if, as hereditarians argue, the great contributions of Jews to science and invention later in history was a result of their genetic advantage for intelligence over northern Europeans and those of African origin.

Of course, northern European gentiles had greater political power and autonomy than European Jews, and even hereditarians concede that environmental factors can make a difference. And yet, the hereditarian claim that recent achievements by Jews and Asians were based on long-standing genetic advantages collapses when comparing their performance to African Americans during the Industrial Revolution. African Americans suffered from political oppression at least as much as Jews and Asians, and despite this, the sons and daughters of escaped or emancipated African American slaves arguably made greater contributions to the Industrial Revolution than Jews or Asians. It is not as improbable as it may seem: Black people in the Northeast had higher literacy rates than either Asians or Jews in 1920, according to census data. It is well documented that African Americans made important contributions in all branches of science, including engineering, chemistry, math, medicine, and quantum theory.[50]

The African Americans Lewis Howard Latimer, Elijah McCoy, and George Washington Carver, for example, were born around the mid-nineteenth century and are now in the National Inventors Hall of Fame. Latimer was born free in 1848 Massachusetts to a runaway slave. He taught himself the art of drafting and drafted the designs for the telephone while working for Alexander Graham Bell. He later made an important improvement to the light bulb while working for a company that rivaled Edison's before getting hired by Edison himself.[51] McCoy's parents escaped slavery and settled in Canada, where Elijah was born. He lived briefly in Edinburgh, Scotland, as an apprentice to an engineer, before moving to Michigan, where he quickly applied inventions to the benefit of railways, before embarking on a successful career as a serial inventor.[52] Carver was born into slavery to an idiosyncratic German American who supported the Union in the Civil War despite being a slave owner.[53] He raised George as his own son and provided the education that eventually led to his academic success as an agricultural scientist and inventor.[54]

These men were not alone. Surveys in 1900 and 1913 by the USPTO of patent attorneys, newspapers, and manufacturing firms identified over one thousand black inventors who held patents, including black women such as Miriam Benjamin and Sarah Boone who were born into slavery but educated in the Northeast.[55] Many more could have registered for patents, according to the research conducted by Henry Baker of the Patent Office, if not for lack of funds to pay attorney fees.[56] Another set of black inventors chose to have the white attorney hold the patent in his name so as not to depress the value of the invention as a result of its association with a black person. The African

American inventor of a clothes drying machine, Ellen Eglin, was explicit about this in an 1890 interview.[57]

By matching patents to census records, a team of University of Chicago economists estimated that 1.8 percent of U.S. inventions during the Golden Age of U.S. Invention (1880–1940) were made by black people, while another group of economic historians put the figure closer to 6 percent (for the 1870–1940 period), showing variation across decades from 3 percent to 10 percent.[58] Overall, these figures suggest that black people were underrepresented in patenting because they comprised 10 percent of the U.S. population in 1920. Yet, black educational and occupational opportunities were severely restricted in the South, home to 82 percent of the black population. Outside of the South, black people comprised just 2.7 percent of the U.S. population, so the estimates above suggest that northern black Americans were about as likely to patent as white Americans—perhaps even considerably more likely.[59] Economic historian Lisa Cook finds that most black inventors lived outside the South and, if born in the South, migrated elsewhere.[60] Moreover, the 2 percent to 6 percent estimates are biased downward, because as mentioned above, black people often had to file patents under the names of white lawyers.

The unmistakable fact is that during one of the most important eras of invention in world history, African Americans played an important role comparable to the average white American. This is all the more incredible given that most of the U.S. black population had been enslaved for many generations.

Even including Southern black people, the number of patents per person was higher among black people than Asians or any other racial group except white Americans during this period, according to the Chicago economists.[61] It is quite possible that black people outside the South patented at higher rates than Jews, but current data cannot test this directly. The patents records also show that black inventors were more productive over their careers—patented more frequently—than non–black people and that patents held by black people were cited more frequently by other patents, which is commonly regarded today as an indicator of higher quality.[62]

Even slaves contributed to innovation, though neither slaves nor their owners were allowed to hold patents for the inventions of slaves. None other than Jefferson Davis, the president of the Confederacy, filed for a patent on the basis of an invention for a boat propeller that he attributed to his slave,

Benjamin T. Montgomery. Davis later promoted legislation in the Confederate Congress to pass a law allowing slave owners to own and patent the inventions of their slaves.[63] Another example comes from Solomon Northrup, who was born free in upstate New York and was later abducted and sold into slavery. His autobiography was eventually adapted into the Academy Award–winning screenplay *Twelve Years a Slave*, but one detail is pertinent here: Northrup saved his owner a large sum of money by applying his engineering skills to devise a cheaper river-based means of transporting the raw timber that was imported into the plantation.[64] Another well-documented and far-reaching example comes from the slave Onesimus, who introduced the practice of inoculation against smallpox to the United States in 1721 by explaining the West African practice to his owner, Cotton Mather, a prominent physician living in Boston.[65] This knowledge saved the lives of countless Americans.

It would take longer for African Americans to gain a foothold in academia, but Jews and Asians were also rarely professors or professional scientists in the early years of the twentieth century. An analysis of the 1,000 top U.S.-based scientists at the beginning of the twentieth century found that just 12.6 percent were foreign born, and almost none were born in Russia or China (0.6 percent and 0.2 percent, respectively).[66] Most of the foreign-born were from England and Canada. U.S. states with high literacy rates and robust public education systems—such as Massachusetts and Connecticut—were the most highly likely to foster scientific leaders.

Mokyr explains the limited Jewish contribution to the Industrial Revolution as resulting from rigid adherence to tradition and authority, which sapped them of creativity as applied to science and engineering. Another explanation is that until the twentieth century, very few Jews or Asians grew up under republican governments that were committed to equality of opportunity, high-quality secular education for the masses, and property rights that would have secured the fruits of invention. A strict adherence to ancient customs at the expense of innovation would have been understandable under such conditions. Britain and especially the United States, by contrast, created the conditions for common people to venture and thrive. Eventually, under republican governments, Asian and Jewish Americans did thrive and went on to make countless contributions to American science and culture.

Free black people were oppressed in many ways, but for a brief time just after the Civil War and Reconstruction and before the full onset of Jim Crow greatly curtailed the rights of black people, the pendulum of liberty swung in favor of political equality. Following amendments to the U.S. Constitution that ended slavery, promised equality before the law, and granted black people the right to vote, Frederick Douglass was moved to say in 1870:

> We are a great nation—not we colored people particularly, but all of us. We are all together now. We are fellow-citizens of a common country. What a country—fortunate in its institutions, in its fifteenth amendment, in its future. We are made up of a variety of nations—Chinese, Jews, Africans, Europeans, and all sorts. These different races give the Government a powerful arm to defend it. They will vie with each other in hardship and peril, and will be united in defending it from all its enemies, whether from within or without.[67]

Even with the diminished incentives afforded by racial discrimination, many black people saw this opportunity and took it. Madam C. J. Walker was born to a black family newly freed by the Civil War. Raised under Reconstruction, she went on to become an extremely wealthy entrepreneur.[68]

These achievements of African Americans should be kept in mind when considering the section that follows. As we will see, the best available evidence suggests that Northern black people had higher IQs than recent Jewish immigrants in the 1920s, which again, is impossible to reconcile with hereditarian theory.

Efforts to Quantify Jewish Intelligence in the 1920s and Beyond

Aside from pointing out disproportionate achievement, hereditarian scholars claim that Jews have higher IQs. Compiling data from a few dozen small-scale studies, Lynn reports that American Jews' IQ scores started at roughly the U.S. average for white people in the 1920s and 1930s (101.5), before gradually increasing to 107 during the 1940s, 1950s, and 1960s, and up to 111 after the 1970s through the early 2000s.[69]

The fact that Jewish IQ increased 10 points over 40 years in his database should be enough to eliminate the possibility that Jewish IQ advantages are genetic in nature. Yet, he argues that it took time for the full nature of Jewish natural genius to reveal itself: "Jewish IQs have increased significantly over this period. It appears that in the earlier studies Jews were handicapped, probably largely because many of them were relatively recent immigrants who were impoverished, had poor nutrition and health, and many spoke Yiddish as their first language."[70] Low social status and unfamiliarity with English were real disadvantages for Jews, but Lynn does not acknowledge any similar environmental "handicaps" for black people suffering from Jim Crow, isolated and dispossessed Native Americans, former gentile serfs from Eastern Europe, oppressed peasants from Mexico and southern Italy, or working-class white people from the U.S. South. Nor does he explain why Yiddish speakers were so impoverished even as he and other (usually gentile) hereditarians extol the centuries of supposed wealth and high status of the Ashkenazi.[71]

Even in his limited compilation, Lynn makes crucial flaws in interpreting the studies he does include, as well as ignoring the problem of selection bias. Most significantly, he ignores or dismisses the highest-quality studies, all three of which contradict the claim that Jews had higher IQs before the 1960s, as I discuss in turn. Instead, he draws heavily on small samples, where, in some cases, the psychologists conducting the study explicitly give an interpretation to the data that does not match Lynn's by pointing out the nonrepresentative nature of either the Jewish population or non-Jewish reference population. Correcting for these errors, the studies Lynn cites provide no evidence that Jewish IQ scores were higher than those of native white people.

IQ Testing in the Early Twentieth Century Contradicts Hereditarian Theory

More significantly, Lynn also dismisses the most famous study from the 1920s and one of the most comprehensive databases ever assembled on American cognitive testing.[72] Understanding its implications for their theories, hereditarian scholars Rushton, Lynn, and Murray have all blithely dismissed the evidence from this research.[73]

The study was one of the most comprehensive IQ exams ever administered, and it was sponsored by the National Academies of Science. In 1919, a Harvard professor of psychology named Robert Yerkes led an effort to perform IQ exams on some 1.75 million American men—those drafted into the military. Unlike most IQ exams before or since, this created data on a representative sample of the U.S. population and its subcomponents because the sample size was so large and the selection process was close to random, relying, as it did, on a military draft. At the request of Yerkes, Carl Brigham, a young scholar, led an analysis of a large sample of the results, which ultimately contained data for 15,543 white officers, 81,465 native-born white people, 23,595 black people, and 12,492 foreign-born soldiers, of whom 2,340 were Russian-born and at least half were Jewish, according to Brigham.

The IQ of Russian immigrants came in at 86, almost a standard deviation below the IQ of native-born white people, immigrants from Germany (100), and the Netherlands (103). Turks and Greeks outscored Russians. Russians scored only slightly higher than the average recently enslaved African American.

For hereditarians, it gets worse. Northern black people, who were slightly less persecuted by Jim Crow than those in the South, outperformed Jews by a comfortable margin (4 IQ points). Northern black people tested only slightly behind Irish, Austrian, and Turkish Americans and ahead of Greek, Russian, Italian, and Polish Americans (table 6.2). Northern black people, moreover, scored almost a full standard deviation higher than Southern black people (12 points), whereas Northern white people scored only 6 points higher than Southern white people. Thus, it would seem that moving north was of greater benefit to black people than white people in terms of enhancing educational opportunities. Other evidence from the period shows that black children born in the South gained roughly 4 IQ points after moving north.[74]

None of the hereditarian critics denies the relevance of these data in the wider IQ debate, but they claim that Russian Christians are mixed up with Russian Jews and so there is nothing to be learned about Jewish intelligence from the Russian results. But this is badly wrong.

First of all, Brigham is correct that the 1920 Census shows that 54 percent of people who listed Russia or an imperial territory as their place of birth listed Yiddish, the language of the Ashkenazi, or Hebrew as their mother tongue, but even this understates the actual percentage who were Jewish. In 1936, according to data from the United States Census of Religious Bodies, there were 4.6 million practicing Jews in the United States but only 54,000 members of the Russian Orthodox Church.[75] Thus, as of 1930, Russian Christians would have constituted a tiny fraction of the 1.1 million American residents born in Russia.[76] More concretely, in 1885, the imperial Russian government—which reigned over Jews in the Pale of Settlement—decreed that only Poles and Jews were allowed to emigrate. The restriction seems to have been strictly enforced at least until 1906. Up to that point, 93 percent of Russian immigrants to the United States were Jewish, according to documents from U.S.

**Table 6.2. Average intelligence test scores
for World War I recruits in 1918, by race
for U.S.-born and by country of origin for
foreign-born**

England	105.8
Scotland	103.0
Holland	102.9
Northern U.S. whites	101.7
Germany	100.6
U.S. whites	100.0
Denmark	99.6
Canada	99.4
Sweden	97.5
Norway	95.9
Belgium	94.9
Southern U.S. whites	94.4
Ireland	92.4
Austria	92.1
Turkey	90.8
Northern U.S. blacks	90.7
Greece	90.2
Russia	87.3
Italy	85.5
Poland	84.1
U.S. blacks	82.4
Southern U.S. blacks	79.2

Source: Carl C. Brigham. *A Study of American Intelligence.*
(Princeton: Princeton University Press, 1923); For comparison,
U.S. officers scores 128.4. Scores by region are from: Alper,
T. G., & Boring, E. G. "Intelligence Test Scores of Northern
and Southern White and Negro Recruits in 1918." *Journal of
Abnormal and Social Psychology* 39.4 (1944): 471–474.

port-of-entry records analyzed by demographer Erich Rosenthal.[77] From 1889
to 1914, the Jewish share of Russian immigrants was at least 84 percent, and
during this period, the majority of Jewish immigrants (72 percent) came from
Russia, with the Austro-Hungarian Empire providing the largest secondary
source.

But whether the Russian sample was 50 percent Jewish or, more likely, over
80 percent Jewish in no way means the data should be discarded or overlooked.
These data are of much higher quality than all the studies described by Lynn
(because of their large size and representative sampling), and simple logic

shows that the maximum possible group average IQ score for Jews was still quite low. Brigham reports detailed distributions of scores, and it is obvious that there were very few outliers among the Russian test-takers. Only 3 percent of Russians scored in the "A" and "B" group, which reflected the highest scores, compared to 12 percent of all test-takers. If only Russian Jews scored in the top group, and they were 50 percent of the total, then 6 percent of Russian Jews scored in the top groups, still half the rate of all other test-takers.[78]

Another issue is whether or not these IQ tests—which were developed by the nation's leading IQ scholars—were biased against Jews more so than other groups. As Brigham argues, the testers went to great lengths to assign people tests based on their language proficiency and literacy. Those who were illiterate in English were assigned the "beta" version of the test, which relied entirely on pictograms and other wordless exercises that tested cognitive ability. Moreover, those who did poorly on the English-based "alpha" version—which was based on the still-used Stanford-Binet IQ test—were often given another chance with the beta version, just in case they were misidentified. Russian Jews did very poorly in both alpha and beta, even compared to other immigrant groups from non-English-speaking countries.

No matter how awkward for hereditarians, the conclusion that Jews born in the former Russian Empire had very low IQ scores in the 1920s is inescapable.

Another massive study ignored by Lynn and hereditarians was conducted by Charles Berry in the early 1920s. Working with the Detroit Public School District, he collected IQ data on 10,000 first-grade students, most of whom were age six. He reported the data by country of father's birth and by language spoken at home. While IQ scores cannot be calculated based on his summary data, his report of the percentage of students who scored at different levels shows that only 13 percent of Yiddish-speaking children scored in the top 20th percentile on the IQ tests, whereas 23 percent of black children and 30 percent of white children who spoke English at home scored in this top group (and 29 percent of all U.S.-born white children).[79] A higher percentage of Yiddish speakers were in the top quintile compared to Italian speakers (6.4 percent), Polish speakers (10 percent), and Russian speakers (10.7 percent), but not German speakers (16.7 percent) or those from miscellaneous language groups (15.6 percent). Again, this is unambiguous evidence that Jewish IQ scores were well below those of native white people, and consistent with Brigham's data, Northern black people outperformed Jews in the same large urban school district. In fact, black students outperformed every group in which children spoke a foreign language at home, even though the test supposedly required no knowledge of written English.

Cognitive Testing in the Mid-Twentieth Century

Sometime between the mid- to late twentieth century, there is evidence to suggest that Jewish Americans began to score consistently higher than black people and eventually native non-Jewish white people on intelligence or other academic tests. The differences with white non-Hispanic gentiles is accounted for by formal education. Young adults who identify as Jewish have the same IQ scores as white non-Jewish young adults with the same education and parental education. This result is found in the only two large-scale surveys that include both IQ and religion: the National Longitudinal Survey (NLS) 1979 (people born from 1957 to 1964) and the NLS 1997 (born between 1980 and 1984).[80] Returning to Lynn's evidence from small, non-random, and non-representative samples, he estimates that American Jews had a mean IQ of around 107 during the middle part of the twentieth century, but the best available evidence shows that scores were similar to native white peers as late as 1960.[81]

Aside from study of the military tests, one other study of IQ stands out from the rest as large in scale and representative. It is called "Project Talent" and was led by University of Pittsburgh psychologist J. C. Flanagan, who founded the American Institutes of Research, which won a major award from the Department of Education to study U.S. students. In 1960, Flanagan and his colleagues collected IQ, demographic, and personality data on a random sample of 440,000 high school students in the United States (5 percent of the population).[82]

The test did not record religion but did ask whether the students' parents could speak a number of non-English languages. One category was Hebrew or Yiddish. As such, the question indirectly asked if the student's parents were Jewish. Certainly, one can imagine that not all Jewish children born in 1945 had parents who still spoke Yiddish or Hebrew, but likely, it was the majority. A 1918 census report estimates that 85 percent of Jews living in New York City reported that Yiddish was their mother tongue.[83] A 1922 study of children in the Detroit Public School District found that 80 percent of Russian-born students spoke Yiddish at home.[84] Finally, in Melbourne,

Australia, a 1967 survey of Jewish children found that 76 percent said that at least one of their parents still spoke Yiddish, and 70 percent said that both spoke Yiddish.[85]

To distinguish families who speak a foreign language based on their ethnicity from people who may pick up a foreign language as a result of exposure, I focus the analysis on children who said their parents spoke the language fairly well, fluently, or very fluently. Nearly 22,000 children of Yiddish speakers fell into this category, or 5 percent of the U.S. population of high school students, which is roughly the Jewish share of U.S. population at the time.[86]

Given the large sample size and random sampling method, this is arguably the highest-quality study of IQ ever conducted in the world for a single country. The results provide rather definitive evidence against the idea that either American Jews or Asians born around 1945 possessed above average intelligence.

African Americans born into Jim Crow and raised in the West or Northeast registered IQ scores that were only slightly lower than those from children whose parents spoke Yiddish or Hebrew and higher than children whose parents spoke "Oriental" languages. In fact, the scores of Northern black people were almost identical to those of Scandinavian immigrants.

The children of Yiddish speakers scored between .33 and .66 standard deviations lower than non-Yiddish-speaking white people. Children selecting the racial category "Oriental" performed roughly the same as white people on the composite IQ tests, but those who said their parents spoke an "Oriental" language at least fairly well—a much larger group than those who selected the race—did quite a bit worse than white people (table 6.3).

The low performance of the children of Yiddish- and Oriental-speaking parents is not explained by the reliance on reading tests for nonnative speakers. Even on abstract tests such as visualization in two or three dimensions, both groups performed much worse than native white people. The designers of the Project Talent database suggested that the Abstract Reasoning subtest was "especially appropriate" for those who had just come to the country and had limited English. On all of these tests, Jews and Asians performed well below average and only slightly better than their composite IQ score. Moreover, even third-generation children whose U.S.-born parents still spoke Yiddish performed well below average. The same is true controlling for paternal occupation. Yiddish-speaking children disproportionately reported that their fathers worked in professional occupations relative to white non-Jewish

Table 6.3. IQ composite score by group for large sample of U.S. high school students in 1960

	IQ	Number of students tested
IQ by how well parents speak "Hebrew or Yiddish"		
Parents speak Hebrew or Yiddish rather poorly	84.6	3,397
Parents speak Hebrew or Yiddish not very well	82.2	3,942
Parents speak Hebrew or Yiddish fairly well	87.5	6,263
Parents speak Hebrew or Yiddish fluently	90.7	5,468
Parents speak Hebrew or Yiddish very fluently	95.6	9,961
Parents speak any Hebrew or Yiddish (poorly or better)	89.5	29,031
Parents speak Hebrew or Yiddish fairly well or better	91.9	21,692
Parents speak Hebrew or Yiddish fairly well or better, at least one parent born abroad	88.0	8,909
Parents speak Hebrew or Yiddish fairly well or better, both parents born in USA	94.7	12,783
IQ for other racial and linguistic groups		
Parents do not speak Yiddish or Hebrew	93.9	308,460
White and parents do not speak Yiddish or Hebrew fairly well or better	100.0	126,128
Parents speak German fairly well or better	93.6	39,090
Parents speak Spanish fairly well or better	90.2	30,151
Parents speak Italian fairly well or better	88.7	28,454
Parents speak a Scandinavian language fairly well or better	86.7	21,131
Parents speak Russian fairly well or better	89.9	17,812
Parents speak Oriental language fairly well or better	80.2	15,991
Blacks in the South	73.4	3,480
Blacks in the Northeast or West	85.3	1,399
Race is Oriental	99.2	975
Race is Mexican American	83.9	312
Race is American Indian	87.4	235

Note: IQ calculated from "IQ composite." To calculate these scores, I first eliminated nonresponses (coded as 999), then calculated mean and standard deviations for the white non-Yiddish-speaking population for each age group, since there were multiple high school ages in the sample (with mean of 15). Then I converted individual scores to age-specific Z-scores before calculating group IQ averages. The white non-Jewish mean is calculated without using sample weights. Applying those weights barely lowers the mean score to 99.9. The question about parental language asks, "How well does your parent speak Hebrew or Yiddish?" Other questions have the same format but use the other languages listed.

Source: American Institutes for Research, "Project Talent, Base Year Data, 1960," May 23, 2015, Ann Arbor, MI: Inter-university Consortium for Political and Social Research [distributor], 2013-05-23, https://doi.org/10.3886/ICPSR33341.v2.

children (12.7 percent vs. 6.3 percent), but while the non-Jewish children of professionals scored 108, the Jewish children of professionals scored just 101.

Still, these results likely understate the IQ of all Jews because more-assimilated Jewish parents—those who no longer spoke Yiddish—would likely hold higher social status and confer educational advantages to their children.[87] One study from Boris Levinson analyzed IQ data from 117 Jewish children whose parents were applying for a competitive Jewish private school in New York City. Since they were endeavoring to enroll their children in an expensive and competitive private school, these parents cannot be thought of as a representative sample of the broader Jewish population, but Levinson found that multilingual Jewish children scored 4 to 5 IQ points lower than monolingual Jewish children. It follows that the scores above for the most-assimilated American-born Jewish children would be roughly 100, if one added 4 to 5 points to account for their Yiddish-speaking parents.[88] In other words, Jewish children scored right at the national benchmark for native non-Jewish white children.

The more famous Coleman Report was also issued around this time and reported test score data for large numbers of people. The report did not distinguish between Jews and non-Jewish white people, but it did report the test scores of Asians ("Orientals") in 12th grade. The average score across five dimensions suggested an IQ score of 97.2. White people scored higher on each dimension, which included math and nonverbal reasoning.[89]

While these data may seem startling to people familiar with hereditarian theory and the IQ literature, the basic argument—if not these specific data—has been made by the economist Thomas Sowell in his review of *The Bell Curve* and his book on ethnic differences.[90] Jewish and Asian IQ gains seem to have occurred largely for people born during and after the 1950s.

In this context, one must also consider another factor in the sudden rise in test scores of Asian Americans and possibly Jewish immigrants from earlier periods. Asian American immigrants—like most immigrant groups—tend to be far more educated than the native population of their home countries. This gap emerges, at least in part, as a result of immigration laws that allocate visas to university students or workers with a college degree. For example, 84 percent of current U.S. residents born in India and 55 percent of U.S. residents born in China who arrived after the age of 21—and so did not grow up in the United States—have a tertiary education compared to only 4 percent in their native countries (table 6.4). The gaps are smaller for some African countries and for Haiti, because people from these countries are more likely

Table 6.4. Tertiary educational attainment rate of U.S. adult immigrants from selected countries compared to adult populations in countries of origin

Country of birth	College attainment rate of U.S. residents aged 30–50 who arrived at age 21 or older	College attainment rate in country of origin, aged 30–50
India	84%	4%
Nigeria	59%	2%
China	55%	4%
Taiwan	80%	30%
Iran	61%	15%
Hong Kong	69%	26%
France	72%	30%
United Kingdom	65%	26%
Ghana	38%	4%
Brazil	40%	7%
Japan	56%	30%
South Korea	64%	45%
Haiti	20%	5%
Honduras	8%	5%
Guatemala	7%	9%
El Salvador	7%	11%
Mexico	6%	15%

Note: Data sorted by difference between educational attainment of emigrant population and home-country population.

Source: Data for U.S. residents are from IPUMS USA, using the 2012–16 American Community Survey. Data is restricted to people born outside the United States who arrived no earlier than age 21 and who are currently aged 30–50. Data from country of origin is from the Gallup World Poll and pools data from 2007–17 for the population aged 30–50.

to gain entry into the United States through refugee programs or family-based programs that do not require high levels of education. For immigrants from Mexico and Central America, the gap is reversed. Through a combination of nonsanctioned entry over the border and visas granted for less-educated seasonal workers, Central American residents who enter the United States are far less likely to be college educated than those who remain in their native country.

Thus, given the many pathways through which people migrate and their motivations for doing so, one must be cautious about comparing test scores and social status of immigrant groups and their native-born children and using that information to draw inferences about a global population.

GLOBAL TEST SCORE PERFORMANCE

Hereditarians like to point to global differences in literacy, test scores, and, where limited data exist, formal IQ scores as evidence that Asians are naturally more gifted than others, but the data are more complicated than they have admitted and ultimately contradict the view that there is any intellectually dominant race or ethnic group.

The educational achievement scores of 15-year-olds enrolled in secondary school who take the OECD's Programme for International Student Assessment (PISA) exam illustrate some of these issues. In general, Japanese and Korean children do very well, but roughly the same as Canadians, Estonians, Finns, and Americans living in Massachusetts.

Likewise, Chinese perform almost as well as these other groups, but the data come from only four provinces: Beijing, Shanghai, Jiangsu, and Guangdong. Eighteen percent of the Chinese population lives in these four provinces, but 43 percent of this population has a postgraduate education. So, it is already an extremely elite group who lives in these places, compared to the rest of China.[91]

Data from the Gallup World Poll illustrate this. From 2012–2016, World Poll data show that 66 percent of the Chinese population aged 30 to 50 had only an elementary education. By contrast, in the 2015 OECD PISA database, only 18 percent of Chinese parents had an elementary education—or 23 percent if you apply their statistical weight. By contrast, in the United States, the Gallup data line up with the PISA data: only 6 percent of U.S. parents in the PISA database had only an elementary education, which nearly matches the Gallup World Poll result of 4 percent for 30 to 50 year olds in the United States.

A further problem with Chinese data is that one has to be very careful about analyzing data by region and applying it to the country as a whole. That is because Chinese cities—including Hong Kong—carefully manage migration from rural areas to cities, and public services such as education are restricted to those who have approved legal status. In Shanghai, this eliminates roughly half of the population from participation in public high schools, and many of the poorest children return to their rural homeland as a result.[92] The Chinese PISA scores, therefore, are not even close to being a representative sample of the national Chinese population.

Even Singapore's data are flawed. Singapore is currently the world's top performer on the PISA. Its scores would suggest an IQ of 113, compared to 109 for Estonia and Japan. Some point to the fact that many students supplement their education with private tutors in response to the country's high-pressure testing.[93] However, one should also consider that as of 2015, 11 percent of Singapore's primary school students failed to gain admission into its high schools, and so they were not included in the OECD PISA exams.[94] That removed the worst-performing students from the sample.

Data from the OECD's other large-scale cognitive exam—one for adults—do not suffer from these flaws because the exam does not require participants to have any special political status—such as eligibility for public educational services. The Programme for the International Study of Adult Competencies (PIAAC) allows for high-quality analysis of cognitive performance by country. The data were collected from 2011 to 2015.[95] While China declined to participate, 346 people born in China but living in a developed country were included. Moreover, residents of Japan, South Korea, Singapore, and Indonesia were explicitly included.

I calculated means and standard deviations within five broad age groups and converted the results into the familiar IQ scores with a mean of 100. The results indicate that adults aged 16 to 65 born in China but living abroad (in one of ten countries that report the country of birth for participants) have a mean IQ of 87.1. Roughly 80 percent live in either South Korea or Singapore. By comparison, African Americans scored higher on literacy and slightly lower on math than this group. Hispanic Americans scored about the same on math and slightly higher on literacy. It is likely that second-generation Chinese immigrants make considerable progress, but that makes a genetic argument hard to sustain.

Except for Japan and Korea, other adults born in other East and South Asian countries also score below the global average, including Singapore (98.3), Malaysia (96.7), Indonesia (94.4), and India (88.9).

Israel was also included on the exam and scored below the global average. Since Israel is not exclusively a Jewish state, the mean score for Israel is not the best available score for its Jewish population. PIAAC data also report scores by the language test-takers speak at home. Hebrew speakers scored right at the international average of 99.6, and their score is estimated with a small margin of error because of the inclusion of Israel in the sample. Hebrew speakers score just ahead of Polish speakers (98.3) but significantly behind Korean speakers (100.5) and English speakers (101.4).

Meanwhile, Yiddish speakers performed well below international norms, with an IQ of 93.6, somewhat below Russian speakers (95.8) and Hungarian speakers (97.2), but their margin of error was large.

Out of all language groups with at least 50 test-takers, Swedish speakers did the best (108.6), but differences with Japanese speakers (108.0) were not statistically significant. Scandinavian and Dutch and Flemish speakers did very well overall. Native Finnish, Dutch/Flemish, Norwegian, and Danish speakers scored between 106.5 and 105. Speakers of southern European and western Asian languages did less well—including Spanish, Croatian, Albanian, Arabic, Persian, and Turkish.

In this context, it is worth reiterating the point stated in the previous chapter that the IQ scores of immigrants are much higher when they arrive as young children and that this illustrates the strong causal effect of exposure to high-quality education. For example, Sub-Saharan Africans who arrived before age ten in New Zealand—itself a high-scoring country—scored as high as the Japanese and Swedes (108.1).

In general, the results in no way suggest that Israeli Jews or East Asians possess uniformly high IQs relative to the global average for residents of developed countries. That makes it all the more difficult to believe that Jews and East Asians living in America today—who once had low IQs themselves—come from some elite racial group.

For that matter, Scandinavian Americans did not perform exceptionally well on IQ tests in the mid-twentieth century either, and, like Jews and Asians, they contributed relatively little to the Industrial Revolution, and yet Scandinavian adults living in Scandinavia today are among the highest scorers globally. This again, undermines any notion that Nordic people are genetically gifted. Rather, their high achievements, like those of the Japanese, as well as those of contemporary American Jews, Native Americans, Korean Americans, and Chinese Americans, are the product of exposure to republican institutions and high-quality learning opportunities from an early age in both their familial life and formal schooling. Like East Asians and Jews, Scandinavians have a long political tradition of valuing early childhood education and literacy, which in their case comes out of their Protestant emphasis on biblical study.[96]

SELECTIVE BREEDING DOES NOT EXPLAIN THE RISE IN IQ

Another lynchpin of Cochran et al.'s theory is that the most successful Jews (and by extension Asians) had more children, which gradually raised the IQ of the population. Could this explain the extraordinary rise in Jewish American intelligence from the early to late twentieth century?

The answer is no. To be clear, no one has proposed that a population's IQ could be radically transformed by genetics over just a handful of generations. Even the most aggressive assumptions about the heritability of IQ and the degree of selective breeding rule that out. It would take hundreds of years to generate a standard deviation change through selective breeding. Moreover, empirical evidence about the degree of selective breeding rules out the idea entirely. According to the Project Talent database, Jews with higher IQs had significantly fewer siblings than those with higher IQs during the 1940s and 1950s. Even worse for hereditarian theory, IQ had a stronger negative effect on reproduction among Jews than it did among other groups. The same is true for Asians. These facts are fundamentally incompatible with a genetic explanation for the rise in Jewish and Asian American test scores during the twentieth century.

Ironically, hereditarian theorists such as Murray and Herrnstein were very concerned by this pattern of "dysgenesis," by which they and others meant the gradual decline in population IQ as a result of parents of lower intelligence out-reproducing parents with higher IQs. They devote an entire chapter to it in *The Bell Curve* as a warning about the decline of Western civilization. They estimate that this process had resulted in a loss of IQ of roughly 0.8 points per generation throughout the twentieth century. In fact, they believe the effect is even worse because racial groups with lower IQs have more children, and they believe racial differences are largely genetic. It is extremely awkward for this theory that actual IQ rose roughly 7.5 points per generation throughout the twentieth century in almost every country.

This pattern of a generally rising IQ for the national population and specific subgroups, even as less-educated parents have more children, illustrates the power that education and nongenetic cultural factors have in shaping cognitive ability. As European Jews and Asian immigrants integrated into American society, their low test scores converged with and later surpassed children from less-educated backgrounds.

EFFECTS OF NONGENETIC AND NONETHNIC CULTURAL
PRACTICES ON IQ

The social scientists Samuel Bowles and Herbert Gintis have defined culture as "preferences and beliefs that are acquired by means other than genetic transmission" and argue that culture affects social success and ultimately the fitness of genes.[97]

The notion that culture affects behavior can, however, be easily misinterpreted as suggesting that long-standing quasi-permanent ethnic traditions—passed on through many generations—are a primary driver of social outcomes. In fact, as Bowles and Gintis's definition suggests, culture can come from anywhere—including political institutions—and changes therein. The economic historian Deirdre McCloskey has presented a compelling argument that the primary force behind the Industrial Revolution in England and northern Europe was the development of a culture that emphasized the dignity and respect of ordinary people—bourgeois life and business.[98] This was a cultural force not primarily tied to family traditions—indeed, the radical changes in occupational and educational mobility were radical departures from family traditions, just as the scientific and entrepreneurial breakthroughs of the Industrial Revolution were radical departures from previous thinking.

To clarify the point, consider the history of English literacy, which grew rapidly during the Industrial Revolution, according to a recent account by historian Adam Fox. In 1500, just 10 percent of adult men and 1 percent of women could write their name, but by 1642, 30 percent of men and 10 percent of women could write, and by 1760, writing ability was demonstrated by 64 percent of men and 39 percent of women. Such rapid large-scale changes didn't come because English parents—who were largely illiterate—were teaching their children at home as part of a family tradition. Rather, as Fox puts it: "New educational provision was both the cause of the effect of the development of religious pluralism, the changing face of the English economy and the more fluid nature of the social order." Religious beliefs—especially that reading the Bible was edifying—combined with practical needs and "bourgeois values"—including respect for the common dignity of others—motivated women such as Alice Heywood of Lancashire, who was the wife of a weaver, to promote literacy in her community. In the words of her son, "It was her usual practice to help many poore children to learning by buying them books, setting to schoole, and paying their master for teacher, whereby many a poore parent blessed god for help by their children reading."[99]

Culture is powerful, but it is fluid, dynamic, and responsive. It is also social and political. Culture cannot be understood as the atomistic and idiosyncratic practices of families, who learned everything from their parents and their parents' parents. The values and practices that sweep through nations, communities, and families arise from social circumstances and publicly agreed-upon norms. Thus, when social norms and ideologies change, one should expect changes in family practices. The political status of ethnic or racial minorities is one such social norm that has profoundly shaped the United States and its culture.

A Cultural War over Education

In the United States, there can be no doubt that cultural views on race have had profound effects on the opportunities for different sections of society. The Civil War could be seen as an experiment that dramatically but only temporarily changed the dominant cultural view toward black people as it changed their political status.

Following the end of slavery, the U.S. government occupied the defeated Southern states. White opposition to the political equality of black people was explicitly based on the theory of black inferiority. "The black man is what God and nature and circumstances have made him. That he is not fit to be invested with these important rights may be no fault of his. But the fact is patent to all that the negro is utterly unfitted to exercise the highest functions of the citizen."[100] According to W. E. B. DuBois, the Southern planters who dominated politics in the region stridently opposed taxation to support public education, even of white people. "Education they regarded as a luxury connected with wealth."[101] They were particularly hostile toward the education of black people.

The occupation of the South by the Northern military temporarily stripped white people who supported slavery of voting rights, and Southern opposition to the political equality of black people was held in check.[102] One consequence was that even during the war, the Northern government made immense changes to U.S. education policy. Southern politicians had voted down efforts to establish public universities, but after the South's secession from the United States, Northern politicians passed the Morrill Act, which established some of the world's leading research universities, including Cornell University, the University of California, Berkeley, Pennsylvania State University, the University of Wisconsin, Purdue University, Virginia Tech, and Texas A&M.

Importantly, after the war, the U.S. government initiated a massive program to increase the literacy of the formerly enslaved population, which also had the effect of creating, for the first time, a system of mass public education in the South.

Many observers of the time noted both the alacrity and aptitude that black people demonstrated for education. DuBois's history of Reconstruction quotes the influential Booker T. Washington, himself a freedman who went to great lengths to acquire an education, on the "intense desire which the people of my race showed for education": "Few were too young, and none too old, to make the attempt to learn. As fast as any kind of teachers could be secured, not only were day-schools filled, but night-schools as well. . . . The great ambition of the older people was to try to learn to read the Bible before they died."[103]

All around the country, white Northern officers—who found a fervor for political equality born out of their opposition to their enemy's creed—formed schools for black soldiers, black folks raised and sacrificed their own limited money for literacy, and the U.S. government's Freedmen's Bureau, as well as Northern philanthropies, all pitched in financially and sometimes personally to give black people opportunities long denied to them.

The French minister of education made some observations in 1870 about the first schools for freed slaves in Washington, DC: "I was well qualified to judge for myself of the differences in intellectual aptitude of the two races. I must say that I have been unable to discover any. . . . All of the teachers . . . that I have consulted on that point are of the same opinion." He recounts other visitors who were also impressed by the "intellectual acuteness" of the black students, including one Englishman, who said: "Never in any school in England, and I have visited many, have I found the pupils able to comprehend so readily the sense of their lessons: never have I heard pupils ask questions which showed a clearer comprehension of the subjects they were studying." At Oberlin College in Ohio, meanwhile, the French minister reported that "14 young colored girls were in the most advanced classes, and they appeared in no way inferior to their white companions." Twenty percent of the student population was black, and they were well integrated and respected by students and faculty alike, according to reports, and re-garded as equals.[104]

During Reconstruction, while Northern educational values predominated, freed Southern black people embraced the culture of learning. Literacy rates for young black adults in the South (aged 20 to 30) went from just 17 percent in 1870 to 34 percent in 1880 and 71 percent by 1910—still far behind the Northern black rate of 96 percent in 1910 but much closer than before Recon-struction.[105] Important research from economist Trevon Logan finds that lit-eracy among black people tended to grow faster under jurisdictions controlled by black politicians, illustrating the social power of political equality.[106]

Eventually, with Lincoln killed and the Klu Klux Klan unchecked, white opposition to Reconstruction, which is typically dated from 1865 to 1877, wore out white Northerners' temporary zeal for republicanism, and they al-lowed Southern white people to snuff out the spark that emancipation had ignited. Black people were barred from voting and thus from being politicians. Black people were shut out of the professions, eviscerating any financial rewards from higher education. Still, as we saw above, what was done could not be undone. Despite immense obstacles, black folks made enormous contributions to the Golden Age of American innovation, and the literacy and intellectual achievements of freed slaves and the second generation of freed people are still with us.

The fervor for equality and education that briefly united a large segment of white Northerners with freed slaves and other black people could be re-garded as a cultural force. It was tied to real relations of power, engaged in a war of ideas and principles. *Culture* is the proper term for family members passing on literacy to their children and encouraging them to become edu-cated, and it is the proper term for a mass political and social movement dedi-cated to that end.

The Culture of Literacy

These society-wide cultural forces—which ebb and flow—should be kept in mind when considering how individual families pass on literacy, motivations for success, and education.

First, we know from adoption studies that family circumstances matter greatly to educational attainment. A fairly consistent result from adoption studies is that the characteristics of nonbiological parents have very large and

Table 6.5. IQ growth and adoption into a professional family for severely disadvantaged children

Occupation of adoptive father	IQ of adopted children, ages 4–6	IQ of adopted children, ages 11–18	IQ gains since adoption
Occupation requires minimal skill or training	77.8	85.5	7.7
Skilled blue collar or low-level manager	76.5	92.2	15.7
Professional or high-level manager	78.5	98	19.5

Source: Duyme, Michel, Annick-Camille Dumaret, and Stanislaw Tomkiewicz. "How Can We Boost IQs of 'Dull children'? A Late Adoption Study." *Proceedings of the National Academy of Sciences* 96.15 (1999): 8790–8794.

significant predictive power for outcomes like income and education.[107] One especially clear study examined cases of abused or neglected children who were tested to have very low IQs between ages four and six and were then adopted into families of varying social class. The IQ of children adopted by fathers who worked as professionals or high-level managers shot up by 19.5 IQ points (1.3 standard deviations) (table 6.5). Being adopted by a father with a low-status job also raised IQ substantially (by 7.7 points), but not nearly as much. The implication is that neglected or abusive homes are disastrous for IQ, that normal working-class homes represent a substantial improvement, and that the homes and access to schooling provided by professional families offer a very large cognitive advantage.

There is further evidence that the social status and education of parents—rather than ethno-specific culture—explain differential development of IQ for Jewish and Asian Americans. The National Longitudinal Survey of Youth 1997 (NLSY97) collected data from a random sample of youth who were 12 to 16 years old as of December 31, 1996. It included a measure of cognitive achievement, the Armed Services Vocational Aptitude Battery (ASVAB). People raised as Jews, Hindus, and Buddhists scored very highly on this test, which is also highly correlated with SAT test score performance. Yet, controlling for parental education, there was no statistically significant difference between Jews and those with East Asian religions and all other groups. In other words, there is a simple explanation for the education and cognitive success of Jews and East Asian children: They have highly educated parents. The children of Christian or other parents who are also highly educated attain essentially the same scores.[108] This implies that there is nothing specific to the ethnic traditions of the parents that translates into high IQ.

The question then becomes what do highly educated parents—whatever their race or religious background—have in common when it comes to parenting their children and preparing them to become highly literate and numerate young adults, and why do some less-educated parents—often immigrants or children of immigrants, but also Southern black people during Reconstruction, and northern Europeans during the Industrial Revolution—motivate their children to invest so heavily in education?

A strong emphasis on early childhood education is, of course, an important cultural factor that certain groups—including highly educated parents—often pass on to their children. Recent survey data in the United States show that black and Hispanic parents of three-year-old children are less likely to incorporate nightly bedtime routines (11 to 10 percentage points) than white parents and much less likely to have a reading component to those routines (20 to 22 percentage points). Taken together, this means that black and Hispanic children are read to much less frequently at home, on average (table 6.6).

This pattern plays an important role in the development of inequality in IQ and school readiness. A large-scale review of dozens of experimental studies concludes that efforts to boost vocabulary and reading ability have large effects on the IQ of young children.[109] Likewise, there is strong and consistent evidence showing that IQ growth is faster when parents consistently read to their children.[110] Being read to literally changes the brain. Children whose brains are scanned while being read to show heightened neurological activity in the regions of the brain associated with decoding meaning.[111]

The fact that some parents read more to their children than others should not be thought of in terms of intrinsic ethnic practices. If that were the case, it would be very difficult to change parenting behavior, when in fact parenting behavior with respect to reading is extremely malleable. Something as simple as a regular text message (three per week over the school year) sent by a school reminding parents to read to their children substantially increases both reading activity by parents and the test scores of their children (by roughly 5 IQ points).[112] The effects were largest for black and Hispanic children, whose parents were less likely to be reading to them routinely before the experiment. These results were from a carefully controlled experiment.

Table 6.6. Nightly reading by parents to three-year-olds by ethnic groups in the United States

Percent who regularly read or tell stories as part of nightly bedtime routine	
Hispanic	36%
Black	37%
White, non-Hispanic	60%

Source: Data are from 3,600 children from the Fragile Families and Child Well Being Study, which oversampled families born to unwed mothers. These statistics are reported in Milan, S., S. Snow, and S. Belay. "The Context of Preschool Children's Sleep: Racial/Ethnic Differences in Sleep Locations, Routines, and Concerns." *Journal of Family Psychology* 21.1 (2007): 20–28.

Mailing books to the homes of low-income families has also proven to be effective.[113] For example, Dolly Parton, a famous southern white American country musician and actress, created a program called "Imagination Library," which mails one book a month to families in eligible areas with children ranging in age from birth to age five. One study concludes that participation in the program increased the percentage of kindergarten children who exceeded benchmark scores on a well-established literacy test from 46 percent to 61 percent.[114] Another study found that it increased IQ by roughly 6.5 points.[115]

Taken together, this evidence demonstrates that family culture is highly dynamic and readily responds to even modest social cues, prompts, and access to resources. Thus, segregation—which cuts off middle-class and low-income communities, including white people, from the cultural practices and often the resources of highly educated parents—inhibits the natural cultural transmission of successful practices across class and race and extends and reinforces the less helpful practices—such as watching television instead of reading or overvaluing the practice of sports relative to the practice of math.

Since children internalize the values of their parents, early reading activities are also likely to promote studious behavior later in life, when ethnic differences in effort are pronounced. Jewish high school students in 1981 reported spending 4.3 hours more per week on studying while away from school than non-Jewish students and 3.4 hours less on watching television, according to my analysis of the National Longitudinal Survey of Youth (table 6.7).

Table 6.7. Hours spent studying away from school per week by group in 1981 among U.S. high school students

	Jewish	Immigrant	U.S.-born, non-Jewish
No parent has four years of college	13.1	7.6	7.2
At least one parent has four years of college	12.3	18.7	10.1
All	12.5	11.3	8.1

Source: NLSY 1979. Restricted to currently enrolled students. Adds minutes and hours spent studying away from school last week and uses 1981 sample weight, which is the year the studying data was collected.

Avoiding television can hardly be regarded as an ethnic trait passed on for centuries. Moreover, non-Jewish children of highly educated parents act much more like Jews in the way that they allocate their time, regardless of race or religion. The most extreme group is the children of college-educated immigrants, who spend an extra 8.6 hours studying per week compared to U.S.-born gentiles.[116]

As it happens, studying predicts higher IQ scores and watching TV predicts lower IQ scores, so these studying habits may very well explain many of the performance differences between groups and give an indication of why the children of immigrants so quickly catch up and often surpass the native population in educational achievements. These findings are consistent with evidence that Asian Americans' academic effort explains their higher academic achievements compared to those of white Americans.[117] High levels of effort and enthusiasm for education have been documented among high-achieving African immigrants to England and the United States, though in both places their cultural history differs dramatically from that of East Asians.[118]

One explanation for why effort is higher in Asians, which may apply to Jews, Africans, and other groups, is that East Asian parents and children are more likely than white people to believe that hard work—not genes or natural ability—explains success.[119] One scholar who has investigated the question asks why Americans have shifted toward crediting innate ability over effort: "It seems likely that the increased attention to genetics and genetic influences on behavior, disease, and human nature has contributed to the belief that genetics matters most. New research on genetic influences is reported quite frequently in the popular press."[120] If so, research efforts to link genetics to social outcomes should be balanced across interdisciplinary approaches, as in the Social Science Genetic Association Consortium, so that findings about genetic effects are put into appropriate theoretical context when communicated to the media and public.

There is clear experimental evidence from social scientists at Stanford and Norwegian universities that belief in one's ability to learn—a "growth mindset"—affects effort and actual math performance, while a hereditarian or "fixed mindset" is poisonous to both effort and performance.[121] In the experiment, Norwegian high school students were classified as having a growth mindset or a fixed mindset for math ability, based on their agreement with statements such as "Your intelligence is something about you that you can't change very much" or "Some people are good at math and other people aren't." Fixed mindsets were more common in students with low grades and students who were on a vocational track that would not lead to a bachelor's degree.

The students were then randomly assigned to either a control group, which received material about brain function but not its malleability, or a treatment group, which received a scientific article about the malleability of the brain written for a general audience for this purpose. They were asked to relate the article to their life and write about how they would use the information to advise a friend struggling in math. These are things that psychologists find help change mindsets.

Then, a few weeks later, both groups were asked to complete algebra exercises and reassess their mindset. People in the treatment group experienced a .56 standard deviation increase in their mindset (becoming more growth-oriented) and outperformed those in the control group (by about .29 standard deviations), even though both began the experiment with a fixed mindset. In other words, this is clear evidence that beliefs affect performance and that beliefs can be changed. A belief that IQ is largely genetic is detrimental.

The implication is that gaps in IQ between classes are reinforced and perpetuated by bad social science. This dynamic has likely played out among the English working class. Recent qualitative studies have focused on the fact that children of the white working class are among the lowest-scoring groups in the country and often suffer from low literacy, little parental engagement in education, and low self-esteem.[122] Interviews with parents, teachers, and students suggest that they believe they are destined to occupy the bottom rungs of society—a view inconsistent with English working-class culture in the nineteenth century and the culture of immigrant groups today who were not exposed to a twentieth-century theory that devalued low-status groups as naturally inferior.

Perhaps, the American and English working classes—whatever their race—could be encouraged to adopt a growth mindset from the achievements of African immigrants such as the Imafidon family. After moving from Nigeria to London, the Imafidons raised five children who have all distinguished themselves with genius-level academic performance. The oldest daughter, Ann Marie Imafidon, broke the record for passing the A-level computer science exam at age 11. She went on to graduate with a master's degree in computer science and mathematics from Oxford at age 20.[123] Her younger siblings had similar accomplishments. Peter and Paula passed A-level math at age seven, breaking the English record and accomplishing a feat attained by only 22 percent of students ten years old or older; they later passed University of Cambridge advanced math exams at age eight.[124] Peter and Paula inspired and even tutored another black girl from their church named Dee Alli, who became the youngest person to ever pass the math General Certificate of Secondary Education at age five.[125] Thus, social contact with the family seems to have raised the achievement of others in their community.

These West African immigrants—with IQ scores that would effectively be off the charts—did not come from a cultural tradition with centuries of literacy or urbanization. The dominant "cultural" perspective that the father, Chris Imafidon, seems to emphasize is a complete rejection of the genetic basis for intelligence: "All children are born bright" is his mantra, which he expresses in various other formulations on a website he has created to inspire learning.[126] This philosophy almost certainly contributed to the success of his children, and it is available to all of us. It is also much closer to scientific reality than hereditarianism.

This is not to say that mere belief or a growth mindset is sufficient to generate upward mobility. Far from it. Children need real, expensive, tangible investments from their parents, community, and governments to learn to read and write or acquire any other advanced skill. When parents lack the resources to invest heavily in their child's education—for want of time, education, or money—then the community and government need to fill the gap. The next chapter discusses the role of neighborhoods in shaping childhood outcomes and how too often political inequality eviscerates chances to obtain equal opportunity.

7

Unequal Access to Housing Markets

AFRICAN AMERICAN SEGREGATION

Like Jewish ghettos in sixteenth-century Italy, African American ghettos in the nineteenth-century United States were created, developed, and sustained by government policies, rather than simply voluntary private action. Thus, one of the most important barriers to racial equality in the United States—residential segregation—has been the direct result of political inequality generally and lack of equal access to housing markets, specifically. It is also important to note that exclusionary policies are not merely past abuses but are active today. Even now, government action and inaction are contributing to racial inequality by preventing African Americans from participating on an equal footing in housing markets.

This argument does not completely deny the importance of decisions made by private individuals, which shape market outcomes under the influence of government policies. Markets, government action, and legislation all require participants, and if those participants value racial discrimination, then market behavior and laws will reflect that. Accordingly, on the side of markets, white people have shown reluctance to live near black people, at least in large numbers. In research I conducted with Andre Perry and David Harshbarger of The Brookings Institution, we estimated that contemporary U.S. homes lose roughly one-quarter of their market value by virtue of their location in a black neighborhood.[1] Our analysis suggests that home buyers undervalue property in black neighborhoods. Real estate agents and private groups have also played a role in creating or sustaining segregation, as I discuss below. With that being said, private actions were not nearly as important in explaining segregation as public actions, and those public actions were often directly in conflict with market dynamics. Moreover, a government committed to equality and market access would penalize and curtail private threats to equal participation, which did not happen throughout most of the twentieth century.

The historic data on segregation bears this out. A detailed study by urban economists on the history of segregation across U.S. metropolitan areas concludes that government collective action, not decentralized private racism, created black ghettos.[2] This is also the conclusion of the leading historical accounts of the causes of segregation, with eminent scholars such as Douglas S. Massey providing one of the clearest and most forceful accounts, and recent investigations by the journalist and writer Ta-Nehisi Coates and the scholar Richard Rothstein also bearing this out.[3]

Moreover, the erroneous theory that extreme segregation is inevitable because black people prefer to live in neighborhoods with different racial makeups than white people has been debunked by history and detailed empirical analysis.[4] Survey data, as well as actual behavior, are quite clear that black people prefer neighborhoods that are far more integrated than their actual living arrangements tend to be, and contemporary white people do not flee from or refuse to live in neighborhoods simply because a few black residents live there.[5]

Black-white segregation was moderate in the early twentieth century, even though racism against black people was terrifically high. Segregation peaked much later—in the 1970s—even as overt racial discrimination waned and racist ideology lost traction. Today, despite some progress toward greater integration, black-white segregation remains extremely high (figure 7.1).[6]

Even into the twenty-first century, black people remain relatively unlikely to have white neighbors, and white people tend to live in overwhelmingly white neighborhoods. In 2010, when non-Hispanic white people constituted 64 percent of the U.S. population, a substantial number of white people—35 percent—lived in extremely isolated census tracts, in which white people comprised 90 percent or more of the population.[7] Meanwhile, just over 30 percent of residents were white in the census tract of the average black or Hispanic American. Asians tended to be more integrated, with roughly half of their neighbors consisting of white people for the average Asian American.

The increasing population share of Asians and Hispanics over the last 30 years has increased the probability that a randomly selected neighbor will also be Asian or Hispanic. This dynamic likely explains why Hispanic exposure to white people—measured as the share of their neighbors who are non-Hispanic white people—has declined relative to 1980 (figure 7.2). As of 2010, Hispanics and black people have converged in their exposure to white neighbors at a low level. Yet, Asians and Hispanics are spread as

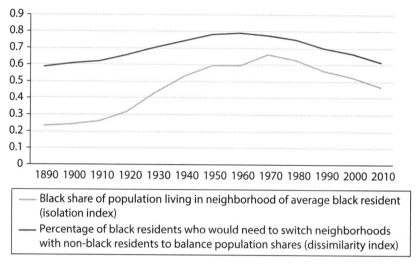

Figure 7.1. African American neighborhood segregation from 1890 to 2010

Sources: David M. Cutler, Edward L. Glaeser, and Jacob L. Vigdor, "The Rise and Decline of the American Ghetto," *Journal of Political Economy* 107.3 (1999): 455–506; Steven Manson, Jonathan Schroeder, David Van Riper, and Steven Ruggles, IPUMS National Historical Geographic Information System: Version 12.0 [1970 Decennial Census]. Minneapolis: University of Minnesota, 2017. http://doi.org/10.18128/D050.V12.0; John Logan, https://s4.ad.brown.edu/projects/diversity/Data/Download1.htm. See John R. Logan, and Brian J. Stults, "The Persistence of Segregation in the Metropolis: New Findings from the 2010 Census," Census brief prepared for Project US2010 (2011).

evenly across neighborhoods as they were in 1980 (which is measured by the index of dissimilarity). By this measure, Asians are only moderately segregated, in that 42 percent would need to switch neighborhoods with someone from another racial group to balance out their distribution; for Hispanics, the corresponding number is 51 percent, and for black people it remains high, at 62 percent, which is nonetheless down from peak years. In summary, black segregation remains high and still exceeds that of all other groups, though Hispanic isolation from white people has converged to black rates after three decades of mass migration.

This racial segregation means that black children grow up in the most disadvantaged neighborhood circumstances, relative to other groups. The Internal Revenue Service publishes data on the average income of families in nearly every zip code in the United States.[8] Zip codes are like neighborhoods and are created by the postal service to facilitate planning for mail delivery within a geographic area. Using Gallup survey data for roughly

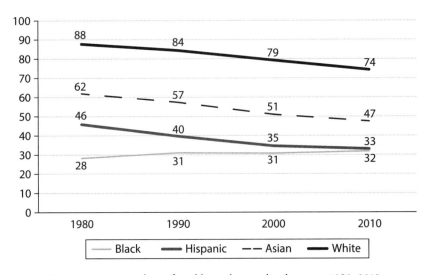

Figure 7.2. Average share of neighbors who are white by group, 1980–2010

Source: Data are from John Logan, available here: https://s4.ad.brown.edu/projects/diversity/Data/Download1.htm; see Logan, John R., and Brian J. Stults. "The Persistence of Segregation in the Metropolis: New Findings from the 2010 Census." Census brief prepared for Project US2010 (2011).

half a million Americans, I calculated whether individuals who have children living at home are in a low-income or high-income neighborhood by comparing zip-code-level income to the median income of the larger local area commuting zones (which are like metropolitan areas but include rural counties).[9] The results show that black people are the most likely group to be raising children in low-income neighborhoods, followed closely by Hispanics. These groups also have very few people living in high-income neighborhoods (table 7.1).

Even the children of low-income white people—families making less than $36,000—are raised in more-prosperous neighborhoods than the children of moderately high-income black people ($90,000–$179,000). On the other hand, upper-income individuals, Jews, people with at least a bachelor's degree, and Asians are highly likely to be raising their children in high-income neighborhoods.

Before Governments Created Ghettos

In the early twentieth century, leading white intellectuals, politicians, business leaders, and professionals were nearly unanimous in arguing that black people were intellectually inferior to white people, and working-class white

Table 7.1. Percentage of population with children living at home who reside in low-income or affluent neighborhoods, by group characteristic

	Top third of neighborhoods	Bottom third of neighborhoods
Upper-income household, ≥$180,000	58%	18%
Jewish	57%	24%
Bachelor's degree or higher	44%	27%
Asian	43%	34%
Moderately high income household, >$90K–$179K	39%	28%
White	35%	29%
Non-Abrahamic religion	33%	38%
Christian	28%	37%
Middle-income household, $60K–$89K	28%	37%
Muslim	26%	53%
Some college, up to two-year degree	26%	40%
Moderately low income, $36K–$59K	24%	43%
Other race and multiracial	23%	44%
White low-income household, <$36K	23%	37%
High school diploma or less	21%	46%
Black moderately high income household, >$90K–$179K	21%	55%
Low-income household, <$36K	18%	51%
Hispanic	18%	60%
Black	17%	62%

Note: Income ranges given in U.S. dollars. Neighborhood income categories were determined by dividing average family income at the zip-code level by median family income at the commuting zone level. Neighborhoods were then coded into thirds within each commuting zone (which is like a metropolitan area).

Source: 2016–2017 Gallup-Sharecare Well-Being Index. Data were collected from January 2016 to December 2017. The data are from a random-digit dialing sample of 426,826 U.S. adults with either a cell phone or landline phone; responses are weighted to reflect demographic characteristics of the U.S. population and the probability of responding. Data by zip code were matched to zip-code-level annual income data published by the Internal Revenue Service for 2014. Commuting zone data were calculated from counties using data from the 2011–2016 Five-Year American Community Survey. Counties were matched to commuting zones using a crosswalk created by David Dorn and made available by the Equality of Opportunity Project. Household income data are from Gallup and refer to annual household income.

people and immigrants agreed.[10] As the great black migrations out of the southern United States commenced and industrial innovations brought about urbanization, white people found that their private racism was grossly inadequate at preventing black people from living near white people. As a result, they created new legal institutions and policies to block integration. In so doing, white people were fully aware that they were working against the market and that market forces were creating pressure for integration. With black neighborhoods being overcrowded and rental prices being extremely high, entrepreneurial white property owners could make large profits by selling to black residents in white areas.

An early example from New York City illustrates the power of markets in pushing integration against the racist inclinations of white people. In the late nineteenth century, black migrants from Jamaica and the U.S. South started moving to New York City in large numbers. According to a *New York Times* article written at the time, black people began to spread out around the city and build churches in formerly white neighborhoods. This caused tension among racist white people. One white gang leader in the Hell's Kitchen area of downtown Manhattan, identified by the police as Thomas Baker, reportedly obtained his "chief delight" by the "indiscriminate punching of colored men and women, whom he should chance to meet upon the street."[11]

The tension between market forces and racism was extremely clear, as racists tried to influence both sides of the market. One local real estate agent named D. Kemper came to the police after receiving a threatening postcard with a skull and crossbones. Meanwhile, the *Times* reported a number of black families who were planning to move out as a result of violent intimidation, including a threat that their homes would be fire-bombed by white people. Despite these threats, white real estate agents were eager to advertise to black residents and have them move in because many of the white people neglected their rental payments. One real estate agent interviewed summed up the situation: "I assure you there is no sentiment about the property owners bringing colored people here. It is purely a matter of dollars and cents and self-interest. The negroes pay their rent regularly, and many of the white people do not."[12]

The observation that black people paid more in housing costs as a result of segregation is consistent with systematic evidence from Harvard economists using Census Bureau data.[13] Controlling for characteristics of the house and other factors, black people paid more when they lived in segregated cities in 1940 and 1970. Detailed evidence from Chicago in the early twentieth century tells the same story. Black people paid more in rent than white immigrants despite living in more dilapidated homes that landlords refused to fix, because black people were forbidden to live elsewhere.[14] Across the country, as late as 1970, black people paid more while living in predominantly black neighborhoods. The implication is that property owners in white neighborhoods stood to gain financially by having black tenants or potential home-buyers. Black people would have bid up rents and home prices in white neighborhoods if social and political pressure allowed them to move in.

Thus, in order to prevent integration, white people pitted themselves against markets.

In 1919, the middle-class African American Clark family moved into a poor white neighborhood in Chicago after purchasing two vacant buildings and renovating them. They rented one of the units to a white family. One day, an older white man observed the Clark family and started yelling that they were shooting at white people and brought an angry white mob to their house. The Clarks, who had been minding their own business, called the police after threatening chants arose from the crowd. The police came but proceeded to arrest the Clarks, not the threatening crowd. Private market forces brought the Clarks to a white neighborhood, but social pressure and government power removed them.[15]

These were not isolated events. In the 17-month period ending in August of 1919, 25 bombs were detonated at black homes or real estate agent offices in Chicago by white terrorists who aimed to keep black people out of their neighborhood, according to documents analyzed by historian Thomas Lee Philpott.[16]

Throughout the early twentieth century, white people fought against market forces that were integrating neighborhoods, but this proved inadequate to their goal of complete apartheid, and so professional white people leveraged their political power to eliminate black people from the market altogether. Their local government action would eventually be aided by a federal government that was dedicated to keeping black people and white people separate.

Segregation as an Anti-Market Policy

Anti-black policy in the post–Civil War and post-Reconstruction eras is known as *Jim Crow*. The origins of the term go back to a show and character invented by a white man named Thomas Dartmouth Rice in Louisville, Kentucky, in 1830.[17] Rice was born in New York City to a poor family and likely got the tune of his signature song, "Jim Crow," from Kentucky slaves. In the show, which was widely popular around the country, Rice acted as an uneducated and unintelligent black man who loved to dance and play the fiddle. The song became linked to populist and racist Democratic Party politics, and Rice himself often advanced that political agenda directly in his shows, such that the name "Jim Crow" came to represent a political agenda associated with white supremacy and status protection.

In a historical context, the Jim Crow system can be thought of as coordinated and collective action taken by white Americans to exclude black Americans from equal citizenship, markets, and public goods and services, including access to Social Security payments, education, and training, which lasted from the period after Reconstruction up until the civil rights movement victories of the 1950s and 1960s.[18] The severity of exclusions from public goods and markets varied by local area and the time period, but many antiblack practices were adopted across the country. Jim Crow was by no means limited to the Southern states that rebelled to preserve slavery during the U.S. Civil War.

When applied to housing, the Jim Crow system had many ways of distorting and controlling the market in an effort to exclude the participation of black people. These included private violence and threats, but they were also perpetrated by nonprofit associations organized to promote the exclusion of black people.

The aggressive pro-segregation efforts of local nonprofits is well documented in U.S. urban history. Consider Chicago, which remains one of the most racially segregated metropolitan areas in the United States. In 1917, in a neighborhood just north of Washington Park, a group called the Community Property Owner's Protective Association met to discuss plans to exclude "undesirables" according to its secretary, a real estate agent. A member was quoted in a local newspaper as stating: "We don't want any gentlemen of color in our midst."[19] Nearby, in the district that surrounds the University of Chicago, the Hyde Park Improvement Association formed in 1918 to "make Hyde Park White" and exclude black people from moving in.[20] The Washington Park Court Improvement Association adopted the same goal.[21] These nonprofit associations used a variety of tactics to achieve their ends, including buying out black residents from white neighborhoods, placing threatening ads in local newspapers to incite mass resistance and violence, and boycotting or blacklisting real estate agents who provided services to black people. These methods were gradually replaced by one that proved most effective of all, because it was considered respectable and, for a time, was legally unassailable: the restrictive covenant.

A *restrictive covenant* is a contractual agreement between a group of homeowners, which in this case bound them to sell or lease their properties only to white people. Previously, some properties had deed restrictions, but those applied to only one property. What made covenants so effective is that they covered entire neighborhoods. They were adamantly antimarket because they explicitly excluded black people from the pool of eligible buyers.

In 1947, 500 homeowners from a southwest neighborhood in Washington, DC, met to organize efforts to block black people from living in their neighborhood with restrictive covenants. The rally was organized by the Congress Heights Citizens Association. Speakers, including the organization's president, Harry Leibrand, passed out pledge cards for homeowners to sign, in which they promised to agree to a covenant when it was presented to them. The covenant would "forever forbid my property from being used by any person not of the Caucasian race," according to the card. Leibrand said they had already collected 800 signatures to loud applause from the audience. One longtime resident, Edward J. Newcomb, urged his neighbors to avoid succumbing to market logic: "Colored persons might offer $1,000 or $2,000 more, and that's a temptation," but if the white homeowners band together, he added, "We will keep them out."[22] A home had just sold for $13,500, so a $1,000 to $2,000 premium offered by an African American would have represented a significant temptation indeed: 7 percent to 15 percent of the home's value.

There are various estimates of the prevalence of covenants from the 1920s to 1940s. In Chicago and in other cities, an estimated 80 percent of properties were restricted by covenants in the 1940s. Contemporary economists analyzed a database of property deeds and found that restrictive covenants were very common in segregated metropolitan areas, where they applied to the majority of properties (68 percent), and less common but still prevalent in somewhat less segregated areas (50 percent of properties).[23] In suburban New York City—including Queens, Nassau, and Westchester Counties—the majority of new developments had deed restrictions between 1935 and 1947. They were also prevalent in Seattle, Washington, as well as in Oklahoma and California.[24]

Covenants were so commonplace that the Chicago Real Estate Board had a model document drafted in 1927 by one of the country's top real estate law experts. It forbade "negroes" from occupying or purchasing a give property and defined anyone who had even one-eighth "negro blood" or was commonly known as a "colored person" as a "negro." Thus, everyone who had even one black great-grandparent was excluded from living in almost every desirable neighborhood in Chicago and every other city with significant black populations.[25]

Aside from indulging in outright racism, homeowners agreed to this policy because they believed doing so would protect their property values. Their concern was that if even one black resident moved into the neighborhood, all the white residents would sell below market value to avoid living in a black neighborhood—never mind that all the available evidence showed that black people were paying more in housing costs than comparable white people were and that these restrictions actually artificially lowered the home prices of white people by removing potential buyers.[26]

U.S. GOVERNMENT EXCLUSION OF BLACK PEOPLE FROM MARKETS, PUBLIC GOODS, AND SUBSIDIES

The federal government, in addition to state and local governments, also actively participated in Jim Crow exclusions. Covenants took on additional power when the newly created Federal Housing Administration (FHA) essentially mandated their inclusion. The FHA dramatically lowered the cost of buying a home by introducing government-backed mortgage insurance. FHA mortgages lengthened the pay-back period, with lower interest rates and a payment schedule that built wealth for homeowners while making monthly payments more affordable. Their practices became the mortgage industry standard.

In 1936 the FHA created a manual that advised how mortgage appraisers should evaluate homes. It explicitly stated that restrictive covenants, combined with exclusionary zoning to prohibit multifamily housing, offered the best protection of a home's value and should get the highest appraisal.[27]

It was not until 1948 that the U.S. Supreme Court case of *Shelly v. Kramer* decided that the enforcement of restrictive covenants—through courts or police power—violated the Equal Protection Clause of the Fourteenth Amendment to the U.S. Constitution (table 7.2).

Aside from promoting covenants, the U.S. federal government also introduced the practice of *red-lining*, or rating the credit-worthiness of a neigh-

Table 7.2. How organizations and governments have excluded African Americans and others from participation in housing markets

Tool	How worked	Period of operation
Violence	Whites threatened or assaulted black residents, and/or vandalized and even incinerated their homes until they left the neighborhood	1890s–1940s
Local associations	Home ownership and neighborhood associations used a variety of means (including covenants) to keep blacks out of neighborhoods; since 1960s, zoning policies have been used	1910–present
Restrictive covenants	Homeowners agreed to contracts stipulating that they were not permitted to sell to blacks	1910–1948
Racial zoning	Neighborhoods were designated as for whites or blacks only	1910–1917 in 24 cities until struck down, though cities persisted through 1920s
Public housing	Public housing was explicitly segregated by race or placed in already segregated neighborhoods	1940s–present
Federal mortgage subsidies for homeowners	Whites but not blacks were eligible for subsidized loans either directly because of race or indirectly because black neighborhoods were deemed too risky	Home Owners' Loan Corporation, 1933, created red-lining; Federal Housing Administration implemented it, 1934–1968
Exclusionary zoning	Housing of different types (single-family vs. multifamily) and densities (multiacre lots vs. small quarter-acre lots) is segregated by law within and across almost every local government	1925–present

Source: Massey, Douglas S., and Nancy A. Denton. *American Apartheid: Segregation and the Making of the Underclass.* Cambridge, MA: Harvard University Press, 1993; Hirsch, Arnold R. *Making the Second Ghetto: Race and Housing in Chicago 1940–1960.* Chicago: University of Chicago Press, 2009; Philpott, Thomas Lee. *Slum and the Ghetto.* Oxford: Oxford University Press, 1978; Rothstein, Richard. *The Color of Law: A Forgotten History of How Our Government Segregated America.* New York: Liveright, 2017; Cutler, David M., Edward L. Glaeser, and Jacob L. Vigdor. "The Rise and Decline of the American Ghetto." *Journal of Political Economy* 107.3 (1999): 455–506; Troesken, Werner, and Randall Walsh. *Collective Action, White Flight, and the Origins of Formal Segregation Laws.* No. w23691. National Bureau of Economic Research, 2017.

borhood based on the racial and ethnic characteristics of the population. Neighborhoods with white immigrants were given lower ratings than those with native white people, and neighborhoods with black residents were given the lowest ratings and were often deemed unworthy of credit. This not only constrained where black people could live but destroyed the wealth of many black families by forcing them to pay for their housing in ways that led to either little or no accumulation of equity (wealth). Finally, the federal government, in conjunction with local housing agencies, actively segregated public housing, setting aside buildings for black people or white people and strategically placing them in already segregated neighborhoods. These facts are well documented.[28]

While white citizens used government to segregate black people, white people also prevented the government from taking any action that would have protected black consumers and allowed them to participate in markets on more equal terms. Two noteworthy examples involved real estate markets and lending markets.

During the Jim Crow era, real estate agents subscribed to a formal code of ethics that required them not to introduce black residents into white neighborhoods. For much of the twentieth century, black people were told by real estate agents that homes in white neighborhoods were not available to them or were deceived into believing that that was the case. These practices were allowed to persist until the Fair Housing Act of 1968 formally banned this type of discrimination, but as Douglas Massey and Nancy Denton have found, Congress blocked antidiscrimination enforcement until 1988.[29]

The U.S. Department of Housing and Urban Development periodically conducts audits to document real estate market discrimination. They send out testers of difference races but with the same income qualifications documents to see how they are treated by real estate agents. The latest evidence finds that black people and white people are treated equally in the majority of cases, but white people are more likely to be told about or shown additional properties.[30] This type of discrimination has fallen since the 1970s, when it was still quite common.

Another important form of discrimination that has persisted into the present day involves mortgage lending terms, such as the value of the interest rate, whether it is fixed or variable, and the length of time available for repayment—all of which affect the monthly payment. As sociologist Jacob Rugh has revealed, prior to the housing crisis that caused the Great Recession of 2007, unscrupulous mortgage-lending companies targeted potential African American and Hispanic buyers in segregated neighborhoods, where lack of financial education and the absence of traditional banking operations made the population especially vulnerable.[31] Similar tactics were used in white working-class neighborhoods, though not to the same extent.[32] Financial crime experts have argued convincingly that the proliferation of these practices was the direct result of a weakening of banking and mortgage regulations and of enforcement practices that were designed to protect consumers and business associates from fraud.[33] By contrast, when poor home buyers with low credit scores were given favorable lending terms and financial advice, they rarely defaulted on their loans.[34]

Market Exclusion through Zoning

Violence, restrictive covenants, outright discrimination by real estate practitioners, the promotion of segregation through public housing, and red-lining are, for the most part, no longer contributing factors to contemporary segregation. Yet, government policy still actively contributes to segregation through zoning laws that delimit neighborhoods and even entire municipalities according to affordability. Typical zoning laws control what land can be used for (e.g., housing, commercial, or industrial property), the number of housing units that are allowed to be built on a parcel of land (e.g., one for a single family home but potentially dozens if a multifamily condominium or apartment), and how much land each housing unit requires (e.g., a quarter-acre or several acres).

This may sound perfectly reasonable, but in practice these laws have been controlled by homeowners in order to accomplish various ends: maximize the value of their home by limiting supply; lower their property tax bill; retain access to certain benefits, as they see them, which may include light traffic congestion or low noise levels; and exclude undesirable people from living near them, which may be racial or ethnic minorities or working-class families. The result of these laws is that housing is more expensive in metropolitan areas than it would be if property owners could use the land more freely, and importantly, housing is more segregated by class and race.

In 2003, an urban planning professor at Cornell University named Rolf Pendall—who is now the director of the Metropolitan Housing and Communities Policy Center at the Urban Institute—launched a survey of local government zoning officials in the 50 largest U.S. metropolitan areas to collect details about the prevalence and type of zoning used in over 1,800 local governments.

To those unfamiliar with zoning, the survey results may shatter misconceptions about how markets operate in the United States. Consistent with similar surveys of zoning, 14 percent of local government zoning officials said that their jurisdiction forbade housing at densities exceeding three units per acre. The median U.S. single-family home sits on a quarter-acre of land, so four units per acre could be considered typical single-family housing. The implication is that hundreds of local governments completely outlawed normal single-family housing. In doing so, they also outlawed housing at a greater level of density, including attached single-family row houses and even low-density apartments or condominiums. In effect, these areas outlawed middle-class families from living under their jurisdiction. Households headed by people in most blue-collar jobs or low-paying professional jobs—such as teaching or office administration—would be unable to afford living in such areas. An additional 12 percent of jurisdictions outlawed housing densities that exceed seven units per acre.

To further clarify how zoning is used, Pendall asked if the prevailing zoning laws would allow for the development of an apartment building with 40 units on five acres. That is a mere eight units per acre—moderately denser than typical single-family detached homes. Nineteen percent of local government zoning officials said their jurisdiction would completely forbid this kind of development. Only 38 percent of governments would allow it without the developer gaining special permission.

Predictably, the local jurisdictions that allowed these sorts of buildings were notably more affordable and had a higher percentage of black and Hispanic residents compared to other jurisdictions within the same metropolitan area (table 7.3). Where apartments were permitted, housing prices tended to be close to what was typical for the metropolitan area; jurisdictions that forbade apartment buildings had median prices that were 25 percent above the typical metropolitan area price.

Detailed academic studies carried out by me and by leading urban economists such as William Fischel and Ed Glaeser also find that zoning laws contribute to higher housing prices and higher levels of residential and economic segregation.[35] Importantly, these laws also keep poor children out of the highest-performing public schools.[36]

Table 7.3. Median home values and racial demographics of U.S. local governments by zoning laws regulating density

	Construction of apartments is illegal	Construction of apartments requires special permission	Construction of apartments is permitted
Median home price in local area/ Median home price in metro area	1.25	1.17	1.08
Percentage black in local area/ Percentage black in metro area	34%	50%	59%
Percentage Hispanic in local area/ Percentage Hispanic in metro area	46%	71%	82%

Source: Via survey, local government land-use planning directors were asked if the zoning ordinances in their jurisdiction would allow the construction of a hypothetical two-story apartment development with 40 units on a five-acre lot by right, by permit, or under no existing law. Fifty of the largest U.S. metropolitan areas captured 1,706 responses. Housing price data from the 2000 Decennial Census were merged to local-government jurisdictions by the author and data on racial demographics were provided by Rolf Pendall. See Pendall, Rolf, Jonathan Martin, and Robert Puentes. "From Traditional to Reformed: A Review of the Land Use Regulations in the Nation's 50 Largest Metropolitan Areas." (Washington: Brookings Institution, 2006).

Where Zoning Came From

As with most regulations, there is a rational and defensible basis for zoning. If used appropriately, zoning laws make housing markets function more fairly. For example, imagine a young couple who just invested their life savings in a modest home on a residential street. They and others in their position would likely feel cheated if their next-door neighbor turned his house into a foul-smelling garbage dump, or a noisy manufacturing plant, or a chicken coop. They may feel their children's development was at risk if a coal plant that belched out toxic smoke was put next door. Legally segregating such uses—those with "negative externalities" in academic jargon—from innocuous residential and commercial uses helps people make mutually beneficial exchanges with far greater confidence and certainty and respects the rights of small property owners to avoid having their homes or health damaged unnecessarily.

Yet, even early on, the fundamentally sound rationale behind the idea of zoning was corrupted in order to protect narrow and racially exclusive self-interest. In 1916 in New York City, the coalition of home and retail owners who formed the Fifth Avenue Association aimed to impose zoning and height limits on Fifth Avenue to suppress nonretail business and the use of upper-level space for low-cost apartments for immigrants. These actions would preserve the exclusivity of their neighborhood by directly impeding market dynamics that were leading to lower-cost housing and a multiplicity of business uses, such as garment manufacturing. The group initiated the New York City Zoning Resolution, which was authored by Robert Whitten, a leader in the city planning movement.[37]

It is clear from Whitten's writing, as well as the public statements that pervaded the early zoning and real estate policy discussions, that the native white leaders who initiated zoning policies were highly motivated by the racial science of the day.[38] The development of modern zoning laws coincided with a time in U.S. and world history that was particularly harsh in its views of lower-class white people and non-Europeans. Just as the Industrial Revolution was pulling people from farms to urban areas in the United States and other developed countries, the myths of "race science" led educated professionals as well as local and national leaders to believe that certain groups of people were inherently inferior. Leading intellectuals—including Supreme Court justices and many top economists—believed less-educated people should be sterilized to prevent them from breeding, such was their disdain for the lower classes and nonwhite races.[39]

Thus, exposure to poor people was considered toxic, just as exposure to loud noise, foul odors, and pollution. Urban historians David Freund and Jason Rhodes have carefully documented these developments. In 1920, Whitten laid out the rationale for segregating the "renting class" from homeowners: "The erection of a single apartment house in a block is almost certain to mean a radical change in the residential population, a decline in the value of the single family houses and a gradual replacement of such houses by apartment houses." This, he argued, was "an injury to the children" raised in them, and "degeneracy" would naturally follow.[40] Elsewhere, Whitten wrote: "A reasonable segregation is normal, inevitable, and desirable."[41]

In 1926, just as the federal government was working on standard zoning guidelines, the U.S. Supreme Court upheld zoning laws, despite their ambiguous relationship to property rights and equal protection before the law.[42] Justice George Sutherland wrote the majority opinion, which follows the logic of Whitten's argument—and those of many other advocates—quite closely:

With particular reference to apartment houses, it is pointed out that the development of detached house sections is greatly retarded by the coming of apartment houses, which has sometimes resulted in destroying the entire section for private house purposes; that, in such sections, very often the apartment house is a mere parasite, constructed in order to take advantage of the open spaces and attractive surroundings created by the residential character of the district. Moreover, the coming of one apartment house is followed by others, interfering by their height and bulk with the free circulation of air and monopolizing the rays of the sun which otherwise would fall upon the smaller homes, and bringing, as their necessary accompaniments, the disturbing noises incident to increased traffic and business, and the occupation, by means of moving and parked automobiles, of larger portions of the streets, thus detracting from their safety and depriving children of the privilege of quiet and open spaces for play, enjoyed by those in more favored localities— until, finally, the residential character of the neighborhood and its desirability as a place of detached residences are utterly destroyed. Under these circumstances, apartment houses, which in a different environment would be not only entirely unobjectionable but highly desirable, come very near to being nuisances.[43]

This view of apartments is very close to the view that white people had about black people moving into their neighborhood. Both a single apartment building and a black household were viewed as contagions: A small dose would spread throughout the neighborhood, quickly and decisively eviscerating all that was healthy and valuable in the area. Thus, as with infectious disease, complete segregation of both black people and lower-class housing from the white middle class was deemed prudent. The exclusionary zoning of neighborhoods or jurisdictions to prevent poor people from living there was deemed constitutional because it is akin to quarantining off a destructive economic and social force.

Zoning spread rapidly during the 1920s and after, complementing efforts to segregate black people. A federal commission found that the number of municipalities with zoning legislation went from 368 to over 1,000 from 1925 to 1930.[44]

The implementation of zoning caused a substantial drop in the development of new housing, which drove up prices by restricting supply. In New

Haven, Connecticut, for example, during the prezoning era of the early 1920s, hundreds of new apartment buildings were permitted each year to accommodate the rising demand for housing following World War I.[45] Yet, after antidensity zoning laws were passed in 1926—against the lobbying efforts of apartment developers—the number of newly permitted apartment dwellings immediately plummeted from roughly 800 units in 1925 and 1926 to around 400 in 1927 and 1928 and less than 200 in 1929.[46] As legal scholar Marie Boyd has documented, the prezoning era in New Haven also saw streets and neighborhoods with lot sizes ranging from 0.1 acres to 9 acres, reflecting the economic diversity of its residents. Most were less than half an acre, but the larger lot sizes made it straightforward to convert one unit on a large lot into a multifamily apartment building.[47]

Zoning surged again in popularity in the 1970s. According to economic historian William Fischel, the reason is that homeowners were concerned about the rapid monetary inflation of the 1970s draining their savings and wealth.[48] Accordingly, they fought for tighter zoning laws to protect their property values. It may only be coincidental that civil rights–era legislation in the 1960s had again opened the door to increased racial integration.

Several political scientists have assembled scholarly evidence on the motivation for zoning and blocking development. An important article from K. Einstein, M. Palmer, and D. Glick systematically collected participation in 2015–2017 local planning and zoning board meetings in metropolitan Boston. Massachusetts requires that these meetings be advertised and that the comments and content of the discussions be made publicly available.[49] Participants' names were matched to voter registration files. The findings derived from these data showed that older and more politically conservative white males were more likely both to speak up at these meetings and to oppose new developments. Homeowners were highly overrepresented as participants as well, and roughly two-thirds (63 percent) of all participants voiced opposition to new housing, while only 15 percent of comments were in favor.

Other evidence on the motivations of zoning comes from political scientist Jessica Trounstine, who finds that local voting precincts in California consistently vote against liberalizing development when they have higher shares of white people and homeowners. In an online survey, she also presented participants with hypothetical development projects and found that the percentage of black residents greatly lowered support: "Respondents reported that developments with more people of color and more poor residents would

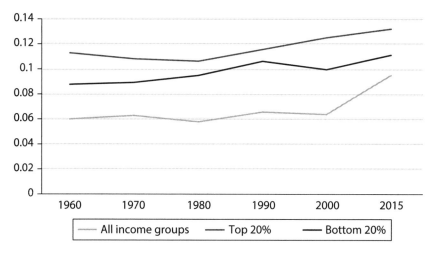

Figure 7.3. Average segregation by income in U.S. local areas, 1960–2015

Note: Segregation is measured by the entropy or Theil information index, using the formula described
  by the U.S. Census Bureau, here: https://www.census.gov/hhes/www/housing/resseg/pdf/app_b
  .pdf. Segregation is measured at the commuting-zone level and the data here are reported for the
  average population weighted commuting zone. Within commuting zones, family incomes were
  reported in categories at the census-tract level. The entropy index measures how the average census
  tract of a commuting zone differs in its composition of families in different income categories from
  the larger commuting zone. A commuting zone is like a metropolitan area in that it is defined by
commuting patterns but includes all rural counties, which fall outside of metropolitan areas, and does
  not require a large central city. The data shown above are from the author's analysis of data from
  IPUMS NHGIS: Steven Manson, Jonathan Schroeder, David Van Riper, and Steven Ruggles.
IPUMS National Historical Geographic Information System: Version 12.0 [Database]. Minneapolis:
  University of Minnesota. 2017. http://doi.org/10.18128/D050.V12.0.

have lower property values, worse schools, and higher crime rates. In short,
they saw these developments as making their neighborhood less desirable."[50]

Whatever the rationale, there is evidence that zoning laws have exacerbated
economic segregation because metropolitan areas with stricter antidensity
zoning laws (i.e., those that limit townhouses, apartments, and other higher-
density forms of housing) are more economically segregated.[51] Likewise, it is
well documented that economic segregation has increased since 1970, even
as the segregation of black people from white people has moderated.[52] My own
calculations of neighborhood census data show that economic segregation has
increased by roughly 50 percent from 1970 to 2015 (figure 7.3). The increases
occurred from 1980 to 1990 and again from 2000 to 2011–2015. Economic
segregation is measured here as the degree to which the proportion of families from different income categories align between neighborhoods and the

broader metropolitan area or county within which families commute to work. In this sense, neighborhoods in 2015 were less reflective of the economic diversity of their local areas than they used to be between 1960 and 1980. I find this is a result of both rising income inequality and more restrictive zoning.[53]

UNITED STATES SEGREGATION IN GLOBAL PERSPECTIVE

Studying segregation in a large number of countries is a challenge because only a few government statistics offices collect and publish data at the neighborhood scale; moreover, the relative shares of either immigrant populations or racial minorities varies widely between countries, which can complicate comparisons, especially since most governments don't collect data by race. An alternative approach would be to compare how perceptions of neighborhood quality vary by income level, which I have done here.

Specifically, I calculated gaps in neighborhood satisfaction and safety for high- and low-income groups for 162 countries included in Gallup's World Poll from 2009 to 2017.[54] I took the average response to six "yes" or "no" questions asked in the World Poll. They were whether respondents with children under 15 living in their households would recommend their city to others as a place to live; whether they are satisfied with their city overall; whether they are satisfied with local access to affordable housing, with the quality of healthcare, and with the quality of schools; and whether they feel safe walking alone at night.[55] I calculated the average responses to these six questions for people in the bottom quintile of the income distribution and people in the top quintile of the income distribution for each country. The underlying rationale is that if people of different income groups live in the same or similar neighborhoods, their level of satisfaction, access to basic resources, and feelings of safety should also be roughly the same. Moreover, neighborhood qualities should affect children more than adults, given the research on how growing up in high- or low-quality neighborhoods affects upward mobility (see next chapter). Differences in favor of richer residents would indicate that economic power translates into better neighborhoods.

By this measure, the country with the largest inequality in neighborhood conditions is Somaliland (with a gap of 24 percentage points between high- and low-income households), which experienced civil war in the 1990s during its struggle for autonomy from Somalia. It is followed by South Africa

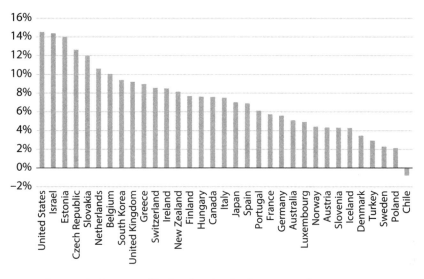

Figure 7.4. Gap in neighborhood quality for the top versus bottom-income quintile, 2009–2017

Source: Gallup World Poll, 2009–2017.

(with a gap of 22 percentage points), which ended its explicit state-sponsored form of segregation (apartheid) only in the 1990s. Another country with extremely high gaps in neighborhood quality is Tunisia. There, segregation between Africans with Sub-Saharan ancestry, many of whom are descended from slaves, and North Africans or Arabs is so intense that children of difference races are bused to school separately in at least one southern town, and racism is so extreme that mixed-race marriages promote outrage among non-Africans.[56] Montenegro and Albania, both of which recently fought in civil wars, also score highly on neighborhood inequality, as do Israel and Pakistan (figure 7.4).

Among the countries with the most inequitable neighborhood conditions is the United States, with a gap of 15 percentage points in the share of people who have high and low satisfaction. According to this measure, the United States ranks 12th in the world out of 162 countries, and it is the most unequal among OECD countries, ahead of Israel and Estonia, which have 14 percentage point gaps. Israel's ethnic conflicts between Palestinians and Jews are well known. Estonia, meanwhile, struggles to integrate its large Russian-speaking ethnic-minority population, which swelled from the 1940s through the 1980s, as residents from Soviet member states moved to

Estonia.[57] The Russian-speaking population disproportionately inhabits less desirable neighborhoods characterized by government-built multifamily housing.

The implication is that around the world, children from low-income families are raised in relatively unsafe and undesirable neighborhoods, with lower-quality housing, schooling, and healthcare. Yet, these gaps are by no means inevitable. Scandinavian countries, as well as Turkey, Chile, and Poland, seem able to limit these gaps.

The United States also stands out on more traditional measures of segregation. To grasp the effects of Jim Crow on residential segregation, consider how the United States differs from the United Kingdom. Both countries are characterized by similar high rates of private home ownership and private construction. One notable difference is that the UK government has made greater investment in public housing, in that public housing (or "council housing") has made up a larger share of total dwellings. For example, in 2001, council housing amounted to 14 percent of all units in the United Kingdom, whereas only 2 percent of housing units were owned by a public housing authority in the United States and 6 percent of occupied homes were subsidized; moreover, in the UK, private nonprofit associations also subsidize a significant share of housing units (7 percent in 2001).[58] More importantly, however, in the United States public housing exacerbated racial segregation, and black people were not allowed to participate in the market on anything like equal terms. In the UK, public housing does not appear to have contributed to segregation, and the private market remained open to immigrants, including black people.

Thus, not surprisingly, black people are far more segregated in the United States than in Great Britain.[59] U.S. black people are essentially three times more segregated than British black people. In Britain, both black immigrants and native-born black people are highly integrated. Foreign-born South Asians are the most segregated group in Great Britain and face similar levels of segregation in the United States, but the level of segregation is still much higher for U.S. black people. Other comparable immigrant and native groups are similarly well integrated in both countries (table 7.4).

Of course, some ethnic segregation is expected because of shared linguistic and cultural characteristics. It is practical for newly arrived immigrants who know little or nothing of the language of the country they have just arrived in to move to an area inhabited by their co-nationals, in order to gain a

Table 7.4. Neighborhood residential segregation of native and foreign-born residents of the United States and Great Britain by region of origin, 2000–2001

	United States	Great Britain
Native-born		
All racial/ethnic groups	0.29	0.12
Asian	0.17	0.22
Black	0.46	0.16
Foreign-born		
Caribbean	0.40	0.18
East Asia	0.22	0.08
Eastern Europe	0.19	0.08
Middle East and North Africa	0.19	0.13
North America	0.08	0.10
Northern and Western Europe	0.06	0.04
South Asia	0.23	0.24
Southern Europe	0.14	0.09
Sub-Saharan Africa	0.33	0.12

Note: Segregation is measured by Theil's H index. H is the weighted average deviation of each unit's "entropy" (or diversity) from the metropolitan-wide entropy, expressed as a fraction of the metropolitan area's total entropy.

Source: Iceland, John, Pablo Mateos, and Gregory Sharp. "Ethnic Residential Segregation by Nativity in Great Britain and the United States." *Journal of Urban Affairs* 33.4 (2011): 409–429.

foothold and to participate in religious services if their religion is in the minority. Yet, this form of practical self-imposed ethnic clustering never reaches anything like the extreme segregation of black people from white people seen in the United States during the twentieth century and into the early twenty-first.

In 2005, France made international news as riots and protests in the suburbs (*banlieue*) brought attention to the segregated conditions in which its immigrant population lives.[60] As in many European countries, the government played a large role in planning the location and characteristics of housing to accommodate postwar population growth and immigration. Rather than allowing decentralized market forces to build more dense housing in desirable neighborhoods, the Communist Party in French cities created massive public housing complexes outside central cities and assigned immigrants to live there.[61]

Table 7.5. Segregation of immigrants in France and in the United States

	Dissimilarity		Isolation	
Area of origin	France	United States	France	United States
Sub-Saharan African	37	64	5	5
North African	38	81	9	2
East Asian	38	54	5	11
Middle Eastern	42	68	3	5
Southern European	22	55	4	3

Note: Dissimilarity index measures the percentage of residents who would need to switch neighborhoods with native-born population to even out distribution across neighborhoods within a metropolitan area. Isolation measures the average share of neighborhood residents who are in the same group as the one referenced. For France, indexes are calculated using 2007 data at census-tract level for urban areas and weighted by population for residents of urban areas with a population of at least 50,000.

Sources: Pan Ké Shon, Jean-Louis, and Gregory Verdugo. "Forty Years of Immigrant Segregation in France, 1968–2007. How Different Is the New Immigration?" *Urban Studies* 52.5 (2015): 823–840. For United States, sample population is limited to metropolitan-area residents. Figures shown are weighted averages of metropolitan-area indexes, using the population of the group shown as the weight. Data from the 2010 U.S. Census via NHGIS; Steven Manson, Jonathan Schroeder, David Van Riper, and Steven Ruggles. IPUMS National Historical Geographic Information System: Version 12.0 [Database] [2010]. Minneapolis: University of Minnesota. 2017. http://doi.org/10.18128/D050.V12.0.

Even so, immigrants in France are not as segregated as those in the United States, at least by standard measures. In France, 37 percent of Sub-Saharan African immigrants and 38 percent of North African immigrants would have to switch places with a French-born resident to even out their distribution within the average metropolitan area. In the United States, the figures are 64 percent and 81 percent, respectively. In general, U.S. immigrants are very unevenly distributed, while in France the segregation is only moderate, by that measure. Moreover, in both countries, isolation is fairly low, in part because the specific immigrant populations typically represent small shares of the total population (table 7.5).

By contrast, black U.S. residents are both unevenly distributed across neighborhoods—56 percent would need to switch neighborhoods with someone from another race to balance out their distribution—and relatively isolated, in that 47 percent of their neighbors are also black on average. Concurrently, they also have limited exposure to white people—and white people to black people. For both black people and Hispanics, just 34 percent of neighbors are white in their average neighborhoods. The white-neighbor share is

Table 7.6. Segregation by race and foreign-born status in the United States, 2010

	Isolation index	Dissimilarity index	White population share in average neighborhood
All residents by race-ethnicity			
Black	0.47	0.56	0.34
Native American	0.17	0.54	0.55
Black or Hispanic	0.59	0.50	0.34
White or Asian	0.80	0.46	0.75
Asian	0.21	0.45	0.49
White	0.78	0.44	0.78
Hispanic	0.50	0.44	0.34
Multiracial	0.05	0.33	0.61
Foreign-born population by region of birth			
Total foreign-born population	0.28	0.32	0.44
Africa	0.04	0.60	0.46
Caribbean	0.19	0.52	0.27
South America	0.08	0.49	0.44
Central America	0.21	0.47	0.32
Asia	0.15	0.44	0.51
Europe	0.06	0.36	0.69

Note: Dissimilarity index measures the percentage of residents who would need to switch neighborhoods with native-born population to even out distribution across neighborhoods within a metropolitan area. Isolation measures the average share of neighborhood residents who are in the same group as the one referenced. Sample population is limited to metropolitan-area residents. Figures shown are weighted averages of metropolitan-area indexes, using the population of the group shown as the weight. For the United States, Europe includes migrants from Canada, New Zealand, and Australia of any race.

Source: Data from the 2010 U.S. Census via NHGIS; Steven Manson, Jonathan Schroeder, David Van Riper, and Steven Ruggles. IPUMS National Historical Geographic Information System: Version 12.0 [Database] [2010]. Minneapolis: University of Minnesota. 2017. http://doi.org/10.18128/D050.V12.0.

44 percent for all immigrants, but it is lowest for those born in the Caribbean and Central American countries and highest for those born in Europe (which, for this calculation, includes the former British colonies of Canada, New Zealand, and Australia), for whom the share is 69 percent. Asian immigrants are in the middle: On average, 51 percent of their neighbors are white (table 7.6).

A comparison of these segregation measures with those in Britain confirms that the United States stands out. The Caribbean dissimilarity index in British cities is 37 versus 52 in U.S. cities. It is 40 for Indians in Britain compared with 65 for Indians in the United States, and it is 51 for British Pakistanis but 82 for U.S. Pakistanis.[62] For its part, Sweden has moderate levels of segregation, with a dissimilarity index of 39 for all non-European immigrants and 24 for European immigrants.[63] Those are considerably lower than the index for Mexican immigrants in the United States (48) and for African immigrants (60).

The mechanisms that created and now sustain ethnic segregation in the United States also elevate segregation by economic class. The urban scholar Sako Musterd has assembled neighborhood-level data from a large number of cities in an effort to document how racial and economic segregation compares across countries.[64] He measured how certain economically distressed groups—such as the poor, the unemployed, or welfare recipients—were unevenly spread relative to all other groups. On these measures, as with ethnic segregation, the United States stands out, alongside Belgium. England is varied, whereas major cities in the Netherlands, Germany, and Scandinavia are relatively integrated economically (table 7.7).

In follow-up work, Musterd and co-authors examined segregation between the richest and poorest 20th percentiles in Stockholm, Oslo, and Amsterdam.[65] In 2000, the dissimilarity index in Amsterdam was roughly 37—implying that 37 percent of poor people would need to switch neighborhoods with affluent people to be evenly distributed across neighborhoods. It was 32 in Stockholm and approximately 23 in Oslo. Using high- versus low-paying occupational data instead of income, they found that London's economic segregation would be around 38. By contrast, for the 100 largest metropolitan areas in the United States in the year 2000, I calculate that the corresponding index was 53, with high scores in places like Philadelphia, Memphis, and Baltimore. The only major metropolitan area with segregation levels comparable to those of Europe was San Jose, with an index of 37. Nearby, San Francisco's score was 48.

ZONING IN EUROPE VERSUS THE UNITED STATES

Zoning offers a potential explanation for why economic segregation is higher in the United States than in Europe. In the early twentieth century, American land-use planners cited Germany as the inspiration for zoning laws, so

Table 7.7. Segregation in European cities and U.S. cities

	Dissimilarity index of segregation
100 largest U.S. cities, poor	36
Antwerp, Belgium, poor	35
Sheffield, England, unemployed residents	23
Oslo, Norway, recipients of social assistance	23
Rotterdam, Netherlands, 1st quintile	21
Amsterdam, Netherlands, 1st quintile	17
Manchester, England, income-support recipients	16
Berlin, Germany, household income < €900	14
Bern, Norway, unemployed	13
Copenhagen, Denmark, 1st quintile	5

Source: Musterd, Sako. "Social and Ethnic Segregation in Europe: Levels, Causes, and Effects." *Journal of Urban Affairs* 27.3 (2005): 331–348.

zoning is certainly not specifically American. Yet, legal scholars have noted that American zoning practice differs from those found in continental Europe in several very important respects that affect economic segregation.

First, control over zoning is far more decentralized in the United States. Municipal governments have tremendous autonomy, given to them by states, with almost no authority imposed from the federal government. In Europe, regional and federal governments have planning requirements to which local governments and developments must conform.[66] Affluent suburban homeowners in the United States, in particular, have a strong incentive to block new development that would allow working-class families with children into their school district because they would have to contribute to the funding of both public education and other services, such as policing and fire prevention. This incentive combined with decentralized authority offers U.S. homeowners the means and motivation to create and enforce antidensity regulations that segregate and impose those costs on the central city or other suburban governments. Affluent European homeowners lack these incentives, because funding for schools is less reliant on local taxes, and they lack the means, because zoning is more centralized.

A second difference between zoning in Europe and the United States, which may follow from the first, is that the two differ in goals and objectives. In the United States, safeguarding single-family homes from exposure to nuisance or other adverse circumstances is the top goal.[67] As legal scholar Matthew Light puts it:

> Clearly absent from German and Swiss regulation is the American goal of segregating single-family homes from other uses. The most restrictive German zones call for duplexes and convenience shops alongside single-family homes, and German law does not require segregation of many services and clean (nonindustrial) workplaces from residential areas.[68]

Instead, the goals from zoning in Germany and Switzerland seem, as Light suggests, to be the opposite: to "*force* people to live relatively near work and shopping, and to encourage citizens to use public transportation to reach these destinations."[69] Likewise, zoning historian Sonia Hirt finds that it is uncommon for areas in England to be designated for single-family-only use.

Exclusive enclaves of affluence, enforced by regulation, are thus much more likely in the United States than in continental Europe. These differing priorities may have their origins in the fact that zoning laws were created in the United States at a time when genetic determinism dominated social and natural science and elites viewed cities as unhealthy and undesirable bastions of immigrants and racial minorities, as Hirt has argued. In Europe, by contrast, cities have had exalted traditions as centers of learning and bastions of political independence from monarchy and rural lords.[70]

Yet, both Europe and the United States fail to provide equitable and open access to housing markets. While affluent areas in Europe are less likely to exclude high-density and lower-cost housing compared with similar areas in the United States, European governments still impose onerous restrictions on what can be built where. The result is that many people who would like to move to particular areas cannot, because private developers are not allowed to acquire and develop the property required to realize their preferences. As the next chapter discusses, these policies limit social and economic opportunity and violate fundamental principles of justice.

8

How Unequal Access to Housing Perpetuates Group Inequality and Injustice

THE IMPOSITION OF SEGREGATION upon black citizens as well as low-income residents of all races has created a society in which equal opportunity for success is impossible. There is now irrefutable evidence that where people grow up greatly affects their chances of achieving a healthy and prosperous life. The importance of local environments—the neighborhood in which a family lives and children grow up—to upward mobility and lifetime success has been proven across a wide range of countries. Thus, governmental institutions that disrupt and block the free and mutually beneficial exchange of residential property and its use fundamentally prevent the realization of a just society.

Limited access to markets for most consumer products may be an annoyance and may be costly, but it is unlikely to affect one's life trajectory. That's not true for housing. Homes are embedded in neighborhoods, and neighborhoods embody a particular geographic space. That space has the potential to open up as well as to constrain social interactions and exposure to opportunities, as well as threats from people and things. If neighborhoods are highly unequal, as they have been in the United States for many decades, opportunity for children will also be highly unequal.

There are several important channels through which neighborhoods affect social and economic opportunities. Most directly, children are assigned to public schools based on their neighborhoods, and the fact that school quality matters is irrefutable evidence that neighborhoods matter. But the effects are far broader. Local governments that represent segregated communities provide lower-quality public services; they spend much less per resident on sewers, policing, parks, roads, social services, and the like.[1] Neighborhoods also shape exposure to culture and peer influences, both good and bad, as well as to crime, police power and practices, and toxic environmental hazards and stress.

HOW NEIGHBORHOODS PASS ON CULTURE

Culture is usually thought of as spreading through families. Parents or extended family pass on their way of living—their habits, adaptations, manners of speaking, and preferences for how they invest time—to children, and the process unfolds over generations. Clearly, neighborhoods also play a role in this process. Sometimes the connection is obvious in that an extended family may actually live in the same neighborhood and contribute to a child's culture, but friends, peers, and nonfamily adult figures also contribute, for good or ill, to a child's development and pattern of behavior.

Some scholars have argued, nonetheless, that children who are predisposed to deviancy may befriend each other or end up in the same neighborhood through choices made by their parents, and whatever predisposes them to crime is the true cause of their behavior—not their social network or neighborhoods. That argument has been proven wrong by a wide variety of academic research, some of which is covered below.

Criminologists, for example, have documented the fact that when someone is exposed to criminal behavior from peers, it greatly increases their odds of engaging in crime.[2] One rich analysis from economists Anne Case and Larry Katz used survey data collected in white and black working-class neighborhoods in Boston to study exposure to unhealthy social behavior. In poor black and poor white neighborhoods, they found very high percentages of young men exposed to deviant behavior.[3] Both groups were more likely to say they knew someone in their neighborhood who sold drugs very well (40 percent of black males and 38 percent of white males) or who was "in jail or in trouble with the police" (42 percent of both black males and white males) than they were likely to know someone who worked in a business or other professional occupations (33 percent of black males and 29 percent of white males). Importantly, Case and Katz found that the probability of committing a crime, using drugs, and attending church were all affected by whether or not neighbors behaved that way, even after controlling for the behavior of parents and family members.

The Cumulative Effect of Neighborhoods

There have been many other studies that attempt to measure how neighborhoods affect life outcomes. By considering how disadvantaged circumstances accumulate over time and affect people differently based on their age, sociologists such as Patrick Sharkey and Geoffrey Wodtke have developed sophisticated techniques to estimate how neighborhoods affect IQ, educational attainment, and teen pregnancy.[4]

My own research with Douglas Massey has used similar methods.[5] Using data on 1,584 children born between 1965 and 1975, we measured their parents' income and the average income in their neighborhood (or neighborhoods if they moved) during their childhood. We then saw how childhood neighborhood income predicted their income as adults between the ages of 30 and 44. To take into account family and genetic effects, we controlled for the incomes of their parents and their siblings. We found that the neighborhood-income effect is larger than the sibling effect. In other words, if you want to predict someone's future income, knowing his or her sibling's future income is less important than knowing the average income in that person's childhood neighborhood. The neighborhood effect was almost as large as the parent-income effect. We estimated that being raised in an affluent neighborhood compared to a poor neighborhood was worth roughly $700,000 dollars in lifetime income.

Another important finding from that research was that the income mobility of African Americans was significantly lower than that for white people. That is, white people were able to move up the income ladder to a greater extent than black people born to parents at similar income levels. Yet, this effect disappeared after controlling for the average income and percentage of black people living in the neighborhood. The implication is that black people are just as upwardly mobile as white people when they grow up in similar neighborhoods.

Yet, much larger-scale research using tax records and census data confirmed that neighborhoods explain most of the variation in upward mobility but contradicted the finding from my research that neighborhoods explain white-black gaps in mobility.[6] Instead, this research team of Harvard and Census Bureau economists found that black women are just as upwardly mobile as white women, but black men consistently earn less income and are less likely to be employed relative to white men who grow up with similar parental incomes.[7] This is true even when they grow up in the same neighborhood. One important factor they mention is that the presence of black fathers in the neighborhood has a large predictive effect on the mobility of black boys but not white children or black girls, suggesting that role models matter but only if they are of the same race and gender. The black-white gap in male mobility falls roughly by half when a substantial number of black fathers are in the neighborhood, and the positive effect holds for black boys whether or not a father actually lives in their home. Instead, something about black fathers living in the neighborhood is driving the results.

The research described above, which is the culmination of work by Raj Chetty, Nathaniel Hendren, and their collaborators, is some of the most powerful social science ever conducted on the effects of neighborhoods on life outcomes. Using tax records for 25 million children born between 1980 and 1993, they studied families who moved to a new city and compared siblings within the same families on various outcomes: income at age 30, college attendance, teenage birth, marriage, and employment. These data, combined with Chetty and Hendren's innovative and methodologically flawless analysis, make their study a classic of social science.

What they found was that each year spent in a local commuting area (a county or group of adjacent counties within which people commute) causes children raised there to be a bit more like people who have always lived there (4 percent of the gap between movers and natives in eventual outcomes goes away with each year spent there in childhood). The implication is that if a poor family moves to an area with great educational outcomes, their children will gradually become like the "native" children. The son raised in the high-success county will have much better outcomes than his older brother who is raised in the low-success county. Chetty and Hendren prove through careful analysis and statistical logic that they can measure the causal effect of place and eliminate confounding statistical factors (such as parental competence and genes), which may systematically induce some families to move and others to stay. For example, their main results hold even when natural disasters—rather than personal reasons—compel large numbers of people to move all at once.[8]

They also found that segregation—both economic and racial—is highly correlated with poor outcomes. For children born to parents with low incomes, every year they spend living in an area with high levels of economic segregation lowers their eventual adult income by 14 percent relative to the average low-income family by the time they reach age 26. The effect is similar

Table 8.1. Percentage gain or loss to income at age 26 of spending one year of childhood living in segregation or integrated commuting zones, for children born to parents at the 25th percentile of the national income distribution

	Economic segregation	Racial segregation
Highest quintile of segregation	−14%	−19%
4	−1%	−4%
3	16%	24%
2	30%	32%
Lowest quintile of segregation	54%	49%

Note: Means for quintile categories are weighted by population.

Source: Summary data from Raj Chetty and Nathaniel Hendren, "The Impacts of Neighborhoods on Intergenerational Mobility I: Childhood Exposure Effects," *Quarterly Journal of Economics* 133.3 (2018): 1107–62.

for those growing up in areas highly segregated by race (−19 percent). By contrast, the low-segregation communities lead to an income gain of 54 percent and 49 percent, respectively, in terms of economic or racial segregation. Their database shows that the probability of attending college follows a similar pattern. On every dimension in life that seems to matter, children born to low-income families do much worse if raised in segregated areas (table 8.1).

Other studies have used quasi-random natural experiments to study how neighborhoods affect behavior. While people are not usually randomly assigned neighborhoods, this does happen under some limited "natural" circumstances, which strengthens confidence that the neighborhood effect is not mixed up with genetic or family effects.

Housing Immigrants

Immigrants are sometimes randomly assigned to neighborhoods by government administrators in receiving countries. This might happen, for example, if the immigrant family applies for refugee status or a special visa while in their home country, and the immigration official assigns them to a subsidized housing project in the host country. Scholars in Sweden and Israel have investigated whether or not the outcomes of immigrants are affected by the quality of their placement under these circumstances.

From 1985 to 1994, the Swedish government came to believe that too many immigrants were settling in Stockholm and other concentrated municipalities, where housing supply was getting scarce and rates of welfare use were increasing among the immigrant population, so they decided to centralize control of which cities immigrants were allowed to settle in. Swedish economists subsequently found that immigrants who were randomly assigned to neighborhoods where other immigrants used welfare at high rates were themselves much more likely to use welfare.[9] A standard deviation increase in the rate of neighborhood welfare use among immigrants increased an individual's likelihood of receiving welfare by 14.5 percentage points roughly ten years later. That is a huge effect considering that just under 40 percent of refugees were receiving welfare payments in 2000. The results were similar using employment as the outcome rather than welfare, and in related work, the same scholars found large neighborhood effects on income.[10]

A similar analysis has been done by Israeli economists. Because of Israel's unique status as the Jewish homeland, immigration policies meant to encourage the settlement of Jews from the diaspora have created conditions that are particularly attractive for social science research. For example, in 1949, roughly 50,000 Jews from Yemen were allowed to settle in Israel. Israeli officials determined whether they were sent to cities or rural areas, which differed in terms of access to electricity and running water. Girls who grew up in the more modern settlements went on to attain higher levels of education than those who did not. They also married at an older age, had fewer children, were more likely to be working at age 55, less likely to be religious, and more likely to express a preference for non-Yemeni music and food.[11] Thus, neighborhoods shaped many of their cultural and social outcomes, despite rather small differences in the quality of the neighborhoods and their shared freedoms and civil rights within Israel.

In 1991, similar circumstances applied to the immigration of 15,000 Ethiopian Jews into Israel, who were again placed into different neighborhoods in ways that were unrelated to their family background. Some children ended up being placed in wealthy suburbs, while others were placed in low-income towns far from city centers. Being placed in an area that led to attendance at a school with high math scores (prior to their arrival) greatly boosted the cognitive ability of children relative to their peers assigned to lower-performing schools. The passage rates on matriculation exams increased by 8.2 percentage points for those placed in high-quality schools against an average of 27 percent.[12]

Randomly Housing the Poor

In the United States, policies designed to provide housing for the poor have also created quasi-experimental conditions with respect to neighborhood assignment. In 1994, the Department of Housing and Urban Development created the Moving to Opportunity (MTO) program. Families living in public housing in a select number of cities were randomly assigned to one of three groups: (1) a control group, which was allowed to continue to live in public housing provided they remained eligible; (2) an experimental group, which was given a rental assistance voucher, allowing them to move; and (3) another experimental group, which was also given a voucher but told they could move only to a low-poverty neighborhood.

At least seven papers were published in prominent academic journals by leading social scientists using data from this experiment.[13] They looked at how being offered the opportunity to move affected educational, health, social, and labor-market outcomes for young adults and youth. The results were disappointing to those, like me, who believe neighborhood environments are important to life outcomes. Other than some effects on mental health and subjective well-being, the results showed no effects on income or employment status for adults and none for educational performance for children.[14]

However, these social scientists did not investigate the effects of growing up in a lower-poverty neighborhood or attending a better-quality school for more than a brief period, because at the time of the research, not enough children had been raised in the new neighborhoods. Moreover, there were other major challenges from a social science perspective. Only half of the people in the experimental group actually moved, and those who did move ended up in schools that were overwhelmingly black (82 percent of students) with low test scores (averaging at the 25th percentile for the state)—only slightly better conditions than those in the control group, which remained in segregated public housing.

Despite these significant limitations, the authors decided that neighborhoods were irrelevant: "Housing mobility by itself does not appear to be an effective antipoverty strategy," read one study's conclusion.[15] Another concluded that "MTO-type policy efforts to improve the neighborhood conditions of poor families would not be part of an effective antipoverty strategy," if judged based on income, but the same study did find that lowering neighborhood poverty greatly increases subjective well-being.[16]

The quality of the analysis was extremely high, but that did not prevent these scholars from arriving at the wrong conclusions, as was demonstrated by the latest follow-up drawing on the same housing study. Enough time had passed for Raj Chetty and Larry Katz (who also contributed to the earlier research) to analyze what happened to young people raised in different neighborhoods when they became adults. Moreover, they were able to measure income more accurately and comprehensively than previous scholars by using data from tax records, rather than surveys. They found that moving before the age of 13 increased future annual income by the mid-twenties by roughly 31 percent, boosted marriage rates by 2 percentage points, and raised college attendance by 2.5 percentage points. It is worth recalling that the neighborhood quality of the movers increased only slightly. These benefits should be thought of as the effect of going from the worst neighborhoods in America to those that are nearly as bad.

Another compelling example comes from a study of public housing in the UK, where, in the 1970s, applicants were also randomly assigned to neighborhoods.[17] Parents who were randomly assigned to neighborhoods with a high rate of educated parents were much more likely to spend time reading to their children—a finding that shows that important and adaptive cultural traits can be readily transmitted across families through neighborhood contact. By age 33, those who had been randomly assigned to neighborhoods with high rates of college attainment and were much more likely to have been read to as children were also more likely to have completed high levels of education. The quality of the neighborhood was particularly important for children whose parents had not completed much education.

Along these lines, a quasi-experimental study in the United States found that children whose low-income parents were admitted into an affordable housing project in an affluent New Jersey community spent more time reading outside of school than peers from their previous community, again suggesting important cultural effects from neighborhoods.[18] Likewise, when public housing applicants were randomly assigned to different neighborhoods by the Montgomery County, Maryland, housing authority, children who were allowed to attend low-poverty schools as a result of their parents' neighborhood assignment earned much higher math scores (0.4 standard deviations after seven years) than those who were placed in less affluent schools in the same county.[19]

THE TOXICITY OF SEGREGATION

Lead is a known toxin and was known as such centuries ago by physicians, even if their warnings went unheeded.[20] Its negative relationship to health and intellectual ability has been well documented across many countries and studies.[21] For even moderate lead exposure (10 micrograms of lead per deciliter of blood [ug/dl]), the estimated effect on IQ has been found to be around 3 IQ points, which translates into a loss of 0.20 standard deviations; other estimates suggest a loss of 7 IQ points (0.5 standard deviations) from going from 1 ug/dl to 10 ug/dl.[22]

In the mid-twentieth century, the majority of American children was experiencing moderate to high levels of toxic lead exposure; housing built before the 1940s was particularly dangerous because of the widespread use of lead paint. Lead was used in the oil refining process starting in the 1920s, despite the fact that its dangers were well known in the medical community. Yet, as a result of lobbying efforts from industry associations that had a financial stake in lead use, it was not until the 1970s that government action was taken to remediate the problem.[23]

In the 1960s, scientists deemed lead exposure in the blood to be dangerous if it measured at 60 ug/dl, but as mentioned earlier, decades of research have demonstrated that exposure at much lower rates is also associated with IQ loss and other ailments. In 1991, the U.S. Centers for Disease Control deemed lead-exposure levels of 10 ug/dl to be of concern for children aged five and under. As of 2012, the CDC has been using a relative standard, based on the 99.5th percentile of exposure, which is currently 5 ug/dl.[24]

Lead poisoning was once deemed to be a problem only for poor neighborhoods, but blood samples from 1976–1980 showed that 85 percent of white children and nearly all black children were suffering from toxic levels of lead exposure. The racial disparities were extreme for what, at the time, was considered a dangerous level (30 ug/dl): this applied to 12.6 percent of black people but only 2 percent of white people.

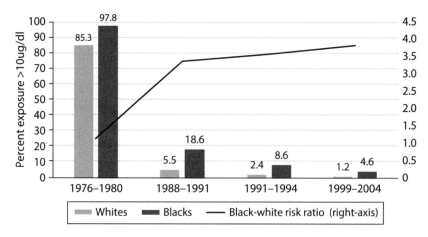

Figure 8.1. Dangerous levels of lead exposure (>10 ug/dl) in blood of U.S. children aged 5 and under, by race and year

Sources: Mahaffey, K. R., J. L. Annest, J. Roberts, and R. S. Murphy. "National Estimates of Blood Lead Levels: United States, 1976–1980: Association with Selected Demographic and Socioeconomic Factors." *New England Journal of Medicine* 307.10 (1982): 573–579; Jones, R. L., Homa, D. M., Meyer, P. A., Brody, D. J., Caldwell, K. L., Pirkle, J. L., & Brown, M. J. (2009). "Trends in Blood Lead Levels and Blood Lead Testing among US Children Aged 1 to 5 years, 1988–2004." *Pediatrics*, 123(3), e376–e385.

Remarkably, in less than ten years the threat was eliminated for all but a small percentage of the population. The primary reason for the decline seems to be the mandatory removal of lead in gasoline starting in 1975, by order of the Environmental Protection Agency.[25] By 1985, less than 50 percent of produced gasoline had lead; by 1990, it was roughly 0 percent. Concurrently, in 1977, the Consumer Product Safety Commission imposed new regulations to remove all but trace elements of lead in paint.[26]

Still, recent data show that race gaps in lead exposure remain large (figure 8.1). Black children are three to four times more likely to have dangerous levels of lead exposure in their blood, using the cutoff of 10 ug/dl (though no safe exposure levels have been found).

The historic and contemporary racial and economic disparities in risk can be directly linked to economic and racial segregation, as a number of scholars have shown. Low-income white people and, to a greater extent black people, have been compelled to live in older homes that were more likely to have lead paint, less likely to have been remediated, and more likely to be located near dangerous environmental hazards.[27] By concentrating toxic exposures and impeding their remediation, government red-lining and zoning directly contributed to well-documented health risks.

Beyond exposure to actual environmental toxins, different neighborhoods also determine exposure to stress, which has its own well-known toxic properties.[28] People living in segregated communities are much more likely to be exposed to violence and other known stressors, but this could be significantly reduced, if not eliminated, if people were given an opportunity to participate in housing markets as equals.

Evidence for this comes from a public housing project that was forced upon the mostly white community of Mt. Laurel, New Jersey, by the New Jersey state Supreme Court. In 1971, the court ruled that the town's zoning laws were racially motivated to exclude black people. The remedy involved the construction of affordable housing units to allow people from nearby low-income and mostly black communities (such as Camden) to move into Mt. Laurel. In 2000, after decades of court battles, the development, built by a nonprofit association, was finally complete and began accepting residents. In 2009 and 2010, sociologists Rebecca Casciano and Douglas Massey surveyed people who had been accepted into the development by the nonprofit and compared their experiences to those who had been wait-listed or rejected for various disqualifying reasons but were otherwise similar.[29] Because acceptance into the program was based on the order in which the application was received and other criteria unlikely to be correlated with social outcomes—the study is quasi-experimental. Living in the housing development significantly lowered the probability of experiencing a wide range of potential stressors and dangers—including exposure to the sale or use of illegal drugs. The residents who moved were also far less likely to be arrested, robbed, or incarcerated. Perhaps, as a result, they were also less likely to report symptoms of stress—such as fearfulness, trouble relaxing, or trouble sleeping (figure 8.2).

Large-scale national surveys confirm that black residents are much more likely to express concerns about their safety and security than other groups and generally express greater dissatisfaction with their home and community. A Gallup survey of 170,000 U.S. residents over the course of 2016 found that black people are twice as likely as white people and over four times as likely as Asians to strongly disagree with the following statement: "You always feel safe and secure." Black people were also much more likely to strongly disagree with statements that their home is ideal or that they can't imagine a better community to live in.[30] These subjective judgments about neighborhood quality

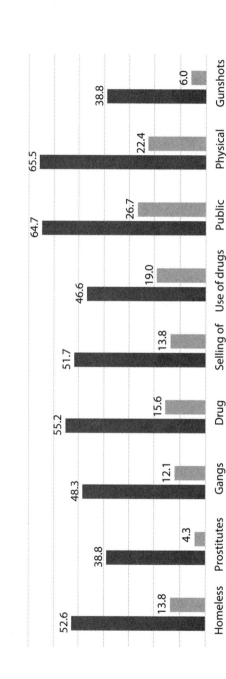

Figure 8.2. Quasi-experimental effect of exposure to disorder or violence within neighborhood

Note: Data are from 2009 survey of current and former residents of an affordable housing project (Ethel Lawrence Homes) in New Jersey, as well as applicants to the program who were either put on a waiting list or rejected. Propensity score-matching was used to address concerns that differences between the experimental group (those who were admitted) and the control group (those who were rejected or wait-listed) were meaningful.

Source: Casciano, Rebecca, and Douglas S. Massey. "Neighborhood Disorder and Anxiety Symptoms: New Evidence from a Quasi-Experimental Study." *Health & Place* 18.2 (2012): 180–190.

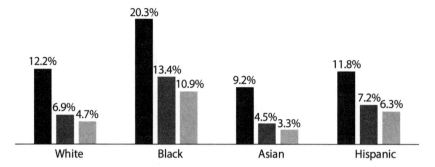

Figure 8.3. Gallup survey on the subjective feelings about neighborhood quality by race and ethnicity of adult respondent, 2016

Source: Gallup-Sharecare Well-Being Index. Data were collected from January 2016 to December 2016. The survey is a random-digit dialing sample of approximately 170,000 U.S. adults with either a cell phone or landline phone; responses are weighted to reflect demographic characteristics of the United States population and the probability of responding.

correspond to objective measures, suggesting that people have an intuitive grasp of whether or not they live in a healthy neighborhood environment. After merging Gallup data with data from the Harvard Opportunity Insights project (created by Raj Chetty and his collaborators), I found that subjective measures of neighborhood quality strongly predict higher intergenerational mobility (figure 8.3).[31]

"Better" neighborhoods are more expensive, which makes economic segregation a real problem for families with lower incomes. Average neighborhood income is a very strong predictor of subjective neighborhood quality— measured as satisfaction with one's community, home, and safety. Thus, 7 percent of those in the lowest third of neighborhoods strongly disagreed with the statement that they "always feels safe and secure" compared to just 3 percent in the middle third and 2 percent in the top third. These results classify neighborhoods based on average incomes relative to the local or metropolitan median income, but similar—even larger gaps—are found when all neighborhoods are simply ranked by income without regard to their broader local or metropolitan area (figure 8.4).

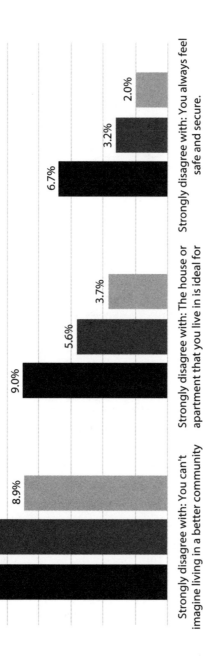

Figure 8.4. Strong dissatisfaction with neighborhood, home, and safety by level of neighborhood income

Note: Neighborhood income categories were determined by dividing average family income at the zip-code level by median family income at the commuting zone level.

Strongly disagree with: You can't imagine living in a better community than the one you live in today.

Strongly disagree with: The house or apartment that you live in is ideal for you and your family.

Strongly disagree with: You always feel safe and secure.

■ Bottom third of neighborhoods ■ Middle third of neighborhoods ■ Top third of neighborhoods

16.8%
12.4%
8.9%
9.0%
5.6%
3.7%
6.7%
3.2%
2.0%

Source of attitudinal data: 2016 Gallup-Sharecare Well-Being Index. Data were collected from January 2016 to December 2016, taken from a random-digit dialing sample of 94,128 U.S. adults with children living at home and either a cell phone or landline phone. Responses are weighted to reflect demographic characteristics of the U.S. population and the probability of responding. Source of zip-code income data: U.S. Department of Treasury, Internal Revenue Service, "SOI Tax Stats—Individual Income Tax Statistics—ZIP Code Data," https://www.irs.gov/statistics/soi-tax-stats -individual-income-tax-statistics-zip-code-data-soi (accessed June 19, 2019). Source of commuting zone data: Median income by county from 2011–2016

Segregation and Crime Victimization

The subjective concerns about neighborhood quality and safety have a corresponding objective basis in that black people are more likely than other groups to be victims of violent crimes—such as sexual assault and robbery—and far more likely to be victims of homicide.[32] This danger is a consequence of the unequal power and long-standing oppression that created and sustains segregation. Even worse, the danger is exacerbated by the often fraught and unjust relationship that exists between the police, the criminal justice system as a whole, and the black community. The result is that segregation puts black people in excessive danger of being harmed by criminals and being harassed or arrested by police for behaviors that are overlooked in white communities.

I know the danger of segregated black neighborhoods from personal experience. Not that I was ever threatened or bothered, despite spending a fair amount of my adult life living near or visiting segregated black neighborhoods. The dangers are much more pronounced for young black males, as I know from both statistics and experience.

A few years ago, I signed up to participate in the Big Brothers/Big Sisters program in Washington, DC, which matches adult mentors to poor children, whose parents would like their children to have greater exposure to positive role models.[33] I was assigned to a 13-year-old boy named Isaiah Harris, who lived in an apartment building in a segregated black neighborhood in DC with his younger brother Xavier and single mother Geneva Harris, who provided security services to downtown office buildings. Isaiah and I played basketball and chess, went bowling, went to DC's Smithsonian museums, saw movies, and had meals together. Despite attending a middle school with zero white children and failing test scores, Isaiah distinguished himself as a strong math student.[34] He was one of only two students in his eighth-grade class to take advanced math courses at a nearby high school.

One warm night in the spring of 2011, when he was 15, Isaiah left his block to talk to a girl he was interested in. A man who harbored a grudge against people from Isaiah's street—apparently related to gang rivalry—decided he was going to kill someone—any young man, it would seem—from Isaiah's street as revenge. Isaiah was murdered.[35] The murderer had never met him, and Isaiah had never participated in any gang activity.

This was a deeply traumatic experience for Isaiah's brother, his sister who lived nearby, his many relatives, including his grandmother who also lived in the neighborhood, his classmates and teachers at school, people in his community, and especially his mother.

At a time when American divisions are thought to be deep and unbridgeable and civic engagement nonexistent, I witnessed an outpouring of support for the family from people representing every race, class, and religion in the DC area. A candlelight vigil was organized at Isaiah's school, which gave the people who knew him best an opportunity to eulogize him and for the community to grieve collectively and reflect on the tragic loss. A few days later, the funeral, which was performed at a neighborhood African American church, was widely attended and allowed for a more formal and ceremonial form of closure for the family and community.

To help the family pay for the steep expenses of burial and the erection of a tombstone at a local cemetery, I assisted Geneva in setting up a nonprofit organization with my local bank. A journalist was kind enough to publicize the address of the nonprofit publicly so people following local news could send in checks, and they did. My records show that 79 different donors contributed a total of nearly $7,000 to the family; many were my former colleagues at The Brookings Institution, as well as friends, some of whom had met Isaiah. Some were also connected to Xavier's "Big Brother," Jay, who also helped fund-raise, and the Big Brothers organization itself. Yet, the majority of the donors were strangers who had no relationship with the family. They often included kind, sympathetic notes. The DC government also provided crucial support that allowed Geneva to move out of the neighborhood to a safer nearby suburb.

The fact that the killer was a black man in no way relieved the trauma and loss experienced by the Harris family and the wider community. Yet, justice was served, in that the killer was quickly arrested and given what seemed to be a fair sentence, and that process—along with unanimous support from the community—did bring a sense of peace that has allowed the family to keep living, to establish and realize new goals, without ever forgetting the loss of their loved one.

In too many other instances, however, black men have been killed not by violent gang members, but by the very people whose income is provided by the black community in order to protect them from such people: the police. Because of the recent proliferation of smartphones—now equipped with video cameras and social media distribution networks—a number of controversial police encounters have been recorded and shared, providing evidence of injustice that otherwise would not have existed.

In 2012, the bizarre death of Trayvon Martin became a focus of national debate. Trayvon, a young black man, was killed while merely walking home from the store, after being confronted by a man who had tried and failed to become a police officer—George Zimmerman—and fancied himself a neighborhood watch volunteer. The details are unclear, but apparently Zimmerman took it upon himself to drive up to Trayvon with his gun to confront what he thought was a suspicious-looking person. They fought and Zimmerman shot and killed him. Zimmerman was later acquitted of even accidental murder.[36]

Though Zimmerman was not a police officer, over a dozen cases over the next five years involved police officers who resorted to excessive force when confronting unarmed black boys or young men out of the very fear and suspicion that motivated George Zimmerman to perform what he thought was his civic duty by accosting a teenage boy going about his legitimate pedestrian business.[37]

Jim Crow is the father of these unjust encounters.

The fear and prejudice that haunts police encounters with black men is in part the result of isolation. One of the strongest and most replicated findings in social science is called *Contact Theory*. It postulates that cooperation and trust between groups of people develop naturally from contact—particularly when that contact is structured between fellow citizens with equal rights, rather than, for example, masters and servants or upper- and lower-caste members of society. In integrated communities, contact between groups arises from commercial interactions, informal exchanges, working relationships, shared extracurricular activities, or friendship. The evidence for its antiprejudicial benefits is overwhelming and cuts across time and country.[38] In the context of the United States, people express more trusting attitudes toward others and are more likely to volunteer if they live in more racially integrated metropolitan areas.[39]

Segregation not only distorts the attitudes of police officers and white citizens, but also provides the practical opportunity to profile and control black people, just as it allowed for the control and oppression of Native Americans in the United States, Jews in premodern Europe, and native black people in apartheid South Africa.

A recent analysis by economist Roland Fryer summarizes estimates from various databases and studies of police shootings. All agree that the probability of being shot by the police while unarmed is much higher for black people than white people. The relative risk ranges from 3.2 to 6.2—meaning that young black men are three to six times more likely than young white men to be victims.[40] In a misunderstood but important finding, Fryer finds that this gap is not explained by the fact that police act differently toward black people than white people after stopping them. Rather, the gap is explained by the much higher likelihood of police stopping black people. The over-stopping of black men—encouraged by policies called "stop-and-frisk," which effectively assert that any young black man on the street should be stopped and searched—seems to be the source of danger, and high-density segregation makes the over-stopping of black men more likely by concentrating them where they can be easily monitored.[41]

Other research from anthropologist Cody Ross of the Max Planck Institute shows that Fryer's findings do not rule out the possibility that black suspects—once encountered—are treated inequitably with respect to use of force. In a mathematical model, Ross and his co-authors show that a small number of strongly antiblack police officers could drive up the number of encounters with black people in situations that would never warrant lethal force, making it seem like the probability of using lethal force is the same for white people and black people, when in fact many of the encounters with black people never should have taken place.[42]

The Unequal Application of Criminal Enforcement

During the peak implementation years of the stop-and-frisk policy in New York City in 2011, local residents were forcibly stopped and searched by the police 685,724 times. The overwhelming majority of these stops were of black people (55 percent) and Latinos (32 percent). In 89 percent of encounters, the suspect was released with no charges.[43] The searches were also concentrated in minority neighborhoods. In 2014, the top precinct for stop-and-frisk searches was the 106th in Queens. Only 4 percent of the population is white in this area.[44]

Defenders of "stop-and-frisk" and similar tactics say it lowers crime, even if it bothers innocent people. There is no obvious evidence that it lowers crime (crime trends show no change as stop-and-frisk waxed and waned), but even if it did—and, in theory, deter crime, as well—it would represent a gross miscarriage of justice through the unequal application of criminal enforcement and the fruitless harassment of innocent people.[45] It is as if the goal is to punish 100 percent of crimes committed by black people but only 30 percent of crimes committed by white people.

In fact, that disproportionate goal is not merely a hypothetical example. The U.S. Department of Health and Human Services conducts a regular survey of health issues, drug use, and criminal behavior. It's the best information available on criminal behavior that does not result in arrest.

I focused on a sample of male respondents aged 18 to 30 because that age group encompasses the majority of arrests in almost every year since 1980, and since the late 1980s, arrest rates have exceeded 1 percent of the population for each age within the years 18 to 29, but are typically below that threshold for all other ages.[46] Men are also far more likely to be arrested than women.

It turns out that black men in this age group are slightly less likely to sell or use drugs compared to white people, though the differences are too small to be statistically significant. Specifically, just 5.7 percent of black men aged 18 to 30 sold illegal drugs, compared to 6.1 percent of white people. People who sell drugs frequently are also no more likely to be black. White people are slightly more likely than black people to have sold drugs ten or more times over the last year than black people (2.2 versus 1.8).

Drug crimes among females are even more disproportionately white. Compared to white women aged 18 to 30, black women are less likely to use drugs (22 percent of black women versus 28 percent of white women) or sell them (1.0 percent versus 2.8 percent, respectively) drugs.

Selling drugs, moreover, is hardly limited to the working class. White men enrolled in college full time are more likely to sell and use drugs than those who aren't enrolled. Fully 43 percent of white male college students reported using a serious illegal drug in the last year, and 6.9 percent reported selling them.[47]

Yet, black men aged 18 to 30 are 3.2 times more likely to be arrested for selling or using drugs than white men in the same age group. Combining arrest rates with selling rates suggests that 81 percent of black men who sell drugs are arrested compared to 24 percent of white men.[48] Drug use by black people is also more aggressively policed. The share of young black men who report using drugs within the last year suggests 12 percent are arrested, compared to 4 percent of white people.

Using more sophisticated methods, I estimate that the odds of being arrested on drug charges for black males aged 18 to 30 is 3.8 times higher than for white males of the same age, controlling for specific age, lifetime drug use, drug use in the last year, and drug sales in the last year.[49] For men over 30, black men are seven times more likely to be arrested on drug charges.

This is what unequal protection under the law looks like. There is a systematic bias toward the punishment and prosecution of black crime relative to white crime. In New York City, 67 percent of people stopped for suspected marijuana possession and 75 percent of those suspected of selling marijuana were black, despite the fact that black people are just 25 percent of the New York City population.[50]

Those who think black people are more likely to lie about drugs than white people on anonymous government surveys will have to reconcile the facts of self-reported drug use with the objective reality that non-Hispanic white Americans died at higher rates from drug use and accidental poisoning from 2007 to 2016 than black people, according to the nation's death records.[51]

Of course, people commit other types of crimes besides those involving drugs, and many of those other crimes have clear victims, who have either been physically harmed or had their property damaged or stolen. Black people are also more likely to be arrested for these crimes as well, and some people assume there is a one-to-one correspondence between a crime and an arrest, but as we saw with drug data that assumption is grossly unfounded (figure 8.5).

Compared to drug crimes, it is harder to measure the population of people who get away with property or violent crimes, because surveys don't typically ask people if they have recently murdered or raped anyone. The #MeToo movement has made it clear that sexual assaults are often unreported or otherwise do not result in arrest. In any case, murder and rape represent just 0.2 percent of all arrests in a given year.[52]

The National Survey on Drug Use and Health does not ask about murder or rape, but it does ask respondents to say whether or not they have stolen or tried to steal anything worth more than $50 in the last 12 months, and it also asks: "During the past 12 months, how many times have you attacked someone with the intent to seriously hurt them?"[53] Relative to white people, black males aged 18 to 30 are less likely to say they have stolen or tried to steal something (2 percent versus 2.3 percent) and 2.4 times more likely to say they have attacked someone (4.9 percent versus 3.7 percent). Yet, black people are

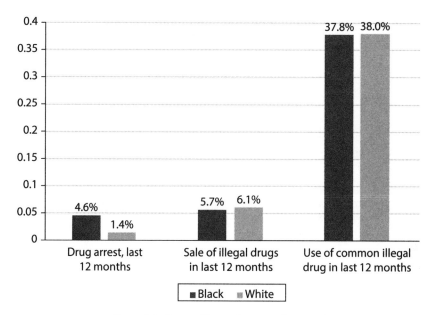

Figure 8.5. Rates of drug sale, use, and arrest of
black and white men aged 18–30, 2013

Source: United States Department of Health and Human Services. Substance Abuse and Mental
Health Services Administration. Center for Behavioral Health Statistics and Quality. National
Survey on Drug Use and Health, 2013. ICPSR35509-v3. Ann Arbor, MI: Inter-university
Consortium for Political and Social Research [distributor], 2015-11-23. https://doi.org/10.3886
/ICPSR35509.v3. I defined common illegal drugs as marijuana, heroin, crack, cocaine, LSD,
and meth. Drug sales question asked: "During the past 12 months, how many times have you
sold illegal drugs?"

3.3 times more likely to be arrested for aggravated assault and 2.6 times more
likely to be arrested for larceny-theft.[54] Again, the story is consistent with uneven enforcement of crime.

Regardless of the apparent disproportionality with respect to nondrug
crimes, the clearly unfair prosecution of black people for drug crimes has tremendous social consequences. For one, the sheer scale of drug arrests is as-
tounding. The U.S. "War on Drugs" has been the predominant source of
arrests and incarcerations in recent years.[55] In 1980, only 7 percent of classifiable arrests were for drug crimes, only slightly more than the share for
violent crimes and far lower than the 21 percent share from property crimes.
Since then, property crime arrests have plummeted and violent crime arrests
have held steady, despite population growth and mass immigration. Yet, drug
crime arrests increased from 0.6 million in 1980 to 1.6 million in 2014 and

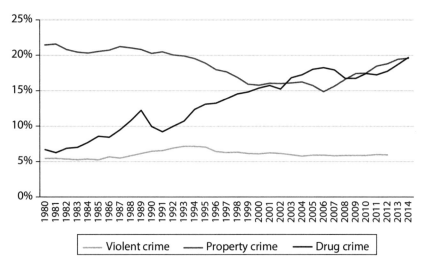

Figure 8.6. Share of U.S. arrests by type of crime for all classifiable offenses, 1980–2014

Source: Bureau of Justice Statistics, Arrest Data Analysis Tool.

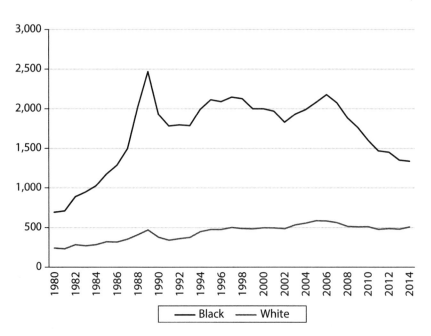

Figure 8.7. Arrests for drugs per 100,000 adults by race, 1980–2014

Source: Bureau of Justice Statistics, Arrest Data Analysis Tool.

now account for 20 percent of all classifiable arrests. In every year since 1993, more people were incarcerated for drug crimes than violent crimes. Nearly one-third of total prison admissions since 1993 were for drug crimes, the largest source of admissions overall (figure 8.6).[56]

The arrests and incarcerations have damaged social mobility and economic opportunity for millions of Americans and their families. There is clear evidence from sociological research that the labor market for ex-offenders is difficult, and as my former colleagues Isabel Sawhill and Scott Winship have shown, getting convicted of a crime in adolescence greatly lowers the probability of reaching the middle class by middle age.[57]

The eruption of drug enforcement activity has been particularly harmful for black people living in segregated communities. From 1980 to 2014, there were 14 million drug-related arrests of black people, averaging over 400,000 per year, and the disproportionate arrest rates for black people have ranged from 2.6 to 5.2 over the years (figure 8.7).

Stepping back, we can see that neighborhood inequality—itself a monumental failure of democracies to protect market access—has played a very important role in creating and sustaining an underclass of Americans. The tools of market manipulation and obstruction that I documented in the last chapter—deed restrictions and then zoning—have lowered the realized intellectual abilities and occupational opportunities of countless children by depriving them of quality schooling, isolating them from the cultural norms of the middle class, exposing them to environmental toxins and damage from the stress of social disorder, and punishing them excessively for crimes committed just as often by the upper-middle class.

9

Unequal Access to the Buying and Selling of Professional Services

THIS BOOK STARTED BY LINKING the rise of far-right nationalism to a strong sense of economic unfairness, which itself is linked to high and growing inequality, a distrust of liberal government, and an underlying belief in racial superiority. I argued that the rise in inequality and the slowdown in economic growth are closely linked to the increasing inefficiency in services and to the rising share of income going to elite professionals who provide services in healthcare, law, finance, and the like. I then sought to demonstrate that there is no scientific basis for believing that racial or ethnic groups differ in any natural or fundamental way in their economically productive characteristics and that in a just society everyone should have an equal opportunity to succeed.

This chapter discusses how elite professionals have managed to appropriate a significant proportion of national income for themselves. The core problem is that professional associations have effectively taken over the governance of markets for many important products and services. These groups have a strong incentive to distort laws to the advantage of their members, and they have the influence to do so.

The results are profoundly negative: Men and women who could ably and profitably provide goods and services are denied the right to do so. This situation violates a core principle of a just society—that people should be able to pursue the occupation that best suits their nature, interests, and skills. Beyond that, the distribution of the good things in life—such as health, income, and social status—is greatly distorted by the rule of professional elites. The rest of society pays dearly in order to shore up the incomes of these groups.

This is not to say that elite professionals do not deserve to be paid well. As described in previous chapters, skills broadly understood—including length of education, the natural and developed traits of personality and cognitive ability—reliably predict income to a greater or lesser degree across developed democracies. Professionals tend to be highly educated and demonstrate relatively high levels of cognitive skill. Those with higher levels of education also score higher on the noncognitive skills that predict success in life (i.e., conscientiousness, enthusiasm, and emotional stability). Along these lines, as discussed in chapter 3, some portion of variation in earnings within democracies can be directly tied to "merit"—the value an individual contributes to an organization, a business, or a society—and to the relative scarcity of the skills brought to bear in creating that value.

Yet, as we've seen, most professions are consistently overpaid even after taking their skill levels into account. In many cases, this is the result of many years of political effort by the various associations that lobby for their interests. Over the last two decades, as developed economies have become more integrated, there have been several attempts to systematically compare the regulations of professional services across countries. In an OECD study published in 2000, the authors noted distinct ways in which professional groups hinder markets from operating efficiently and effectively, to the benefit of their professions and the expense of the public.[1]

Common control mechanisms used by professional groups across countries include (1) excessive entry barriers, (2) collusion in setting fees or deterring advertising that might lower prices, (3) limits on how firms are organized and on the extent to which professionals can be employed by outsiders, and (4) the establishment of a legal monopoly on service provision.

In many cases, these laws and practices are controlled by professional associations, which practitioners are often required to join. Such associations also provide important information and networking opportunities to members, at the expense of outsiders. If that sounds similar to the way the craft and merchant guilds operated, it is no coincidence. The same antimarket tools have been used for centuries across many different countries and economies.[2]

HEALTHCARE

Being a doctor pays very well in all rich countries. In Spain, Sweden, and Iceland, general practice doctors typically earn twice as much as the average worker. In the UK, Ireland, and Canada, it is three times as much.[3] But doctors' pay in the United States truly stands out: Physicians and surgeons earn

Table 9.1. Average pay of health professionals divided by average worker pay, by country, 2000–2016

	Specialists	General practitioners	Nurses
Belgium	6.0	2.1	1.1
United States	5.0	3.6	1.3
Austria	4.6	2.9	
Luxembourg	4.5	2.9	1.4
Canada	4.5	2.9	1.1
Australia	4.2	1.8	1.2
Germany	4.0	3.8	1.2
Netherlands	3.9	2.3	1.1
Ireland	3.6	2.8	1.0
United Kingdom	3.5	2.9	1.1
Mexico	3.2	2.6	1.7
New Zealand	3.0	2.5	1.2
Chile	3.0	2.4	1.7
Israel	3.0	1.9	1.3
France	2.9	3.0	1.0
Denmark	2.6	2.9	1.1
Finland	2.5	1.8	1.0
Slovenia	2.4	2.2	1.0
Sweden	2.4	2.2	
Spain	2.3	2.1	1.3
Czech Republic	2.1	3.1	1.0
Iceland	2.1	2.1	0.9
Estonia	2.1	1.8	1.0
Hungary	1.8	1.6	0.9
Latvia	1.5	1.1	0.8
Poland	1.5	2.1	1.0

Note: Numbers in table show relative pay, expressed as the ratio of average pay for the group shown to average pay of all workers in country.

Source: Data from OECD.STAT. "Health Care Resources: Remuneration of Health Professionals," accessed April 3, 2018. Salary ratios are averaged from 2000 to 2016 using all available data for each country.

4.9 times as much as the average worker.[4] Only Belgium provides higher relative compensation to specialists, but the United States compensates general practitioners much higher, so the average physician in the United States receives higher relative pay than a physician in any other OECD country (table 9.1).[5]

Of 480 occupational categories in the United States, census data from 2012–2016 shows that physicians and surgeons possess, by far, the highest average income ($219,000), home values ($706,000), and probability of being in the top 1 percent of income earners (31 percent).[6]

There are several reasons why doctors in the United States are so over-represented among top earners. U.S. physicians, more so than their European peers, have created large entry barriers, including at the hospital level; they have more aggressively suppressed lower-cost professional competitors; and they have eliminated more efficient ways of organizing health services.

Let us start with entry barriers. High pay creates incentives for more people to enter a field. Yet, becoming a physician is an extremely lengthy and costly process. In the United States, it takes a minimum of 11 years of constant work and study to complete medical school, including a bachelor's degree program, four years of graduate study, and at least three years of residency training, depending on the specialization, plus state licensing exams. Typical medical school tuition, meanwhile, is over $200,000, which comes on top of the roughly $120,000 required to complete a bachelor's degree.[7] In the nineteenth century, it took only eight months of study to complete medical school and earn a doctorate in medicine.[8] While eight months is surely too short a period, 11 years of formal study strikes me as excessive.

These entry barriers lower the number of people willing or able to become physicians, thereby artificially raising the salaries of physicians. In 2016, the average salary for a family practitioner was $184,240, and that is among the lowest-paid physician specialties. Anesthesiologists—who provide pharmacological pain relief before and after surgery—are the highest-paid specialty, even ahead of surgeons, with average salaries of $270,000 (table 9.2).

Meanwhile, nurse anesthetists and nurse practitioners are trained to provide essentially the same services as anesthesiologists and family practitioners, but their salaries are between 50 percent and 60 percent of those of their counterparts. The nursing pathway requires four years of nursing school and licensure as a registered nurse, plus the completion of a master's degree program in nursing, which has clinical and classroom components. Becoming a nurse practitioner or anesthetist does not require additional years of residency training for those who have experience working as a nurse. Thus, a nurse can start practicing five years earlier than a physician, without paying nearly as much in educational fees or foregone income from being out of the labor force.

There is no question about the competency of nurse practitioners at providing family and general practice medical care. After reviewing the extensive

Table 9.2. Salary comparisons of healthcare professionals

	Mean salary, 2016
Elite healthcare professions with high entry barriers	
Anesthesiologists	$269,600
Surgeons	$252,910
Obstetricians and gynecologists	$234,310
Physicians and surgeons, all other	$205,560
Internists, general	$201,840
Family and general practitioners	$200,810
Psychiatrists	$200,220
Pediatricians, general	$184,240
Dentists	$178,670
Healthcare professions with lower entry barriers	
Nurse anesthetists	$164,030
Optometrists	$117,580
Nurse practitioners	$104,610
Nurse midwives	$102,390
Chiropractors	$81,210
Dental hygienists	$73,440
Registered nurses	$72,180

Source: Bureau of Labor Statistics, Occupational Employment Statistics, 2016. Source does not include self-employed workers or owners of unincorporated businesses.

medical literature showing that patient outcomes are just as high for nurse practitioners as they are for physicians, the Institute of Medicine at the National Academies strongly recommended that states grant them full independence to practice family and general practice medicine.[9] Likewise, a recent study by Dutch- and British-based healthcare experts reviewed 25 studies of nurse-practitioner efficacy, which used randomized controlled experiments—the gold standard in social science—and the conclusion was extremely clear: "The findings suggest that appropriately trained nurses can produce as high quality care as primary care doctors and achieve as good health outcomes for patients."[10]

Nurse midwives are similar to nurse practitioners in terms of their educational requirements and average pay, but focus on reproductive issues, birth, and early childcare. A review of the literature finds that low- to moderate-risk home births attended by midwives are at least as safe as hospital births, whether attended by a physician or midwife.[11] Indeed, births attended by midwives utilize far fewer costly interventions—dramatically lower rates of epidurals, induction, and Caesarean sections—with comparable mortality rates, and in this way midwife-attended births would be far more efficient even if midwives were paid as much as their physician counterparts.[12] Patient safety, according to another study, is in no way harmed when nurse anesthetists work without the supervision of physician anesthesiologists.[13]

Despite this empirical evidence, many states impose heavy restrictions on the practice of nursing in ways that explicitly benefit physicians. The District of Columbia and 22 of the 50 states allow nurse practitioners to work independently of physicians in accord with their training and the interests of the public;[14] 27 states allow midwives to practice independently; and only 16 states allow independence from supervision for nurse anesthetists.[15] Even worse, the richest and most populous states, such as California, Texas, New York, Florida, and Illinois, tend to be the most restrictive.

The result is that the services provided by one elite professional group—to which access is extremely restricted—are not allowed to be provided by less elite professional groups, even when those groups meet state licensing requirements and scientific evidence demonstrates their efficacy and competence. One can imagine that gender inequality has more to do with this imbalance than professional mastery, given the historic barriers to women becoming doctors but not nurses.

The Physician Lobby

State political representatives are duty bound to represent the interests of their constituents, but they routinely side with the interests of elite professionals—such as doctors—over the interests of citizens. It's no mystery why. Representatives of physicians wield considerable power in opposing the interests of nurses, as well as the interests of the consumers and taxpayers who pay for healthcare. And there's no need to take my word for it. Physician lobbies are quite open about their anticonsumer advocacy and boast about their power to persuade legislators and the public that paying excessive healthcare costs is necessary to guarantee their health and safety.

In 2012, a physician's advocacy association, the Physicians Foundation, wrote a candid report entitled "Accept No Substitute: A Report on Scope of Practice." As the title implies, the report identified potential competition from nonphysicians as a key concern for physicians. The report describes political momentum to grant greater scope of practice or autonomy to nonphysicians such as nurse practitioners, optometrists, and psychologists. It mentions pressure to lower costs as one of the primary motivations behind these changes as well as "the lack of hard evidence that physicians do in fact provide better care than non-physician providers."[16]

The report's authors list concrete steps that their lobbyists are taking to protect the power of physicians in concert with the largest physician lobby of all, the American Medical Association (AMA):

> In the face of all these challenges—both external and internal—medical society leaders have taken a number of steps that include: strengthening their lobbying capacity, working more closely with specialty societies, stepping up their fundraising and campaign contributions, fostering strong relationships with key legislators, and keeping the focus solely and relentlessly on patient safety. In addition, they have worked with the American Medical Association and other national medical organizations through the Scope of Practice Partnership. The AMA, in turn, has been active on federal policy issues related to scope of practice; produced its Scope of Practice data series on ten non-physician professions; launched a national Truth in Advertising campaign that has already generated new laws in fourteen states; and funded a major mapping study to document where non-physician providers are actually practicing.[17]

The report makes it abundantly clear that the physician lobby, including the authors who are affiliated with the Physician Foundation, are stridently opposed to state laws that would lower the cost of healthcare and increase the efficiency of accessing it.[18] Their motivation, to be fair, may very well be patient safety, as they understand it, but insofar as that is a genuine concern, I'd argue it is based on prejudice rather than science. Whatever the true motive, the report documents specific efforts by physician groups to uphold the following prohibitions: on optometrists treating glaucoma, on podiatrists treating ankles, on nurse anesthetists practicing independently of physicians, and on pharmacists providing routine vaccinations.

Citing anonymous interviews with medical executives, it quotes one as bragging about holding back the tide of consumer-friendly deregulation by wielding "sheer political muscle." Another boasted of a victory over nurse anesthetists: "We beat them back in the legislature."[19] The report notes with some satisfaction that only a tiny fraction of nurse practitioners are operating independently as a result of the political opposition of medical societies. This same group laments the disappointing lack of evidence in its favor and suggests the need to commission studies that will be more favorable to its mission.

The California Medical Association—the largest physician lobby in the state—spent $13 million on state campaign finance contributions from 2010 to 2016. Total spending by physicians and their associations reached $26 million in the state over the same period. Nurses also have associations, but their political resources are dwarfed by those of physicians, even though there are far more nurses. Nurses and their associations spent only $1.3 million on campaign finance in California during the period.[20] This physician spending was apparently effective. In 2015, California legislators introduced a bill that would allow nurse practitioners to work independently of physicians. On May 7, 2015, the bill passed the California State Senate by a margin of 25 to 9.[21] All of the nine senators voting against the bill received substantial donations from the California Medical Association, which openly lobbied against it, saying it would "put Californians at risk."[22] Despite this initial success, on June 30, 2015, the bill officially died in the other legislative body, the California State Assembly, where it lost a vote in the Business and Professions Committee by a margin of nine to four. The average assembly member voting to move the bill forward received $13,000 from physicians' organizations, mostly the California Medical Association, whereas those voting to kill the bill received an average of $20,000 from those groups.[23]

The California Medical Association (CMA) was quite open about its hostility to the bill, calling it "dangerous" in a press release from the CMA's president, Paul R. Phinney, M.D. In referring to the bill back in August 2013, when it passed a senate committee vote, Dr. Phinney stated:

> Patients should be deeply concerned that SB 491 was able to move forward today. If SB 491 becomes law, nurse practitioners will be allowed to practice without any supervision by a physician, despite the enormous differences in education and training between the two. SB 491 allows nurse practitioners to diagnose and treat patients beyond their capabilities and without any additional training, jeopardizing patient safety.[24]

Finally, in 2017, the AMA's House of Delegates formally passed a resolution with the intention of suppressing the right of nurses to practice medicine without physician supervision. It states that the AMA should

(1) effectively oppose the continual, nationwide efforts to grant independent practice to non-physician practitioners; (2) effectively educate the public, legislators, regulators, and healthcare administrators; and (3) effectively oppose state and national level legislative efforts aimed at inappropriate scope of practice expansion of non-physician healthcare practitioners.[25]

This is consistent with material on the AMA website in 2018.[26]

It might be considered malpractice if a physician knowingly prescribed a treatment that contradicts the scientific literature, and yet, when it comes to public policy, there is no accountability for a doctor—or association leader—publicly contradicting the scientific literature by falsely stoking fear.

Aside from nurse practitioners, the AMA and other physician groups have also made enemies out of other allied health professions, including optometrists, who typically complete four years of graduate school, after science-based undergraduate training, which is similar to the premedicine track taken by physicians. Optometrists would like to practice independently of physicians, prescribe medication, and treat eye disease, but ophthalmologists, who go to medical school, argue that they are not qualified to so.

As it happens, optometrists get paid roughly 60 cents for every dollar earned by ophthalmologists, so the public would see huge savings if medical services shifted toward optometrists. Thus, in 2015, ophthalmologists spoke out against state legislation in Texas aimed at allowing optometrists to provide more services.[27] Even two years later, the Texas Ophthalmologist Association (TOA) website was blunt: "TOA will not sit idly by while a small, radical faction of non-physicians seeks authority to treat patients with surgical and medical modalities in which they are not trained and which require a comprehensive medical education to fully manage."[28]

The American Medical Association's Historic Victories against the Public

The California Medical Association is a subsidiary of the AMA, which has a long and well-documented history of limiting entry to markets to the advantage of its members and to the expense of the public.

In 2016, only five organizations outspent the AMA on lobbying, three of which were healthcare related: Blue Cross/Blue Shield, an insurer, with close ties to medical associations; the American Hospital Association; and the Pharmaceutical Research and Manufacturers Association of America. The AMA invested $19 million in lobbying, according to the Center for Responsive Politics.[29]

To appreciate how the AMA limits and restricts entry to markets for healthcare today, consider a few of its historic activities. As medical science advanced in the late nineteenth century, physicians gained newfound respect from the public and began to win out against less-professional and less-organized providers of healthcare services. State licensing laws, which had been repealed for decades, were reestablished after the Civil War in many states.

In the early nineteenth century, orthodox medicine consisted of bloodletting and the inducement of mineral poisons. Homeopathic medicine and eclecticism—which recommended rest, herbal remedies, and baths—developed as competing models and established their own medical schools. The orthodoxy fought back through the creation of the American Medical Association in 1847, which nationally organized state- and university-level organizations. Its goal, according to historian Ronald Hamowy, was largely to reduce the supply of competing schools and physicians.[30] In 1867, the AMA made the introduction of state licensing restrictions a high priority through the establishment of AMA-controlled licensing boards and eventually won enough control to deny licensure to graduates from non-AMA-approved colleges, causing them to close down. AMA power to control institutions was particularly strong in the early twentieth century, and they used it to reduce the number of medical schools from 131 in 1910 to 88 in 1920 and 77 in 1939.[31]

Controlling How Healthcare Is Paid For

With the power to decide who could practice medicine established, the AMA went on to dictate how medical services were paid for and by whom.

In the 1920s and 1930s, medicine was becoming increasingly expensive, and many consumers could not afford it. Doctors had long respected the need to treat people who could not afford care and had a variety of pricing schemes in order to do so, which mostly involved having richer people pay more to subsidize the care of low-income people. Still, as medical science deepened, research hospitals became more common, and specializations grew, doctors figured out more efficient and effective ways to organize healthcare to help the poor and improve the quality of care.

In her powerful book on the origins of U.S. health insurance, historian Christy Ford Chapin documents how unions, large businesses, and other private organizations hired doctors on staff or otherwise pooled money from their members to collectively pay for certain medical expenses as needed.[32] This group medical care model was a radical departure from the basic business model supported by the AMA in that it paid doctors a fixed salary—from union or membership dues in some cases—unrelated to the services performed, and thereby exerted much greater control over doctors than they were accustomed to. The basic model had been that doctors worked independently at their own clinics and charged whatever fees they deemed appropriate.

Two examples illustrate the superiority of the cooperative or group model. In 1929, a Lebanese-born doctor named Michael Shadid launched a healthcare cooperative in Elk City, Oklahoma, to better meet the needs of poor agricultural workers and other rural residents. For an entry fee ($50) to build and equip a hospital and a modest annual membership fee ($25), families had access to free clinical and hospital care.[33] An annual fee of $25 in 1929 would have been 4 percent of the average annual income of Americans living at that time. As of 2018, family health insurance costs employers and workers an average of $19,600, which amounts to 37 percent of average income.[34] Over 2,000 families signed up for Shadid's plan and the model spread such that 101 rural cooperatives were in place by 1950. Shadid published books about his philosophy of healthcare, emphasizing that group practice encouraged doctors to share knowledge, discuss cases, and practice preventive medicine, while creating an affordable way for patients to get treatment.[35] Also in 1929, municipal workers in Los Angeles convinced Drs. Donald Ross and Clifford Loos to create a prepaid medical group for roughly 2,000 workers and their families. As Ford Chapin relates, the group created eventually included salaried doctors from different specialties who could all work together to discuss individual cases and make contractual arrangements with hospitals for emergency cases. Thus, for a small fee, all of the patients' healthcare needs could be met in an integrated system that did not require getting referrals from one independent doctor to another and did not rely on arbitrary and unpredictable fee schedules. By 1935, the Ross-Loos clinic had 50 employed doctors and 40,000 patients, a drugstore, a staff library, and a surgery office. Moreover, in additional to salary payments, the doctors were given a percentage of profits. Since revenue depended on attracting and retaining members—and not on providing excessive services—the doctors had a strong incentive to control expenditures by not providing unnecessary procedures, but like independent doctors, they also had a strong incentive to keep patients happy and healthy, so patients would remain paying members.[36]

The AMA opposed these models. At a time when corporations were gaining prominence and employing other professionals—such as engineers—doctors did not like the idea of becoming mere employees under the control of some businessman in either a corporate or government bureaucracy. Although group practices were run by doctors, the doctors did not set the prices of treatments, and AMA leaders worried that groups of doctors would eventually be managed by outsiders if the principle of autonomy wasn't held sacrosanct.

In the 1930s, the AMA launched a systematic campaign to wipe out group practice and preserve the autonomous fee-for-service model. The AMA went so far to as expel Dr. Shadid from membership. This was a clear signal of where it stood on cooperatives, but the conspiracy was far more serious: The AMA lobbied aggressively and successfully to change state laws to make group cooperatives either illegal or effectively impossible to organize.[37]

Similar tactics were used to crush group practice. In 1938, the AMA was indicted by a federal grand jury for violating the Sherman Anti-Trust Act. The AMA and its state affiliates, in this case the Medical Society of the District of Columbia and the Washington Academy of Surgery, conspired to ostracize and coerce any doctors who formed such a group and restrain them from practicing.[38] Ostracism by the AMA was economically fatal to doctors because, with few exceptions, only doctors with AMA membership were allowed to treat patients in hospitals, and AMA members were discouraged from consulting with and making or taking referrals to or from non-AMA members. The net result was that group practice and cooperatives were almost annihilated, while preserving physician autonomy to overcharge patients as they saw fit.

The AMA's hostility to group practice also had an unintended and deeply unfortunate result. Insurance companies and eventually, in the 1960s, the U.S. government began paying for healthcare to deal with the rising costs, but they had to do so according to the AMA's rules, creating a fundamental conflict that still haunts the United States between service providers (practitioners) and payment providers (insurers).

Insurance companies were very reluctant to enter the market, according to Ford Chapin, but were gradually convinced to do so. At first, they viewed health insurance as a losing proposition because they had no way to control doctors—who insisted on total autonomy and fee-for-service payments. Insurance company concerns that fee-for-service payments would encourage the over-provisioning of services have proven valid in the face of careful academic study.[39]

The health insurance model did begin to gain traction, however, as citizens and the government grew increasingly frustrated with the high fees charged by physicians at hospitals and in private practice, especially as reports of billing malfeasance and the use of unnecessary hospital admissions and surgical procedures became widespread. The insurance companies and federal bureaucracies in charge of health insurance responded by subjecting physician billing claims to intense scrutiny and audits. Physicians began spending hours per week on paperwork with the hope of using just the right codes and language to get approval for payment.[40]

Physicians' offices and hospitals now routinely employee people who attend college and obtain certifications in the field of either medical coding—transforming a doctor's notes into billable codes—or medical billing—entering codes into complex insurance-company or government-insurance records systems.[41] According to the U.S. Bureau of Labor Statistics, over 200,000 U.S. adults worked in the occupation of "medical records and health information technician" as of 2017.[42] Another 135,000 workers were classified as "billing and posting clerks" and worked in either physicians' offices or hospitals.[43] The same database reports 666,000 physicians and surgeons, which suggests that one billing professional is required for every two doctors.[44]

Current estimates suggest that U.S. consumers and taxpayers spend 4.6 times as much on healthcare administration as the average resident of a rich country (in the OECD).[45] A detailed comparison between the United States and Canada found that U.S. nurses in physician's offices spend an additional 18 hours per week processing billing codes and claims compared with their Canadian counterparts and administrative staff spend an additional 27 hours per week.[46] Healthcare economists estimate that U.S. residents waste hundreds of billions of dollars per year in administrative expenses that contribute nothing to the quality of care.[47]

Thus, the United States healthcare system exhibits two massive inefficiencies, which when combined, largely explain why U.S. residents spend around twice as much per capita on healthcare as residents of other rich countries without getting higher-quality care: The AMA-supported inefficiency of the fee-for-service system encourages physicians to provide excessive services, while the inefficiency of the claims and billing system forces physicians to waste massive resources on administrative paperwork. The latter is deemed a necessary evil to counteract the bad incentives created by the former. Both problems would have been avoidable if the AMA had allowed cooperatives and group practice to flourish. Unfortunately, the AMA viewed such organizations as competitive threats, and rather than rise to the challenge, the AMA hobbled its competition, with disastrous implications for the country, which now spends 18 cents of every dollar on healthcare services.[48]

Restraining group practice in favor of a fee-for-service insurance model is only one way that the AMA has controlled the development of U.S. healthcare. Another crucial way in which the physician lobby has harmed the public and exacerbated inefficiency in healthcare delivery is by insisting that doctors cannot be employees or even independent contractors of nondoctors. This set of laws is called the *corporate practice of medicine*. In nearly every state—including the largest ones of California, Florida, Texas, and New York—it is against the law for a nondoctor to manage a business that employs doctors.[49] Thus, a brilliant software designer or business management expert with ideas about how to provide healthcare more efficiently is forbidden from raising venture capital money, starting a new model, and scaling it up if it involves the employment of physicians. The only common exception is that hospitals and medical universities are allowed to be managed by nondoctors in many states. The law is justified as a means of removing financial incentives from medical decision-making, but as we've seen, the current model essentially encourages physicians to overcharge patients and insurers, and the AMA has a long history of restricting entry into markets to benefit physicians.

Medical Associations in Other Developed Countries

As noted, healthcare is inordinately expensive in the United States, and while doctors are well paid in every country, they are particularly well paid in the United States, making them the largest source of top-1-percent income earners by occupation—even more than chief executives. Other countries have medical lobbies, but they have not been as influential in steering policies to favor physicians as the AMA.

While the educational requirements for those who wish to become physicians are similar across developed countries, they tend to require fewer years of training outside the United States. Many developed countries do not require that someone first earn a bachelor's degree to enter medical school, as is the case in the United States. Instead, students in Australia, Canada, Ireland, the UK, and the Netherlands can enter medical school straight from secondary school, though that route requires an extra two years compared to those with a four-year degree. On average, that saves two years of formal college instruction. In Italy, the Netherlands, and Canada physicians are not required to spend as many years in post–medical school training, saving what amounts to roughly two years, depending on the specialty.[50]

Similarly, countries outside the United States are often more favorably disposed to professions that compete with physicians. In Canada nurse practitioners practice independently without any need for supervision from physicians.[51] The same is true in Australia and the UK, despite opposition from the Australian Medical Association and the British Medical Association.[52]

In a 1960 book about the British Medical Association (BMA), which is organized like the AMA in many respects but has been far less political, the late Harry Eckstein, a political scientist, wrote:

> The plain fact is that the BMA has lost all the crucial public disputes over medical policy in which it has engaged during this century. Twice the government has passed over BMA opposition legislation affecting the whole structure of medicine—opposition which was intense despite the broad area of agreement between the profession and the government. From this standpoint, the BMA emerges as a political group considerably weaker than the American Medical Association.[53]

It is unclear why the AMA has been so much more effective than its counterparts. One factor may be the decentralized power of American market regulation, which largely rests in the hands of states, not the central government. Doctors and lawyers provide local services and tend to be diffused across cities and counties, and they rarely have to contend with other powerful groups at the local and even state level, whereas pro-consumer and pro-labor interest groups can often successfully mobilize to influence federal regulations. The AMA has blocked federal legislation to expand government healthcare, but in my opinion, as discussed above, its most blatant suppression of competition occurs at the state level.

DENTAL SERVICES

Dentists operating in the United States enjoy income advantages that are almost as large as those of physicians. From 2012 to 2016, 19 percent of dentists were earning incomes that put them in the top one percent. That makes dentists second only to physicians and surgeons in terms of the likelihood of being in the top one percent, among 480 detailed occupational categories. The high wage and salary income translates into substantial wealth. The average home value of dentists is $638,000, which puts them ahead of chief executives and legislators ($621,000).

It is not unusual for countries to impose limitations on the supply of dentists; nor is it unusual for dentist associations to control or at least heavily influence this process. In the Netherlands, for example, the Royal Dutch Dentistry Association helps determine the national quota for the number of students admitted to dental school. As a result, the number of people graduating with the ability to practice dentistry has barely changed over the past three decades. There is a relatively small number of dentists in the Netherlands compared to its overall population, and a large number of people who apply for dental school never gain admission. The Dutch Health Care Authority sets maximum fees that dentists can charge, but they nonetheless enjoy a major earnings advantage—of about $68,000, or 55,000 euros per year—over people who work similar hours and who have similar cognitive performance on a nationwide secondary exam, according to Dutch economists.[54]

In the United States and elsewhere the high earning premium for dentists gives the public strong incentives to shift tasks to other professionals who could provide similar services at a lower cost. Dental hygienists play that role to a large extent, and they require fewer years of postsecondary education. Not surprisingly, the American Dental Association has aggressively lobbied to block dental hygienists from opening their own clinics and practicing without their supervision.[55] As a result, there are many services that dental hygienists are not allowed to perform despite possessing the requisite training, or that they can perform only under various levels of supervision.[56] For example, in 41 states and the District of Columbia, dental hygienists cannot administer local anesthesia without a dentist on site, and in Texas, they cannot administer under any circumstances.[57] Only a small number of states permit dental hygienists to provide services to patients without supervision by a dentist, even in schools, hospitals, and long-term care facilities, where having a dentist on staff would be prohibitively expensive.

Seeing a need for lower-cost access to dental services, Alaska, Minnesota, and Maine have created a new dental therapist license, which permits dental professionals with similar training to that of a dental hygienist to provide basic preventative dental care. With pioneering efforts credited to New Zealand, one 2012 report finds that 54 countries use dental therapists as auxiliary providers of oral healthcare, usually in public school settings.[58] Despite the obvious and well-documented public health benefits of such programs, the American Dental Association has stridently opposed efforts to grant legal status to these practitioners.[59]

One reason why dentists have successfully blocked their competitors is that they are given broad powers to decide what constitutes the practice of dentistry and prevent nondentists from performing those activities. In one example, the Federal Trade Commission—which is charged with protecting the public from uncompetitive business practices—successfully won a case in the U.S. Supreme Court against the North Carolina Board of Dental Examiners. The board was stacked with practicing dentists—as most licensing boards are—and used that power to crack down on the provision of teeth-whitening services by nondentists after dentists complained to the board about losing business to more affordable competitors.[60]

LEGAL SERVICES

Given the training and skill requirements, it is not surprising that lawyers tend to receive relatively high compensation compared to other professions. Yet, as with doctors, dentists, and financial-sector workers, both straightforward evidence (examining pay as it relates to education or cognitive ability) and advanced statistical analysis (controlling for even unobserved skills) show that lawyers are overpaid, even after accounting for their skills.[61]

Comparable international data on lawyers is difficult to find, but the Luxembourg Income Study provides information on incomes for lawyers in a handful of countries and further provides earnings in a number of countries for "legal, social, and cultural professionals," which includes lawyers, librarians, social scientists, authors, and journalists.[62] These data indicate that lawyers and related professionals are often highly likely to be top income earners and comprise a substantial share of top income earners in many countries. In Luxembourg, legal, social, and cultural professionals comprise 18.2 percent of top earners. In the United States, the narrower category of lawyers and judges comprises 7.7 percent, which is the highest in the Luxembourg Database for narrowly defined lawyers. Indeed, the probability of a lawyer being a top-1-percent income earner is higher in the United States (at 14.2 percent) than in any other country that reports lawyers narrowly. Though lower, the top-1-percent rate is also high in Germany and Denmark, where 12 percent and 10 percent, respectively, of lawyers are top earners. Yet, it is not inevitable that lawyers are concentrated at the top of the income distribution. In the Netherlands, Finland, and Switzerland, very few top earners (5 percent or less) are in the broad category of "legal, social, and cultural professionals." This variation suggests that country-specific institutions and political factors shape the compensation of lawyers (table 9.3).

An OECD report on professional service competition notes that lawyers benefit from a monopoly on representing clients in court in almost every OECD country, and in many, they also have a monopoly on providing paid legal advice or applying for patents. In some countries, lawyers are required even to make routine real estate transactions or deal with the allocation of assets following the death of a family member.[63]

Notably, Finland and Sweden have the least restrictions on the provision of legal services among developed countries. In Sweden, nonlawyers can represent defendants in court, and that was also true in Finland until 2002.[64] In both countries, a license is not required to provide legal advice, tax advice, or patent filing, which is also the case in the Netherlands. In the United Kingdom, Belgium, Ireland, and Italy nonlawyers may provide tax advice. In Austria, Denmark, France, Germany, Greece, Luxembourg, Portugal, Spain, and the United States, only lawyers can represent people in court or provide legal advice.[65] Notably, lawyers appear to be less prevalent among top income earners in Finland and the Netherlands, where markets are more open, compared to the United States, Luxembourg, Denmark, Germany, and Spain.

The Control of Legal Services in the United States

The American Bar Association (ABA) was developed, in part, with the worthy aim of raising the quality of legal services in the United States, but from

Table 9.3. Probability of lawyers being in top 1 percent of income earners, by country

Country	Title	Year of data collection	Percentage of lawyers who are top-1% earners	Percentage of top-1% earners who are lawyers
Luxembourg	Legal, social, cultural professions	2013	14.3%	18.2%
United States	Lawyers and judges	2012–2016	14.2%	7.7%
Germany	Lawyers	2013	12.1%	6.6%
Denmark	Lawyers	2013	9.7%	2.5%
Estonia	Lawyers	2013	7.1%	2.0%
Uruguay	Lawyers	2013	5.7%	2.9%
Poland	Legal, social, cultural professions	2013	5.7%	8.8%
Spain	Legal, social, cultural professions	2013	5.6%	13.6%
Israel	Lawyers	2012	5.0%	7.8%
Russia	Lawyers	2013	4.7%	4.9%
Ireland	Legal, social, cultural professions	2010	2.6%	9.4%
Czech Republic	Legal, social, cultural professions	2013	2.1%	3.3%
Greece	Legal, social, cultural professions	2013	2.1%	5.4%
Switzerland	Legal, social, cultural professions	2013	1.4%	4.6%
Austria	Legal, social, cultural professions	2013	1.2%	3.8%
Finland	Legal, social, cultural professions	2013	0.8%	5.1%
Netherlands	Legal, social, cultural professions	2013	0.8%	5.3%

Sources: All data is from the Luxembourg Income Study, except for the United States. Those data are from IPUMS USA. Luxembourg Income Study (LIS) Database, http://www.lisdatacenter.org (multiple countries; run May 24, 2017–June 17, 2017). Luxembourg: LIS.

its beginning it also had the destructive and harmful goal of raising the cost of becoming a lawyer and limiting competition for existing lawyers. The second goal is in direct conflict with the public good but highly valuable to lawyers, and so the ABA's efforts have resulted in unreasonable limitations on legal practice. The seductive power of the second goal has, in fact, overwhelmed even the first. Little effort is made by the ABA to provide the public with information about the quality of legal services or even the quality of law schools.

If the ABA really wanted students to get the best-possible legal training, it would publish a user-friendly database that would allow people to assess the quality of law schools. This could entail releasing data at the institutional level on bar-exam passage rates by state as well as more sophisticated metrics that adjust for the difficulty of state exams and take into account differences in test scores and income of entering students. It could even collect and report data from alumni surveys, with basic questions on a Likert scale such as "How would you rate the quality of your legal education?" or "How likely would you be to recommend your law school to others?"

If the ABA wanted the public to employ the best lawyers, it would create a website that would allow an individual to more readily find a lawyer who is the right match for him or her. Nothing is stopping the ABA from creating a searchable website that allows the public to find licensed lawyers by their specialty, discover when they obtained their license, and maybe even where they attended law school. Lawyers could even enter resume-like information highlighting their accomplishments and experience—even their hourly rates. Of course, the ABA does not do any of this—nor does the AMA.

By contrast, if you want to hire a domestic worker, companies such as Care .com allow you to make these sorts of comparisons. If you want a designer, you can use something like 99 Designs to have designers bid for your project and submit prototypes. Websites such as Upwork are designed for a broad range of professionals—including accountants and software developers. You will not, however, find lawyers and doctors on these websites.

Instead, the ABA focuses its considerable resources and energy on ensuring that the public continues to transfer a large and excessive share of income to lawyers. It does this in several ways. First, the ABA's actions support a high barrier to entering the profession. To practice law one must graduate from an accredited law school and pass a state-specific bar exam that usually does not allow one to practice outside that state. In 2015, 59 percent of exam takers passed in the average state.[66] Aside from the anti-competitive issues raised by the bar exam, the Society of American Law Teachers points out that it is deeply flawed in several other dimensions. According to the society, the test measures one's ability to memorize a wide swath of legal principles and procedures, but it does not test the skills actually used by lawyers, which include research. It would be considered malpractice to give a client advice based solely on memory, without performing legal research, but the test does not demand competency in this area.[67] Unsurprisingly, passage rates are lower for lower-income groups, who are less likely to be able to afford a bar exam class or devote many hours to preparation for the exam.

Second, the ABA defines the practice of law in an expansive way such that even mundane services require a licensed legal attorney. For example, some states actually require an attorney to be physically present when the deed of a house is transferred, whereas others require attorneys to prepare the documentation.[68] In any case, this raises the costs of "closing" on a house significantly, regardless of the fact that the tasks involved require very specific bureaucratic knowledge but in no way require a comprehensive grasp of American legal matters—much less the passage of a bar exam. If it were up to the ABA, the situation would be even worse, because not only would such services require an attorney, they would require high and fixed prices. In 1975, plaintiffs purchasing a home in Virginia won a lawsuit against the Virginia Bar Association for inflating the price of title examinations. The Bar Association had been publishing pricing guidelines for such services and disciplining members if they did not adhere to those prices.[69]

Third, the ABA, like many of its international counterparts, prevents nonlawyers from operating legal services firms. The American Bar Association's Model Rules of Professional Conduct prohibit nonlawyers from owning or even managing law firms, as well as preventing lawyers from sharing fees with nonlawyers.[70] This is the law prevailing in every state, though not in the District of Columbia, where nonlawyers may have an ownership stake in a legal services firm.[71] Outside of the United States, Australia has allowed nonlawyers to own law firms since 2001, and England and Wales since 2007. Other European countries allow nonlawyers to own a minority stake.[72] As with rules barring the corporate practice of medicine, the stated goal is to preserve the integrity and independence of legal judgment and advice, but, like the corporate practice of medicine prohibitions, the idea that the practice of law would be corrupted if lawyers had to work for a nonlawyer is specious. Law firms owned by lawyers face just as much pressure to make money as law firms owned by entrepreneurs who are not lawyers. In effect, the rule ensures that ownership profits related to legal services are appropriated exclusively by lawyers, and it mitigates potential downward pressure on fees that more efficient business organizations might create.

Unmet Legal Needs

The American public does not seem to think highly of lawyers. Since 1976, Gallup has asked a random sample of U.S. adults to say how they would rate "the honesty and ethical standards of people in these fields."[73] Lawyers are consistently ranked near the bottom. The highest percentage of U.S. adults who answer "high" or "very high" with respect to lawyers has never been more than 27 percent; it stood at 19 percent in the latest poll from 2018. By contrast, 84 percent of U.S. adults rate the honesty and ethical standards of nurses as at least "high," and roughly two out of three give that rating to medical doctors, pharmacists, military officers, and teachers at high school and grade school levels. Even with the high-profile controversies over policing discussed in the previous chapter, 54 percent of U.S. adults rate police officers as having high or very high honesty and ethical standards.

This negative reputation of lawyers is unfortunate because legal services are massively important and often under-sought and under-provided. The legal community has long known that low- and moderate-income individuals are particularly likely to have unmet civil legal needs. Legal needs, in this sense, are defined as noncriminal situations that involve possible violations of rights or responsibilities recognized by laws, where a person might benefit from legal advice or action.

A major survey by the American Bar Association in 1992 concluded that approximately half of low- and moderate-income U.S. residents faced a noncriminal (or "civil") legal need during the year.[74] The most-common legal needs involved consumer financial problems, such as problems with creditors, taxing authorities, or insurance companies or inability to obtain credit or tax; housing problems, such as unsafe or problematic living conditions; and domestic problems, such as divorce mediation or disputes over childcare support. Seventy-one percent of low-income households and 61 percent of moderate-income households with legal needs did not take formal legal action, citing cost concerns as one of the most important reasons.

More recently, in 2003, Washington State published a landmark study with an improved methodology, which found that roughly 80 percent of low-income Washington households experienced at least one situation that would call for noncriminal legal counsel within a year; most had multiple needs. In all but 15 percent of cases, low-income people confronted their noncriminal legal challenges without help from an attorney, according to the study.[75] A 2015 follow-up study found similar results.[76] Efforts to measure unmet civil legal needs in the UK have reached similar conclusions.[77]

Additionally, the functioning of the criminal justice system is greatly hindered by inadequate funding. Most criminals cannot afford attorneys, and the public defenders—to whom they are entitled—are massively overburdened, understaffed, and underpaid, as the ABA and U.S. government have long admitted.[78] Simple and routine cases drag on for years, holding even innocent people's lives in forced abeyance, while delaying justice for both victims and guilty parties.

Though the problem is national, Washington is arguably the only U.S. state to take substantial action to tackle this issue. First of all, it is one of a small number of states that allows nonattorneys to prepare and complete legal documents related to real estate transactions. Since 1983, the Washington State Supreme Court has allowed "limited practice officers" to do this, after passing an exam and obtaining the appropriate license, whereas most states require a licensed attorney.[79] Since then, it has taken even more radical action, with far-reaching implications, but the opposition to the court reveals the power of professional elites to preserve their economic privileges and explains why these changes have not occurred elsewhere in the United States.

In 2001, the Washington State Supreme Court created the Practice of Law Board to investigate the unauthorized practice of law, advise the state court and legal community, and recommend ways to increase access to legal services.[80] The board was administered and funded by the Washington State Bar Association, and in 2006 it proposed the creation of legal technicians who could provide some limited legal services, after completing at least an associate's degree in relevant legal studies, passing various exams, and working under the supervision of a lawyer.[81] The proposal was rejected by the Washington State Bar Association's board of governors in 2006 and again in 2008, after revisions. Perhaps as a result, the state Supreme Court repeatedly delayed votes.

Many lawyers in Washington and California, which was also considering a similar policy, wrote letters or otherwise publicly criticized the proposal. The criticisms reveal the low regard that elite professionals have for those who have not gone through their same level of training: "The class of individuals described is not going to have the competency to actually do for the poor what needs to be done," one partner in a Washington law firm argued. "The state bar proposal now under consideration would simply give the veneer of legality to these unauthorized, ill-trained practitioners who do more damage than good," argued a California lawyer about a similar proposal in his state.[82]

Finally, in 2012, the Washington State Supreme Court adopted the recommendation and created a Limited License Legal Technician (LLLT), who is licensed to provide legal counsel and prepare legal documents but not represent clients in court or negotiate on their behalf.[83] Currently the license is applicable only to domestic legal affairs, such as divorce and child support and custody issues, but the plan is to gradually expand the scope. Importantly, the LLLT's educational requirements are far more streamlined, and similar to those of a paralegal, with a few additional steps.

In the Seattle, Washington, metropolitan area, the average lawyer earns a salary of $139,000, compared to $64,200 for a paralegal, so the LLLT license has the power to overcome many of the cost barriers that currently deter people from seeking legal assistance.[84] Divorce mediation, to offer but one example, is an important legal service that an LLLT can provide and save a household thousands of dollars. The mediator serves an important function by guiding a divorcing couple through the various issues they are likely to confront, such as childcare arrangements and the allocation of financial assets and responsibilities. The mediator helps them reach a solution that is mutually aggreeable and able to withstand scrutiny from a judge in divorce court. These issues can be complex and contentious, but they do not require years of case study or courtroom experience. Rather, the issues require someone who is skilled at understanding and addressing people's concerns, walking them through various options, and condensing the final information into a fairly standardized and routine document.

After its members proposed the LLLT to the Supreme Court, the state bar association's Board of Governors reportedly voted to defund and eliminate the Practice of Law Board, according to the Practice of Law Board's former members.[85] In an open letter to the Washington State Supreme Court, the chairman and three other board members resigned in protest, stating that "the Washington State Bar Association has a long record of opposing efforts that threaten to undermine its monopoly on the delivery of legal services."[86]

The LLLT program is not old enough and the number of licensees not large enough for the sort of detailed studies that compare nurse practitioners to physicians, but qualitative evidence gathered by scholars at the National Center for State Courts and the American Bar Foundation contradicts the elitist concerns raised by lawyers opposed to the license. The authors interviewed

13 of the 15 LLLTs who had been licensed and several of their clients and colleagues. They concluded that "clients uniformly reported that the LLLTs provided competent assistance" and that their "legal outcomes were improved by utilizing the services of the LLLTs." The authors recommended that the program be expanded to other states.[87] Roughly a year after that report was published, the number of LLLTs doubled in Washington, where there are presently 30 people with LLLT licenses in Washington, according to the state bar association directory.[88]

FINANCIAL SERVICES RESERVED FOR THE RICH

Any study of income inequality in the United States must take into account the role of the financial sector and the fact that most of the inordinate income gains go to those working in securities, commodity contracts, and investments.

In 2016, average compensation for all workers in the United States was $75,000, but more than three times that amount for workers in the securities and investment industry ($255,000). That makes it by far the highest-paid industry.[89] Compensation is even well ahead of other high-paying industries such as oil and gas ($202,000), as well as tech industries, including information and data-processing services ($155,000), software and other publishing ($149,000), computer and electronics manufacturing ($138,000), and professional, scientific, and technical services ($111,000). In fact, workers in the securities and investment industry are paid more than double what workers in banking are paid, which is just $97,000.

Data from the Census Bureau from 2012 to 2016 shows that the securities and investment industry had the highest percentage of workers in the top one percent (10.5 percent); that is notably higher than the medical (7.8 percent) and legal professionals (7.7 percent), which were the second- and third-highest paying, respectively, although those two accounted for a larger absolute number of top earners as a result of their larger base of workers.[90] It is also worth noting that workers in the consumer banking industry are rarely in the top one percent (only 2.4 percent).

Investment banks and hedge funds make up the majority of businesses in the securities and investment industry. At Goldman Sachs, one of the highest-paying firms in the industry, average compensation per worker in 2016 was

$339,000.[91] But even Goldman's extraordinary compensation falls below estimates for the median hedge fund, where median salaries after bonus payments amount to $350,000.[92] The average would be substantially higher. In fact, large investment banks were increasingly integrated with hedge funds until the regulatory changes that followed the Great Recession made it difficult for firms such as Goldman Sachs to operate hedge funds. Now, Goldman collects fees to refer clients to hedge funds, often those managed by former Goldman employees who broke away after the regulatory changes.[93]

I have come to believe that these extraordinary salaries exist only because of very specific regulations that both shelter hedge funds fees from market competition and prevent mutual funds from using the same strategies.[94] Skill alone doesn't explain the high salaries, because workers with the same or higher levels of skill in other industries are paid less. Instead, there are good reasons to believe that hedge funds and investment banks are operating in a market that is fundamentally not competitive.[95]

To be sure, like doctors and lawyers, workers at investment banks— including JPMorgan, Goldman Sachs, Morgan Stanley, and Credit Suisse— possess specialized and valuable skills. They provide extremely complex services to large, sophisticated clients, such as multinational corporations, start-ups in the midst of an initial public offering, massive pension funds, university endowments, and governments. The richest and largest clients of investment banks genuinely benefit from the expertise that these firms possess. The fact that financial-sector workers who serve large organizations earn relatively high salaries compared to workers with no specialized knowledge or education is not itself a scandal. The problem is that the size of the salary advantage is disproportionate to the value of the underlying skills and thus serves as a tax on the economy, as I will explain.

In analyzing finance, it is important to distinguish between the activities that serve institutions and rich investors and those that serve ordinary individuals. In contrast to investment banks, the big retail banks do not make vast profits from the basic routine transactions that retail consumers conduct on a regular basis—such as getting a home loan, refinancing a mortgage, buying and selling stocks, or maintaining a checking account. Those are relatively low-profit-margin activities. With appropriate regulation and oversight to protect against fraud and abuse—which was missing during the housing bubble—people can readily get these financial products at a reasonably low cost. Evidence for this comes from the U.S. Bureau of Economic Analysis

Table 9.4. Change in prices of various goods and services, 1980–2016, in the United States

	Price index 2016/ Price index 1980
All goods and services	2.5
Goods	1.5
Electronic equipment and media	0
Motor vehicles and parts	1.7
Clothing and footwear	1.1
Services	3.4
Housing	3.6
Healthcare	4.8
Financial services	1.8
Communication	1.4
Higher education	11.4
Legal, accounting, and other professional services	5.7

Source: U.S. Bureau of Economic Analysis, Table 2.4.4. Price Indexes for Personal Consumption Expenditures by Type of Product.

(table 9.4). The price of financial services has been rising more slowly than overall inflation—in sharp contrast to other services such as housing, healthcare, education, and legal services.

Financial services prices have faced downward pressure for two reasons: The first is information technology—including automated teller machines and online banking, which have streamlined access, increased competition, and lowered costs; the second is the deregulation of banking within and across states, which occurred largely from the 1970s through the 1990s.

Up until the 1970s, most states prohibited banks headquartered in other states from opening branches. One reason for this is that state taxing authorities could charge charter fees and often owned part of the banks, and so competition from banks from other states weakened their tax base. States also prohibited branching within their own state, so that their preferred banks could benefit from monopoly prices. Technological changes—including telephone banking—allowed customers to bank outside their local areas, and this and information technology helped create pressure for reform.[96] The economics literature generally finds that these regulatory reforms benefited economic performance by improving the quality of banking services.[97]

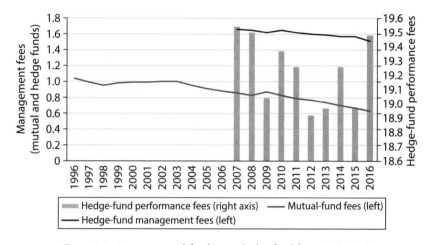

Figure 9.1. Average mutual-fund versus hedge-fund fees, 1996–2016

Sources: Mutual-fund fees expressed as expense ratio for long-term funds using data from Collins, Sean, and James Duvall. 2017. "Trends in the Expenses and Fees of Funds, 2016." *ICI Research Perspective* 23, no. 3 (May). Available at www.ici.org/pdf/per23-03.pdf. Hedge-fund fee data are from Preqin Hedge Fund Online. Available at http://docs.preqin.com/newsletters/hf/Preqin-HFSL -March-2017-Hedge-Fund-Fees.pdf.

Beyond retail banking, retail investment fees have plummeted. In 1996, for every $1,000 the average person invested in a stock-based mutual fund, he or she had to pay 1 percent each year, or $10. That's not outrageously high but adds up over time. With the rise of low-cost funds such as Vanguard—which was started in 1975 by John Bogle, a champion of the common investor—and other index funds with little or no active management, that fee steadily declined. As of 2016, the average mutual fund takes just .63 percent, or $6.30 (figure 9.1). Moreover, for a Vanguard fund that gives a return based on the 500 largest publicly traded companies in the United States, the cost is just 0.04 percent, or $0.40 per year.[98]

Remarkably, nothing like this has occurred for hedge funds. Fees are roughly the same now as they were when modern hedge funds were invented in the 1950s and are orders of magnitude higher than fees for mutual funds, because hedge funds take a much larger percentage of an initial investment (close to 2 percent) and a massive share of the profits from investment (close to 20 percent).

The first modern hedge fund was credited to Alfred Winslow Jones, a former financial journalist turned investor, who got the idea in 1949. He charged his investors 20 percent of profits, which ended up being substantial.[99] Mutual funds are not even allowed to charge a performance fee. How is it possible that mutual funds are so much cheaper than hedge funds? The answer lies in the only meaningful difference between the two.

A fund, first of all, is an investment portfolio managed by a firm. "Hedge fund" is not a legal term, but refers to a fund that is less regulated than other funds, with the core distinction being that only rich individuals—those with $1 million in assets or an annual income of $200,000 or more for at least two years—or institutional investors (e.g., pension funds, university endowments) can invest.[100] These eligible investors are known legally as *accredited investors*, and in addition to hedge funds, they have access to private equity and venture capital markets that are not available to those who are not wealthy. This means they can buy stocks of companies that are not publicly traded or buy stocks before a company goes public or gets acquired.

Moreover, private funds—hedge funds or otherwise—that explicitly refuse money from anyone except the very rich are automatically exempt from most securities regulations. These investors—called *qualified purchasers*— must have a net worth of $5 million or more.[101] Indeed, these investors are preferred by hedge funds because hedge funds are allowed to charge them performance fees, not just management fees.[102]

So, a hedge fund is like a normal fund, except it can do almost anything it wants and is available only to rich people or large investment organizations. This regulatory advantage allows hedge funds to take more risk and use a variety of strategies unavailable to mutual funds. The main advantage is the use of leverage, which means using borrowed money and in some cases borrowed money that greatly exceeds the firm's assets by many multiples. This is a huge advantage, which is why hedge funds outperform traditional funds.[103]

A large study of global hedge funds from 1994 to 2011 calculated the yearly average return on investment as just over 9 percent, after fees, compared with 7 percent for stocks and 6 percent for bonds.[104] For large investments, two to three percentage points means millions if not billions of dollars. And for an individual investor, that premium is also substantial, even with the large fee.

Leverage—the ability to borrow in order to invest—is so advantageous because paying back a loan is cheap compared to a great investment strategy. Say you have you a good investment strategy that can easily scale into the millions—buying or shorting commodities, for example—and you expect a return of 20 percent. Let's compare a hedge fund to a mutual fund for a fund with $1 million in investments from individuals.

The mutual fund uses exactly the same strategy as the hedge fund but can't borrow, so its return is simply 20 percent of $1 million, or $200,000. The mutual fund earns 1 percent from management fees for a profit of $10,000. The hedge fund, however, gets a loan from some big bank for $100 million at 3 percent interest. At the end of the year, it pays the bank $3 million, but has turned the $1 million investment into $17.2 million in gains. The hedge fund managers get $20,000 in management fees plus $3.4 million in performance fees. That's why hedge fund managers are so rich. So, why doesn't competition among hedge funds drive down the price of management fees? I believe there are two reasons.

First, the Securities and Exchange Commission (SEC) made it illegal for hedge funds to advertise before 2013.[105] The implication is that rich people and institutional investors had a hard time finding "better deals." There was no reason for any one fund to lower its prices, because the anti-advertising rule would have blocked it from using its lower prices to attract more investors. The SEC justified the rule as a way to protect consumers, but the commission made a huge mistake. The prevention of advertising is really a way to keep consumers in the dark and encourage price collusion. The mutual fund price drop shows what could have happened. Mutual funds fees are public knowledge and easily found, and companies such as Vanguard advertise those low fees regularly.

The second reason that hedge funds fees have remained so high is that most of the payments of those fees are indirect, from institutional investors. Institutional investors manage money from ordinary people, such as union workers and various retirement funds. Data from the SEC show that pension funds are the largest owners of hedge funds.[106] If one excludes other private funds—which include hedge funds and are also owned primarily by pension funds—and unclassified investors, over two-thirds of hedge-fund ownership comes from the following: private pension funds (such as those collected for union members), state or municipal pension funds, sovereign wealth funds, SEC-regulated funds (such as mutual funds), or nonprofits, such as university endowments. The managers of these funds have very little incentive to push down fees. Using SEC data, I estimate that only 20 percent of the ownership stake in hedge funds is attributable to individuals.

Institutional investors who manage pension funds cannot charge their clients fees based on performance; their revenue is based on how much money they manage. Thus, they have almost no incentive to negotiate with hedge funds for lower performance or management fees, unless their client—a union or a state government bureaucrat—threatens to replace them for poor performance. Since hedge funds often "beat the market," no one seems to notice or care if huge percentages are siphoned away.

In short, the problem is that institutional investors are managing other people's money with no "skin in the game," to borrow a relevant phrase from Nassim Taleb.[107] Just as healthcare consumers have little incentive to haggle with their doctor over the cost of a surgery paid for by an insurer, so a pension-fund manager has no incentive to tell a hedge-fund manager to stop unnecessarily gouging his clients so he can buy another painting from the Italian Renaissance for his summer mansion.

As of 2017, private, state, and municipal pensions had roughly $686 billion invested in hedge funds, according to SEC data. If the hedge funds earned a 10 percent return, which is near the historical average, the pension plans would have given the hedge funds $161 billion over the next year at average prevailing fees.[108] By contrast, if the pension plans had negotiated the fees down to mutual-fund levels, they would have had to pay only $4 billion over the year. Say hedge-fund performance fees could be negotiated down to 5 percent (from 19.5 percent) with the same elevated 1.5 percent management fee. That would result in roughly $100 billion in annual savings for pension holders and would represent a massive redistribution of capital income from elite professionals to ordinary workers.

Mutual funds could never get away with these expenses—even if they could charge performance fees—because individual "retail" investors are often heavily involved in picking them and the prices and fees are transparent, even openly advertised.

The bottom line is that the SEC's authentic but misplaced concern for ordinary Americans has resulted in the wholesale transfer of trillions of dollars from plumbers, pipefitters, teachers, automakers, and families with retirement accounts to super-elite billionaires. Rich investors, like other elite professionals, are given privileged access to markets.

In sum, then, the largest and richest groups among elite income earners in the United States benefit greatly from specific unjust laws. This political arrangement results in the mundane redistribution of money from the bottom 99 percent of income earners to the top one percent and is unrelated to the things that scholars often attribute to the causes of inequality: skills, technology, and globalization.

10

Creating a Just Society

THE ARGUMENT, RESTATED

Humans are endowed with an innate sense of fairness and reciprocity. Though shaped by history and culture, this understanding and appreciation of fairness is broadly shared across societies. The only consistently approved violation of reciprocity found across cultures is a preference to give the interests of the worst off greater weight. Sympathy for the plight of those who are suffering, whether their circumstances are the result of bad luck or not, has evidently proven beneficial to communities throughout the world and across time, likely by strengthening solidarity. These innate tendencies, which provide the evolutionary and cultural foundations for a just society, were forged in relatively egalitarian communities, according to the best efforts of scholars to measure inequality in the hunter-gather societies that characterized roughly 90 percent of human history.[1]

Yet, the world is profoundly unequal politically and economically, even in democratic countries such as the United States with universal suffrage and robust civil rights. Health and income are highly unequal across racial and ethnic groups, social class, and occupation. Moreover, after declining during the middle of the twentieth century, income inequality has grown in the United States and most developed countries.

There are many theories as to why inequality is large and persistent and why it has recently increased in rich democracies: fundamental differences between racial and ethnic groups, globalization, trade, immigration, technological changes. On both the Left and the Right, it is assumed that free exchange ("markets") naturally generates inequality, either because the fundamental source of productivity varies dramatically between individuals (and groups) or because business owners exploit workers. There are deep flaws with each of these theories, as I have discussed in earlier chapters.

First, racial diversity predicts higher income inequality across developed countries, and it is no coincidence that the United States stands out among rich democracies as having excessive inequality and that it relied heavily on slave labor for much of its history. Any theory of inequality that ignores race is fundamentally flawed.

Race is essential to the analysis of inequality in income and social status because racial prejudice provided the ideological and cultural justification for denying people of recent African ancestry basic liberties. Even after the end of slavery in the United States, African Americans were denied political equality in three fundamental ways: disenfranchisement, unequal access to public goods, and severe restrictions on their participation in markets. The first of these three was corrected with the end of Jim Crow and the civil rights movement, but the second two, while affected by the civil rights movement, persist to this day, as I demonstrated in chapters 6, 7, and 8. Black people are denied the equal provision of education and policing services, and they are denied participation in housing markets. The restriction on participation in housing markets applies to many non-rich Americans regardless of race, but zoning laws emerged in such a way so as to disproportionately regulate and curtail the residency of black people. Given the power of neighborhoods in shaping economic opportunity, the oppressive regulation of housing markets by local factions of mostly white homeowners is a profound injustice that runs through all spheres of American economic and social life.

As for changes in the income distribution, if high and rising inequality was primarily the result of great innovations and entrepreneurial success that benefited the public broadly but allowed certain economic stars to get rich, it would arguably be of little concern. This does not characterize the situation in the United States for several reasons. First, most individuals in the top one percent of income earners are not innovators: They have not invented products or systems, and the services that they sell—financial, medical, or legal—have not raised the value to cost ratio for society. Second, rising inequality has not caused a surge in economic growth. Rising inequality has coincided with—and perhaps even contributed to—a slowdown in productivity growth. As economist Robert Gordon has shown, the last few decades have been characterized by weak productivity growth and lackluster innovation, relative to the 100-year period lasting from 1870 to 1970.[2] It cannot be true that the top one percent have only been reaping gains from their own innovations—because the innovations that have actually materialized have been of little economic value.

Thus, across most rich democracies, slow economic growth combined with rising inequality has resulted in very weak income growth for ordinary people. In many of these countries far-right nationalist politicians and, in some cases, far-left populist politicians have gained traction with middle-income voters whose financial circumstances have not improved nearly as much as those of professional elites.

Slow growth and rising inequality are linked to the same underlying cause: the rise of the service industries as a share of production (as opposed to manufacturing, energy, and agriculture) and the glaring inefficiencies in elite professional services, which are created by their powerful interest groups. Across the developed world, a disproportionate percentage of the gains from economic growth are going to elite professionals, and inequality is highly correlated with the overpayment of elite professionals. As I have shown, merit—genes, intelligence, and work ethic—does not explain why elite professionals are doing so well. There is an alternative explanation: the influence of the professional associations, and in finance, the influence of regulators, who defer to the industry. As the economic theorist Mancur Olson famously argued, interest groups—such as lobbying associations—can often win against the interests of the public because they have strong incentives to take "collective action," or to shape the laws that affect their members, so they will invest heavily in doing so.[3] For the average citizen, any one industry or product is a very small factor in his or her life, accounting for but a modest fraction of expenses and absorbing even less as a matter for concern and attention. In short, we are all busy with our families, friends, work, and lives and can't possibly guard against distortions to markets for this or that product or service, unless it is how we make a living. Thus, lobbying associations present their arguments to legislatures largely unopposed, and the arguments seem even more convincing when they are accompanied by campaign donations, as they typically are.

In a recent book, Steven Teles and Brink Lindsey update and extend Olson's argument to point out the way in which the economy is "captured" by interest groups, including homeowners' associations that oppose open housing markets; large banks that lobby for bailouts and regulations that make it impossible for small banks to compete with them; and pharmaceutical companies that lobby for patent rules that preserve their monopoly rights for vital medicines and allow them to charge as much as insurance companies can bear to pay.[4] They point to the need for countervailing forces that represent the public, as well as well-staffed professional legislative teams and analytic organizations that are sophisticated enough to see through and challenge the arguments of lobbyists.

I agree with these points and offer my own vision for what specifically should be changed to make democracies more just and egalitarian. I focus on the United States because it is the country I know best, but I view these proposals as having much broader applications.

THE NEED FOR INSTITUTIONS THAT OPERATE
IN THE PUBLIC INTEREST

U.S. leaders across political parties have called for smarter regulations. In 2011, President Obama signed Executive Order 13563, which states: "[The regulatory system] must identify and use the best, most innovative, and least burdensome tools for achieving regulatory ends."[5] The Progressive Policy Institute, a think tank, has sensibly proposed creating a federal regulatory improvement commission to address regulatory accumulation, and a current bill in the Senate would create such a commission.[6] Another proposal from the Brookings Institution would create a permanent Congressional Regulation Office, complementing the work of the Congressional Budget Office.[7]

Of course, reforming regulations does not mean eliminating them. Markets cannot function without rules. Regulations should be designed to make markets function optimally. In the early twentieth century, "muckraking" journalists such as Ida Tarbell inspired the creation of the Federal Trade Commission and antitrust legislation by documenting how large corporations were distorting markets by eliminating competition and raising prices on consumers.[8] Today, the Federal Trade Commission and other regulatory bodies serve the public and enhance productivity by advocating for competition in healthcare and other markets.[9] The capacity and influence of these bodies should be strengthened and their scope expanded.

The much-maligned media also needs to be strengthened, as the example of Ida Tarbell indicates. Challenges to collective business interests are likely to fail unless accompanied by focused public attention. Sometimes, it must be said, the interests of businesses also need to be defended against a misinformed public. The internet and social media companies have weakened newspapers by eliminating much of their advertising revenue. Solutions must involve finding new ways for high-quality news to be identified, recognized, and financially supported by a broad cross-section of interests so that no one funding source (e.g., government, industry, or philanthropist) can exert dominance on the news.

Crucially, the above institutions also need to be in place in state and local governments. Presently, a little bit of lobbying money—and organizational expertise—can go a long way in influencing state legislators or city council members. It is not an exaggeration to suggest that state professional licensing laws and market-access regulations are written largely by the most powerful member associations. Likewise, homeowner associations often mobilize opposition to affordable housing projects or zoning reforms. For these reasons, states need their own institutions to seek out and challenge laws or political efforts that distort markets at the expense of the public.

MARKET-ACCESS REFORMS OF SPECIFIC INDUSTRIES

Because industry-specific rules have been distorted by the shared interests of those most affected, the solutions to income inequality must also be industry-specific. The overarching theme of these reforms is to open markets so that currently prohibited mutually beneficial exchanges are allowed to take place.

For workers, market access means allowing nonelite professionals to offer goods and services that they are appropriately trained to offer. Their training is appropriate if it allows them to consistently and reliably provide the service. While some take a dim view of all licensing, especially the licensing of nonelite professions, licensing laws do afford important protections to buyers, which elevates market efficiency, and the introduction of licensing restrictions often predicts greater entry, especially for women and black people in the United States, as sociologist Beth Redbird's analysis concludes, because it clarifies the skills, credentials, and pathway needed to gain entry.[10] The challenge with such rules is to make sure they are relevant to legitimate concerns about quality and do not systematically block beneficial exchanges.

For consumers, market access means being free to buy the goods or services from foreign or domestic providers that can reliably provide those products at the highest quality-to-cost ratio that consumers are willing to pay for. As a result, incomes go up, because real income is nothing more than purchasing power. Opening up markets to greater foreign or domestic competition tends to accelerate business closings (and often openings), but when citizens are empowered by education and training, they readily find new work. Since eliminating foreign and domestic competition would be a disaster for the least off—who, like everyone else but more so, benefit greatly from innovation and greater purchasing power—trade protectionism is immoral from the perspective of justice. Layoffs are often damaging, but employers, unions, training institutions, and regional and federal policymakers can and should work cooperatively to ease transitions for workers to another job or a new field. One challenge that must be overcome is the high and rapidly growing cost for higher education. Freeing up public funding for high-quality but low-cost training providers—particularly those offering online courses—would be one way of overcoming this challenge.

Aside from competition from foreign goods producers, competition from foreign workers brings its own set of concerns, as I argued in chapter 4. A complete deference to markets would eliminate borders entirely, allowing migrants to come and go and work as they please, but this would be unjust for two reasons: First, it would expose low-income workers to excessive competition, transferring income to the rich, and second, it would greatly weaken political equality, because noncitizens would not have the full set of rights and entitlements as citizens, since the basis for those rights rests on the reciprocal obligations of citizenship. A solution that acknowledges both the market's needs and its social limitations would be to greatly expand the availability of legal pathways for low-income workers—especially to Mexican and Central American populations—while empowering those workers and other immigrant groups to gradually attain the rights of full citizenship after meeting reasonable criteria. Counterintuitively, the best available evidence shows that legalizing the flow of migration would result in a net decrease relative to the current situation, which deters undocumented migrants from returning to their home country.

Healthcare and Law

The most far-reaching reform of the U.S. healthcare system that would lower costs and enhance its value would be the replacement of the insurance model with a group-practitioner membership model. This would lower healthcare costs by eliminating the wasteful overhead associated with insurance payment processing and removing the incentives for physicians to overprescribe treatments and tests. Competition between groups to attract and retain patients would keep quality high. The government could pay all or some portion of the membership fee for low-income households or even provide something like universal membership vouchers for the entire population.

A second-best solution would be to either move to a more efficient single-payer system, which is common in other rich countries, or to implement a streamlined universal billing and payment system that would apply to government- and privately funded insurance. Either one would greatly increase the efficiency of information-technology solutions in healthcare, which are currently limited by the idiosyncratic complexities of each insurance provider—complexities that themselves serve as a way for insurance providers to limit treatment and payment to providers. Whether group cooperatives or single-payer insurance manages healthcare financing, eliminating arbitrary limits on hospital competition is another much-needed reform.[11] These changes—like many innovations—would reduce income inequality by bolstering the purchasing power of all Americans. Innovations—defined as increases in the quality-to-cost ratio of goods or services—tend to disproportionately benefit lower-income groups because lower-income households spend a larger share of their income than the affluent.

Other policy changes directed at making occupational licensing rules serve the public would both lower the cost of healthcare and legal services and more directly redistribute money away from top-income earners to middle-income workers, patients, and clients. These changes would reduce income inequality in almost every democratic country, while also raising living standards more broadly.

The most urgent needs for licensing reform entail empowering licensed nonelite professionals—such as dental hygienists and nurses—to practice fully and independently, when justified by their training and expertise. This would break up the monopoly of service provision by elite professionals. A related reform would be to allow physicians and lawyers to become employees of organizations that are owned by nonphysicians or nonlawyers.

Finance

Most of the discussion of finance reforms concerns eliminating the too-big-to-fail dynamics whereby mega-banks take too many risks with other people's money, squander it, and then threaten catastrophe if not bailed out. Finance journalist Rana Foroohar makes this and other points about the negative and often unintended consequences of an excessively large and concentrated financial sector.[12] Likewise, the economists Anat Admati and Martin Hellwig's elegant reform proposal—require banks to use a larger share of their own money—would enhance stability and protect consumers from painful financial recessions.[13]

These are surely important issues, but when it comes to reducing income inequality and redistributing money from the top one percent to ordinary investors and retirement account holders, the most consequential reforms must deal with access to hedge, private equity, and venture capital funds. It is grossly unfair that only rich people are allowed to invest in and profit from start-ups, initial public offerings, and acquisitions.

The most beneficial policy change would create a retail market for hedge-fund and related products. The legal scholar Houman Shadab has developed a number of compelling arguments in favor of this for those concerned about the consequences.[14]

My preferred approach would be to allow SEC-regulated companies to offer a new, less-regulated product—a hedge, private equity, or venture capital fund—to any customer. These products would have the same disclosure and reporting requirements as mutual funds (including transparency about the general strategy, withdrawal limitations, estimated risk, and fees), but they would be free from mutual-fund restrictions on leverage or use of derivatives, and the managers would be allowed to charge a performance fee, which would end up being much less than 20 percent.

A second-best approach would be to regulate the 20 percent fee structure for cases when individual investors are not the ones picking the hedge fund. It is unseemly that pension funds and other institutional investors are handing over 20 percent of retirement profits from school teachers and blue-collar union workers to billionaire hedge-fund owners and advisors from Goldman Sachs, often without the consent of the investors. A consumer protection agency could directly outlaw high fees, or, better still, force hedge funds to disclose their fees publicly, so that institutional investors could at least shop around and their investors could be informed about alternative, lower-cost arrangements.

Intellectual Property

Patenting law is another instance where the market is wildly distorted at the expense of the public. Two reforms are needed.

Patents should not be granted for "functions"; instead, they should be granted only for specific means of achieving things. The current practice is a massive problem for software patents, and most should be nullified according to an analysis by the intellectual property scholar Mark Lemley.[15] The presence of these functional patents creates legal uncertainty, invites petty but terribly expensive lawsuits, and discourages entrepreneurs, who might be threatened by patent trolls, who buy up these meritless patents and use them to extort payments.[16]

A second and more radical reform would be to stipulate that patents grant an exclusive right not to entirely own a given product but rather to own some small share of it, such as a percentage of profits sold. For example, pharmaceutical companies now use patents to block generic drug-makers from reproducing and selling a drug at a tiny fraction of the current price. This is a disaster for the public. U.S. taxpayers and the public typically pay over $100,000 per year for a single anticancer medication for a single patient, and many of these medications have to be taken in combination.[17] Under a reformed patent system, the original patent holder would have no right to prevent the sale of that drug by anyone but would be entitled to collect some percentage of the generic drug-makers' profits off those sales. This would preserve much of the incentive to invest in research and development while substantially lowering prices.

Antiracism

The most proven and effective cure for racism and other forms of prejudice is contact, particularly among political equals.[18] The channels include market exchange, voluntary cooperation, and working and romantic relationships. In addition to the harm it inflicts on its victims, prejudice lowers trust, depresses collective action, weakens government quality, and distorts public policy. Eliminating artificial barriers to contact is thus of vital public importance.

One of the most important artificial barriers to interracial contact is created through land use laws or zoning. Local government should be prohibited from regulating the density of residential housing, with few exceptions. Investments in the renovation of old housing and the development of new housing would be more rational and efficient if zoning laws did not impede them. Rational, in this case, means building at higher density where land is more valuable and where housing is scarce relative to demand. Often, this situation is found in suburban areas with access to good schools. If density were permitted everywhere, it would diffuse affordability and gradually eliminate most of the economic and racial segregation that exists. Evidence for this is easy to find. Less-regulated metropolitan areas are more integrated, U.S. metropolitan areas were more integrated before zoning was widely adopted, and the United States is more segregated than Europe and uses antidensity zoning more aggressively.

Since local homeowner associations are a powerful interest group, higher levels of government must take the lead in prying open markets from their fists. Here, I list a number of possible remedies, which range in how much they would give in to the power of homeowners; actual bills would need to consider the legitimate cases where land use must be regulated—to protect green space, for example, or mitigate traffic congestion.

1. Pass state constitutional laws that universally ban land-use density regulations and police loopholes that would otherwise allow local governments to block market forces.
2. Provide state tax relief—perhaps in the form of property tax rates—to local governments that agree to open up their market by eliminating antidensity restrictions, since density growth would likely result in greater per capita government expenses.

I believe state governments are best suited to make zoning policy changes through amendments to their constitutions that bolster property rights by limiting zoning to rules that explicitly regulate harm and permit any level of housing density as the default condition. Local governments could, of course, adopt these changes, but the mayor or city council members would likely face a backlash and possible reversal if homeowner groups were largely against the changes. Moreover, even if large cities manage to pass zoning deregulations, citizens are still constrained by the rules put in place by suburban governments, which are even more antidensity. The federal government could also entice states or local governments to act by providing federal grants or other incentives. Finally, the U.S. Supreme Court could overturn a century of precedent on the validity of zoning rules, but that would require justices with much stronger respect for property rights than the current mix.

I'm justifying zoning reform as a way to reduce racism and spark healthier civic relations, but other justifications are also important: eliminating anti-density zoning laws would make housing more affordable at the same or higher levels of quality, spurring economic growth, and it would enhance the cognitive ability and lower the crime rates of groups that live in highly segregated high-poverty communities.

Information—grounded in science—is also a cure for racism, as this book argues.

First, scientific advances in genomics have reversed our understanding of the genetic origins of IQ. Whereas throughout the twentieth century and into the early twenty-first, IQ was thought to be mostly genetic by leading experts, now the best evidence suggests that cognitive ability is mostly environmental for a given age cohort within a given country. The actual percentage varies widely across time, region, and population, but the importance of the environment becomes clearer still after considering that environmental effects alone account for the increase by two standard deviations in IQ from the early twentieth century to the early twenty-first (the Flynn effect), and environmental conditions alone explain the fact that growing up in Western Europe as opposed to India or Sub-Saharan Africa enhances IQ by roughly one standard deviation, as we see by comparing children who arrive at different ages. The addition of multiple cohorts across multiple countries multiplies the variation in IQ that cannot be explained by genes.

Moreover, there is no rational basis for believing group differences are in any significant way genetic. The social status of large ethnic groups has changed places over the last 2,000 years of human history, which itself rules out the possibility of long-standing genetic differences that are important for determining living standards. The most ambitious hereditarian estimates suggest that group differences could theoretically emerge with selective breeding over 500 years, but historical facts rule out this possibility. European Jews and East Asians demonstrated lower cognitive ability than non-Jewish European Americans and Northern African Americans in the early twentieth century and were less likely than both white people and northern black people to contribute scientific and product innovations to the Industrial Revolution during the period. This pattern seems to have reversed sometime in the second half of the twentieth century for Jews and slightly later for East Asians, as parents from those groups became more educated. Those dynamics rule out simple hereditarian explanations, but at the same time, there is absolutely no evidence consistent with selective breeding. If anything, those with higher cognitive ability were having the fewest children, especially if they were Jewish. And yet, Jewish American and Asian American IQ levels gradually increased; the most recent large-scale survey data show that non-Jewish white people, Asians, and Jews have equivalent cognitive scores after adjusting for parental education, which is higher, on average, in the latter two groups. Meanwhile, African Americans were under the boot of Jim Crow, which lasted as late as the 1970s and lingers on in the form of unfair policing and lower-quality schooling and neighborhood conditions.

These shifting patterns in social status are impossible to reconcile with any cogent genetic theory of group differences. Asian and Jewish Americans could not have significantly changed their genes relative to other groups within the span of only a few generations. Moreover, the larger global population of Asians and Jews—meaning adults living in East Asia or Israel—exhibits average intelligence, with the exception of the Japanese, who perform the same as Scandinavians and share with them a politically and economically egalitarian political system that could be replicated around the world.

East Asians, Jewish Europeans, and recent African immigrants seem to succeed academically at similar high levels in the United States and England, despite coming from distinct racial groups.

While we can confidently rule out genetics at the group level, the explanation for their success may partly be that migrants tend to exhibit cultural behaviors that are conducive to success compared to those who do not migrate, but these practices do not require the adoption of ancient religious or ethnic practices or worldviews. Instead, the practices are quite simple: They include behaviors such as implementing routines that are proven to boost cognitive performance of children, such as the practice of conversing, reading books, writing, solving puzzles, and performing math exercises.

Many parents did not inherit these cultural practices from their own parents, and in the case of illiterate slaves, serfs, or peasants, it would have been nearly impossible to gain literacy, without external help. Still, poor parents have shown remarkable willingness and ability to adopt cognitively stimulating behaviors and apply them to their children when given even the slightest encouragement in that direction—from things as simple as periodic text messages. More sustained interventions, therefore, would be more helpful still, such as regular home visits from nurses who are experts in childhood development. Recall how in the aftermath of the U.S. Civil War, there was an explosion in literacy and enthusiasm for learning among recently freed slaves; their children frequently became inventors and entrepreneurs, at least if raised in the North, and thereby made massive contributions to economic development.

Education

At this heart of this book is the claim that equal access to education would have profoundly pro-egalitarian effects on the distribution of IQ, income, and health, among other good things.

Because of segregation by class and race, equal access to high-quality education is a significant problem in the United States and elsewhere. Moreover, early childhood education is typically not publicly funded, though the benefits to the public greatly exceed the costs and benefit children with less-educated parents disproportionately.[19]

A more general problem with education in the United States is that the teaching profession is unattractive to top students.[20] One issue is pay. Teachers are paid much less than workers with similar levels of education and cognitive ability. This is especially the case for teachers of the youngest students. Primary school teacher salaries are 63 percent of the salaries of other workers with a tertiary degree. It is barely higher for secondary school teachers. The average OECD country pays teachers closer to the "market" level for their education—78 percent. Top-scoring countries like Finland pay teachers much better; there, primary school teachers earn 91 percent of the average for tertiary workers, and upper secondary teachers are paid above the average. The same is true of Korea.[21]

Moreover, pay in the United States is closely linked to seniority, rather than performance, making the teaching profession particularly unattractive to those who expect to be top performers. Using a combination of best-practice observational evaluations, perhaps supplemented with test scores and personal judgment from supervisors, could go a long way to aligning pay incentives with merit.

Low pay is not the only unattractive feature of the teaching profession in the United States. Well-intentioned efforts to reduce racial inequality and hold schools more accountable have led to excessive testing. Instead of one test at the beginning of the year and one at the end, teachers have to administer standardized federal, state, and district exams throughout the year, some with high stakes for the school and teacher. This creates strong incentives to teach to the test. Students, meanwhile, are not actively learning while taking tests, and explicit test preparation is likely less useful than the deeper development of cognitive skills.

With both lower and higher education, excessive administrative costs have crowded out funding that should be going to teachers, while still increasing the private and public burden of financing education. Universities now employ more highly paid professionals who do not teach than they do teachers, and the administrative staff, whose contribution to learning is at best indirect, commands the highest salaries.[22] Rapid inflation in the cost of higher education over the last three decades is primarily the result of this shift toward excessive nonteaching expenses, which itself is encouraged by the indiscriminate public subsidization of higher education through federal student loan and aid programs. The public should contribute to higher education financing, because it benefits greatly from it, but government funding agencies need to be much more sophisticated about aligning pay with performance and accrediting innovative lower-cost models.

Another key problem in education is how to help students who are at risk to pursue their education to the fullest or develop high levels of cognitive ability. As discussed earlier, the environmental experiences that lead to character and cognitive development will never be exactly equal, nor should they be. Children with greater natural ability or proclivity for certain fields should be given opportunities to develop those talents at the expense of other areas, and parents should be free to have authority over the educational and cultural development of their children.

A politically egalitarian society respects differences in natural abilities and family circumstances and offers help to those who need it to maximize natural talents from whatever starting point. Thus, parents, particularly those with low levels of education, should be offered access to proven programs on how to create a healthy pregnancy and postnatal home life. Scalable low-cost interventions such as book-giving programs and text-messaging reminders appropriately balance parental autonomy with the solicitude that comes from understanding the vulnerable as worthy of respect and support.

The controversial educational reform efforts undertaken in the United States—pay based on test scores, expansion of de-unionized charter schools, and experiments with publicly funded vouchers that can be used for private schools—should be seen in this light. Insofar as the political goal is to weaken unions or lower public expenditures on education, the reforms should be opposed. But if legislatures can come to a fair solution for how to align pay with performance for unionized teachers, there is no reason why charter schools could not be governed by the same structure. Without weakening the commitment to public universal education, vouchers, meanwhile, could be reserved for students in special circumstances, such as those with special education needs that could be better met in a private school or low-income children who live near a high-performing private school but are assigned to a low-performing public school. In addition to these modest reforms, financial support for validated teacher and principal training or certification programs would enhance teacher quality.

Respecting genetic, cultural, or personality differences in a politically egalitarian community, while rejecting the unfounded idea that IQ is a measure of genetic potential, has another important implication for policy: There is no reason to consider career and technical education as undignified. There are many skilled jobs that typically do not require a bachelor's degree. These jobs may be as nurses, mechanics, medical or laboratory technicians, electricians, or information-technology systems analysts or technicians.[23] In addition to preserving health and maintaining the machines and infrastructure that the public relies upon, people in these roles make fundamental contributions to research and development and innovation, through their expert advice and support of academically trained professionals, as Phillip Toner has documented.[24]

Policymakers would do well to recognize the value of these roles and provide secondary school students a clear pathway to acquiring these skills and working in these fields, if they so choose. The Virginia Beach School District on the coast of southeastern Virginia provides an excellent example of what is possible. The district allows any student in its 11 secondary schools to take career and technically focused classes at a state-of-the-art community college. The educators are confident that the classes are directly linked to practical skills because the course work prepares them for certification exams created by businesses or associations. In the 2014–2015 school year, the district tested secondary students in 111 different industry and professional certification exams, 105 of which were for technical subjects related to science, engineering, or technology. Of 12,000 exams taken by just over 2,000 students, 81 percent were passed, resulting in a valuable and meaningful credential and set of skills that secondary school students can immediately use to demonstrate competency to employers or use as a foundation for further education or entrepreneurship.[25]

Antipoverty

I've argued that reciprocal ethical norms require that a just society provides everyone the opportunity to do the work that aligns with their natural ability. Nonetheless, it needs to be recognized that bad luck—including genetic or environmental disadvantages that weaken the cognitive ability or character traits conducive to success—or bad choices sometimes lead to sustained poverty, disease, mental illness, or disability, even for those who have been born into highly advantaged circumstances.

A just society protects its most vulnerable members by drawing from the resources of its strongest. This is in the long-run interests of everyone because bad luck can strike either oneself or one's descendants, and it is fair because it balances rewards for merit with the partial amelioration of misfortune.

The "welfare states" of Europe and the United States recognize these principles and have built institutions in accordance with them. The challenge is to make them both effective at promoting well-being and sustainable financially. In general, aligning these programs to foster decentralized mutually beneficial exchanges will accomplish those ends better than top-down strategies that create complicated rules about who gets benefits, who provides them, and how they can be used. For example, requiring housing developers to build affordable housing for the poor is a less effective and financially sustainable strategy than a program that gives poor people a housing voucher to support their rent (or lower their mortgage payment) wherever they choose to live. It is unfair to force private businesses to shoulder the burden of public welfare beyond their mandated tax payments, and it is less effective, because it gives them strong incentives either to avoid certain projects that would benefit others or to overcharge other customers to make up for the revenue loss. Similar logic could apply to employer requirements to pay healthcare benefits.

Another aspect of antipoverty policy relates to adult training. Egalitarian countries such as Denmark have been successful in combining unemployment insurance with requirements to undergo publicly funded training in pursuit of a new line of work for people who can no longer find a job in their chosen field. This demonstrates a strong reciprocal norm: Able-bodied beneficiaries of public generosity are expected to give something back by investing in skills that will be useful to society. Accordingly, because common people are valued and not seen as genetically inferior, the public has confidence that investing in their retraining will be worthwhile.

MARKET EGALITARIANISM

I define a just society as one that grants its members equal opportunity to realize and apply their talents under conditions of political equality, defined by basic civil liberties and access to markets. I maintain that this background structure leads to a relatively egalitarian distribution of income and health. The set of ideas behind this could be thought of as market egalitarianism, because of the dual emphasis on equality of rules and the reliance on mutually beneficial market exchanges.

People today are rightly skeptical about claims about justice. On the Left, there is suspicion of power; in recent history, powerful white-dominated nations have imposed their will on others—via slavery and colonialism—at the expense of justice, even while claiming to represent it. On the Right, there seems to be an exhaustion and frustration with claims that racism is behind every unfavorable outcome for black people or other nonwhite groups. The phrase "social justice warrior" has become a derogatory term to describe people on the Left, who, from the perspective of conservatives, engage in self-righteous, illogical, and emotionally laden public discourse.

I have a very different starting point. Market egalitarianism is the foundation, and a just end is what naturally follows from it. This starting point aligns most closely with experiences that shaped our DNA and our moral cooperative culture and institutions. From there, reciprocity toward community members and even strangers follows naturally, as does generosity toward the weak.

As I've argued throughout, market egalitarianism does not set out to guarantee equal economic or social outcomes, but it would make society far more egalitarian economically and thus accomplish many of the goals of the socialist Left. The reason is that when decentralized mutually beneficial exchanges are allowed to govern markets, people tend to be rewarded on merit rather than political power, and merit is distributed equitably when given a chance to develop. This distribution is not perfectly equal, of course, but equal enough such that everyone except the most profoundly disabled can find jobs that are broadly productive and socially useful. The most productive and clever among us—even the luckiest—should be rewarded when their inventions and ventures increase the ratio of product quality to cost, but doing so will never lead to the massive inequality observed today in the United States, Latin America, and much of the world.

Extremes in inequality arise when pay is systematically divorced from merit. Even in highly egalitarian societies—such as Scandinavia and Japan—entrepreneurs, executives, and elite performers have opportunities to distinguish themselves and make much higher incomes than ordinary professionals. The difference between these countries and the United States is that there are far fewer people who reach that level as a result of antimarket distortions, so overall inequality remains much lower.

As for more conservative goals, market egalitarianism provides a defense of liberty, private property, and mutually beneficial exchanges, as well as a protection against excesses and abuses of government power. From a cultural perspective, market egalitarianism creates conditions that allow people to solve their problems and meet their needs as they see fit. For many, that will involve the continued embrace of religious and cultural traditions that guide their values. At the same time, the integration of people, culture, and information that comes from decentralized housing market choices, from migration, from trade, and from mundane exchanges within cities tends toward harmonious cooperative interactions, trust, and mutual respect. Insofar as the religious and cultural traditions valued by conservative Europeans promote healthy and appealing lifestyles, they are likely to be embraced by immigrants and those from other cultures. At the same time, the native Christian populations could benefit by adopting some of the parenting practices of European Jews, Asians, or Sub-Saharan Africans with regard to actively promoting literacy and numeracy in their children. A diverse society allows groups to learn from each other and allows good ideas—whether ancient or modern—to emerge from cultural competition.

One cultural tradition that deserves to be rejected is the doctrine of racial superiority, which is closely linked to hereditarian theory. It has haunted European and American society like an intellectual plague for several centuries now and spread outside it to Asia and elsewhere. It has caused tremendous harm by justifying political inequality, even genocide; it has created and sustained an underclass of citizens, squandering their natural ability; it has deprived millions of would-be immigrants of the opportunity to migrate; and it has drastically eroded trust and cooperation not only between European white people and nonwhite people and European Jews and non-Jews, but even among them. Political dysfunction in the United States and much of Europe is closely tied to differences in opinions about how to relate to minorities and the foreign born, and hereditarianism exacerbates those differences.

Less seriously, the doctrine is to blame for the stifling awkwardness and fear that permeate college campuses with respect to open discussions of group social status differences and how to mitigate them. The painful implications of white supremacy as a doctrine makes it poisonous to take in and dwell upon at length. The problem then is that sophisticated theoretical claims made by hereditarian social scientists and intellectuals are never engaged openly and appear edgy and seductive to many who come across them on the internet unaware of their weaknesses.

As I've argued, there is no logical or scientific basis for hereditarianism. The best available genetic research shows that the heritability of IQ has been greatly exaggerated, even within the same age group and by greater amounts across generations or societies at different levels of economic development. The environmental origins of the massive two-standard-deviation increase in cognitive ability over the past 100 years are themselves powerful evidence that genes cannot account for more than a modest share of variation across individuals.

Most importantly, there is no logical basis for believing that group differences are genetic in nature, in any important way. The instability in group social status and intellectual achievements over the last 100 years disproves it; the consistently low and then high performance of American Jews and Asians disproves it; the intellectual achievements of African Americans after the Civil War but before Jim Crow disprove it; the current intellectual achievements of African immigrants in England and the United States disprove it; and the clearly demonstrated, replicable, and undeniable gains in IQ that come from exposure to high-quality education and educated parenting disprove it.

Cognitive ability, like every important human trait, has a genetic basis, but exercise, practice, and training are most important in determining the expression of fitness, and most people can become fit—fit enough to perform any occupation.

Moreover, noncognitive character traits such as conscientiousness, emotional stability, enthusiasm, and integrity are at least as important as IQ in preparing people for success in life, measured through income or health, and the evidence presented here shows that these traits are distributed evenly across race, ethnicity, and gender, despite wide variation in the parenting behaviors that foster IQ development. If people are going to reach their optimal potential, we would do well to foster these noncognitive skills in those at risk of not fully developing them. We know they are fostered by a loving upbringing, and it seems likely that they are enriched by the best artistic and religious elements of culture: great books, films, plays, works of art, sermons, and religious teachings. The discipline and grounded moral tradition of military life may also boost noncognitive skills. Quite likely school-based practices and therapeutic interventions can help remediate deficits, as the scholarly literature indicates.[26] This is an area in great need of additional research, as the focus of education has been almost exclusively on cognitive skills. In a promising development school districts in California have begun measuring social-emotional skills—such as self-management—alongside traditional cognitive performance as a first step in understanding how to effectively develop them.[27]

The malleability of cognitive ability, the even spread of psychological traits conducive to realizing one's capacity, and the responsiveness of people to educational opportunities all suggest that the vast gaps in social and economic power that exist in modern democracies are not inevitable. Nor are they desirable. The large gaps have come about primarily through the enactment of deeply harmful barriers to free exchange, put in place by powerful interest groups.

The nineteenth century saw a bourgeois revolution against the hereditary elite. The professional class won that revolution, and billions of people have benefited greatly as a result. Yet, the professional elites have become too entrenched and are the new landed gentry, claiming entitlement to special privileges such as the right to work without being an employee and the right to own a monopoly on services others could do quite well. Quite likely, a feeling of natural superiority set in, given that many of the professional associations gained prominence at the same time that racial science gained traction.

The nonelite professions—those not afforded monopoly privileges, including engineers, computer programmers, midlevel managers, technicians, nurses, and educators, as well as various para-professionals—need to take part in the next stage of revolution. They, like the working class, would stand to benefit by eliminating the privileges that siphon away their spending power to elite professionals, restoring a common understanding that everyone has something to contribute, and creating the political equality promised by republican ideals.

APPENDIX

THIS APPENDIX IS WRITTEN for scholars, students, journalists, and anyone else interested in the technical details of the data used in the book. Readers should be aware that much of the data and related replication code (written for STATA software) are available freely for download at https://github.com/jtrothwell/Republic_Equals/, and the source and description of each variable accompany those files. The files (or supplemental materials, as I will refer to them below) include topics that are not addressed in what follows, such as my analysis of National Longitudinal Survey of Youth (personality, IQ, and their relationship to health, income, race, and ethnicity) and pre-kindergarten schooling and test score data.

The text below discusses the following topics:

1. Analyzing who is in the top one percent in the United States and around the world presents methodological challenges. These are explained, along with why I think my analysis is valid.
2. For people skeptical that inequality is a meaningful summary measure or curious about the relationship between different measures of inequality (top 1 percent shares versus Gini coefficient), I provide a brief discussion and analysis that aims to show that inequality can be measured reliably across methods and offers valid insight into living conditions.
3. The section "Inequality, Slow Growth, and Falling National Confidence" presents results from a simple regression analysis. The full results are available in the supplemental materials and are consistent with my argument that slow growth and inequality predict low levels of confidence in national government.

4. The section "What Explains Inequality?" sketches the main theoretical argument of the book and presents empirical results from a historical accounting exercise of which occupations and industries explain the rise in the U.S. one percent. It then turns to an international analysis and discusses correlations and regression results that look at the most-robust predictors of inequality across OECD countries. These findings suggest that elite professional power and racial diversity predict higher inequality; meanwhile, government spending (as a share of GDP) and innovation (measured by patenting rates) predict lower inequality.

This evidence is consistent with the arguments made in the main text. Measures of globalization, the power of business owners as opposed to workers, and gaps in cognitive ability are unrelated to inequality, which is consistent with my fundamental argument: Markets do not inherently lead to mass inequality; mass inequality has been created through racial oppression and isolation—blocking minorities from public services and markets—and the disruption and control of certain markets by elite professionals.

IDENTIFYING WHO IS IN THE TOP ONE PERCENT

For levels and trends in top-one-percent income shares and for analysis of thresholds, I rely on the World Inequality Database (WID), which is assembled by Thomas Piketty and his collaborators using national tax data.[1] Unfortunately, tax records do not usually record information about the occupation or industry of those who file their taxes, and these data are not available in the WID.

Thus, to analyze top earnings by occupation and industry, I relied on government surveys. The American Community Survey (ACS), with the data packaged and managed by IPUMS USA, was my primary data source for analyzing the U.S. one percent.[2] For international analysis, I relied primarily on the Luxembourg Income Study (LIS).[3]

There are several issues that arise with these sources, which warrant comment and clarification.

Issue 1: Reporting Thresholds for Income Sources

One limitation of the American Community Survey is that underlying income sources (wage/salary, investment, and business being the most important for the affluent) are top-coded at the 99.5th percentile (the top 0.5 percent) for each state to make it difficult to identify individuals. For the analysis of the one percent in this book, I have concluded that it is not a significant problem for several reasons.

First, total income is not top-coded, only the underlying sources, so the only way someone who is really in the top one percent can be misclassified is if he or she happens to have top-coded business income or wage income in a state where the top codes fall below the national one-percent threshold (of $315,700) but still does not make it to the top one percent, once all other income sources are included (table A.1).

There are only four states for which the wage/salary income top code for 2016 falls below the national top-income threshold of $316,000 for the entire period of 2012–2016 (West Virginia, Alaska, Mississippi, and Vermont), but almost everyone with top-coded wage income makes it into the one percent when their salary income is combined with another income source. The business income threshold falls below $316,000 for 36 states in 2016, but again, there are very few people who have top-coded business income and do not reach the one percent.

To be more precise, only 216 respondents out of 12 million with income data are potentially misclassified as not being in the one percent despite having top-coded salaries in the 2012–2016 census database. Another 1,789 are potentially misclassified because they have top-coded business income data, but do not reach the one percent. This is 0.01 percent of U.S. residents with income. A higher number (7,447) have top-coded investment income, but are not in the one percent. They appear to be mostly retirees living off their investment income, as 81 percent are out of the labor force and 62 percent are at least 65 years old. This leaves just 1,139 workers who, based on investment income alone, could be misclassified as not being in the top one percent.

Second, if you believe that the one-percent threshold is best established through fiscal income (defined as the income people must report to tax authorities) measured from the World Inequality Database, then identifying the top one percent of fiscal income holders from the American Community Survey is even more straightforward because the threshold is lower. In the World

Table A.1. Income thresholds to qualify as a top-one-percent earner in the United States using World Inequality Database and Census in 2014

American Community Survey

Wage and salary income	$221,616
Total income	$315,700

World Inequality Database

Capital income reported on tax returns per adult on return	$242,775
Labor (or employee) income reported in tax returns per adult on return	$264,286
Total income reported on tax returns per adult on return	$283,749
Total national income (including nontaxable labor and capital income) per adult on return	$469,256

Source: World Inequality Database, accessed via WID STATA program on May 10, 2018. The population is adults aged 20 and over. Steven Ruggles, Katie Genadek, Ronald Goeken, Josiah Grover, and Matthew Sobek. Integrated Public Use Microdata Series: Version 7.0, 2012–2016 American Community Survey. Minneapolis: University of Minnesota, 2017. https://doi.org/10.18128/D010.V7.0.

In the 2014 American Community Survey, every state's top-code threshold for labor income is above the labor-income threshold for the one percent except West Virginia. Additionally Montana and New Mexico's thresholds fall below the total-income threshold in the WID. For both, almost any amount of income from business ownership or dividends would be enough to push a high wage earner into the top 1%.

Inequality Database, the U.S. national one-percent threshold per adult house member for taxable (fiscal) income is $284,000 for 2014, which is below every 2016 wage and salary top code in the census and greater than only three states for 2012 top codes. The census threshold is likely somewhat higher because the tax records are often not measured for individuals, but rather for tax returns, which often have multiple adults (e.g., a husband and wife). This is akin to measuring household income per capita, which will tend to be lower than individual income for top earners, since the other adults with whom they share a household will typically earn less (table A.1).

I conclude that census reporting thresholds are not a serious obstacle to accurate analysis of who is in the one percent. With 119,130 individuals over the age of 20 identified as being in the top one percent, those who are potentially misclassified amount to a tiny fraction of the total.

Issue 2: Missing Capital Income in the Census Data

Another limitation of the American Community Survey is that it does not include income data from the sale or exchange of a "capital asset," such as a stock or ownership stake in a company. It does, however, include data from business income, including dividends, royalty payments, and rental payments. In effect, this means that the ACS includes only income that flows to individuals as either owners or workers, but does not include income from sales of property unless directly tied to a business controlled by the individual. It also does not include employer or government allocations of funds to an individual's retirement account, the implicit value of owning a home ("owner-occupied rent"), the distribution of taxes on business, or the value of compensation through public or private health insurance plans. Recent work from Thomas Piketty, Emanuel Saez, and Gabriel Zucman includes these concepts as part of income (they call it "national income") and reports that the U.S. top-one-percent threshold for individual pretax income is $470,000 for 2014.[4] The threshold greatly exceeds taxable income because it includes all of these other concepts, which, in most cases, are not like income that one can use to buy products, at least in the present.

The important point is that the sale of assets could be an important source of income for rich people and be systematically allocated to certain occupations, such as executives, in ways that bias my earlier results.

To better understand how different income concepts and sources relate, I combine IRS zip-code data—which is available to the public—with census data. I use adjusted gross income, which corresponds with what Piketty and co-authors describe as fiscal income. At the zip-code level, mean census income has a very high correlation of 0.87 with mean IRS adjusted gross income—and a correlation of 0.91 between the share of residents in the top one percent (incomes above $284,000) and mean census income. IRS gross income is also highly correlated with median home values (0.71). In addition, IRS data distinguish income from capital gains and business partnerships. Average capital-gains income at the zip-code level has a correlation of 0.58 with mean census income, while income from partnerships has a correlation of 0.72 with mean income (table A.2). These correlations use zip-code population as a weight, but the results are similar when giving equal weight to all zip codes.

To further explore the relationship between census income at the individual level and fiscal income, I match IRS data by zip codes to the census-relevant Zip Code Tabulation Areas (ZCTAs) using the Uniform Data Systems (UDS) zip mapper.[5] The next step is to match ZCTAs to a unit available in the census microdata. The smallest such unit of analysis is a Public Use Microdata Area (PUMA), which has 100,000 people. I do this using an application published by Missouri Census Data Center.[6]

Table A.2. Correlation between census income and other income concepts, 2015

	Home value	Total income, census	Total family income, census	Average adjusted gross income from IRS in zip code	Percent of residents in zip code with IRS adjusted gross income of $284,000 or higher
Home value	1.00				
Total income, census	0.30	1.00			
Total family income, census	0.43	0.64	1.00		
Average adjusted gross income from IRS in zip code	0.52	0.26	0.33	1.00	
Percent of residents in zip code with IRS adjusted gross income of $284,000 or higher	0.51	0.26	0.33	0.96	1.00

Sources: Correlations based on 1,176,360 individual observations. U.S. Internal Revenue Service, Individual Income Tax Statistics, 2015; Steven Ruggles, Katie Genadek, Ronald Goeken, Josiah Grover, and Matthew Sobek. Integrated Public Use Microdata Series: Version 7.0, 2012–2016 American Community Survey. Minneapolis: University of Minnesota, 2017. https://doi.org/10.18128/D010.V7.0.

The results show a high correlation between home values at the household level and IRS adjusted-gross-income levels at the PUMA level. IRS income is also highly correlated with family income (.64). The correlation between IRS income and individual income is lower, but this is not surprising, because variation within PUMAs and within households creates noise that lowers these correlations.

The high correlation between IRS zip-code income data and home values (0.52) implies that home values may be an important proxy measure for the income sources not captured by the American Community Survey (e.g., capital income). Thus, as a robustness check, I report how occupations vary by home value. At the detailed level, the census data are grouped into 480 occupational categories by IPUMS USA (using "occsoc"). The correlation between the percentage of workers in each occupation who are in the top one percent of income and the percentage who live in a home valued in the top one percent is 0.73. It is likewise high (0.65) between the percentage living in a top-one-percent home and a top-one-percent zip code.

Consistent with my earlier analysis, physicians and surgeons, dentists, lawyers, and securities traders are heavily overrepresented among top-one-percent homeowners. While chief executives and other managerial groups are also heavily represented, the additional consideration of home value does not appear to substantially change the analysis. In other words, while it would be desirable to explicitly include all forms of capital income in the analysis of which occupations are most overrepresented among top earners, doing so probably would have little effect on the actual composition of top one-percent earners. Doctors, dentists, lawyers, and finance-related workers are at or near the top any which way you measure income (table A.3).

International Estimates

The same two issues with U.S. census data apply to census data from other countries, which I access through the Luxembourg Income Study, but I conclude they are not serious obstacles to accurate analysis.

First, maximum income reported in each country in the LIS exceeds national top-one-percent thresholds in all 12 cases that I could compare against WID data using LIS income data from 2010 or later. Thus, reporting restrictions are not an actual problem for describing who is in the one percent outside the United States using these data. For LIS and U.S. Census

Table A.3. Occupations ranked by share in top one percent of home values, 2012–2016

	Top 1%— home value	Top 1%—zip code, IRS income	Top 1%—individual income, census
Physicians and surgeons	6.4%	13.3%	30.3%
Chief executives	6.0%	12.9%	16.4%
Actors	5.8%	11.8%	1.9%
Securities, commodities, and financial services sales agents	5.6%	12.8%	10.6%
Financial analysts	5.0%	14.2%	6.9%
Dentists	5.0%	11.8%	18.4%
Lawyers, judges, magistrates, and other judicial workers	4.8%	13.8%	13.7%
Agents and business managers of artists, performers, and athletes	4.1%	11.4%	2.6%
Producers and directors	4.0%	12.8%	2.6%
Personal financial advisors	3.8%	12.9%	11.6%
Writers and authors	3.6%	12.6%	2.1%
Property, real estate, and community association managers	3.4%	9.6%	3.2%
Economists	3.0%	14.4%	6.0%
Financial specialists, all other	2.8%	9.5%	5.6%
Management analysts	2.8%	13.0%	4.5%
Real estate brokers and sales agents	2.8%	10.3%	3.3%
Public relations specialists	2.7%	12.1%	2.7%
Psychologists	2.6%	12.5%	1.7%
Lodging managers	2.5%	8.2%	1.4%
Market research analysts and marketing specialists	2.4%	13.7%	2.4%

Sources: Correlations based on 1,176,360 individual observations. U.S. Internal Revenue Service, Individual Income Tax Statistics, 2015; Steven Ruggles, Katie Genadek, Ronald Goeken, Josiah Grover, and Matthew Sobek. Integrated Public Use Microdata Series: Version 7.0, 2012–2016 American Community Survey. Minneapolis: University of Minnesota, 2017. https://doi.org/10.18128/D010.V7.0.

Bureau sources, the data do not allow for accurate calculations of the share of national income that goes to the one percent, since it would cut off a large chunk of money flowing to people whose income exceeds the reporting thresholds, but that limitation does not affect the description of who is in the one percent, which is the focus of this book.

As for the capital gains issue, nonlabor income is roughly the same share of national income in the United States as in other OECD countries, according to data from the Penn World Table.[7] It is unlikely that including capital income would substantially affect the occupational rankings, since efforts to do so made little difference in the United States. One reason that capital versus labor income distinctions are unlikely to affect the occupational distribution is that with the exception of those who inherit large fortunes, capital income amounts to the profits of invested savings from labor income. In this sense, capital income is, in large part, earnings from past labor income. Analysis from Robert Carroll of the Tax Foundation finds that capital income is also far more transitory than labor income at the individual level. Roughly, half of taxpayers with over $1 million in taxable income reach millionaire status only once in a nine-year period.[8] Labor income, however, is more stable, which makes comparisons that exclude capital gains—as in the census—relatively attractive when describing the characteristics of top earners over time.

THE VALIDITY OF INCOME INEQUALITY MEASURES

Whether measured by the top-one-percent share of taxable income using tax records or by the Gini coefficient using household survey data, countries that are more unequal on one measure tend to be more unequal on others. This is true for 26 countries with data from the United Nations World Income Inequality Database (UN WIID), LIS, and WID. The survey-based UN and LIS measures are highly correlated (0.91), and both are highly correlated with top-one-percent income shares (0.74 and 0.79, respectively). Within the 16 countries in the OECD with data from all three sources, the correlations are similar (0.65 and 0.74) between top-one-percent shares and UN and LIS Gini coefficients, respectively.

In this sense, the measures used in this book are reliable across data sources and methods.

Inequality measures are also clearly associated with bad outcomes, such as low health and low subjective well-being. In this sense, they are valid.

For example, the Gallup World Poll asks several questions related to financial well-being, including the following:

- Are you satisfied or dissatisfied with your standard of living, all the things you can buy and do?
- Which one of these phrases comes closest to your own feelings about your household's income these days: living comfortably on present income, getting by on present income, finding it difficult on present income, or finding it very difficult on present income?

Both of these questions are highly correlated with inequality measured across all three data sources. The most unequal countries in the world—using the UN database—are in Latin America, followed by Sub-Saharan Africa. In these regions, people tend to be dissatisfied with their living standard and many find living difficult (table A.4). By contrast, in egalitarian northern and western Europe, people are highly satisfied with their living standard, and few find living difficult. The global correlation (for 101 countries) between income inequality and the percent satisfied with their living standard is −0.27. The correlation between income inequality and difficulty living on income is 0.42.

Among OECD countries, Norway, Sweden, Denmark, and Japan have the lowest percentage of people who report difficulty living comfortably on their household income, ranging from 10.3 percent in Japan to 6 percent in Norway. Meanwhile, in countries with higher income inequality, such as Canada, the United Kingdom, and the United States, 15 percent, 19.1 percent, and 19.7 percent, respectively, report difficulty. The OECD correlation between income inequality and the percent satisfied with their living standard for 30 countries is −0.37. The correlation between income inequality and difficulty living on income is 0.33. There is also a statistically significant correlation between inequality and healthy life expectancy (−.22) and life evaluation (−.34) within the OECD.[9]

The poor performance of the United States on subjective financial well-being is particularly surprising considering that the United States is richer on a per capita basis than all but five OECD countries but ranks 17th on this measure of subjective financial well-being. The latest World Bank data from

Table A.4. Inequality and subjective financial well-being by world region

	Income inequality, UN database, standardized to mean zero	Percent satisfied with standard of living	Percent finding living difficult with household income
Western Europe	−1.11	0.87	0.17
Northern Europe	−0.97	0.74	0.20
Eastern Europe	−0.83	0.53	0.37
Southern Europe	−0.77	0.56	0.37
Australia and New Zealand	−0.45	0.87	0.13
Northern America	−0.39	0.81	0.17
Western Asia	−0.38	0.62	0.41
Central Asia	−0.31	0.78	0.22
Southern Asia	−0.28	0.67	0.42
Northern Africa	−0.18	0.67	0.41
Eastern Asia	−0.08	0.73	0.25
Southeast Asia	0.26	0.77	0.30
Sub-Saharan Africa	0.63	0.41	0.64
Latin America and the Caribbean	1.16	0.68	0.41

Source: Data from the Gallup World Poll (columns 2 and 3) are for years 2013–2017, with sample sizes of roughly 1,000 per country per year. UN data (column 1) average the ten most recent observations up to 2017 and are from the World Income Inequality Database, Version 3.4.

2016 show that only Luxembourg, Singapore, Ireland, Switzerland, and Norway have higher incomes per capita than the United States, after adjusting for purchasing power.[10] High income inequality, presumably, is the chief explanation for why such a high percentage of U.S. residents do not feel comfortable with their living standard, despite living in such a rich country.

INEQUALITY, SLOW GROWTH, AND FALLING NATIONAL CONFIDENCE

To test whether growth and inequality predict political dissatisfaction, I regress the change in national government confidence on income inequality and per capita income growth from 2008 and 2017. There is a strong negative and significant relationship between inequality and rising confidence (t-stat is −3.2), and a strong positive relationship between rising confidence and higher growth (t-stat is 3.3). The r-squared is 0.34 for this model, which uses data from 35 OECD member countries.

WHAT EXPLAINS INEQUALITY?

A Theoretical Sketch

To provide a somewhat more formal theoretical framework for my argument, I refer readers to a summary of growth theory from Stanford University economist Charles Jones, as well as a working paper he has developed with Chang-Tai Hsieh, Erik Hurst, and Peter Klenow.[11] Drawing on their analysis, I will lay out some of the logic of my own theory.

Modern economic growth theory links long-run growth in living standards to productivity growth, which describes changes in how efficiently each factor of production (usually labor and capital) is being utilized. Productivity is often represented as either knowledge or technology, but Jones describes a new branch of growth theory that allows for the misallocation of resources (such as people) to govern productivity growth. It is straightforward to represent this idea in the mathematical language and context of macroeconomic growth literature. For my purposes, the misallocation of talent can result from inequitable political power, and this, in turn, will result in both slower productivity growth and high-income inequality, as people work in the wrong careers.

To see how the misallocation of talent may arise in ways that correspond to the broad themes of this book, imagine that people choose their career in early adulthood in such a way as to maximize their lifetime health and income. To the best of their knowledge, income and health are determined by how productively they can perform the tasks of a given occupation in the economy. When choosing a career, they thus aim to pick the set of tasks that will allow them to work most productively, given what they know about their preferences and talent. Talent at young adulthood, meanwhile, is determined by genetics, private environmental circumstances (such as neighborhood and familial influences), and public influences, such as environmental security, law enforcement, and education. In a politically egalitarian society, people choose careers that line up closely with their talent profile, given these factors, but in a politically unequal society, power can have a large influence in several ways. Power is determined by group membership, which is determined by ascribed characteristics (e.g., race, ethnicity, and gender), as well as malleable characteristics (e.g., occupational or industry membership). When ascribed characteristics affect power, the accumulation of talent is distorted through the nongenetic channels mentioned (access to optimal private and public environmental circumstances), and this has a direct effect on career choice by lowering talent from what it would otherwise be. Another channel by which inequitable power distorts career choice is by taxing away the income of members of low-power groups. To elaborate, prejudice against religious or racial minorities, women, and workers in nonelite professions has resulted in lower earnings and fewer entrepreneurial possibilities than would be the case with a more equitable distribution of power. These income losses are predictable and deter low-power groups from performing their most productive tasks.

For members of powerful groups, the obverse of this dynamic dominates, and they are encouraged to over-pursue high-paying careers, even when other careers may have been a better use of their talents, because they receive an earnings benefit in doing so. Thus, people who would have been excellent plumbers, machinists, teachers, or scientists become doctors, lawyers, dentists, and hedge-fund managers instead. Members of powerful groups may enjoy somewhat higher talent insofar as they can better leverage private and public resources, but they also enjoy over-compensation for their talents as a result of access to privileged industrial or occupational groups.

In this way, political inequality creates income inequality that favors the members of politically powerful groups and results in slower economic growth than would otherwise be the case: Too many people in the low-power group are working in low-productivity jobs that fail to utilize their talent, and too many people in the high-power group are working in jobs that have high productivity but low macroeconomic efficiency (e.g., lawyers and plastic surgeons instead of engineers and software developers).[12]

To extend this to my theory of politics, right-wing populism will become more attractive in this kind of society because those who share partial membership advantages (say, middle-class white males) but not the full advantages of industrial or occupational status will develop deep distrust of elites and be more willing to embrace xenophobia, especially if they come to believe that increasing numbers of members of the elite are from foreign groups who do not traditionally hold power. The chief political opponents for this group are the subset of elites who are minority members of occupational and industrial groups. Left-wing populism will also become more attractive and its chief political opponents will be white male members of privileged occupational and industrial groups. In both cases, however, the shared distrust of elites will make it hard for populists to distinguish between successful individuals who have earned their status through talent and those who have merely cashed in on their power. This makes a large segment of the voting population open to spurious policy analysis that links inequality and slow growth to salient trends (such as globalization, immigration, and technology) even when they are unrelated from a causal perspective.

Empirical Analysis of the Political Economy of Inequality

One way to study the factors that relate to rising income inequality is to see how the composition of the one percent has changed over time by sector (the products firms produce) and occupation (the type of work people do for their firm). I focus on 1980 as the starting point because that is when top-one- percent income shares began to rise after a long-term fall, as documented in the World Income Database and by Census Bureau measures of inequality.

The one percent have increasingly consisted of financial-sector managers, professional and other business service managers, healthcare professionals and managers, and legal service providers. If you add up the total increase in workers from 1980 to 2015 in these categories you get 98 percent of the total increase in top-one-percent earners (table A.5).

Keep in mind that other sectors and occupations also contributed statistically to the rise of the one percent because some sectors had a negative effect. Large reductions in the number of top income earners were found among craft and construction workers, farmers, and retail and wholesale managers.

Overall, this provides more evidence that a fairly narrow group of domestically focused professionals and managers—particularly managers in the financial and healthcare sectors—explains the rise of the one percent in the United States. Any coherent theory of income inequality must focus on why elite healthcare professionals, financial-sector managers and professionals, and lawyers are so overrepresented now and account for such a large share of the increase. This makes the globalization story look rather weak.

Table A.5. Accounting for change in number of workers in top one percent of U.S. income earners by high-level occupation and sector from 1980 to 2015

Broad occupational category	Broad sector	Share of increase in top 1% population, 1980–2015
Managerial	Financial services	40%
Managerial	Other professional and social services (e.g., engineering, accounting)	17%
Professional specialists	Healthcare services	15%
Managerial	Business and repair services (e.g., advertising, computer services)	14%
Professional specialists	Legal services	7%
Managerial	Healthcare services	6%
Professional specialists	Business and repair services (e.g., advertising, computer services)	6%
Managerial	Transportation, communication, and utilities	5%
Professional specialists	Financial services	4%
Professional specialists	Other professional and social services (e.g., engineering, accounting, computer)	4%
Finance and sales	Business and repair services (e.g., advertising, computer services)	4%
Professional specialists	Agriculture, mining, and manufacturing	4%
Professional specialists	Education services	3%
Professional specialists	Retail and wholesale trade	3%
Professional specialists	Transportation, communication, and utilities	2%
Finance and sales	Transportation, communication, and utilities	2%
Managerial	Education services	1%
Administrative	Financial services	1%
Managerial	Construction services	1%
Finance and sales	Other professional and social services (e.g., engineering, accounting)	1%

Source: Author analysis of IPUMS USA. See replication code and related files for how categories were created using "ind1990" and "occ1990." The column shows the change for each occupation-sector group in the number of workers in the top 1% from 2015 to 1980 divided by the total U.S. change in the number of workers in the top 1%.

International Analysis

Another approach to testing different theories on what predicts the level and rise in income inequality is to look across countries. This has the advantage of allowing for comparisons across different institutional regimes and countries with different characteristics and laws.

I compiled 61 variables that I classified into nine different theoretical viewpoints. Later, I will discuss some of the individual variables in each.

The evidence suggests that inequality is closely linked to racial diversity, measured as the share of population from various continents. The supplemental materials discuss the sources in more detail. Given that races do not differ by their inherent capacity for work, as I argued in detail in the preceding chapters, the fact that racial diversity predicts inequality is likely the result of discrimination, segregation, and other ways in which racial minorities are cut off from full participation in markets and denied full access to high-quality public services.

Demographic structure is also predictive of more inequality, particularly if the working-age population is large relative to the retirement-age population, but we will see this result is not robust.

What I refer to as *political economy variables* perform moderately well on average, though some of the individual measures are among the top performers. These measure the structure of earnings through the lens of occupations and industries. A summary measure of regulations on professional occupations that limit competition predicts greater inequality.

The capital-versus-labor variables perform rather poorly. Minimum-wage regulations, union membership, the capital-labor share of income, and regulations on firing workers are not well correlated with inequality.

The same is true for globalization measures, which include the share of the population that is foreign born, how it has changed, and measures of openness to trade.

Institutional quality, skill, technological innovation—measured by patenting—and the overall level of economic development all predict lower income inequality and lower growth inequality. This makes it unlikely that skill-based technological change is a serious driving force of inequality. Countries with more educated and inventive citizens, who have higher cognitive ability, tend to have low inequality (table A.6).

Table A.6. Correlations with level and change in inequality by theoretical concept

	Correlation with level of income inequality	Correlation with change in income inequality, 1980–2016 approx.
Racial diversity	0.78	0.18
Demographic structure	0.48	0.07
Political economy	0.22	0.09
Capital vs. labor	−0.15	−0.13
Globalization	−0.17	−0.10
Institutional quality	−0.30	−0.04
Skill	−0.35	0.06
Technology	−0.36	−0.11
Level of development	−0.42	−0.20

Source: See online supplemental materials for details on sources and methods: https://github.com /jtrothwell.

The individual variable with the highest absolute value correlation with inequality within the OECD is my preferred measure of professional elite economic power: the 90th percentile of earnings for professional workers relative to the national median. This has an incredibly high correlation of 0.91 with the level of inequality and 0.32 with the change in inequality (table A.7).

Racial diversity is also highly predictive, as noted, followed by another measure of elite-professional dominance (median salary of professionals divided by median salary of all workers). Managerial dominance is also highly correlated, but the relationship is weaker than the professional-worker relationship. Countries with larger tax revenue as a share of GDP—which may indicate their commitment to high-quality public services—have lower inequality today and have seen lower growth in inequality.

These correlations should not be interpreted as causal, since omitted-variables bias is prevalent in all of them, but they do provide a baseline sense of what plausible causal relationships might look like.

To further investigate, I regressed inequality on the list of 61 variables, while controlling for racial diversity, the percentage of children raised by single parents, the patenting rate, the tertiary degree attainment rate, a trade freedom index, and the mean income, adjusted for purchasing power. The

Table A.7. Correlations with level and change in inequality by theoretical concept

	Correlation with level of income inequality	Number of countries for level calculation	Correlation with change in income inequality, 1980–2016 approx.	Number of countries for change calculation
90th percentile of income of professional occupations/ Median income of all workers 18–65	0.91	20	0.32	20
Racial diversity of country	0.78	35	0.18	35
Medium income of professional occupations/ Median income of all workers 18–65	0.75	20	0.22	20
90th percentile of income of managerial occupations/ Median income of all workers 18–65	0.73	21	−0.02	21
Tax revenue as share of GDP	−0.72	35	−0.20	35
Number of people of working age per number of retirement age	0.71	33	−0.12	33
Political stability and absence of violence/ terrorism	−0.69	35	−0.14	35
Number of physicians with income in top 1%/total number of workers in top 1%	0.67	8	0.37	8
Mean test scores, 15-year-olds	−0.67	34	−0.03	34
Medium income of managerial occupations/ Median income of all workers 18–65	0.64	21	−0.08	21

Note: See online supplemental materials for details on sources and methods. These materials are available at https://github.com/jtrothwell/Republic_Equals.

sources are documented in the supplemental materials (https://github.com/jtrothwell/Republic_Equals).

I used three measures of inequality: the UN Gini coefficient for the latest available year; the top-one-percent share of income from the World Inequality Database, and a composite measure of the UN Gini, the WID top-one-percent share, and the Luxembourg Income Study Gini coefficient. This index should capture multiple related dimensions of inequality, given the different sources, and offers a robust summary measure.

In the OECD, only Chile, Mexico, and Turkey are more unequal than the United States, which is 1.7 standard deviations above the mean on the average of its three inequality measures. Israel is close behind at 1.2. Denmark has the lowest inequality at −1.1 standard deviations below the mean. Notably, racial diversity and elite professional power are much more prevalent in the most unequal countries. For example, in Denmark, professionals at the 90th percentile are paid only two times as much (100 percent more) as the median worker, but in the United States they are paid 3.5 times as much (250 percent more). Only Mexico and Israel exhibit greater economic advantage for professionals than the United States (table A.8).

The regression results (which are available in the supplemental materials) reveal only four variables to be consistently significant (5 percent p-values or lower) across the models: racial diversity (higher inequality), patenting (lower inequality), elite professional power (higher inequality), and tax burden as a share of GDP (lower inequality).

The following variables are all consistently insignificant: the labor share of income, the change in the labor share of income, the number of union members as a share of all workers, changes in unionization, the minimum wage, labor protections, the skill of the workforce, the gap in skills between top-scoring students and the median student, the corporate tax rate, the individual tax rate, the progressivity of individual taxation, institutional quality as measured by the Heritage Foundation and World Bank, trade openness, and exposure to globalization.

These correlations and regression results do not provide direct evidence of a causal relationship. I rely on the logic of the book—and the history and form of the regulations responsible—rather than country-level statistical analysis to make that case. I make all the data publicly available.

In short, the results are strongly consistent with the main theme of this book: Providing high-quality public services—funded by government—and

Table A.8. Summary data on inequality, racial diversity, and elite professional power

	Inequality index	UN Gini	Top 1% share of income	Racial diversity	Elite professional power
Chile	3.2	53.3		0.51	
Mexico	3.0	50.8		0.52	6.0
Turkey	2.0	42.4	21%	0.20	
United States	1.7	39.9	20%	0.43	3.5
Israel	1.2	39.4		0.46	4.5
Estonia	0.5	36.5		0.02	3.1
United Kingdom	0.5	34.5	13%	0.10	3.1
Greece	0.5	36.3		0.00	2.9
Canada	0.4	34.2	14%	0.32	
Poland	0.3	34.8	12%	0.01	3.1
Portugal	0.2	38.2	10%	0.03	
Latvia	0.2	35.1		0.05	
Australia	0.2	37.4	9%	0.20	
Japan	0.1	36.3	10%	0.00	
Korea	0.1	33.0	12%	0.00	
Spain	0.1	34.1	9%	0.02	3.2
Italy	0.0	34.2	9%	0.00	
Ireland	0.0	35.1	11%	0.00	3.0
Germany	−0.1	30.2	13%	0.06	3.3
France	−0.2	31.4	11%	0.13	3.3
New Zealand	−0.2	35.6	8%	0.31	
Switzerland	−0.3	30.3	11%	0.03	2.4
Hungary	−0.5	27.6	10%	0.07	2.7
Austria	−0.6	30.0		0.03	2.7
Luxembourg	−0.6	30.0		0.02	3.0
Belgium	−0.6	30.1		0.04	
Czech Republic	−0.7	29.9	9%	0.00	
Slovakia	−0.8	29.2		0.01	
Finland	−0.9	29.2	7%	0.00	2.2
Norway	−0.9	29.3	8%	0.00	
Netherlands	−0.9	29.8	6%	0.08	2.3
Sweden	−1.0	25.5	9%	0.01	
Iceland	−1.0	28.8		0.00	2.1
Slovenia	−1.0	26.7		0.00	2.3
Denmark	−1.1	27.8	6%	0.02	2.0

Note: Elite professional power is measured as the 90th percentile of earnings for professional workers relative to the national median. Racial diversity is the share of population from each continent. See online supplemental materials for details on sources and methods, available at https://github.com/jtrothwell/Republic_Equals.

curbing the power of elite professionals will lower income inequality. Racial diversity predicts higher inequality only because prejudice and the doctrine of white supremacy have led to the exclusion of black minorities and Native Americans from public services and markets. The patent finding suggests that innovation lowers inequality, but it could also be the case that egalitarian societies are more innovative. I believe both are true. Combating racism and curbing professional privilege will sap the motivation and support for the unfair laws and behavior that generate and perpetuate inequality.

To conclude the arguments, markets that allow mutually beneficial exchange do not naturally lead to extreme inequality. They tend to reward more productive people, but nearly everyone can contribute to society productively. The distribution of talent is naturally egalitarian across individuals and completely so across groups. This is not to deny that some people are born more conscientious and brighter than others, but the extra rewards generated by these advantages are modest relative to the enormous gaps in income observed in many democracies today.

NOTES

1. BEHIND THE DISCONTENT

1. Time Staff, "Here's Donald Trump's Presidential Announcement Speech," *Time*, June 15, 2016, http://time.com/3923128/donald-trump-announcement-speech/.

2. Cas Mudde, "The Far Right in the 2014 European Elections: Of Earthquakes, Cartels, and Designer Fascists," *Washington Post*, May 30, 2014, https://www.washingtonpost.com/news/monkey-cage/wp/2014/05/30/the-far-right-in-the-2014-european-elections-of-earthquakes-cartels-and-designer-fascists/?utm_term=.774be9678793; Brian Wheeler, Paul Seddon, and Richard Morris, "Brexit: All You Need to Know about the UK Leaving the EU," *BBC News*, May 10, 2019, http://www.bbc.com/news/uk-politics-32810887.

3. Bryony Jones and Hillary Clarke, "Le Pen Faces Macron in Final Round of Presidential Election," CNN, April 24, 2017, http://www.cnn.com/2017/04/23/europe/french-presidential-election-results/.

4. My analysis of data from Gallup World Poll, https://www.gallup.com/analytics/232838/world-poll.aspx (accessed May 29, 2019).

5. Mudde, "The Far Right in the 2014 European Elections."

6. "France Fuel Protests: Who Are the 'Gilets Jaunes' (Yellow Vests)?" *BBC News*, December 6, 2018.

7. Simon Schutz, "Germany's Far-Right AfD Party Now Polls Second," National Public Radio, September 30, 2018, https://www.npr.org/2018/09/30/652284976/germanys-far-right-afd-party-now-polls-second.

8. Annual growth rates are weighted by population. Data are from Penn World Tables 9.0; see Robert C. Feenstra, Robert Inklaar, and Marcel P. Timmer, "The Next Generation of the Penn World Table," *American Economic Review* 105.10 (2015): 3150–82, www.ggdc.net/pwt.

9. These numbers are disputed by two other economists: Gerald Auten and David Splinter, "Top 1% Income Shares: Comparing Estimates Using Tax Data," *AEA Papers & Proceedings*, forthcoming 2019, https://www.aeaweb.org/conference/2019/preliminary/paper/k3bn5Qak. I analyzed appendix data from this research posted by Splinter and note two things: First, the Auten-Splinter measure of fiscal income (which is essentially all taxable income from labor or capital) showed an increase in top one-percent income shares of 9.9 percent to 21.8 percent from 1979 to 2014, which essentially matches data from the Congressional Budget Office, as well as Thomas Piketty, Emmanuel Saez, and Gabriel Zucman, "Distributional National Accounts: Methods and Estimates for the United States," *Quarterly*

Journal of Economics 133.2 (2017): 553–609. Second, the dispute comes in considering pretax nonfiscal income, which includes concepts such as imputed rent to homeowners, unrealized pension contributions, realized capital gains, corporate retained earnings, and underreported income, all of which are much harder to measure and impute to individual tax filers relative to fiscal income. Auten-Splinter estimate a top one-percent share of just 13.1 percent after including nonfiscal income. After making various assumptions, their calculations imply that the top one percent's share of nonfiscal income went from 10.3 percent in 1979 to just 3.7 percent, despite a doubling of fiscal income. I agree with Piketty, Saez, and Zucman that this is highly implausible and contradicts reasonable assumptions about underreported income. But even if Auten and Splinter are closer to the truth, everyone agrees that there was a large increase in income inequality and that the top one percent control roughly 20 percent of taxable income.

10. Piketty, Saez, and Zucman, "Distributional National Accounts." Table B3 in appendix 2 shows that from 1980 to 2014, average pretax income growth was as follows for all tax units aged 20 and over (with income split equally for those filing jointly): 61 percent for total population, 1 percent for the bottom 50 percent, 42 percent for the middle 50th–90th income earners, 121 percent for the top 10 percent, and 204 percent for the top 1 percent. This income concept includes all labor and capital income, as well as Social Security, retirement income, disability, and unemployment insurance income. It does not include government taxes and transfers. The Census Bureau collects self-reported income data from these sources (excluding capital gains) and finds that median income for full-time year-round workers increased by only 3 percent for men and 34 percent for women from 1980 to 2017; see "Table P-36. Full-Time, Year-Round All Workers by Median Income and Sex: 1955 to 2017," https://www.census.gov/data/tables/time-series/demo/income-poverty/historical-income-people.html (accessed May 13, 2019).

11. See appendix 2, table E3, in Piketty, Saez, and Zucman, "Distributional National Accounts."

12. Edward N. Wolff, "Household Wealth Trends in the United States, 1962 to 2016: Has Middle Class Wealth Recovered?," NBER Working Paper No. 24085, Cambridge, MA: National Bureau of Economic Research, 2017. National Accounts data show the national savings rate is also at historical lows, much lower than in the 1960s and 1970s; see U.S. Bureau of Economic Analysis, "Table 2.1. Personal Income and Its Disposition," https://www.bea.gov/ (accessed June 20, 2019).

13. See Appendix Table "Composition of Bottom 90%, Bottom 50%, and Middle 40% Pre-Tax Income Shares: Taxable vs. Tax-Exempt Income," in Thomas Piketty, Emmanuel Saez, and Gabriel Zucman, "Distributional National Accounts: Methods and Estimates for the United States," *Quarterly Journal of Economics* 133.2 (2017): 553–609.

14. Piketty, Saez, and Zucman, "Distributional National Accounts."

15. It should be noted these data go beyond tax records to impute income from nontaxable benefits, such as those from employers and the government, as well as home ownership; see Piketty, Saez, and Zucman, "Distributional National Accounts." They are the best and most comprehensive measures of income available, because they combine survey data with detailed tax data and detailed national accounting data.

16. The four Gallup World Poll questions are as follows: "(1) Which one of these phrases comes closest to your own feelings about your household's income these days: living comfortably on present income, getting by on present income, finding it difficult on present income,

or finding it very difficult on present income? (2) Are you satisfied or dissatisfied with your standard of living, all the things you can buy and do? (3) Right now, do you feel your standard of living is getting better or getting worse? (4) Right now, do you think that economic conditions in the city or area where you live, as a whole, are getting better or getting worse?" I standardized responses to each question—coded so negative responses have higher values—and took the mean. The resulting financial anxiety index is highly correlated with confidence in government and approval of the president or prime minister, depending on the country. To establish this, I regress political satisfaction (measured by either confidence in government or approval of leaders) on financial anxiety, the log of income, the quintile income rank, educational attainment binary variables, age, age^2, and age^3, gender, foreign-born status, and employment status in OECD countries, controlling for country-fixed effects and year-fixed effects, during the years 2013–2017. The sample size is 129,551. A one standard deviation increase in financial anxiety increases probability of lacking confidence by 18 percentage points and increases probability of disapproval of government by 16 percentage points.

17. Benjamin M. Friedman, "The Moral Consequences of Economic Growth," *Society* 43.2 (2006): 15–22; Francis Fukuyama, "Dealing with Inequality," *Journal of Democracy* 22.3 (2011): 79–89.

18. Daron Acemoglu, "Import Competition and the Great US Employment Sag of the 2000s," *Journal of Labor Economics* 34.S1 (2016): S141–98.

19. David Autor, David Dorn, Gordon H. Hanson, and Jae Song, "Trade Adjustment: Worker-Level Evidence," *Quarterly Journal of Economics* 129.4 (2014): 1799–1860. According to the authors' data, the average wage in manufacturing was roughly $38,000 around 1990. They say the cumulative effect over 16 years was 46 percent of that baseline amount, which is roughly $1,100 per year.

20. Jonathan T. Rothwell, "Cutting the Losses: Reassessing the Costs of Import Competition to Workers and Communities," Working Paper, March 22, 2017, https://ssrn.com /abstract=2920188, or http://dx.doi.org/10.2139/ssrn.2920188.

21. Christian Broda and John Romalis, *Inequality and Prices: Does China Benefit the Poor in America?* (Chicago: University of Chicago Press, 2008).

22. See U.S. Bureau of Labor Statistics, "Table 1110. Deciles of Income before Taxes: Annual Expenditure Means, Shares, Standard Errors, and Coefficients of Variation," *Consumer Expenditure Survey*, 2017, https://www.bls.gov/cex/tables.htm.

23. Michael A. Clemens and Jennifer Hunt, *The Labor Market Effects of Refugee Waves: Reconciling Conflicting Results*, No. w23433 (Cambridge, MA: National Bureau of Economic Research, 2017). For an opposing argument, see George J. Borjas, *We Wanted Workers: Unraveling the Immigration Narrative* (New York: W. W. Norton, 2016).

24. G. I. P. Ottaviano and G. Peri, "Rethinking the Effect of Immigration on Wages," *Journal of the European Economic Association* 10.1 (2012): 152–97; National Academies of Sciences, Engineering, and Medicine, *The Economic and Fiscal Consequences of Immigration* (Washington, DC: The National Academies Press, 2017), doi: https://doi.org/10.17226 /23550.

25. Borjas, *We Wanted Workers*.

26. See Table 5-1 in National Academies of Sciences, Engineering, and Medicine, *The Economic and Fiscal Consequences of Immigration*.

27. George J. Borjas, "Yes, Immigration Hurts American Workers; The Candidates Tell Drastically Different Stories about Immigration. They're Both Skipping Half the Truth,"

Politico, October 2016, https://www.politico.com/magazine/story/2016/09/trump-clinton
-immigration-economy-unemployment-jobs-214216.

28. National Academies of Sciences, Engineering, and Medicine, *The Economic and Fiscal Consequences of Immigration*, "Table 8-12. 75-Year Net Present Value Flows for Consolidated Federal, State, and Local Governments for Two Future Budget Scenarios," and Table 8-13, which shows the fiscal effects compared with natives.

29. Raj Chetty, Nathaniel Hendren, Maggie R. Jones, and Sonya R. Porter, *Race and Economic Opportunity in the United States: An Intergenerational Perspective*, No. w24441 (Cambridge, MA: National Bureau of Economic Research, 2018).

30. The methods appendix describes this analysis, and external data files available online reproduce it.

31. Bernie 2020, Issues, "Fight for Working Families," https://berniesanders.com/issues /fight-for-working-families/ (accessed May 29, 2019).

32. Loukas Karabarbounis and Brent Neiman, "The Global Decline of the Labor Share," *Quarterly Journal of Economics* 129.1 (2013): 61–103.

33. Jared Bernstein, "Why Labor's Share of Income Is Falling," *New York Times*, Economix Blog, September 9, 2013.

34. International Labor Organization, "Global Wage Report 2012/13: Wages and Equitable Growth" (Geneva: International Labour Office, 2013).

35. U.S. Census Bureau, "P23-212, 65+ in the United States: 2010" (Washington, DC: U.S. Government Printing Office, 2014).

36. OECD, "Annual Survey of Large Pension Funds and Public Pension Reserve Funds: Report on Pension Funds' Long-Term Investments," 2005, http://www.oecd.org/daf/fin /private-pensions/2015-Large-Pension-Funds-Survey.pdf.

37. Louise Story, "G.M.'s Unit for Investing to Attract Pay Scrutiny," *New York Times*, August 13, 2009, https://www.nytimes.com/2009/08/14/business/14pay.html.

38. Matthew Rognlie, "Deciphering the Fall and Rise in the Net Capital Share: Accumulation or Scarcity?" *Brookings Papers on Economic Activity* 2015.1 (2016): 1–69, 2.

39. OECD, "HM1.3 Housing Tenures," OECD Affordable Housing Database, n.d., https://www.oecd.org/els/family/HM1-3-Housing-tenures.pdf (accessed April 17, 2019).

40. Josh Bivens and Lawrence Mishel, "Understanding the Historic Divergence between Productivity and a Typical Worker's Pay: Why It Matters and Why It's Real" (Washington, DC: Economic Policy Institute, 2015).

41. For a definition of foreign versus domestic corporate profits, see Douglas R. Fox et al., "Chapter 13 Corporate Profits," in *NIPA Handbook: Concepts and Methods of the U.S. National Income and Product Accounts*," U.S. Bureau of Economic Analysis, https://www.bea .gov/system/files/2019-05/Chapter-13.pdf (accessed May 29, 2019).

42. My analysis of data from appendix tables A2 and A2b in Piketty, Saez, and Zucman, "Distributional National Accounts." Specifically, I added up the bottom 90 percent and top 10 percent shares of national income that come from equities. This equals the value of equities divided by national income. I then divided the top 1 percent share of national income from equities by the total to get 64 percent in 2014. As it happens, 21 percent goes to the top 90 to 99 percent, and the rest, 15 percent, goes to the bottom 90 percent, according to their data.

43. My analysis of data from appendix tables A2, A2b, and A2c in Piketty, Saez, and Zucman, "Distributional National Accounts."

44. My analysis of data from appendix table A2b in Piketty, Saez, and Zucman, "Distributional National Accounts." Specifically, I divided the top 1 percent share of total income by the top 1 percent share of equity income in 1980 and 2014.

45. U.S. Internal Revenue Services, "U.S. Individual Income Tax: Personal Exemptions and Lowest and Highest Bracket Tax Rates, and Tax Base for Regular Tax," https://www .irs.gov/statistics/soi-tax-stats-historical-table-23 (accessed May 29, 2019). For data on effective payments, see Piketty, Saez, and Zucman, "Distributional National Accounts," Appendix Table TG1.

46. My analysis of raw data from the World Inequality Database's STATA download tool, "wid," which pulls in raw data from the website wid.world.

47. Richard V. Reeves, *Dream Hoarders: How the American Upper Middle Class Is Leaving Everyone Else in the Dust, Why That Is A Problem, and What to Do About It* (Washington, DC: Brookings Institution Press, 2018).

48. David Autor, "Skills, Education, and the Rise of Earnings Inequality among the 'Other 99 Percent,'" *Science* 344.6186 (2014): 843–51. See also Philip Oreopoulos and Uros Petronijevic, "Making College Worth It: A Review of the Returns to Higher Education," *Future of Children* 23.1 (2013): 41–65, http://www.jstor.org/stable/23409488.

49. Patricia Cohen, "'Superstar Firms' May Have Shrunk Workers' Share of Income," *New York Times*, March 8, 2017; David Autor, David Dorn, Lawrence Katz, Christina Patterson, and John van Reenen, "The Fall of the Labor Share and the Rise of Superstar Firms," National Bureau of Economic Research Working Paper No. 23396 (2017).

50. David Card, "The Causal Effect of Education on Earnings," in *Handbook of Labor Economics*, 3: 1801–63 (Elsevier, 1999).

51. N. Gregory Mankiw, "Defending the One Percent," *Journal of Economic Perspectives* 27.3 (2013): 21–34.

52. For evidence of large industry effects on earnings, controlling for human capital, see John Abowd, Francis Kramarz, Paul Lengermann, Kevin McKinney, and Sébastien Roux, "Persistent Inter-Industry Wage Differences: Rent Sharing and Opportunity Costs," *IZA Journal of Labor Economics* 1.1 (2012): 1–25.

53. Jason M. Thomas, "Where Have All the Public Companies Gone?," *Wall Street Journal*, November 16, 2017; Ian Hathaway and Robert E. Litan, "The Other Aging of America: The Increasing Dominance of Older Firms" (Washington, DC: The Brookings Institution, 2014).

54. Christina Starmans, Mark Sheskin, and Paul Bloom, "Why People Prefer Unequal Societies," *Nature Human Behaviour* 1 (2017): 0082.

55. Jon Bakija, Adam Cole, and Bradley T. Heim, "Jobs and Income Growth of Top Earners and the Causes of Changing Income Inequality: Evidence from US Tax Return Data," unpublished manuscript, Williams College, 2012.

56. Luxembourg Income Study (LIS) Database, 2019, http://www.lisdatacenter.org.

57. Sherwin Rosen, "The Economics of Superstars," *American Economic Review* 71.5 (1981): 845–58; Autor et al., "The Fall of the Labor Share and the Rise of Superstar Firms."

58. World Trade Organization, "Trade and Tariffs," n.d., https://www.wto.org/english /thewto_e/20y_e/wto_20_brochure_e.pdf (accessed April 17, 2019).

59. This is the population-weighted average share of workers in the top 1 percent of income earners in the mining, manufacturing, transportation, storage, and communications sectors for 24 OECD countries with available data. Data are from the Luxembourg Income Study (2019), using its sector classifications. The countries included use data from 2010 or later with the exception of Sweden, where the latest year is 2005.

60. Using data from the U.S. Bureau of Economic Analysis, this calculation divides exports of financial services (roughly $100 billion) by the value added by the financial and insurance services sector for 2015 ($1.3 trillion). Manufacturing exports, valued at just over $1.1 trillion, and divided by GDP, $2.2 trillion, were calculated from the United States International Trade Commission DataWeb.

61. This relationship holds using the World Income Database (https://wid.world), which is from tax records, or the Luxembourg Income Study, which is from survey-based sources. The correlation coefficient with the healthcare, education, and public administration share of the one percent using "GiniAll" from the latter database is 0.63 for 19 countries. For changes, it is 0.68 for 13 countries. This is calculated using Gini coefficient changes from 1979–1981 to 2008–2014, averaging within each time period. See appendix for more information.

62. Japan has the lowest share of the one percent from these domestic service industries, but not because it has a high percentage of top earners in global industries. Rather, Japan has a disproportionate share of top earners in other domestic industries such as construction (14 percent) and unclassifiable services (16 percent).

63. Analysis of 2015 American Community Survey via IPUMS USA, University of Minnesota, www.ipums.org. Steven Ruggles, Sarah Flood, Ronald Goeken, Josiah Grover, Erin Meyer, Jose Pacas, and Matthew Sobek, IPUMS USA: Version 9.0 [dataset] (Minneapolis, MN: IPUMS, 2019; https://doi.org/10.18128/D010.V9.0).

64. Lawrence Mishel and Natalie Sabadish, "CEO Pay and the Top 1%: How Executive Compensation and Financial-Sector Pay Have Fueled Income Inequality," *EPI Issue Brief* 331 (2012).

65. Analysis of 2015 American Community Survey via IPUMS USA.

66. These figures use the latest available data from the Luxembourg Income Study (2019), using the most-detailed occupational categories.

67. It's also worth pointing out that most managers in the top 1 percent work in domestic sectors. In the United States, only 28 percent of managers in the top 1 percent work in the export or tech-oriented sectors of agriculture, mining, manufacturing, and communications.

68. Analysis of 2015 American Community Survey via IPUMS USA.

69. 2011 data from Statistics Canada via Minnesota Population Center, Integrated Public Use Microdata Series, International: Version 7.1 [dataset] (Minneapolis, MN: IPUMS, 2018. https://doi.org/10.18128/D020.V7.1).

70. Electronic Health Records Incentives Program, Centers for Medicare and Medicaid Services, https://www.cms.gov/Regulations-and-Guidance/Legislation/EHRIncentivePrograms /index.html?redirect=/ehrincentiveprograms/ (accessed June 20, 2017). As late as 2007, two-thirds of physician's offices did not use electronic medical records; the share of physicians in the top 1 percent has not substantially changed since use became more widespread; see Chun-Ju Hsaio and Esther Hing, "Trends in Electronic Health Record System Use among Office-Based Physicians: United States, 2007–2012," National Health Statistics Report 75 (May 20, 2014), https://www.cdc.gov/nchs/data/nhsr/nhsr075.pdf#x2013.

71. The OECD's Programme for the International Assessment of Adult Competencies (PIAAC) survey collected cognitive performance data from approximately 5,000 U.S. residents in 2012. I excluded occupational categories with fewer than 50 respondents. Among the remainder, the highest-scoring occupational group was information and communications

technology (ICT) professionals, who scored .95 standard deviations above the mean U.S. score for combined results across three subjects (literacy, numeracy, and problem-solving). Science and engineering professionals' scores were the next highest (0.88 standard deviations above the mean). Business and administrative professions, legal, social, and cultural professions, and health professions all scored lower: 0.76, 0.68, and 0.54, respectively. Teaching professionals scored 0.58. Respondents were also asked to report their "level of computer use": 66 percent of ICT professionals reported complex computer use (as opposed to straightforward or moderate), compared with 27 percent of science and engineering professionals, 9 percent of business professionals, 3 percent of legal, social, and cultural professionals, and just 1 percent of health professionals.

72. Jonathan Rothwell, "Still Searching: Job Vacancies and STEM Skills" (Washington, DC: The Brookings Institution, 2014).

73. The U.S. total reported here adds legal occupations to arts, design, entertainment, sports, and media and social service and community occupations.

74. Luxembourg Income Study (2109), most recent year of data by country.

75. Autor et al., "The Fall of the Labor Share and the Rise of Superstar Firms."

76. Another, more sophisticated approach takes into account the amount the company spends on things like machines and energy, which complement workers. This is called "multifactor productivity" or "total-factor productivity." Multifactor productivity and worker productivity are highly correlated, at least in the United States, and I use worker productivity because of the data challenges of measuring multifactor productivity across countries and sectors.

77. Tesla, n.d. https://www.tesla.com/ (accessed June 19, 2017).

78. Technically, the key ratio is quality to cost, not price, but I wrote price above to simplify the discussion. In textbook microeconomic theory, prices and costs converge, but in real life this is not always the case, especially in the short term or if an industry is not very competitive. For example, a company could keep prices the same but reduce costs by shifting its supply chain to a lower-cost provider of the same quality. This would still result in economic growth, but the gains would go to the company's owners, not its customers.

79. The list is: Austria, Belgium, Denmark, Finland, France, Germany, Greece, Ireland, Italy, Luxembourg, Netherlands, Portugal, Spain, Sweden, United Kingdom. Data analyzed here are from Eurostat National Accounts data, https://ec.europa.eu/eurostat/data/database; productivity is calculated by dividing inflation-adjusted gross value added by the number of employees for each industry. Data for the United States is from the Bureau of Economic Analysis, https://www.bea.gov/, using the same formula.

80. One explanation for rising returns to capital is the large and growing foreign trade deficits run by the United States. Trade deficits mean that foreign banks accumulate U.S. dollars and are essentially forced to find something to do with them, often buying U.S. securities or, during the housing bubble of the early 2000s, purchasing mortgage backed securities.

81. Analysis of real GDP and employment data from Statistics Canada, https://www150.statcan.gc.ca/t1/tbl1/en/tv.action?pid=3610020701. Total GDP per worker growth in Canada over the same 2000–2015 period was 10 percent. Healthcare experienced −12 percent growth, whereas education experienced 4 percent growth. Professional services saw just 1 percent growth. Manufacturing registered 16 percent growth.

82. Jonathan Rothwell, "The Declining Productivity of Education," Washington, DC: The Brookings Institution, 2016.

83. Jonathan Rothwell, "No Recovery: An Analysis of Long-Term U.S. Productivity Decline" (Washington, DC: Gallup, 2016).

84. Kristopher J. Hult, Sonia Jaffe, and Tomas J. Philipson, *How Does Technological Change Affect Quality-Adjusted Prices in Health Care? Systematic Evidence from Thousands of Innovations*, No. w22986 (Cambridge, MA: National Bureau of Economic Research, 2016).

85. Robert J. Gordon, *The Rise and Fall of American Growth: The US Standard of Living Since the Civil War* (Princeton, NJ: Princeton University Press, 2017).

86. My analysis of data from "Confidence in Institutions," Gallup Poll, https://news .gallup.com/poll/1597/Confidence-Institutions.aspx (accessed May 31, 2019).

87. Sarah Flood, Miriam King, Renae Rodgers, Steven Ruggles, and J. Robert Warren, "Integrated Public Use Microdata Series, Current Population Survey: Version 6.0 [dataset]" (Minneapolis, MN: IPUMS, 2018), https://doi.org/10.18128/D030.V6.0.

88. Benjamin I. Page, Larry M. Bartels, and Jason Seawright, "Democracy and the Policy Preferences of Wealthy Americans," *Perspectives on Politics* 11.1 (2013): 51–73.

89. Centers for Medicare and Medicaid Services, The National Health Expenditure Accounts, 2018, https://www.cms.gov/Research-Statistics-Data-and-Systems/Statistics-Trends -and-Reports/NationalHealthExpendData/NationalHealthAccountsHistorical.html.

90. My analysis of Gallup Political/Economic Daily track data, asked January 9–10, 2017.

91. Jonathan Rothwell, "The Minuscule Importance of Manufacturing in Far-Right Politics," *New York Times*, Upshot, September 15, 2017.

92. Jonathan T. Rothwell and Pablo Diego-Rosell, "Explaining Nationalist Political Views: The Case of Donald Trump," November 2, 2016, https://ssrn.com/abstract=2822059, or http://dx.doi.org/10.2139/ssrn.2822059.

93. European Social Survey (ESS) Round 8 Data (2016), data file edition 2.1. NSD (Norwegian Centre for Research Data), Norway, Data Archive and distributor of ESS data for ESS European Research Infrastructure Consortium (ERIC), https://www.euro peansocialsurvey.org/data/conditions_of_use.html.

94. Frank Newport, "Republicans Upgrade Views of Their Own Financial Situation," Gallup Poll, March 22, 2017, https://news.gallup.com/poll/206792/republicans-upgrade -views-own-financial-situation.aspx; Frank Newport, "Americans View Finances through Lens of Political Identity," April 30, 2018, Gallup Poll, https://news.gallup.com/poll/233576 /americans-view-finances-lens-political-identity.aspx (emphasis in original).

95. For this analysis, I updated my previous work by using zip code population data from the 2016 5-Year American Community Survey. The sample size for this estimate is 73,950 white non-Hispanic Americans randomly selected by phone in 2016. Rothwell and Diego-Rosell, "Explaining Nationalist Political Views."

96. Results are based on author's analysis of European Social Survey Round 7 Data (2014), data file edition 2.2. https://www.europeansocialsurvey.org/.

The question about immigration policy requests: "Please tell me how important you think each of these things should be in deciding whether someone born, brought up and living outside [country] should be able to come and live here." On a scale of 0 to 10, where 10 is "extremely important," I coded people who answered that white race is important above 5. Questions about racial intelligence and work ethic were: "Do you think some races or ethnic groups are born less intelligent than others?" and "Do you think some races or ethnic groups are born harder working than others?" In both cases, far-right supporters were more likely to say yes than those who did not vote for the far right by a statistically significant margin at 95 percent confidence intervals. Among far-right supporters, 24 percent and

47 percent answered yes to the question about intelligence and work ethic, respectively. Among those who did not vote for a far-right party, only 14 percent and 40 percent, respectively, agreed with racist views. Far-right party support was coded as 1 if the respondent indicated that he or she voted for a party that was described as far right in the ESS7 documentation. I further checked this for consistency against a useful summary analysis by Mudde, "The Far Right in the 2014 European Elections."

97. Aaron Blake, "Republicans' Views of Blacks' Intelligence, Work Ethic Lag behind Democrats,'" *Washington Post*, March 31, 2017, https://www.washingtonpost.com/news/the -fix/wp/2017/03/31/the-gap-between-republicans-and-democrats-views-of-african -americans-just-hit-a-new-high/?utm_term=.e4d391c72273.

98. Blake, "Republicans' Views of Blacks' Intelligence."

99. My analysis of Gallup data, conducted June 7–July 1, 2016, from the Minority Rights and Relations poll.

100. John Sides, Michael Tesler, and Lynn Vavreck, *Identity Crisis: The 2016 Presidential Campaign and the Battle for the Meaning of America* (Princeton, NJ: Princeton University Press, 2018).

101. Louis Putterman and David N. Weil, "Post-1500 Population Flows and the Long-Run Determinants of Economic Growth and Inequality," *Quarterly Journal of Economics* 125.4 (2010): 1627–82.

102. My analysis of Gallup data, conducted June 7–July 1, 2016, for the Minority Rights and Relations poll. The sample included 2,314 non-Hispanic black respondents who were asked to answer yes or no to "Do you think racism against blacks is or is not widespread in the U.S.?"

103. ESS Round 8: European Social Survey Round 8 Data (2016).

104. Pew Research Center, "A Fragile Rebound for EU Image on Eve of European Parliamentary Elections," May 2014, Washington, DC, https://www.pewresearch.org/wp-content /uploads/sites/2/2014/05/2014-05-12_Pew-Global-Attitudes-European-Union.pdf.

105. Pew Research Center, p. 27.

106. Alberto Alesina, Michela Carlana, Eliana La Ferrara, and Paolo Pinotti, *Revealing Stereotypes: Evidence from Immigrants in Schools*, No. w25333 (Cambridge, MA: National Bureau of Economic Research, 2018).

107. Alberto Alesina, Armando Miano, and Stefanie Stantcheva, *Immigration and Redistribution*, No. w24733 (Cambridge, MA: National Bureau of Economic Research, 2018).

108. Allum Bokhari and Milo Yiannopoulos, "An Establishment Conservative's Guide to the Alt-Right," *Breitbart*, March 29, 2016.

109. P. S. Forscher and N. Kteily, "A Psychological Profile of the Alt-Right," Working Paper, August 10, 2017, https://osf.io/preprints/psyarxiv/c9uvw.

110. Ashley Jardina, Sean McElwee, and Spencer Piston, "How Do Trump Supporters See Black People? 'Less Evolved,'" *Slate*, November 7, 2016, http://www.slate.com/articles /news_and_politics/politics/2016/11/the_majority_of_trump_supporters_surveyed _described_black_people_as_less.html.

111. Leonie Huddy and Stanley Feldman, "On Assessing the Political Effects of Racial Prejudice," *Annual Review of Political Science* 12 (February 6, 2009): 423–47.

112. Forscher and Kteily, "A Psychological Profile of the Alt-Right."

113. My analysis of Gallup data, conducted June 7–July 1, 2016, for the Minority Rights and Relations poll. Among non-Hispanic whites, 40 percent of Trump supporters say the government should have no role in improving the social and economic position of black people. For non-Hispanic white Republicans with an unfavorable view of Trump, the share

is 29 percent, and it is 13 percent for non-Hispanic white Democrats. The sample sizes are 531, 199, and 2,178, respectively. Those who lean toward one party were allocated to that party but the results are similar without leaners.

2. THE NATURAL FOUNDATIONS OF A JUST SOCIETY

1. James Baldwin, *Notes of a Native Son* (Boston: Beacon Press, 1984), 13.

2. Anton-Hermann Chroust and David L. Osborn, "Aristotle's Conception of Justice," *Notre Dame Law Review* 17.129 (1942): 129–43, http://scholarship.law.nd.edu/ndlr/vol17/iss2/2.

3. The Hebrew god is quoted as commanding followers to use "just balances" and just currency. An unjust balance (or scale for measuring weight) would presumably favor the merchant at the expense of the producer or customer, by not measuring the true weight and undervaluing the market price of the product, as well as the materials and labor that went into it. Hence, to intentionally distort market prices is unjust. Even today, a common symbol of justice is a picture with a balanced scale. See Ezekiel 45:10, Bible, King James Version, https://quod.lib.umich.edu/cgi/k/kjv/kjv-idx?type=DIV2&byte=3276983; Leviticus 19:36, Bible, King James Version, http://quod.lib.umich.edu/cgi/k/kjv/kjv-idx?type=DIV2&byte=497716. On conformity with law, Ezekiel 18 defines a just man as one who does what is "lawful and right," and mentions following God's laws as examples; Bible, King James Version, https://quod.lib.umich.edu/cgi/k/kjv/kjv-idx?type=DIV2&byte=3140652.

4. Donald E. Brown, "Human Universals, Human Nature, and Human Culture," *Daedalus* 133.4 (2004): 47–54. See Brown's full list in Steven Pinker, *The Blank Slate: The Modern Denial of Human Nature* (New York: Penguin, 2003).

5. "Golden Rule," Wikipedia.com, n.d., https://en.wikipedia.org/wiki/Golden_Rule (accessed April 17, 2019).

6. Quoted in Abdusalam A. Guseinov, "The Golden Rule of Morality," *Russian Social Science Review* 55.6 (2014): 84–100; Ikechukwu Anthony Kanu, "Igwebuike as an Igbo-African Ethic of Reciprocity," *Igwebuike: An African Journal of Arts and Humanities* 3.2 (2017): 24.

7. Marcus Tullius Cicero, *Ethical Writings of Cicero: De Officiis, De Senecture, De Amicitia, and Scorpio's Dream* (Veritatis Splendor Publications, 2014), 305, 507, 466 (Kindle ed.).

8. Marcus Tullius Cicero, "On Duties III," in *Selected Works*, trans. Michael Grant (London: Penguin, 1960), 167.

9. Cicero, *Ethical Writings*.

10. While short of calling for the abolition of slavery, this is the most anti-slavery sentiment I've been able to find anywhere in the ancient world, including in the words of the Jewish prophets, Jesus, and Muhammed, though all held generous attitudes toward those with low social status. It is also worth pointing out that unlike in modern America, Roman slavery was neither a hereditary condition in the ancient world nor even permanent for many slaves. A few former slaves even went on to be emperors.

11. Pope John Paul II, *On Social Concern* (Vatican City: Vatican Press, 1987), sec. 42, http://www.vatican.va/holy_father/john_paul_ii/encyclicals/documents/hf_jp-ii_enc_30121987_sollicitudo-rei-socialis_en.html.

12. "The Teaching of Amenemhat I: Section 3," Digital Egypt for Universities, n.d., http://www.ucl.ac.uk/museums-static/digitalegypt/literature/teachingaisec3.html (accessed May 2,

2018). I am indebted to Dominic Perry's "The History of Egypt Podcast" for this insight; https://egyptianhistorypodcast.com/.

13. Sarah F. Brosnan and Frans B. M. de Waal, "Monkeys Reject Unequal Pay," *Nature* 425.6955 (2003): 297–99.

14. Frans de Waal, "Moral Behavior in Animals," TEDxPeachtree, November 2011, https://www.ted.com/talks/frans_de_waal_do_animals_have_morals/transcript?language=en.

15. Frans B. M. de Waal, Kristin Leimgruber, and Amanda R. Greenberg, "Giving Is Self-Rewarding for Monkeys," *Proceedings of the National Academy of Sciences* 105.36 (2008): 13685–89.

16. J. M. Burkart, E. Fehr, C. Efferson, and C. P. van Schaik, "Other-Regarding Preferences in a Non-Human Primate: Common Marmosets Provision Food Altruistically," *Proceedings of the National Academy of Sciences* 104.50 (2007): 19762–66.

17. Juliane Bräuer and Daniel Hanus, "Fairness in Non-Human Primates?" *Social Justice Research* 25.3 (2012): 256–76.

18. Ernst Fehr and Simon Gächter, "Cooperation and Punishment in Public Goods Experiments," *American Economic Review* 90.4 (2000): 980–94.

19. Samuel Bowles and Herbert Gintis, *A Cooperative Species: Human Reciprocity and Its Evolution* (Princeton, NJ: Princeton University Press, 2011).

20. Ernst Fehr and Simon Gächter, "Altruistic Punishment in Humans," *Nature* 415.6868 (2002): 137–40.

21. Joseph Henrich, Robert Boyd, Samuel Bowles, Colin Camerer, Ernst Fehr, Herbert Gintis, and Richard McElreath, "In Search of Homo Economicus: Behavioral Experiments in 15 Small-Scale Societies," *American Economic Review* 91.2 (2001): 73–78; P. R. Blake, K. McAuliffe, J. Corbit, T. C. Callaghan, O. Barry, A. Bowie, L. Kleutsch, et al., "The Ontogeny of Fairness in Seven Societies," *Nature* 528.7581 (2015): 258–61.

22. Bowles and Gintis, *A Cooperative Species*.

23. Grit Hein, Yosuke Morishima, Susanne Leiberg, Sunhae Sul, and Ernst Fehr, "The Brain's Functional Network Architecture Reveals Human Motives," *Science* 351.6277 (2016): 1074–78.

24. Amy Dawel, Richard O'Kearney, Elinor McKone, and Romina Palermo, "Not Just Fear and Sadness: Meta-Analytic Evidence of Pervasive Emotion Recognition Deficits for Facial and Vocal Expressions in Psychopathy," *Neuroscience & Biobehavioral Reviews* 36.10 (2012): 2288–2304.

25. Abigail A. Marsh, Sarah A. Stoycos, Kristin M. Brethel-Haurwitz, Paul Robinson, John W. VanMeter, and Elise M. Cardinale, "Neural and Cognitive Characteristics of Extraordinary Altruists," *Proceedings of the National Academy of Sciences* 111.42 (2014): 15036–41.

26. K. E. Langergraber, J. C. Mitani, and L. Vigilant, "The Limited Impact of Kinship on Cooperation in Wild Chimpanzees," *Proceedings of the National Academy of Sciences* 104.19 (2007): 7786–90.

27. Bowles and Gintis, *A Cooperative Species*.

28. Katherine McAuliffe, Natalie Shelton, and Lauren Stone, "Does Effort Influence Inequity Aversion in Cotton-Top Tamarins (*Saguinus oedipus*)?" *Animal Cognition* 17.6 (2014): 1289–1301; Sarah F. Brosnan and Frans B. M. de Waal, "Evolution of Responses to (Un)Fairness," *Science* 346.6207 (2014): 1251776.

29. Edward O. Wilson, *The Social Conquest of Earth* (New York: W. W. Norton, 2012), 4142 (Kindle ed.).

30. Jung-Kyoo Choi and Samuel Bowles, "The Coevolution of Parochial Altruism and War," *Science* 318.5850 (2007): 636–40.

31. My analysis of 61 hunter-gatherer cultures from the "Standard Cross-Cultural Sample" shows that only four were reported as not conducting intergroup trade; data are from George P. Murdock and Douglas R. White, "Standard Cross-Cultural Sample," *Ethnology* 8.4 (1969): 329–69.

32. Fotini Christia, *Alliance Formation in Civil Wars* (Cambridge: Cambridge University Press, 2012).

33. Thomas F. Pettigrew and Linda R. Tropp, "A Meta-Analytic Test of Intergroup Contact Theory," *Journal of Personality and Social Psychology* 90.5 (2006): 751; Jonathan T. Rothwell, "The Effects of Racial Segregation on Trust and Volunteering in US Cities," *Urban Studies* 49.10 (2012): 2109–36; Marcus Alexander and Fotini Christia, "Context Modularity of Human Altruism," *Science* 334.6061 (2011): 1392–94.

34. Cicero, *Ethical Writings*, 389, 383.

35. Plato, *The Republic*, trans. Benjamin Jowett (Titan Classics, 2015), 989 (Kindle ed.).

36. Plato, *The Republic*, 349.

37. Plato, *Laws*, in *Plato: The Complete Works* (e-artnow, 2015), 42816 (Kindle ed.).

38. Plato, *The Republic*, 989.

39. Steven Michels, "Democracy in Plato's *Laws*," Government, Politics, and Global Studies Faculty Publications, Paper 24, 2004, http://digitalcommons.sacredheart.edu /gov_fac/24.

40. First, Sparta initiated a rule by two rather than just one king. Then, Sparta make the kings equal in power to a parliamentary council of 28 elders "in the most important matters." Third, Sparta enacted some mechanism of electing "Ephors" who seemed to hold considerable legislative power. More important is that in laying out his ideal city, Plato departs somewhat from *The Republic* in advocating for a mix of monarchy and democracy, suggesting that the best attributes of Persia's monarchy—under a wise king such as Cyrus the Great—should be combined with Athenian democracy.

41. Michels, "Democracy in Plato's *Laws*"; Plato, *Laws*.

42. Plato, *The Republic*.

43. John Rawls, *Justice as Fairness: A Restatement* (Cambridge, MA: Harvard University Press, 2001), 42–43.

44. Kristin F. Butcher, *Assessing the Long-Run Benefits of Transfers to Low-Income Families* (Washington, DC: Brookings Institution Hutchins Center Working Paper 26, 2017), https://www.brookings.edu/research/assessing-the-long-run-benefits-of-transfers-to-low -income-families/.

45. Cicero, *Ethical Writings*, 350.

46. Leif Wenar, "John Rawls," in *The Stanford Encyclopedia of Philosophy*, ed. Edward N. Zalta, 2017, https://plato.stanford.edu/archives/spr2017/entries/rawls.

47. Paul Ricoeur, *The Just*, trans. David Pellauer (Chicago: University of Chicago Press, 2003), 54.

48. John Rawls, *A Theory of Justice* (Cambridge, MA: Harvard University Press, 1971), 3.

49. Karl Marx, "Critique of the Gotha Program," in *Marx/Engels Selected Works* (Moscow: Progress Publishers, 1970), 3:13–30.

50. Lars J. Lefgren, David P. Sims, and Olga B. Stoddard, "Effort, Luck, and Voting for Redistribution," *Journal of Public Economics* 143 (November 2016): 89–97.

51. Philip Taubman, "Soviet Law Widens Private Business," *New York Times*, November 20, 1986, https://www.nytimes.com/1986/11/20/world/soviet-law-widens-private-business.html.

52. Timothy Garton Ash, *The Magic Lantern: The Revolution of '89 Witnessed in Warsaw, Budapest, Berlin and Prague* (New York: Atlantic Books, 2014).

53. Rawls, *Justice as Fairness*.

54. Robert Nozick, *Anarchy, State, and Utopia* (New York: Basic Books, 2013); Friedrich August Hayek, *The Fatal Conceit: The Errors of Socialism*, vol. 1 (Chicago: University of Chicago Press, 2011).

55. R. P. Saller, *Personal Patronage under the Early Empire* (Cambridge: Cambridge University Press, 2002).

56. William V. Harris, *Ancient Literacy* (Cambridge, MA: Harvard University Press, 1991).

57. Amartya Sen, *Development as Freedom* (Oxford: Oxford University Press, 2001).

58. Martha Nussbaum, "Capabilities as Fundamental Entitlements: Sen and Social Justice," *Feminist Economics* 9.2–3 (2003): 33–59.

3. MERIT-BASED EGALITARIANISM

1. Bart de Langhe, Philip M. Fernbach, and Donald R. Lichtenstein, "Navigating by the Stars: Investigating the Actual and Perceived Validity of Online User Ratings," *Journal of Consumer Research* 42.6 (2016): 817–83; Abhijit Gosavi, William Daughton, Ozge Senoz, and V. A. Samaranayake, "Consumer Perception of US and Japanese Automobiles: A Statistical Comparison via Consumer Reports and J. D. Power & Associates Data," *International Journal of Engineering Management and Economics* 6.1 (2016): 1–18; Jose A. Guajardo, Morris A. Cohen, and Serguei Netessine, "Service Competition and Product Quality in the US Automobile Industry," *Management Science* 62.7 (2016): 1860–77, doi: 10.1287/mnsc.2015.2195.

2. Jonathan T. Rothwell, "Assessing the Validity of Consumer Ratings for Higher Education: Evidence from a New Survey," October 20, 2017. https://ssrn.com/abstract=2982395.

3. Patrick Kampkötter and Dirk Sliwka, "The Complementary Use of Experiments and Field Data to Evaluate Management Practices: The Case of Subjective Performance Evaluations," *Journal of Institutional and Theoretical Economics* 172.2 (2016): 364–89.

4. Nicholas Bloom, Christos Genakos, Raffaella Sadun, and John Van Reenen, "Management Practices across Firms and Countries," *Academy of Management Perspectives* 26.1 (2012): 12–33.

5. Anders Frederiksen, Fabian Lange, and Ben Kriechel, "Subjective Performance Evaluations and Employee Careers," *Journal of Economic Behavior & Organization* 134 (2017): 408–29.

6. T. J. Kane and D. O. Staiger, "Gathering Feedback for Teaching: Combining High-Quality Observations with Student Surveys and Achievement Gains" (Seattle, WA: Bill and Melinda Gates Foundation, 2012); M. Caridad Araujo, Pedro Carneiro, Yyannú Cruz-Aguayo, and Norbert Schady, "Teacher Quality and Learning Outcomes in Kindergarten," *Quarterly Journal of Economics* 131.3 (2016): 1415–53.

7. Alan Manning, "We Can Work It Out: The Impact of Technological Change on the Demand for Low-Skill Workers," *Scottish Journal of Political Economy* 51.5 (2004): 581–608.

8. To measure IQ, I used the percentile scores from a variety of different IQ tests because subjects were not all given the same test. The list is available on the NLSY website (https://www.nlsinfo.org/investigator/pages/search.jsp?s=NLSY79) and includes the Stanford-Binet, Henmon-Nelson, Wechsler, Lorge-Thorndike, and a few others, all administered in 1979.

9. This is consistent with other evidence that crystalized intelligence is more important than fluid intelligence in terms of predicting life outcomes, such as years of education. Mathilde Almlund, Angela Lee Duckworth, James J. Heckman, and Tim D. Kautz, "Personality Psychology and Economics," in *Handbook of the Economics of Education* (Elsevier, 2014), 4: 1–181.

10. These results can be replicated using the NLSY 1997 database and including a squared term for the Armed Services Vocational Aptitude Battery (ASVAB) score that combines math and verbal performance; see https://www.nlsinfo.org/investigator/pages/search.jsp?s=NLSY79.

11. I supplement this with "Program for the International Assessment of Adult Competencies (PIAAC) 2012/2014: U.S. National Supplement Public Use Data Files—Household," a U.S. file not originally included in the PIAAC release. It is available through the U.S. National Center for Educational Statistics, https://nces.ed.gov/pubsearch/pubsinfo.asp?pubid=2016667REV. I remove the prison population to maintain a consistent population for comparison.

12. For a regression of log earnings (which includes salary, wages, and bonuses) on age, age^2, age^3, and age^4, measured in five-year bands, the adjusted r-squared is 0.235. For a regression of log earnings on cognitive ability, it is 0.225. For educational attainment and for gender, the r-squared is 0.23. These regressions include country-fixed effects. When combining all of the variables, the coefficient on cognitive ability is 0.13, and all the other terms remain highly significant.

13. To make this calculation, I regress the log of earnings on cognitive ability, educational attainment (measured as binary variables for primary and secondary school completion and associate's, bachelor's, and graduate degrees), age, age^2, age^3, and age^4, and an indicator for male for 72,000 individuals. I do the same for health status, measured on a 1–5 scale. I then predict both outcomes based on the underlying variables. The Gini coefficients for income and health are .47 and .52, respectively. The Gini coefficients for predicted income and predicted health (based on IQ and the other factors) are .17 and .21, respectively.

14. My analysis of IPUMS CPS; Sarah Flood, Miriam King, Renae Rodgers, Steven Ruggles, and J. Robert Warren, Integrated Public Use Microdata Series, Current Population Survey: Version 6.0 [dataset] (Minneapolis, MN: IPUMS, 2018), https://doi.org/10.18128/D030.V6.0.

15. To calculate this, I use $50,000 for the average salary in the PIAAC database (the mean is actually $41,000 in purchasing power parity adjusted dollars but would be higher in actual dollars because Europe tends to be more expensive). I multiply the standardized IQ score (3.27 for IQ of 149) by .13, which is the average predicted effect of IQ on income, which yields 0.42. The natural log of $50,000 is 10.8; 10.8 plus .42 yields 11.23, which amounts to $76,000. The 149 IQ figure for the top 0.1 percent comes from Jack Cox, "Smarter than 99.9% of the Rest of Us," *Denver Post*, June 20, 2005, https://www.denverpost.com/2005/06/20/smarter-than-99-9-of-the-rest-of-us/. The average predicted effect comes from the regression described above.

16. On the basis of the NLSY 1997, the Gini coefficients for personality, cognitive ability, income, and health are 0.22, 0.37, 0.41, and 0.49, respectively.

17. I calculate an age-cohort-adjusted measure of IQ by combining PIAAC test scores for the math, literacy, and technology sections of the test; ages were grouped into 11 categories. I further removed the incarcerated population. The raw data with race variables included are available through the U.S. National Center for Educational Statistics, https://nces.ed.gov /pubsearch/pubsinfo.asp?pubid=2016667REV.

18. Richard J. Herrnstein and Charles Murray, *The Bell Curve: Intelligence and Class Structure in American Life* (New York: Simon and Schuster, 2010).

19. This NLS 1997 finding was generated by regressing the log of income in 2013 on the summary ASVAB score and binary variables for being male, having a mother with a bachelor's degree or higher education, black, Jewish, Asian, Hispanic, or multiracial, relative to a reference group of white non-Hispanics. The coefficient on black is negative and significant, and the reverse is true for the coefficients on maternal education and male. The implication is that pay gaps would be reduced for females, black people, and those born with less-educated mothers if pay were based only on the ASVAB score. The finding from the PIAAC used a similar model but adjusted for region by including binary variables for the South, Midwest, and West (with the Northeast as reference) categories, and controlling for suburban, town, and rural, with city being the reference category. The variable for male and maternal education of bachelor's degree or higher were statistically significant and positive. The variable for black was negative but not significant.

20. These data combine O*NET Version 19 scores on knowledge domains by occupation with American Community Survey data from the 2011–2015 sample, as produced and made available through IPUMS USA (University of Minnesota, www.ipums.org). I created the crosswalk between them using methods similar to those discussed in Jonathan Rothwell, "Defining Skilled Technical Work," prepared for the National Academies Board on Science, Technology, and Economic Policy Project on "The Supply Chain for Middle-Skilled Jobs: Education, Training and Certification Pathways," September 1, 2015, https://sites.national academies.org/cs/groups/pgasite/documents/webpage/pga_167744.pdf.

21. Lawrence H. Summers, "Remarks at NBER Conference on Diversifying the Science & Engineering Workforce," Cambridge, MA, January 14, 2005, https://www.harvard.edu /president/speeches/summers_2005/nber.php.

22. National Science Foundation, National Center for Science and Engineering Statistics, "Women, Minorities, and Persons with Disabilities in Science and Engineering," special tabulations of U.S. Department of Education, National Center for Education Statistics, Integrated Postsecondary Education Data System, Completions Survey, table 7-2, "Doctoral Degrees Awarded to Women, by field: 2004–2014," https://www.nsf.gov/statistics/2017 /nsf17310/data.cfm.

23. Charlotte Witt and Lisa Shapiro, "Feminist History of Philosophy," in *The Stanford Encyclopedia of Philosophy*, ed. Edward N. Zalta (2017), https://plato.stanford.edu/archives /spr2017/entries/feminism-femhist/.

24. Jonathan Wai, David Lubinski, and Camilla P. Benbow, "Spatial Ability for STEM Domains: Aligning over 50 Years of Cumulative Psychological Knowledge Solidifies Its Importance," *Journal of Educational Psychology* 101.4 (2009): 817; Lloyd G. Humphreys, David Lubinski, and Grace Yao, "Utility of Predicting Group Membership and the Role of Spatial Visualization in Becoming an Engineer, Physical Scientist, or Artist," *Journal of Applied Psychology* 78.2 (1993): 250.

25. PISA 2015 database, http://www.oecd.org/pisa/data/2015database/.

26. Among 15-year-olds who score 2 standard deviations or higher (using international means and variation) in the United States, 41 percent are female for science, 37 percent for math, and 55 percent for reading.

27. To test this, I regressed science and math scores separately on a variable that is the gap between paternal and maternal education levels (dad-mom) for girls and then for boys. A positive gap predicted lower scores for girls but higher scores for boys. The differences were statistically significant in three of the four cases (science for girls and math and science for boys).

28. Michel Duyme, Annick-Camille Dumaret, and Stanislaw Tomkiewicz, "How Can We Boost IQs of 'Dull Children'? A Late Adoption Study," *Proceedings of the National Academy of Sciences* 96.15 (1999): 8790–94.

29. For comprehensive discussion of personality, cognitive ability, and some of the evidence on their determinants, see Almlund et al., "Personality Psychology and Economics."

30. Almlund et al., "Personality Psychology and Economics."

31. Frederiksen, Lange, and Kriechel, "Subjective Performance Evaluations and Employee Careers."

32. Almlund et al., "Personality Psychology and Economics." For discussion of the relationship between job performance and cognitive ability, see Frank L. Schmidt and John Hunter, "General Mental Ability in the World of Work: Occupational Attainment and Job Performance," *Journal of Personality and Social Psychology* 86.1 (2004): 162–73.

33. Frank L. Schmidt, In-Sue Oh, and Jonathan A. Shaffer, "The Validity and Utility of Selection Methods in Personnel Psychology: Practical and Theoretical Implications of 100 Years of Research Findings," Fox School of Business Research Paper, October 17, 2016, https://ssrn.com/abstract=2853669.

34. This literature finds that conscientiousness has a negative correlation with IQ (General Mental Ability) of −0.07. The correlation between IQ and integrity is positive but only 0.05. Emotional stability is correlated with IQ at .16. The other "Big 5" personality traits (extroversion, openness to experience, and agreeableness) have very low correlations with performance, but some have incremental validity in that they add to the predictive power of selection when combined with IQ.

35. Schmidt, Oh, and Shaffer, "The Validity and Utility of Selection Methods in Personnel Psychology."

36. Patrick F. McKay and Michael A. McDaniel, "A Reexamination of Black-White Mean Differences in Work Performance: More Data, More Moderators," *Journal of Applied Psychology* 91.3 (2006): 538.

37. Philip Bobko, Philip L. Roth, and Denise Potosky, "Derivation and Implications of a Meta-Analytic Matrix Incorporating Cognitive Ability, Alternative Predictors, and Job Performance," *Personnel Psychology* 52.3 (1999): 561–89.

38. James K. Harter, Frank Schmidt, Sangeeta Agrawal, Stephanie Plowman, and Anthony Blue, "The Relationship between Engagement at Work and Organizational Outcomes: 2016 Q12 Meta-Analysis: Ninth Edition" (Washington, DC: Gallup, 2016).

39. J. K. Harter, F. L. Schmidt, J. W. Asplund, E. A. Killham, and S. Agrawal, "Causal Impact of Employee Work Perceptions on the Bottom Line of Organizations," *Perspectives on Psychological Science* 5.4 (2010): 378–89.

40. For information on how Gallup measures engagement, see Gallup Q12 Employee Engagement Survey, https://q12.gallup.com/public/en-us/Features. Gallup survey sources used here are described at the following links: Gallup Panel, https://www.gallup.com

/analytics/213695/gallup-panel.aspx; Gallup Healthways, https://www.gallup.com/175196 /gallup-healthways-index-methodology.aspx.

41. These gaps (.10 standard deviations) were calculated by regressing a summary mean index of the 12 Q12 items after standardizing each one on dummy variables for each racial group and for gender, controlling for age, age-squared, and age-cubed. The sample was limited to workers, but relaxing that makes little difference. The main finding was robust to controls for educational attainment and part-time work status. Similar results were found using the larger Gallup Healthways Wellbeing Index sample of 85,000 workers, https://www.gallup .com/175196/gallup-healthways-index-methodology.aspx (accessed June 1, 2019).

42. This analysis regresses three items from the Q12 (standardized) on age (age squared and cubed), gender, racial binary variables, education variables, marital status, the presence of children in the home, and employment status (full-time self-employed and full-time employed). I also control for whether the respondent reports that the company is hiring or reducing staff. People working at firms in which employment is being reduced score 0.42 standard deviations lower on engagement; at growing firms, engagement is 0.19 standard deviations higher. The religious, racial, and gender differences are not substantially affected by including or removing these controls, but including a control for education does reduce the predicted Jewish score.

43. Similar results can be found using the three items from the larger survey. Since one Q12 item could be seen as directly measuring performance, I examine that separately. On receiving praise for good work, 43 percent of black workers answered with a 4 or 5, suggesting agreement or strong agreement, compared to 44 percent of Asians, 52 percent of white people, and 55 percent of Hispanics. Again, this suggests small gaps that are inconsistent with typical social status perceptions of these groups.

44. Patrick F. McKay, Derek R. Avery, and Mark A. Morris, "Mean Racial-Ethnic Differences in Employee Sales Performance: The Moderating Role of Diversity Climate," *Personnel Psychology* 61.2 (2008): 349–74.

45. Kim Mai-Cutler, "Here's a Detailed Breakdown of Racial and Gender Diversity Data across U.S. Venture Capital Firms," *TechCrunch*, October 6, 2015, https://techcrunch.com /2015/10/06/s23p-racial-gender-diversity-venture/.

46. S. B. Badal and J. H. Streur, "Builder Profile 10: Methodology Report" (Washington, DC: Gallup, 2014), https://www.gallupstrengthscenter.com/EP10/en-US/GetFile ?fileName=EP10%2FEP10_TalentDefinitions.pdf&language=en-US.

47. Jonathan Rothwell, "No Recovery: An Analysis of Long-Term U.S. Productivity Decline" (Washington, DC: Gallup, 2016).

48. Pamela Villarreal, *How Much Are Teachers Really Paid? A Nationwide Analysis of Teacher Pay* (Madison, WI: McIver Institute, 2014).

4. THE IMPORTANCE OF EQUAL ACCESS TO PUBLIC GOODS AND MARKETS

1. Adult education is considered a quasi-public good and should be partly subsidized with public money. It is partly private because there are large private benefits to education that immediately prepares adults for a certain occupation or career path, in the form of higher pay, for example. But is also public, because everyone is more productive when they are allowed to specialize and exchange with other specialists.

2. Earl J. Hamilton, "The Role of Monopoly in the Overseas Expansion and Colonial Trade of Europe before 1800," *American Economic Review* 38.2 (1948): 33–53.

3. Sheilagh Ogilvie, "The Economics of Guilds," *Journal of Economic Perspectives* 28.4 (2014): 169–92; Sheilagh Ogilvie, *Institutions and European Trade: Merchant Guilds, 1000–1800* (Cambridge: Cambridge University Press, 2011); Sheilagh Ogilvie, *The European Guilds: An Economic Analysis* (Princeton, NJ: Princeton University Press, 2019).

4. Ronald M. Davis and James Rohack, "The AMA & the NMA: Past, Present, and Future" (2008), https://www.ama-assn.org/sites/default/files/media-browser/public/ama-history/ama-nma-past-present-future_0.pdf; https://www.ama-assn.org/sites/default/files/media-browser/public/ama-history/african-american-physicians3-v2.pdf.

5. American Bar Association, timelines, http://www.americanbar.org/about_the_aba/timeline.html (accessed May 18, 2017).

6. Steven J. Jager, "William Henry Lewis, 1868–1949," *Black Past*, July 31, 2012, http://www.blackpast.org/aah/lewis-william-henry-1868-1949.

7. Tad Banicoff, "African Americans and Princeton University: A Brief History," Princeton University Library Guide, March 11, 2005, http://libguides.princeton.edu/c.php?g=84056&p=544526.

8. Douglas S. Massey and Nancy A. Denton, *American Apartheid: Segregation and the Making of the Underclass* (Cambridge, MA: Harvard University Press, 1993).

9. Kenneth T. Jackson, *Crabgrass Frontier: The Suburbanization of the United States* (New York: Oxford University Press, 1987).

10. Testimony of Robert D. Atkinson, President, Information Technology and Innovation Foundation, before the House Committee on Oversight and Government Reform Subcommittee on Information Technology, September 26, 2018, http://www2.itif.org/2018-testimony-atkinson-countering-china.pdf; Denis Blair and John Huntsman, "Update to the IP Commission Report: The Report of the Commission on the Theft of American Intellectual Property" (Seattle, WA: The National Bureau of Asian Research, February 2017).

11. Victor Nee and Sonja Opper, *Capitalism from Below: Markets and Institutional Change in China* (Cambridge, MA: Harvard University Press, 2012).

12. J. Fang, H. He, and N. Li, *China's Rising IQ (Innovation Quotient) and Growth: Firm-Level Evidence* (Washington, DC: International Monetary Fund, 2016).

13. K. Couch and D. Placzek, "Earnings Losses of Displaced Workers Revisited," *American Economic Review* 100.1 (2010): 572–89.

14. See historic data from the Job Openings and Labor Turnover Survey from the U.S. Bureau of Labor Statistics. My analysis of these data is in Jonathan T. Rothwell, "Cutting the Losses: Reassessing the Costs of Import Competition to Workers and Communities," October 19, 2017, https://ssrn.com/abstract=2920188.

15. Nancy M. Birdsall, Jose Edgardo L. Campos, Chang-Shik Kim, W. Max Corden, Howard Pack, John Page, Richard Sabor, and Joseph E. Stiglitz, *The East Asian Miracle: Economic Growth and Public Policy: Main Report*, ed. Lawrence MacDonald, World Bank policy research report (New York: Oxford University Press, 1993), http://documents.worldbank.org/curated/en/975081468244550798/Main-report.

16. M. Mazzucato, *The Entrepreneurial State: Debunking Public vs. Private Sector Myths*, vol. 1 (London: Anthem Press, 2015).

17. G. J. Borjas, *We Wanted Workers: Unraveling the Immigration Narrative* (New York: W. W. Norton, 2016).

18. Raj Chetty, Nathaniel Hendren, Maggie R. Jones, and Sonya R. Porter, *Race and Economic Opportunity in the United States: An Intergenerational Perspective*, No. w24441

(Cambridge, MA: National Bureau of Economic Research, 2018). See chapter 5 for my discussion of African immigrants to the United States (and Europe), which includes evidence that those raised in the United States exceed the education levels of U.S. natives.

19. The econometric model is restricted to the employed U.S.-born workforce. It regresses the log of total income on binary variables for education, race, and gender. It also includes age, age-squared, and age-cubed as controls and year-fixed effects, state-fixed effects, and broad occupational-fixed effects. Errors are clustered at state level. I use a definition of occupations that is consistent over the entire period (which is the occupational variable "occ1990" in the IPUMS database), but for the purposes of occupational-fixed effects, I use an aggregation of this into 24 broad occupations. To measure competition from foreign-born workers, I calculate the percentage of workers who are foreign born by state and occupation. This variable is negative and significantly correlated with the log of income. The coefficient is −0.2. If I use the broad occupational categories instead of the more detailed ones to measure competition from immigration, I get similar results. The data are from Sarah Flood, Miriam King, Renae Rodgers, Steven Ruggles, and J. Robert Warren, *Integrated Public Use Microdata Series, Current Population Survey: Version 6.0* [dataset] (Minneapolis, MN: IPUMS, 2018). https://doi.org/10.18128/D030.V6.0.

20. Simonetta Longhi, Peter Nijkamp, and Jacques Poot, "A Meta-Analytic Assessment of the Effect of Immigration on Wages," *Journal of Economic Surveys* 19.3 (2005): 451–77.

21. Marcus Tullius Cicero, *Ethical Writings of Cicero: De Officiis, De Senecture, De Amicitia, and Scorpio's Dream* (Veritatis Splendor Publications, 2014), 498 (Kindle ed.).

22. Cicero, *Ethical Writings*, 492.

23. Cicero, *Ethical Writings*, 446.

24. Migration Policy Institute (MPI) tabulation of data from U.S. Census Bureau, 2010–2017 American Community Surveys (ACS), and 1970, 1990, and 2000 Decennial Census. All other data are from Campbell J. Gibson and Emily Lennon, "Historical Census Statistics on the Foreign-Born Population of the United States: 1850 to 1990," Working Paper no. 29 (Washington, DC: U.S. Census Bureau, 1999).

25. Ashley S. Timmer and Jeffrey G. Williamson, "Immigration Policy prior to the Thirties: Labor Markets, Policy Interaction, and Globalization Backlash," *Population and Development Review* 24.4 (1998): 739–71; P. H. Lindert and J. G. Williamson, *Unequal Gains: American Growth and Inequality since 1700* (Princeton, NJ: Princeton University Press, 2016).

26. Immigrant population data from 1850 to 1990 come from the U.S. Census Bureau, https://www.census.gov/population/www/documentation/twps0029/tab01.html, and American Fact Finder for 2000, 2010, and 2017, https://factfinder.census.gov/faces/nav/jsf/pages/index.xhtml. Birth data are from the National Center for Health Statistics, NCHS Data Visualization Gallery: Natality Trends in the United States, 1909–2015, https://www.cdc.gov/nchs/data-visualization/natality-trends/index.htm.

27. U.S. Census Bureau, American Community Survey, 2017, https://factfinder.census.gov/faces/nav/jsf/pages/index.xhtml.

28. Douglas S. Massey, Jorge Durand, and Karen A. Pren, "Border Enforcement and Return Migration by Documented and Undocumented Mexicans," *Journal of Ethnic and Migration Studies* 41.7 (2015): 1015–40, doi: 10.1080/1369183X.2014.986079.

29. Jonathan Rothwell, "Still Searching: Job Vacancies and STEM Skills" (Washington, DC: The Brookings Institution Metropolitan Policy Program, 2014).

30. Eric Alden Smith, Kim Hill, Frank W. Marlowe, David Nolin, Polly Wiessner, Michael Gurven, Samuel Bowles, Monique Borgerhoff Mulder, Tom Hertz, and Adrian Bell,

"Wealth Transmission and Inequality among Hunter-Gatherers," *Current Anthropology* 51.1 (2010): 19–34. These authors estimate a Gini coefficient of inequality of 0.25 for wealth. That is comparable to Denmark's Gini coefficient for income and roughly half of the U.S. Gini coefficient for household income reported by the Census Bureau for 2017 of 0.48. U.S. wealth inequality, however, is much more severe, with a Gini coefficient of 0.88, according to Wolff's analysis of the Survey of Consumer Finances, U.S. Census Bureau, Historical Income Tables, "Table H-4. Gini Indexes for Households, by Race and Hispanic Origin of Householder: 1967 to 2017," https://www.census.gov/data/tables/time-series/demo/income-poverty /historical-income-inequality.html; Edward N. Wolff, "Household Wealth Trends in the United States, 1962 to 2016: Has Middle Class Wealth Recovered?" No. w24085 (Cambridge, MA: National Bureau of Economic Research, 2017).

5. UNEQUAL ACCESS TO EDUCATION

1. Frederick Douglass, *Narrative of the Life of Frederick Douglass* [1845] (Word Wise, 2012).

2. Civil Rights Act, 1964, transcript, https://www.ourdocuments.gov/doc.php?flash =false&doc=97&page=transcript.

3. James Coleman et al., *Equality of Educational Opportunity* (Washington, DC: U.S. Department of Health, Wealth, and Education, 1966).

4. Coleman et al., *Equality of Educational Opportunity*, 21–22.

5. Robert D. Putnam, *Our Kids: The American Dream in Crisis* (New York: Simon and Schuster, 2016), 182.

6. Gary Ravani, "Why No Excuses Makes No Sense: Revisiting the Coleman Report," *Washington Post*, July 23, 2011, https://www.washingtonpost.com/blogs/answer-sheet/post /why-no-excuses-makes-no-sense-revisiting-the-coleman-report/2011/07/23 /gIQAo7W7UI_blog.html?utm_term=.92a1692cb522.

7. Diane Ravitch, "Education: Achievement Gap Starts before School Starts," *mySA*, Thursday, October 13, 2011, https://www.mysanantonio.com/community/northwest/news /article/Education-Achievement-gap-starts-before-school-2213710.php.

8. Richard J. Herrnstein and Charles Murray, *The Bell Curve: Intelligence and Class Structure in American Life* (New York: Simon and Schuster, 1994), 394–96.

9. Charles Murray, *Coming Apart: The State of White America, 1960–2010* (New York: Crown Forum, 2012), 60.

10. Murray, *Coming Apart*, 62.

11. Caroline Hoxby, "The Immensity of the Coleman Data Project," *Education Next* 16.2 (2016).

12. Coleman et al., *Equality of Educational Opportunity*, table 3.221.1, 299.

13. Coleman et al., *Equality of Educational Opportunity*, table 3.221.1, 310.

14. Coleman et al., *Equality of Educational Opportunity*, table 2.41.1, 184.

15. As it happens, he uses many variables to attempt to measure family background; these include parental education, whether a father is present in the home, parental and student attitudes toward education. Together with school effects, these variables explain 42 percent to 53 percent of the variation in test scores, which still leaves roughly half of the variation to be explained. In other words, Coleman's analysis shows that schools are the most important measured factor in predicting black test scores. It seems a bit strange to then say that schools are of minor importance in his analysis.

16. Precisely a one-standard-deviation increase in teacher value-added predicts a 0.27 standard deviation increase in exam scores. A highly effective teacher (at the 75th percentile) can explain a large effect—.33 standard deviations—relative to a weakly effective teacher (at the 25th percentile). This analysis is particularly impressive because it controls for test scores at age 14 in the same subject as well as other subjects, thereby allowing the researchers to isolate the effect of subject-specific teachers. See Helen Slater, Neil M. Davies, and Simon Burgess, "Do Teachers Matter? Measuring the Variation in Teacher Effectiveness in England," *Oxford Bulletin of Economics and Statistics* 74.5 (2012): 629–45.

17. Marion F. Shaycoft, "Project TALENT. The High School Years: Growth in Cognitive Skills. Interim Report 3" (Washington, DC: Office of Education (DHEW), Bureau of Research, 1967).

18. Stuart J. Ritchie and Elliot Tucker-Drob, "How Much Does Education Improve Intelligence? A Meta-Analysis," *Psychological Science* 29.8 (2018): 1358–69.

19. I took the average of their reported effect using the raw study-level data that the authors posted online at https://osf.io/r8a24/.

20. Shaycoft, "Project TALENT."

21. James R. Flynn, "The Mean IQ of Americans: Massive Gains 1932 to 1978," *Psychological Bulletin* 95.1 (1984): 29.

22. Jakob Pietschnig and Martin Voracek, "One Century of Global IQ Gains: A Formal Meta-Analysis of the Flynn Effect (1909–2013)," *Perspectives on Psychological Science* 10.3 (2015): 282–306.

23. Tamara C. Daley, Shannon E. Whaley, Marian D. Sigman, Michael P. Espinosa, and Charlotte Neumann, "IQ on the Rise: The Flynn Effect in Rural Kenyan Children," *Psychological Science* 14.3 (2003): 215–19. The authors report an increase in IQ of 26.3 using the standard deviation from the 1984 sample. The raw increase corresponds to an increase of 11.2 using standard deviations observed in industrialized countries.

24. Jonathan Rothwell, José Lobo, Deborah Strumsky, and Mark Muro, "Patenting Prosperity: Invention and Economic Performance in the United States and Its Metropolitan Areas" (Washington, DC: The Brookings Institution, 2016).

25. M. A. Woodley of Menie, M. Peñaherrera-Aguirre, H. B. F. Fernandes, and A.-J. Figueredo, "What Causes the Anti-Flynn Effect? A Data Synthesis and Analysis of Predictors," *Evolutionary Behavioral Sciences* 12.4, 276–95 (forthcoming).

26. Pietschnig and Voracek, "One Century of Global IQ Gains."

27. OECD, "Pisa 2015 Results in Focus," *PISA in Focus* 67 (2016), https://www.oecd.org/pisa/pisa-2015-results-in-focus.pdf.

28. Edward Dutton and Richard Lynn, "A Negative Flynn Effect in Finland, 1997–2009," *Intelligence* 41.6 (2013): 817–20.

29. Bernt Bratsberg and Ole Rogeberg, "Flynn Effect and Its Reversal Are Both Environmentally Caused," *Proceedings of the National Academy of Sciences* 115.26 (2018): 6674–78.

30. Jungho Kim, "Female Education and Its Impact on Fertility," *IZA World of Labor* (2016), https://wol.iza.org/uploads/articles/228/pdfs/female-education-and-its-impact-on-fertility.one-pager.pdf.

31. This analysis compared math test scores in 2003 to those in 2015 using summary data for the country overall and by foreign-born status via the U.S National Center for Education Statistics International Data Explorer, https://nces.ed.gov/surveys/pisa/idepisa/ (accessed June 23, 2018).

32. Raj Chetty, John N. Friedman, and Jonah E. Rockoff, "Measuring the Impacts of Teachers I: Evaluating Bias in Teacher Value-Added Estimates," *American Economic Review* 104.9 (2014): 2593– 2632.

33. Raj Chetty, John N. Friedman, and Jonah E. Rockoff, "Measuring the Impacts of Teachers II: Teacher Value-Added and Student Outcomes in Adulthood," *American Economic Review* 104.9 (2014): 2633–79.

34. Andrew J. Mashburn, Robert C. Pianta, Bridget K. Hamre, Jason T. Downer, Oscar A. Barbarin, Donna Bryant, Margaret Burchinal, Diane M. Early, and Carollee Howes, "Measures of Classroom Quality in Prekindergarten and Children's Development of Academic, Language, and Social Skills," *Child Development* 79.3 (2008): 732–49.

35. Specifically, the difference in math learning between a teacher at the 25th percentile on the CLASS rating and one in the 75th percentile is 0.10 standard deviations for math, 0.05 for language, and 0.23 for student effort. The cognitive effect increases considerably when combined with two other quality measures—student ratings and the test score gains of prior students—to .24, .12, and .22 for math, language, and student effort, respectively. Student effort was measured by self-reported willingness to do work outside of the classroom. See Thomas J. Kane and Douglas O. Staiger, "Gathering Feedback for Teaching: Combining High-Quality Observations with Student Surveys and Achievement Gains," Measure of Effective Teaching (MET) Project (Seattle, WA: Bill & Melinda Gates Foundation, 2012).

36. A one-standard-deviation increase in the CLASS score caused a .11, .11, and .07 standard deviation increase in math, language, and executive functioning, respectively. See M. Caridad Araujo, Pedro Carneiro, Yyannú Cruz-Aguayo, and Norbert Schady, "Teacher Quality and Learning Outcomes in Kindergarten," *Quarterly Journal of Economics* 131.3 (2016): 1415–53.

37. For my analysis, see Jonathan T. Rothwell, "Classroom Inequality and the Cognitive Race Gap: Evidence from 4-Year-Olds in Public PreK," March 1, 2016, https://ssrn.com /abstract=2740527. For raw data, see D. Early, M. Burchinal, O. Barbarin, D. Bryant, F. Chang, R. Clifford, et al., *Pre-Kindergarten in Eleven States: NCEDL's Multi-State Study of Pre-Kindergarten and Study of State-Wide Early Education Programs (SWEEP)*, ICPSR34877-v1 (Ann Arbor, MI: Inter-university Consortium for Political and Social Research [distributor], 2013-10-02), http://doi.org/10.3886/ICPSR34877.v1.

38. Raw IQ scores were available for the Peabody Picture Vocabulary and Woodcock to Johnson III (math); see Early et al., *Pre-Kindergarten in Eleven States*.

39. Black students in top-quartile classes closed roughly 20 percent of the achievement gap on the Peabody vocabulary IQ test when compared to white people in top-quartile classes and 30 percent of the gap when compared to white students who did not attend top-quartile classes. The text refers to a mean of standardized scores across three IQ tests and four learning tests. For related analysis, see Jonathan T. Rothwell, "Classroom Inequality and the Cognitive Race Gap: Evidence from 4-Year-Olds in Public PreK," (March 1, 2016), https://ssrn .com/abstract=2740527 or http://dx.doi.org/10.2139/ssrn.2740527.

40. Dan Goldhaber, Lesley Lavery, and Roddy Theobald, "Uneven Playing Field? Assessing the Teacher Quality Gap between Advantaged and Disadvantaged Students," *Educational Researcher* 44.5 (2015): 293–307.

41. Bridget K. Hamre, Robert C. Pianta, Margaret Burchinal, Samuel Field, Jennifer LoCasale-Crouch, Jason T. Downer, et al., "A Course on Effective Teacher-Child Interactions: Effects on Teacher Beliefs, Knowledge, and Observed Practice," *American Educational Research Journal* 49.1 (2012): 88–123.

42. H. J. Kitzman, D. L. Olds, R. E. Cole, C. A. Hanks, E. A. Anson, K. J. Arcoleo, et al., "Enduring Effects of Prenatal and Infancy Home Visiting by Nurses on Children: Follow-Up of a Randomized Trial among Children at Age 12 Years," *Archives of Pediatrics & Adolescent Medicine* 164.5 (2010): 412–18.

43. Timothy J. Bartik, *From Preschool to Prosperity: The Economic Payoff to Early Childhood Education* (Kalamazoo, MI: Upjohn Institute for Employment Research, 2014), https://doi.org/10.17848/9780880994835.

44. Greg J. Duncan and Aaron J. Sojourner, "Can Intensive Early Childhood Intervention Programs Eliminate Income-Based Cognitive and Achievement Gaps?" *Journal of Human Resources* 48.4 (2013): 945–68.

45. Arthur J. Reynolds, Judy A. Temple, Dylan L. Robertson, and Emily A. Mann, "Long-Term Effects of an Early Childhood Intervention on Educational Achievement and Juvenile Arrest: A 15-Year Follow-Up of Low-Income Children in Public Schools," *Journal of the American Medical Association* 285.18 (2001): 2339–46.

46. Josh Dawsey, "Trump Derides Protections for Immigrants from 'Shithole' Countries," *Washington Post*, January 12, 2018, https://www.washingtonpost.com/politics/trump-attacks-protections-for-immigrants-from-shithole-countries-in-oval-office-meeting/2018/01/11/bfc0725c-f711-11e7-91af-31ac729add94_story.html?utm_term=.0ce470468b30.

47. For compelling evidence on the low quality of educational opportunities in poor countries, see UNESCO, "More Than One-Half of Children and Adolescents Are Not Learning Worldwide" (Paris: UNESCO Institute for Statistics, 2017), http://uis.unesco.org/sites/default/files/documents/fs46-more-than-half-children-not-learning-en-2017.pdf; Tessa Bold, Deon Filmer, Gayle Martin, Ezequiel Molina, Brian Stacy, Christophe Rockmore, et al., "Enrollment without Learning: Teacher Effort, Knowledge, and Skill in Primary Schools in Africa," *Journal of Economic Perspectives* 31.4 (2017): 185–204; Nazmul Chaudhury, Jeffrey Hammer, Michael Kremer, Karthik Muralidharan, and F. Halsey Rogers, "Missing in Action: Teacher and Health Worker Absence in Developing Countries," *Journal of Economic Perspectives* 20.1 (2006): 91–116.

48. Deborah Wilson, Simon Burgess, and Adam Briggs, "The Dynamics of School Attainment of England's Ethnic Minorities," *Journal of Population Economics* 24.2 (2011): 681–700; see working paper version at http://eprints.lse.ac.uk/6245/1/The_Dynamics_of_School_Attainment_of_England's_Ethnic_Minorities.pdf. I used their summary statistics in tables 2 and 3 to calculate IQ scores.

49. Feyisa Demie, "Raising the Achievement of Black African Pupils: Good Practice in Schools" (London: Lambeth Research and Statistics Unit, 2013), https://www.lambeth.gov.uk/rsu/sites/lambeth.gov.uk.rsu/files/Raising_the_Achievement_of_Black_African_Pupils-Good_Practice_in_Schools_2013.pdf.

50. Demie, "Raising the Achievement of Black African Pupils."

51. Jenny Easby, "GCSE and Equivalent Attainment by Pupil Characteristics, 2013 to 2014 (Revised)," United Kingdom Department of Education, January 29, 2015, figure 2, https://www.gov.uk/government/uploads/system/uploads/attachment_data/file/399005/SFR06_2015_Text.pdf.

52. Dominique Lemmermann and Regina T. Riphahn, "The Causal Effect of Age at Migration on Youth Educational Attainment," *Economics of Education Review* 63 (2018): 78–99.

53. Lemmermann and Riphahn, "The Causal Effect of Age at Migration on Youth Educational Attainment."

54. See UNESCO, "More Than One-Half of Children and Adolescents Are Not Learning Worldwide"; Bold et al., "Enrollment without Learning"; Chaudhury et al., "Missing in Action." For evidence that gray-matter volume in the frontal lobe of the brain levels off around ages 11 for females and 12 for males, see Jay N. Giedd, Jonathan Blumenthal, Neal O. Jeffries, F. Xavier Castellanos, Hong Liu, Alex Zijdenbos, et al., "Brain Development during Childhood and Adolescence: A Longitudinal MRI Study," *Nature Neuroscience* 2.10 (1999): 861.

55. Linda S. Gottfredson, "Mainstream Science on Intelligence: An Editorial with 52 Signatories, History, and Bibliography," *Intelligence* 24.1 (1997): 13–23.

56. Robert Plomin and Ian J. Deary, "Genetics and Intelligence Differences: Five Special Findings," *Molecular Psychiatry* 20.1 (2015): 98.

57. A. J. F. Griffiths, Susan R. Wessler, Richard C. Lewontin, William M. Gelbart, David T. Suzuki, and Jeffrey H. Miller, "Quantifying Heritability," in *An Introduction to Genetic Analysis*, 7th ed. (New York: W. H. Freeman, 2000), https://www.ncbi.nlm.nih.gov/books/NBK21866/.

58. Tinca Polderman, Beben Benyamin, Christiaan A. De Leeuw, Patrick F. Sullivan, Arjen Van Bochoven, Peter M. Visscher, and Danielle Posthuma, "Meta-Analysis of the Heritability of Human Traits Based on Fifty Years of Twin Studies," *Nature Genetics* 47 (2015): 702–9, http://match.ctglab.nl/.

59. MaTCH, Meta-Analysis of Twin Correlations and Heritability, http://match.ctglab.nl/#/specific/plot1 (accessed June 2, 2019). Despite common claims to the contrary, the heritability estimates do not show a tendency to increase with age. They are lowest for children at or below 11 and adults over 65, with no increase from teen years to prime working years.

60. Amelia R. Branigan, Kenneth J. McCallum, and Jeremy Freese, "Variation in the Heritability of Educational Attainment: An International Meta-Analysis," *Social Forces* 92.1 (2013): 109–40.

61. Hannah Gordon, Frederik Trier Moller, Vibeke Andersen, and Marcus Harbord, "Heritability in Inflammatory Bowel Disease: From the First Twin Study to Genome-Wide Association Studies," *Inflammatory Bowel Diseases* 21.6 (2015): 1428–34.

62. Richard E. Nisbett, Joshua Aronson, Clancy Blair, William Dickens, James Flynn, Diane F. Halpern, and Eric Turkheimer, "Intelligence: New Findings and Theoretical Developments," *American Psychologist* 67.2 (2012): 130.

63. Eric Turkheimer, Andreana Haley, Mary Waldron, Brian d'Onofrio, and Irving I. Gottesman, "Socioeconomic Status Modifies Heritability of IQ in Young Children," *Psychological Science* 14. 6 (2003): 623–28.

64. I am grateful to Eric Turkheimer and Dalton Conley for helping me clarify this over personal communication.

65. Roar Fosse, Jay Joseph, and Ken Richardson, "A Critical Assessment of the Equal-Environment Assumption of the Twin Method for Schizophrenia," *Frontiers in Psychiatry* 6 (2015): 62.

66. MaTCH, Meta-Analysis of Twin Correlations and Heritability, http://match.ctglab.nl/#/specific/plot1 (accessed June 2, 2019).

67. Elizabeth Suhay, Nathan P. Kalmoe, Leon Porter, Perry Silverschanz, Abby Stewart, Laura Stoker, Jennifer Talarico, et al., "The Equal Environment Assumption in Twin Studies of Political Traits: Social Confounds and Suggested Remedies," unpublished manuscript, 2010, http://sites.lafayette.edu/suhaye/files/2011/01/Violations-ofthe-EEA-Suhay-Kalmoe.pdf.

68. T. J. Bouchard, D. T. Lykken, M. McGue, N. L. Segal, and A. Tellegen, "Sources of Human Psychological Differences: The Minnesota Study of Twins Reared Apart," *Science* 250.4978 (1990): 223–28. The education of adopted mothers is strongly similar (0.41) for twins reared apart. The authors suggest that this doesn't matter because they find no correlation between twin IQ and adopted mother education, but that is surely a fault of the database's low sample size (56 twin pairs) and does not reflect the reality of the relationship. Adoption studies consistently find that the educational attainment of the adopted mother (and father) strongly predicts IQ. For example, see Mikael Lindahl, Anders Björklund, and Erik Plug, *Intergenerational Effects in Sweden: What Can We Learn from Adoption Data?* IZA Discussion paper series, No. 1194, 2004.

69. Peter M. Visscher, Sarah E. Medland, Manuel A. R. Ferreira, Katherine I. Morley, Gu Zhu, Belinda K. Cornes, Grant W. Montgomery, et al., "Assumption-Free Estimation of Heritability from Genome-Wide Identity-by-Descent Sharing between Full Siblings," *PLoS Genetics* 2.3 (2006): e41.

70. Alexander I. Young, Michael L. Frigge, Daniel F. Gudbjartsson, Gudmar Thorleifsson, Gyda Bjornsdottir, Patrick Sulem, Gisli Masson, et al., "Estimating Heritability without Environmental Bias," *bioRxiv* (Novermber 14, 2017): 218883, https://www.biorxiv.org/content/10.1101/218883v1. See also Alexander I. Young, Michael L. Frigge, Daniel F. Gudbjartsson, Gudmar Thorleifsson, Patrick Sulem, Gisli Masson, Unnur Thorsteinsdottir, et al., "Relatedness Disequilibrium Regression Estimates Heritability without Environmental Bias," *Nature Genetics* 50 (2018): 1304–10.

71. Cornelius A. Rietveld, Sarah E. Medland, Jaime Derringer, Jian Yang, Tõnu Esko, Nicolas W. Martin, Harm-Jan Westra, et al., "GWAS of 126,559 Individuals Identifies Genetic Variants Associated with Educational Attainment," *Science* 340.6139 (2013): 1467–71.

72. Rietveld et al., "GWAS of 126,559 Individuals Identifies Genetic Variants"; for details see supplemental materials at https://doi.org/10.1126/science.1235488.

73. Aysu Okbay, Jonathan P. Beauchamp, Mark Alan Fontana, James J. Lee, Tune H. Pers, Cornelius A. Rietveld, Patrick Turley, et al., "Genome-Wide Association Study Identifies 74 Loci Associated with Educational Attainment," *Nature (London)* 533.7604 (2016): 53.

74. Okbay et al., "Genome-Wide Association Study Identifies 74 Loci"; supplemental information available at http://ssgac.org/documents/SI_74_loci_educational_attainment.pdf.

75. James J. Lee, Robbee Wedow, Aysu Okbay, Edward Kong, Omeed Maghzian, Megan Zacher, Tuan Ahn Nguyen-Viet, et al., "Gene Discovery and Polygenic Prediction from a 1.1-Million-Person GWAS of Educational Attainment," *Nature Genetics* 50.8 (2018): 1112–21.

76. Social Science Genetic Association Consortium, Frequently Asked Questions, https://www.thessgac.org/faqs (accessed May 26, 2018).

77. Augustine Kong, Gudmar Thorleifsson, Michael L. Frigge, Bjarni J. Vilhjalmsson, Alexander I. Young, Thorgeir E. Thorgeirsson, Stefania Benonisdottir, et al., "The Nature of Nurture: Effects of Parental Genotypes," *Science* 359.6374 (2018): 424–28.

78. D. Belsky, B. Domingue, R. Wedow, L. Arseneault, J. Boardman, A. Caspi, D. Conley, et al., "Genetic Analysis of Social Class Mobility: Evidence from Five Longitudinal Studies," *Proceedings of the National Academy of Sciences* (2018), doi:10.1073/pnas.1801238115.

79. See supplementary text for Lee et al., "Gene Discovery and Polygenic Prediction."

80. Nicholas Papageorge and Kevin Thom, "Genes, Education, and Labor Market Outcomes: Evidence from the Health and Retirement Study" (May 31, 2017), https://ssrn.com/abstract=2982606 or http://dx.doi.org/10.2139/ssrn.2982606.

81. Belsky et al., "Genetic Analysis of Social Class Mobility."

82. Belsky et al., "Genetic Analysis of Social Class Mobility," found a correlation of 0.28 between parental education and genes for education (measured as the polygenic score) in two samples. This value squared is 8 percent, which is the amount of variation explained. They also found a correlation of just 0.12 between "social origins" (parental education, household income, and father's occupation) and the polygenic score in their largest sample, which suggests that a more comprehensive measure of class explains only 1 percent of the variation in genes that predict education.

83. Plato, *The Republic*, trans. Benjamin Jowett (Titan Classics, 2015), 1765 (Kindle ed.).

84. Riccardo E. Marioni, Lars Penke, Gail Davies, Jennifer E. Huffman, Caroline Hayward, and Ian J. Deary, "The Total Burden of Rare, Non-Synonymous Exome Genetic Variants Is Not Associated with Childhood or Late-Life Cognitive Ability," *Proceedings of the Royal Society B* 281.1781 (2014): 20140117. "Rare" in this case meant that the allele was present in less than 1 percent of the population under study; changing that to 5 percent did not change the results.

85. This is based on my analysis of supplementary table 13 in Lee et al., "Gene Discovery and Polygenic Prediction." The average SNP that reaches genome-wide significance has an allele frequency of 0.47. I separately analyzed all ten million SNPs in the authors' file "GWAS_CP_all.txt." The average frequency is the same for all SNPs (.50) as for 13,175 SNPs with p-values below 5×10^{-8} (0.5), all of which are common, with allele frequencies above 1 percent. The analysis won't be applicable to non-Europeans until the polygenic scores can be calculated in larger samples.

86. World Bank data (https://data.worldbank.org/ [accessed May 29, 2019]) show that in 2016, 164 countries had per capita income levels that were lower than the average for high-income countries in 1960, adjusted for inflation, and that many countries had income levels that were a tiny fraction of even the 1960 level for rich countries. Thus, one could reasonably expect that IQ scores for these countries would be well below the IQ scores of rich countries 50 years ago (15 IQ points).

6. THE HISTORICAL CONTINGENCIES OF GROUP DIFFERENCES IN SKILLS

1. Aristotle, *Politics*, trans. Benjamin Jowett, book 3, http://classics.mit.edu/Aristotle /politics.3.three.html.

2. Aristotle, *Politics*, book 1.

3. Quoted in W. E. B. Du Bois, ed., *Black Reconstruction in America: Toward a History of the Part Which Black Folk Played in the Attempt to Reconstruct Democracy in America, 1860–1880* (New York: Routledge, 2017), 2000 (Kindle ed.).

4. Nell Irvin Painter, *The History of White People* (New York: W. W. Norton, 2010); Louis Menand, *The Metaphysical Club* (New York: Macmillan, 2001).

5. Elyce Zenoff Ferster, "Eliminating the Unfit—Is Sterilization the Answer?" *Ohio State Law Journal* 27 (1966): 591.

6. "One Hundred and Forty-Fourth Session," *New York Legislative Documents*, 5: 12–43 (Albany, NY: J. B. Lyon Company, 1921).

7. Pearce Baily, Charles Johnson, and Frank Utter, "State Commission for Mental Defectives, Second Annual Report," in "One Hundred and Forty-Fourth Session," *New York Legislative Documents*, 5: 12–43 (Albany, NY: J. B. Lyon Company, 1921).

8. Thomas C. Leonard, *Illiberal Reformers: Race, Eugenics, and American Economics in the Progressive Era* (Princeton, NJ: Princeton University Press, 2016).

9. Ezra Klein, "The Sam Harris Debate," Vox, April 9, 2018, https://www.vox.com/2018/4/9/17210248/sam-harris-ezra-klein-charles-murray-transcript-podcast.

10. George M. Fredrickson, *Racism: A Short History* (Princeton, NJ: Princeton University Press, 2002).

11. Arthur Jensen, "How Much Can We Boost IQ and Scholastic Achievement?" *Harvard Educational Review* 39.1 (1969): 1–123.

12. Arthur Jensen and J. Phillipe Rushton, "Thirty Years of Research on Race Differences in Cognitive Ability," *Psychology, Public Policy, and Law* 11.2 (2005): 235–94.

13. Richard Herrnstein and Charles Murray, *The Bell Curve: Intelligence and Class Structure in American Life* (New York: Free Press: 1994).

14. Linda S. Gottfredson, "Mainstream Science on Intelligence: An Editorial with 52 Signatories, History, and Bibliography," *Intelligence* 24.1 (1997) 13–23.

15. Heiner Rindermann, David Becker, and Thomas R. Coyle, "Survey of Expert Opinion on Intelligence: Causes of International Differences in Cognitive Ability Tests," *Frontiers in Psychology* 7 (2016): 399.

16. Author's analysis of National Assessment of Education Progress (NAEP) Data Explorer, https://www.nationsreportcard.gov/. Science and reading scores have overlapping 95 percent confidence intervals and differed very slightly.

17. National Center for Education Statistics, *Digest of Education Statistics, 2015*, NCES 2016–014 (Washington, DC: U.S. Department of Education, 2016), chapter 2, https://nces.ed.gov/fastfacts/display.asp?id=171.

18. Anemona Hartocollis and Stephanie Saul, "Affirmative Action Battle Has a New Focus: Asian-Americans," *New York Times*, August 2, 2017. Economist David Card submitted an analysis for the defense in a lawsuit against Harvard, and he concluded that Harvard did not discriminate against Asians because Asian candidates scored lower on nonacademic criteria that are valued by the university. See https://projects.iq.harvard.edu/files/diverse-education/files/expert_report_-_2017-12-15_dr._david_card_expert_report_updated_confid_desigs_redacted.pdf.

19. "Jewish Nobel Prize Winners," JINFO.org, http://www.jinfo.org/Nobel_Prizes.html (accessed May 29, 2019); Charles Murray, "Jewish Genius," *Commentary—New York–American Jewish Committee* 123.4 (2007): 29.

20. Gregory Cochran, Jason Hardy, and Henry Harpending, "Natural History of Ashkenazi Intelligence," *Journal of Biosocial Science* 38.5 (2006): 1–35; Richard Lynn, "IQ, Socio-Economic and Intellectual Achievements of Ashkenazi Jews," *Mankind Quarterly* 52.1 (2011): 3–34; Steven Pinker, "Groups and Genes," *New Republic*, June 26, 2006; Murray, "Jewish Genius"; Nicholas Wade, *A Troublesome Inheritance: Genes, Race and Human History* (New York: Penguin, 2015).

21. Max Roser and Esteban Ortiz-Ospina, "Global Rise of Education," Our World in Data (2019), https://ourworldindata.org/global-rise-of-education, using data from the Wittgenstein Centre for Demography and Global Human Capital (2015), Wittgenstein Centre Data Explorer Version 1.2.

22. Roser and Ortiz-Ospina, "Global Rise of Education."

23. In 1937, Jews comprised 3.7 percent of the U.S. population and remained above 3 percent until the late 1960s. Sidney Goldstein, "American Jewry, 1970: A Demographic Profile," *The American Jewish Yearbook* 72 (1971), 3–88, http://www.jewishdatabank.org/Studies/downloadFile.cfm?FileID=1447. In 1946, Jews comprised 4.4 percent of the U.S.

workforce; "Statistics of Jews," *The American Jewish Yearbook* 42 (1940), 589–632, http://www.ajcarchives.org/AJC_DATA/Files/1940_1941_8_Statistics.pdf.

24. Alvin Chenkin, "National Jewish Population Study, Demographic Highlights" (New York: Council of Jewish Federations and Welfare Funds, 1971), https://www.jewishdatabank.org/databank/search-results/study/304.

25. Maristella Botticini and Zvi Eckstein, *The Chosen Few: How Education Shaped Jewish History, 70-1492* (Princeton, NJ: Princeton University Press, 2012).

26. Botticini and Eckstein, *The Chosen Few.*

27. William V. Harris, *Ancient Literacy* (Cambridge, MA: Harvard University Press, 1989).

28. Harris, *Ancient Literacy.*

29. Botticini and Eckstein, *The Chosen Few*, 72.

30. Murray, "Jewish Genius"; Wade, *A Troublesome Inheritance.*

31. Michael Goldfarb, *Emancipation: How Liberating Europe's Jews from the Ghetto Led to Revolution and Renaissance* (New York: Simon and Schuster, 2009).

32. Lynn, "IQ, Socio-Economic and Intellectual Achievements of Ashkenazi Jews."

33. Herman Rosenthal, J. G. Lipman, Vasili Rosenthal, L. Wygodsky, M. Mysh, and Abraham Galante, "Russia," *Jewish Encyclopedia*, 1906, http://www.jewishencyclopedia.com/articles/12943-russia.

34. Rosenthal et al., "Russia."

35. "Statistics of the Jews," *The American Jewish Year Book*, 20 (1918–1919): 339–352, http://www.ajcarchives.org/AJC_DATA/Files/1918_1919_7_Statistics.pdf.

36. Bernard Wasserstein, *On the Eve: The Jews of Europe before the Second World War* (New York: Simon and Schuster, 2012).

37. Joseph Jacobs and M. Grunwald, "Occupations," The Jewish Encyclopedia, 1906, http://www.jewishencyclopedia.com/articles/11652-occupations.

38. Fabian Waldinger, "Quality Matters: The Expulsion of Professors and the Consequences for PhD Student Outcomes in Nazi Germany," *Journal of Political Economy* 118.4 (2010): 787–831; Petra Moser, Alessandra Voena, and Fabian Waldinger, "German Jewish Émigrés and US Invention," *American Economic Review* 104.10 (2014): 3222–55.

39. Paul Windolf, "The German-Jewish Economic Elite (1900 to 1930)," *Zeitschrift für Unternehmensgeschichte* 56.2 (2011): 135–62.

40. Harry S. Linfield, "The Communal Organization of the Jews in the United States, 1927," *The American Jewish Year Book* 31 (1929): 99–254.

41. Kaufmann Kohler and Joseph Jacobs, "Intermarriage," The Jewish Encyclopedia, 1906, http://www.jewishencyclopedia.com/articles/8137-intermarriage.

42. Petra Moser, "Taste-Based Discrimination at the NYSE—Empirical Evidence from a Shock to Preferences after WWI" (August 20, 2010), https://ssrn.com/abstract=930237 or http://dx.doi.org/10.2139/ssrn.930237.

43. Linfield, "The Communal Organization of the Jews."

44. Windolf, "The German-Jewish Economic Elite."

45. I estimate that there were 1.8 million Episcopalians and 2.3 million Presbyterians living in the United States in 1926, based on data from the 1926 Census of Religious Bodies, from the Association of Religious Data Archives, http://www.thearda.com/Archive/Files/Downloads/1936CENSCT_DL2.asp. There were 4.2 million Jews according to Harry S. Linfield, "The Communal Organization of the Jews in the United States, 1927," *The American Jewish Year Book* 31 (1929): 99–254.

46. Moser, Voena, and Waldinger, "German Jewish Émigrés."

47. Ross Thomson, *Structures of Change in the Mechanical Age: Technological Innovation in the United States, 1790–1865* (Baltimore, MD: Johns Hopkins University Press, 2009); B. Zorina Khan, *The Democratization of Invention: Patents and Copyrights in American Economic Development, 1790–1920* (Cambridge: Cambridge University Press, 2005).

48. Joel Mokyr, "The Economics of Being Jewish," *Critical Review* 23.1–2 (2011): 195–206.

49. "Willem Einthoven," Wikipedia, The Free Encyclopedia, https://en.wikipedia.org/w/index.php?title=Willem_Einthoven&oldid=895209158 (accessed May 19, 2019).

50. Robin Walker, *African American Contributions to Science and Technology*, Reklaw Education Lecture Series Book 12 (Reklaw Education, 2012).

51. "Lewis Howard Latimer," Wikipedia, The Free Encyclopedia, https://en.wikipedia.org/w/index.php?title=Lewis_Howard_Latimer&oldid=897120552 (accessed May 19, 2019); National Inventor's Hall of Fame, https://www.invent.org/inductees/lewis-latimer.

52. National Inventor's Hall of Fame, https://www.invent.org/inductees/elijah-mccoy.

53. "George Washington Carver," Wikipedia, The Free Encyclopedia, https://en.wikipedia.org/w/index.php?title=George_Washington_Carver&oldid=893757901 (accessed May 19, 2019).

54. National Inventor's Hall of Fame, https://www.invent.org/inductees/george-washington-carver.

55. "Sarah Boone," Wikipedia, The Free Encyclopedia, https://en.wikipedia.org/w/index.php?title=Sarah_Boone&oldid=893843422 (accessed May 19, 2019); "Miriam Benjamin," Wikipedia, The Free Encyclopedia, https://en.wikipedia.org/w/index.php?title=Miriam_Benjamin&oldid=887264204 (accessed May 19, 2019).

56. Henry E. Baker, "The Negro in the Field of Invention," *Journal of Negro History* 2.1 (1917): 21–36. See also U.S. Patent and Trademark Office, "African Americans Hold Patents on Important Inventions," February 9, 2002, https://www.uspto.gov/about-us/news-updates/african-americans-hold-patents-important-inventions.

57. "Ellen Eglin," Wikipedia, The Free Encyclopedia, https://en.wikipedia.org/w/index.php?title=Ellen_Eglin&oldid=889447040 (accessed May 19, 2019).

58. The 1.8 percent figure is from Ufuk Akcigit, John Grigsby, and Tom Nicholas, *The Rise of American Ingenuity: Innovation and Inventors of the Golden Age*, no. w23047 (Cambridge, MA: National Bureau of Economic Research, 2017). The 3–10 percent figure is from Sarada, Michael Andrews, and Nicola Ziebarth, "Historical Changes in the Demographics of Inventors in the United States" (January 30, 2017), https://ssrn.com/abstract=2908160.

59. I used full-count 1920 census data from IPUMS USA to estimate black population shares in the South and outside of it. Steven Ruggles, Sarah Flood, Ronald Goeken, Josiah Grover, Erin Meyer, Jose Pacas, and Matthew Sobek. IPUMS USA: Version 9.0 [1920] (Minneapolis, MN: IPUMS, 2019), https://doi.org/10.18128/D010.V9.0.

60. Lisa D. Cook, "Inventing Social Capital: Evidence from African American Inventors, 1843–1930," *Explorations in Economic History* 48.4 (2011): 507–18.

61. Akcigit, Grigsby, and Nicholas, *The Rise of American Ingenuity*, figure 4B.

62. Akcigit, Grigsby, and Nicholas, "Immigration and the Rise of American Ingenuity," 327–31.

63. Baker, "The Negro in the Field of Invention."

64. Solomon Northrup and David Wilson, "Twelve Years a Slave: Narrative of Solomon Northrup, a Citizen of New-York, Kidnapped in Washington City in 1841, and Rescued in

1853, from a Cotton Plantation Near the Red River, Louisiana," in *I Was Born a Slave: An Anthology of Classic Slave Narratives*, ed. Yuval Taylor and Marshall Joseph Becker, repr. in *African Diaspora Archaeology Newsletter* 6.3 (1999): article 7, https://scholarworks.umass.edu /adan/vol6/iss3/7.

65. Christianna Elrene and Thomas Hurford, "'In His Arm the Scar': Medicine, Race, and the Social Implications of the 1721 Inoculation Controversy on Boston," PhD dissertation, Ohio State University, 2010.

66. J. McKeen Cattell, "A Further Statistical Study of American Men of Science," *Science* 32.827 (1910): 633–48; J. McKeen Cattell, "A Statistical Study of American Men of Science III. The Distribution of American Men of Science," *Science* 24.623 (1906): 732–42.

67. Frederick Douglass, "At Last, at Last, the Black Man Has a Future: An Address Delivered in Albany, NY, on 22 April 1870," *Albany Evening Journal*, April 23, 1970, http:// frederickdouglass.infoset.io/islandora/object/islandora%3A2429.

68. "Madam C. J. Walker," Wikipedia, The Free Encyclopedia, https://en.wikipedia.org /w/index.php?title=Madam_C._J._Walker&oldid=896974633 (accessed May 19, 2019).

69. Lynn, "IQ, Socio-Economic and Intellectual Achievements of Ashkenazi Jews."

70. Lynn, "IQ, Socio-Economic and Intellectual Achievements of Ashkenazi Jews."

71. Richard Lynn, *The Chosen People: A Study of Jewish Intelligence and Achievement* (Augusta, GA: Washington Summit Publishers, 2011).

72. Lynn, *The Chosen People.*

73. J. Philippe Rushton, "Race, Intelligence, and the Brain: The Errors and Omissions of the 'Revised' Edition of S. J. Gould's *The Mismeasure of Man* (1996)," *Personality and Individual Differences* 23.1 (1997): 169–80; Lynn, "IQ, Socio-Economic and Intellectual Achievements of Ashkenazi Jews"; Murray, "Jewish Genius."

74. Audrey M. Shuey, *The Testing of Negro Intelligence* (New York: Social Science Press, 1966).

75. Data from the 1936 Census of Religious Bodies is from the Association of Religious Data Archives, http://www.thearda.com/Archive/Files/Downloads/1936CENSCT_DL2 .asp.

76. This figure is from the 1930 U.S. Census, using data from IPUMS NHGIS (Steven Manson, Jonathan Schroeder, David Van Riper, and Steven Ruggles. IPUMS National Historical Geographic Information System: Version 13.0 [Database] (Minneapolis: University of Minnesota, 2018), http://doi.org/10.18128/D050.V13.0.

77. Erich Rosenthal, "The Equivalence of United States Census Data for Persons of Russian Stock or Descent with American Jews: An Evaluation," *Demography* 12.2 (1975): 275–90.

78. Carl C. Brigham, *A Study of American Intelligence* (Princeton, NJ: Princeton University Press, 1923), table 28.

79. Charles S. Berry, "The Classification by Tests of Intelligence of Ten Thousand First-Grade Pupils," *Journal of Educational Research* 6.3 (1922): 185–203.

80. U. S. Bureau of Labor Statistics, National Longitudinal Surveys, https://www.bls.gov /nls/home.htm.

81. For a cautious analysis ignored by Lynn of the scores of Anglo-Saxons in New York compared to Jews, see Zecharia Dershowitz, Yaakov Frankel, and Brendan A. Maher, "Jewish Culture and the WISC and WAIS Test Patterns," *Journal of Consulting and Clinical Psychology* 43.2 (1975): 126–34; Z. Dershowitz, "Influences of Cultural Patterns on the Thinking of Children in Certain Ethnic Groups: A Study of the Effect of Jewish Subculture on the Field-Dependence-Independence Dimension of Cognition," unpublished doctoral dis-

sertation, New York University, 1966. Dershowitz's results provide evidence that Jewish children had the same IQ scores as Anglo-Saxon children with the same class background.

82. Lauress L. Wise and Donald Hatch McLaughlin, *The Project TALENT Data Bank Handbook* (Palo Alto, CA: American Institutes for Research, 1977), https://www.projecttalent.org/about/history/. The IQ score is labeled "IQ composite" in the database and consists of 25 percent abstract reasoning, 24 percent mathematical reasoning, and 51 percent reading comprehension.

83. Samson D. Oppenheim, "The Jewish Population of the United States," *The American Jewish Year Book* 20 (1918), 31–74.

84. Berry, "The Classification by Tests of Intelligence."

85. Yiddish Melbourne, Monash University, http://future.arts.monash.edu/yiddish-melbourne/statistics/ (accessed February 20, 2018).

86. The entire U.S. population was estimated to be 3 percent Jewish at the time, according to World Jewish Population, http://www.ajcarchives.org/AJC_DATA/Files/1961_16_WJP.pdf.

87. In other ways, the Project Talent data appear to be representative of the Jewish population. Among the children of Yiddish speakers in the database, 28 percent have at least one parent with a bachelor's degree, compared with 19 percent of children from non-Yiddish-speaking households. Likewise, 36 percent of the fathers of Yiddish-speaking children worked in a job as a professional, manager, or business owner, compared to 21 percent of non-Yiddish-speaking white fathers. Boris Levinson, "A Comparison of the Performance of Bilingual and Monolingual Native-Born Jewish Preschool Children of Traditional Parentage on Four Intelligence Tests," *Journal of Clinical Psychology* 15.1 (1959): 74–76, finds that the fathers of applicants to private school in New York City had a similar share working in professional and managerial roles (37 percent).

88. Levinson, "A Comparison of the Performance of Bilingual and Monolingual Native-Born Jewish Preschool Children." I adjusted the WISC scores by 1 IQ point to adjust for the Flynn effect, since Levinson used the 1949 standard on a 1959 population.

89. James Coleman et al., *Equality of Educational Opportunity* (Washington, DC: U.S. Department of Health, Wealth, and Education: 1966), table 9. Asian first-grade students scored higher than white people on nonverbal, but all other scores shown suggest lower Asian scores. The mean is 50 and standard deviation is 10, according to Coleman. Translating this into an IQ score with mean 100 and standard deviation 15 is straightforward.

90. Thomas Sowell, "Ethnicity and IQ," *American Spectator* 28 (February 1, 1995), 32; Thomas Sowell, *Ethnic America: A History* (New York: Basic Books, 1981).

91. Chinese National Statistics, "[Table] 2–14 Population Aged 6 and Over by Sex, Educational Attainment and Region" (2015), http://www.stats.gov.cn/tjsj/ndsj/2016/indexeh.htm.

92. Tom Loveless, "PISA's China Problem" (Washington, DC: The Brown Center Chalkboard, The Brookings Institution, 2013); Duoduo Xu and Jaap Dronkers, "Migrant Children in Shanghai: A Research Note on the PISA-Shanghai Controversy," *Chinese Sociological Review* 48.3 (2016): 271–95.

93. Amanda Wise, "Behind Singapore's PISA Rankings Success and Why Other Countries May Not Want to Join the Race," *The Conversation*, December 8, 2016, http://www.abc.net.au/news/2016-12-08/behind-singapore-pisa-rankings-success/8104074.

94. Singapore, Ministry of Education, *Education Statistics Digest* (2017), xiv, https://www.moe.gov.sg/docs/default-source/document/publications/education-statistics-digest/esd_2017.pdf.

95. Survey of Adult Skills, OECD Skills Surveys, 2011–2015, https://www.oecd.org /skills/piaac/data/.

96. Knut Tveit, "The Development of Popular Literacy in the Nordic Countries. A Comparative Historical Study," *Scandinavian Journal of Educational Research* 35.4 (1991): 241–52.

97. Samuel Bowles and Herbert Gintis, *A Cooperative Species: Human Reciprocity and Its Evolution* (Princeton, NJ: Princeton University Press, 2011), 449–50.

98. Deirdre N. McCloskey, *Bourgeois Dignity: Why Economics Can't Explain the Modern World* (Chicago: University of Chicago Press, 2010).

99. Adam Fox, "Words, Words, Words: Education and Literacy and Print," in *A Social History of England, 1500–1750*, ed. Keith Wrightson (Cambridge: Cambridge University Press, 2017), 134.

100. J. S. Reynolds, "Virtue and Intelligence under Foot: Reconstruction in South Carolina," in Walter Lynwood Fleming, *Documentary History of Reconstruction, Political, Military, Social, Religious, Educational & Industrial, 1865 to the Present Time*, ed. Walter Lynwood Fleming (Cleveland, OH: A. H. Clark Company, 1907), 1: 424–25.

101. Du Bois, *Black Reconstruction in America*.

102. Eric Foner, *Reconstruction: America's Unfinished Revolution, 1863–1877* (New York: Harper Collins, 2011).

103. Du Bois, *Black Reconstruction in America*, 15149 (Kindle ed.).

104. Walter Lynwood Fleming, *Documentary History of Reconstruction, Political, Military, Social, Religious, Educational & Industrial, 1865 to the Present Time*, vol. 2 (Cleveland, OH: A.H. Clark Company, 1907), 184–85.

105. IPUMS-USA, Version 9.0 [Datasets for 1870, 1880, 1890, 1900, 1910]. Minneapolis, MN: IPUMS, 2019, https://doi.org/10.18128/D010.V9.0; restricted to population with at least one U.S.-born parent between ages 20 and 30.

106. Trevon D. Logan, *Do Black Politicians Matter?* no. w24190 (Cambridge, MA: National Bureau of Economic Research, 2018).

107. Nicole Spear, "Adopted Children's Outcomes as Young Adults in Regards to Educational Attainment and Income," *Park Place Economist* 17 (2009), http://digitalcommons .iwu.edu/parkplace/vol17/iss1/16; Anders Björklund, Mikael Lindahl, and Erik Plug, "The Origins of Intergenerational Associations: Lessons from Swedish Adoption Data," *Quarterly Journal of Economics* 121.3 (2006): 999–1028.

108. Data analyzed are from the U.S. Bureau of Labor Statistics, National Longitudinal Survey of Youth (NLSY) 1997 cohort, 1997–2013 (rounds 1–16), https://www.bls.gov/nls /nlsy97.htm. We can also use this for the 1979 version: U.S. Bureau of Labor Statistics, National Longitudinal Survey of Youth (NLSY) 1979 cohort, 1979–2012 (rounds 1–25), https://www.bls.gov/nls/nlsy79.htm.

109. Loren M. Marulis and Susan B. Neuman, "The Effects of Vocabulary Intervention on Young Children's Word Learning: A Meta-Analysis," *Review of Educational Research* 80.3 (2010): 300–35.

110. David K. Dickinson, Julie A. Griffith, Roberta Michnick Golinkoff, and Kathy Hirsh-Pasek, "How Reading Books Fosters Language Development around the World," *Child Development Research* (2012): 1–15, https://www.hindawi.com/journals/cdr /2012/602807/. Eileen T. Rodriguez, Catherine S. Tamis-LeMonda, Mark E. Spellman, Barbara A. Pan, Helen Raikes, Julieta Lugo-Gil, and Gayle Luze, "The Formative Role of Home Literacy Experiences across the First Three Years of Life in Children from

Low-Income Families," *Journal of Applied Developmental Psychology* 30.6 (2009): 677–94.

111. John S. Hutton, Tzipi Horowitz-Kraus, Alan L. Mendelsohn, Tom DeWitt, Scott K. Holland, and the C-MIND Authorship Consortium, "Home Reading Environment and Brain Activation in Preschool Children Listening to Stories," *Pediatrics* 136.3 (2015): 466–78.

112. Benjamin N. York, Susanna Loeb, and Christopher Doss, "One Step at a Time: The Effects of an Early Literacy Text Messaging Program for Parents of Preschoolers," *Journal of Human Resources* (2018): 0517-8756R, http://jhr.uwpress.org/content/early/2018/01/03/jhr .54.3.0517-8756R; Matthew A. Kraft and Manuel Monti-Nussbaum, "Can Schools Enable Parents to Prevent Summer Learning Loss? A Text-Messaging Field Experiment to Promote Literacy Skills," *Annals of the American Academy of Political and Social Science* 674.1 (2017): 85–112.

113. Dickinson et al., "How Reading Books Fosters Language Development."

114. Frank Ridzi, Monica Sylvia, Xiaofen Qiao, and Jeff Craig, "The Imagination Library Program and Kindergarten Readiness: Evaluating the Impact of Monthly Book Distribution," *Journal of Applied Social Science* 11.1 (2017): 11–24.

115. Shahin Samiei, Andrew J. Bush, Marie Sell, and Doug Imig, "Examining the Association between the Imagination Library Early Childhood Literacy Program and Kindergarten Readiness," *Reading Psychology* 37.4 (2016): 601–26. The authors report a standard deviation effect of 0.43 on literacy tests, which translates into 6.45 IQ points. The effect was also significant but not as large for math (0.27 standard deviations).

116. These data are from the National Longitudinal Survey of Youth, 1979, https://www .bls.gov/nls/nlsy79.htm.

117. Amy Hsin and Yu Xie, "Explaining Asian Americans' Academic Advantage over Whites," *Proceedings of the National Academy of Sciences* 111.23 (2014): 8416–21.

118. Feyisa Demie and Christabel McLean, "Raising the Achievement of African-Heritage Pupils: A Case Study of Good Practice in British Schools," *Educational Studies* 33.4 (2007): 415–34; Osagie Festus Amayo, "Dimensions of Challenging Parenting Practices: Nigerian Immigrants in the United States," *Journal of Pan-African Studies* 3.2 (2009): 83–100.

119. David H. Uttal, "Beliefs about Genetic Influences on Mathematics Achievement: A Cross-Cultural Comparison," *Genetica* 99.2–3 (1997): 165–72.

120. Uttal, "Beliefs about Genetic Influences on Mathematics Achievement," 171.

121. E. Bettinger, S. Ludvigsen, M. Rege, I. F. Solli, and D. Yeager, "Increasing Perseverance in Math: Evidence from a Field Experiment in Norway," *Journal of Economic Behavior & Organization* 146 (2018): 1–15.

122. Feyisa Demie and Kirstin Lewis, "White Working Class Achievement: An Ethnographic Study of Barriers to Learning in Schools," *Educational Studies* 37.3 (2011): 245–64.

123. "About Dr Anne-Marie Imafidon MBE," http://aimafidon.com/about/.

124. "Wonder Twins: Seven-Year-Olds Are Youngest Ever to Pass A-Level Maths," *Daily Mail*, January 15, 2009, http://www.dailymail.co.uk/news/article-1116584/Wonder-twins -Seven-year-olds-youngest-pass-AS-level-maths.html#ixzz5B4FoArs6; http://ireport.cnn .com/docs/DOC-317180.

125. Laura Roberts and John Bingham, "GCSE Results: Girl, Five, Claims Record While Seven-Year-Old Boy Receives A*," *Daily Telegraph*, August 25, 2010, https://www.telegraph

.co.uk/education/educationnews/7962546/GCSE-results-Girl-five-claims-record-while
-seven-year-old-boy-receives-A.html.

126. "A-Level Success for Twins, Eight," *BBC News*, August 20, 2009, http://news.bbc.co
.uk/2/hi/uk_news/england/berkshire/8211160.stm (accessed May 29, 2019).

7. UNEQUAL ACCESS TO HOUSING MARKETS

1. Andre M. Perry, Jonathan Rothwell, and David Harshbarger, "The Devaluation of Assets in Black Neighborhoods: The Case of Residential Property" (Washington, DC: The Brookings Institution, 2018).

2. David M. Cutler, Edward L. Glaeser, and Jacob L. Vigdor, "The Rise and Decline of the American Ghetto," *Journal of Political Economy* 107.3 (1999): 455–506.

3. Douglas S. Massey and Nancy A. Denton, *American Apartheid: Segregation and the Making of the Underclass* (Cambridge, MA: Harvard University Press, 1993); Ta-Nehisi Coates, "The Case for Reparations," *Atlantic*, June 2014; Richard Rothstein, *The Color of Law: A Forgotten History of How Our Government Segregated America* (New York: Liveright, 2017).

4. William Easterly, "Empirics of Strategic Interdependence: The Case of the Racial Tipping Point," *The BE Journal of Macroeconomics* 9.1 (2009), https://www.degruyter.com/view
/j/bejm.2009.9.1/bejm.2009.9.1.1492/bejm.2009.9.1.1492.xml.

5. Jonathan T. Rothwell, "Racial Enclaves and Density Zoning: The Institutionalized Segregation of Racial Minorities in the United States," *American Law and Economics Review* 13.1 (2011): 290–358.

6. Data from 1890–1960 are from Cutler, Glaeser, and Vigdor, "The Rise and Decline of the American Ghetto." Jacob Vigdor graciously shared data with me. Their 1890–1930 data rely on census wards, which are local voting districts; from 1940–2010, all estimates are based on census tracts, which are like neighborhoods. Wards are much larger and therefore artificially more encompassing, suggesting less segregation. For example, in the District of Columbia, in 2010, there were only 8 wards, with populations ranging from 70,000 to 80,000, but there were 179 census tracts with populations ranging from just under 1,000 to 7,500. To make the ward data comparable, I follow Douglas S. Massey, Jonathan Rothwell, and Thurston Domina, "The Changing Bases of Segregation in the United States," *Annals of the American Academy of Political and Social Science* 626.1 (2009): 74–90, and regress tract segregation measures on ward segregation measures for 1940, when both are available. The resulting equation is used to adjust ward data upward by multiplying by a coefficient (.5 for dissimilarity and .96 for isolation) and adding a constant term (.436 and .166, respectively). Data from 1980–2010 are from John Logan, available at https://s4.ad.brown.edu
/projects/diversity/Data/Download1.htm; see also John R. Logan and Brian J. Stults, "The Persistence of Segregation in the Metropolis: New Findings from the 2010 Census," census brief prepared for Project US2010 (2011), https://s4.ad.brown.edu/Projects/Diversity
/Data/Report/report2.pdf. Data for 1970 were calculated by the author using Steven Manson, Jonathan Schroeder, David Van Riper, and Steven Ruggles, *IPUMS National Historical Geographic Information System [NHGIS]: Version 12.0* [Database] (Minneapolis: University of Minnesota Press, 2017), http://doi.org/10.18128/D050.V12.0.

7. Author analysis of IPUMS NHGIS, www.nhgis.org.

8. U.S. Department of the Treasury, Internal Revenue Service, "SOI Tax Stats—Individual Income Tax Statistics—ZIP Code Data," https://www.irs.gov/statistics/soi-tax-stats-indi
vidual-income-tax-statistics-zip-code-data-soi (accessed June 19, 2019).

9. Gallup-Sharecare Well-Being Index, 2016–2017, https://wellbeingindex.sharecare.com/.

10. Louis Menand, *The Metaphysical Club* (London: Macmillan, 2001); Nell Irvin Painter, *The History of White People* (New York: W. W. Norton, 2010).

11. "WAR IN 'HELL'S KITCHEN': Negroes and Whites Renew Rioting in Eighth Avenue and Many Are Hurt," *New York Times*, August 4, 1898.

12. "WAR IN 'HELL'S KITCHEN.'"

13. Cutler, Glaeser, and Vigdor, "The Rise and Decline of the American Ghetto."

14. Thomas Lee Philpott, *The Slum and the Ghetto* (New York: Oxford University Press, 1978), 159.

15. Philpott, *The Slum and the Ghetto*.

16. Philpott, *The Slum and the Ghetto*, 169.

17. Dale Cockrell, "Jim Crow, Demon of Disorder," *American Music* 14.2 (1996): 161–84.

18. Ira Katznelson, *When Affirmative Action Was White: An Untold History of Racial Inequality in Twentieth-Century America* (New York: W. W. Norton, 2005).

19. "Whites Object to People of Color in the Third Ward," *Chicago Defender*, September 22, 1917, 1.

20. Philpott, *The Slum and the Ghetto*, 165.

21. Gunnar Myrdal, *An American Dilemma: The Negro Problem and Modern Democracy* (New York: Harper Brothers Publishers, 1944), 82.

22. Sam Stavinsky, "500 Attend Rally to Prevent Sale of Homes to Negroes: 500 Protest Home Sales to Negroes," *Washington Post*, November 9, 1947, M1.

23. Cutler, Glaeser, and Vigdor, "The Rise and Decline of the American Ghetto."

24. Rothstein, *The Color of Law*.

25. Philpott, *The Slum and the Ghetto*, 353.

26. Rothstein, *The Color of Law*.

27. Rothstein, *The Color of Law*; Swedish economist Gunnar Myrdal also emphasized the importance of covenants in this influential study. Gunnar Myrdal, *An American Dilemma: The Negro Problem and Modern Democracy* (New York: Harper Brothers, 1944).

28. Massey and Denton, *American Apartheid*; Arnold R. Hirsch, *Making the Second Ghetto: Race and Housing in Chicago, 1940–1960* (Chicago: University of Chicago Press, 2009); Rothstein, *The Color of Law*.

29. Massey and Denton, *American Apartheid*.

30. Margery Austin Turner, Robert Santos, Diane K. Levy, Douglas A. Wissoker, Claudia Aranda, Robb Pitingolo, "Housing Discrimination against Racial and Ethnic Minorities, 2012. Washington, DC: US Department of Housing and Urban Development," *Policy Development and Research*, June 11, 2013, https://www.urban.org/research/publication/housing-discrimination-against-racial-and-ethnic-minorities-2012-full-report.

31. Jacob S. Rugh and Douglas S. Massey, "Racial Segregation and the American Foreclosure Crisis," *American Sociological Review* 75.5 (2010): 629–51.

32. Marvin M. Smith and Christy Chung Hevener, "Subprime Lending over Time: The Role of Race," *Journal of Economics and Finance* 38.2 (2014): 321–44.

33. Henry N. Pontell, William K. Black, and Gilbert Geis, "Too Big to Fail, Too Powerful to Jail? On the Absence of Criminal Prosecutions after the 2008 Financial Meltdown," *Crime, Law and Social Change* 61.1 (2014): 1–13; see also William K. Black discussion with Russ Roberts, "William Black on Financial Fraud," Library of Economics and Liberty, February 6, 2010, http://www.econtalk.org/archives/2012/02/william_black_o.html.

34. Binyamin Applebaum, "A Nonprofit Lender Revives the Hopes of Subprime Borrowers," *New York Times*, February 25, 2014.

35. William A. Fischel, "Zoning Rules" (Cambridge, MA: Lincoln Institute of Land Policy, 2015); Edward L. Glaeser and Bryce A. Ward, "The Causes and Consequences of Land Use Regulation: Evidence from Greater Boston," *Journal of Urban Economics* 65.3 (2009): 265–78; Edward Glaeser, *Triumph of the City: How Urban Spaces Make Us Human* (London: Pan Macmillan, 2011).

36. Jonathan T. Rothwell, "Racial Enclaves and Density Zoning: The Institutionalized Segregation of Racial Minorities in the United States," *American Law and Economics Review* 13.1 (2011): 290–358; Jonathan T. Rothwell and Douglas S. Massey, "Density Zoning and Class Segregation in US Metropolitan Areas," *Social Science Quarterly* 91.5 (2010): 1123–43; Jonathan Rothwell and Douglas S. Massey, "The Effect of Density Zoning on Racial Segregation in US Urban Areas," *Urban Affairs Review* 44.6 (2009): 779–806; Jonathan Rothwell, *Housing Costs, Zoning, and Access to High-Scoring Schools* (Washington, DC: The Brookings Institution, 2012).

37. Jason Rhodes, "The Value of Exclusion: Chasing Scarcity through Social Exclusion in Early Twentieth-Century Atlanta," *Human Geography* 9.1 (2016): 46–67.

38. David M. P. Freund, *Colored Property: State Policy and White Racial Politics in Suburban America* (Chicago: University of Chicago Press, 2010).

39. Thomas C. Leonard, "American Economic Reform in the Progressive Era: Its Foundational Beliefs and Their Relation to Eugenics," *History of Political Economy* 41.1 (2009): 109–41.

40. Rhodes, "The Value of Exclusion," 57.

41. Quoted in Freund, *Colored Property*, 66.

42. Ruth Knack, Stuart Meck, and Israel Stollman, "The Real Story behind the Standard Planning and Zoning Acts of the 1920s," *Land Use Law & Zoning Digest* 48.2 (1996): 3–9.

43. *Village of Euclid v. Ambler Realty Co.*, 272 U.S. 365 (1926).

44. United States National Commission on Urban Problems, *Building the American City—Report of the National Commission on Urban Problems to the Congress and to the President of the United States* (Washington, DC, 1968).

45. Marie Boyd, "Zoning for Apartments: A Study of the Role of Law in the Control of Apartment Houses in New Haven, Connecticut, 1912–1932," *Pace Law Review* 33 (2013): 600.

46. Boyd, "Zoning for Apartments."

47. Boyd, "Zoning for Apartments."

48. Fischel, "Zoning Rules."

49. K. Einstein, M. Palmer, and D. Glick, "Who Participates in Local Government? Evidence from Meeting Minutes," *Perspectives on Politics* 17.1 (2018): 1–19.

50. Jessica Trounstine, "The Geography of Inequality: How Land Use Regulation Produces Segregation and Polarization," University of California Merced Working Paper, July 2018.

51. Rothwell and Massey, "Density Zoning and Class Segregation."

52. Kendra Bischoff and Sean F. Reardon, "Residential Segregation by Income, 1970–2009," in *Diversity and Disparities: America Enters a New Century*, ed. John Logan (New York: Russell Sage, 2014), 208–33.

53. Rothwell and Massey, "Density Zoning and Class Segregation."

54. Gallup World Poll, https://www.gallup.com/analytics/232838/world-poll.aspx (accessed June 19, 2019).

55. The detailed wording is as follows: "Would you recommend the city or area where you live to a friend or associate as a place to live, or not?" "Are you satisfied or dissatisfied with the city or area where you live?" "Do you feel safe walking alone at night in the city or area where you live?" Finally, three questions use the same preface: "In the city or area where you live, are you satisfied or dissatisfied with (1) the educational system or the schools? (2) the availability of good affordable housing? (3) the availability of quality healthcare?"

56. Nada Issa, "Tunisia's Dirty Secret: Five Years after the Revolution, Tunisia's Black Minority Has Yet to Experience the Freedoms Enjoyed by Other Citizens," *Al Jazeera*, March 17, 2016, http://www.aljazeera.com/programmes/peopleandpower/2016/03/tunisia -dirty-secret-160316153815980.html.

57. Siiri Silm and Rein Ahas, "The Temporal Variation of Ethnic Segregation in a City: Evidence from a Mobile Phone Use Dataset," *Social Science Research* 47 (2014): 30–43.

58. David Beckett, "Trends in the United Kingdom Housing Market, 2014" (London: UK Office of National Statistics, 2014), http://webarchive.nationalarchives.gov.uk /20160109144125/http://www.ons.gov.uk/ons/dcp171766_373513.pdf. U.S. data are from the U.S. Agency for Housing and Urban Development, "American Housing Survey for the United States: 2001" (Washington, DC: 2002), https://www.census.gov/prod/2002pubs /h150-01.pdf.

59. John Iceland, Pablo Mateos, and Gregory Sharp, "Ethnic Residential Segregation by Nativity in Great Britain and the United States," *Journal of Urban Affairs* 33.4 (2011): 409–29.

60. Jonathan Laurence and Justin Vaisse, "Understanding Urban Riots in France" (Washington, DC: The Brookings Institution, December 1, 2005), https://www.brookings .edu/articles/understanding-urban-riots-in-france/.

61. Tanvi Misra, "The Othered Paris," *City Lab*, November 16, 2016, https://www.citylab .com/equity/2017/11/the-othered-paris/543597/.

62. British data are from Ceri Peach, "Slippery Segregation: Discovering or Manufacturing Ghettos?" *Journal of Ethnic and Migration Studies* 35.9 (2009): 1381–95. U.S. data are from analysis using IPUMS National Historical Geographic Information System, Version 12.0 (Minneapolis: University of Minnesota, 2017).

63. I use the K = 6,400 threshold, which measures the number of neighbors used in the neighborhood; of those published this is closest to the U.S. census tract median of 4,000 residents. Smaller definitions also yield smaller segregation measures. See B. Malmberg, M. M. Nielsen, E. Andersson, and K. Haandrikman, "Residential Segregation of European and Non-European Migrants in Sweden: 1990–2012," *European Journal of Population* 34.2 (2018): 169–93.

64. Sako Musterd, "Social and Ethnic Segregation in Europe: Levels, Causes, and Effects," *Journal of Urban Affairs* 27.3 (2005): 331–48.

65. Sako Musterd, Szymon Marcińczak, Maarten Van Ham, and Tjit Tammaru, "Socioeconomic Segregation in European Capital Cities. Increasing Separation between Poor and Rich," *Urban Geography* 38.7 (2017): 1062–83.

66. Matthew A. Light, "Different Ideas of the City: Origins of Metropolitan Land-Use Regimes in the United States, Germany, and Switzerland," *Yale Journal of International Law* 24 (1999): 577–611; Sonia Hirt, "Mixed Use by Default: How the Europeans (Don't) Zone," *Journal of Planning Literature* 27.4 (2012): 375–93.

67. Hirt, "Mixed Use by Default."

68. Light, "Different Ideas of the City," 594.

69. Light, "Different Ideas of the City," 595. Emphasis in original.

70. Sonia Hirt, "Home, Sweet Home: American Residential Zoning in Comparative Perspective," *Journal of Planning Education and Research* 33.3 (2013): 292–309; Hirt, "Mixed Use by Default."

8. HOW UNEQUAL ACCESS TO HOUSING PERPETUATES GROUP INEQUALITY AND INJUSTICE

1. Jessica Trounstine, "Segregation and Inequality in Public Goods," *American Journal of Political Science* 60.3 (2016): 709–25.

2. R. Paternoster, J. M. McGloin, H. Nguyen, and K. J. Thomas, "The Causal Impact of Exposure to Deviant Peers: An Experimental Investigation," *Journal of Research in Crime and Delinquency* 50.4 (2013): 476–503.

3. Anne C. Case and Lawrence F. Katz, *The Company You Keep: The Effects of Family and Neighborhood on Disadvantaged Youths*, no. w3705 (Cambridge, MA: National Bureau of Economic Research, 1991).

4. Geoffrey T. Wodtke, David J. Harding, and Felix Elwert, "Neighborhood Effects in Temporal Perspective: The Impact of Long-Term Exposure to Concentrated Disadvantage on High School Graduation," *American Sociological Review* 76.5 (2011): 713–36; Patrick Sharkey and Felix Elwert, "The Legacy of Disadvantage: Multigenerational Neighborhood Effects on Cognitive Ability," *American Journal of Sociology* 116.6 (2011): 1934–81; Geoffrey T. Wodtke, "Duration and Timing of Exposure to Neighborhood Poverty and the Risk of Adolescent Parenthood," *Demography* 50.5 (2013): 1765–88.

5. Jonathan Rothwell and Douglas Massey, "Geographic Effects on Intergenerational Income Mobility," *Economic Geography* 91.1 (2015): 83–106.

6. Raj Chetty, John N. Friedman, Nathaniel Hendren, Maggie R. Jones, and Sonya R. Porter, *The Opportunity Atlas: Mapping the Childhood Roots of Social Mobility*, no. w25147 (Cambridge, MA: National Bureau of Economic Research, 2018), see figure 3, "Geographic Decomposition of Variance in Upward Mobility."

7. Raj Chetty, Nathaniel Hendren, Maggie R. Jones, and Sonya R. Porter, *Race and Economic Opportunity in the United States: An Intergenerational Perspective*, no. w24441 (Cambridge, MA: National Bureau of Economic Research, 2018).

8. Raj Chetty and Nathaniel Hendren, "The Impacts of Neighborhoods on Intergenerational Mobility I: Childhood Exposure Effects," *Quarterly Journal of Economics* 133.3 (2018): 1107–62; Raj Chetty and Nathaniel Hendren, "The Impacts of Neighborhoods on Intergenerational Mobility II: County-Level Estimates," *Quarterly Journal of Economics* 133.3 (2018): 1163–1228.

9. O. Åslund, P.-A. Edin, P. Fredriksson, and H. Gronqvist, "Peers, Neighborhoods, and Immigrant Student Achievement: Evidence from a Placement Policy," *American Economic Journal: Applied Economics* 3.2 (2011): 67–95.

10. P.-A. Edin, P. Fredriksson, and O. Åslund, "Ethnic Enclaves and the Economic Success of Immigrants—Evidence from a Natural Experiment," *Quarterly Journal of Economics* 118.1 (2003): 329–57.

11. Eric D. Gould, Victor Lavy, and M. Daniele Paserman, "Sixty Years after the Magic Carpet Ride: The Long-Run Effect of the Early Childhood Environment on Social and Economic Outcomes," *Review of Economic Studies* 78.3 (2011): 938–73.

12. E. D. Gould, V. Lavy, and M. D. Paserman, "Immigrating to Opportunity: Estimating the Effect of School Quality Using a Natural Experiment on Ethiopians in Israel," *Quarterly Journal of Economics* 119.2 (2004): 489–526.

13. Jonathan Rothwell, "Sociology's Revenge: Moving to Opportunity (MTO) Revisited," The Brookings Institution, Social Mobility Memos, May 6, 2015, https://www.brookings.edu /blog/social-mobility-memos/2015/05/06/sociologys-revenge-moving-to-opportunity -mto-revisited/.

14. Rothwell, "Sociology's Revenge."

15. Jeffrey R. Kling, Jeffrey B. Liebman, and Lawrence F. Katz, "Experimental Analysis of Neighborhood Effects," *Econometrica* 75.1 (2007): 108.

16. J. Ludwig, G. J. Duncan, L. A. Gennetian, L. F. Katz, R. C. Kessler, J. R. Kling, and L. Sanbonmatsu, "Neighborhood Effects on the Long-Term Well-Being of Low-Income Adults," *Science* 337.6101 (2012): 1509.

17. Eleonora Patacchini and Yves Zenou, "Neighborhood Effects and Parental Involvement in the Intergenerational Transmission of Education," *Journal of Regional Science* 51.5 (2011): 987–1013.

18. Rebecca Casciano and Douglas S. Massey, "School Context and Educational Outcomes: Results from a Quasi-Experimental Study," *Urban Affairs Review* 48.2 (2012): 180–204; https://ssrn.com/abstract=1865232 or http://dx.doi.org/10.2139/ssrn.1865232.

19. Heather Schwartz, "Housing Policy Is School Policy: Economically Integrative Housing Promotes Academic Success in Montgomery County, MD," *Education Digest* 76.6 (2011): 42.

20. Sven Hernberg, "Lead Poisoning in a Historical Perspective," *American Journal of Industrial Medicine* 38.3 (2000): 244–54; Herbert Needleman, "Lead Poisoning," *Annual Review of Medicine* 55 (2004): 209–22.

21. Joel Schwartz, "Low-Level Lead Exposure and Children's IQ: A Meta-Analysis and Search for a Threshold," *Environmental Research* 65.1 (1994): 42–55; J. Liu, L. Li, Y. Wang, C. Yan, and X. Liu, "Impact of Low Blood Lead Concentrations on IQ and School Performance in Chinese Children," *PLoS One* 8.5 (2013): e65230.

22. Bruce P. Lanphear, Richard Hornung, Jane Khoury, Kimberly Yolton, Peter Baghurst, David C. Bellinger, Richard L. Canfield, et al., "Low-Level Environmental Lead Exposure and Children's Intellectual Function: An International Pooled Analysis," *Environmental Health Perspectives* 113.7 (2005): 894–99.

23. David C. Bellinger and Andrew M. Bellinger, "Childhood Lead Poisoning: The Torturous Path from Science to Policy," *Journal of Clinical Investigation* 116.4 (2006): 853–57; David Rosner and Gerald Markowitz, "Building the World That Kills Us: The Politics of Lead, Science, and Polluted Homes, 1970 to 2000," *Journal of Urban History* 42.2 (2016): 323–45; Richard Rabin, "Warnings Unheeded: A History of Child Lead Poisoning," *American Journal of Public Health* 79.12 (1989): 1668–74.

24. Centers for Disease Control and Prevention (CDC), "Blood Lead Levels in Children Aged 1–5 Years—United States, 1999–2010," *MMWR: Morbidity and Mortality Weekly Report* 62.13 (2013): 245.

25. Richard G. Newell and Kristian Rogers, "The US Experience with the Phasedown of Lead in Gasoline" (Washington, DC: Resources for the Future, 2003).

26. Bellinger and Bellinger, "Childhood Lead Poisoning."

27. This is also true to some extent for Hispanics. Ingrid Gould Ellen, David M. Cutler, and William Dickens, "Is Segregation Bad for Your Health? The Case of Low Birth Weight [with comments]," *Brookings-Wharton Papers on Urban Affairs* (2000): 203–38.

28. Douglas S. Massey, "Why Death Haunts Black Lives," *Proceedings of the National Academy of Sciences* 114.5 (2017): 800–802.

29. Rebecca Casciano and Douglas S. Massey, "Neighborhood Disorder and Anxiety Symptoms: New Evidence from a Quasi-Experimental Study," *Health & Place* 18.2 (2012): 180–90.

30. Gallup. For description, see "How Does the Gallup U.S. Daily Work?," https://www .gallup.com/174146/gallup-daily-methodology.aspx (accessed May 23, 2019).

31. See Opportunity Insights, https://opportunityinsights.org/ (accessed May 23, 2019). Chetty et al., *The Opportunity Atlas*; Jonathan Rothwell, "The Biggest Economic Divides Aren't Regional. They're Local. (Just Ask Parents.)," *New York Times*, February 12, 2019.

32. Rachel E. Morgan and Grace Kena, "Criminal Victimization, 2016: Revised," U.S. Department of Justice, Bureau of Justice Statistics, NCJ 251150 (October 2018), https://www .bjs.gov/content/pub/pdf/cv16.pdf. For homicide data, see the Federal Bureau of Investigation, *Crime in the USA, 2015, Uniform Crime Report*, expanded table 6, https://ucr.fbi.gov /crime-in-the-u.s/2015/crime-in-the-u.s.-2015/tables/expanded_homicide_data_table_6 _murder_race_and_sex_of_vicitm_by_race_and_sex_of_offender_2015.xls.

33. David J. De Wit, Ellen Lipman, Maria Manzano-Munguia, Jeffrey Bisanz, Kathryn Graham, David R. Offord, Elizabeth O'Neill, et al., "Feasibility of a Randomized Controlled Trial for Evaluating the Effectiveness of the Big Brothers Big Sisters Community Match Program at the National Level," *Children and Youth Services Review* 29.3 (2007): 383–404.

34. District of Columbia Public Schools, Shaw Middle School, 2012–2013 School Scorecard, http://profiles.dcps.dc.gov/pdf/shaw2012.pdf (accessed May 23, 2019).

35. Theola Labbé-DeBose, "Mourners Gather after Fatal Shooting of a Promising 15-Year-Old Boy," *Washington Post*, June 3, 2011.

36. Lizette Alvarez and Cara Buckley, "Zimmerman Is Acquitted in Killing of Trayvon Martin," *New York Times*, July 14, 2013, http://www.nytimes.com/2013/07/15/us/george -zimmerman-verdict-trayvon-martin.html.

37. Jasmine C. Lee and Haeyoun Park, "15 Black Lives Ended in Confrontations with Police. 3 Officers Convicted," *New York Times*, October 5, 2018, https://www.nytimes.com /interactive/2017/05/17/us/black-deaths-police.html.

38. Thomas F. Pettigrew and Linda R. Tropp, *When Groups Meet: The Dynamics of Intergroup Contact* (London: Psychology Press, 2013).

39. Jonathan T. Rothwell, "The Effects of Racial Segregation on Trust and Volunteering in US Cities," *Urban Studies* 49.10 (2012): 2109–36.

40. Roland G. Fryer Jr., *Reconciling Results on Racial Differences in Police Shootings*, no. w24238 (Cambridge, MA: National Bureau of Economic Research, 2018).

41. Roland G. Fryer Jr., "An Empirical Analysis of Racial Differences in Police Use of Force," *Journal of Political Economy* 127.3 (2019), https://www.journals.uchicago.edu/doi /full/10.1086/701423.

42. Cody T. Ross, Bruce Winterhalder, and Richard McElreath, "Resolution of Apparent Paradoxes in the Race-Specific Frequency of Use-of-Force by Police," *Palgrave Communications* 4.1 (2018): 61.

43. New York Civil Liberties Union, "Stop-and-Frisk-Data," https://www.nyclu.org/en /stop-and-Frisk-data (accessed May 23, 2019).

44. Demographic data are from New York City Department of City Planning, http:// maps.nyc.gov/census/, using the precinct office address as the neighborhood; search data are

from author analysis of raw 2014 data from Stop-and-Frisk Data, released by the New York City Police Department and posted online by the New York City Civil Liberties Union, https://www.nyclu.org/en/stop-and-frisk-data.

45. Philip Bump, "The Facts about Stop-and-Frisk in New York City," *Washington Post*, September 26, 2016.

46. Author analysis of data from Howard N. Snyder, Alexia D. Cooper, and Joseph Mulako-Wangota, "Arrests in the United States, 1980–2014," FBI, Uniform Crime Reporting Program, Bureau of Justice Statistics, August 2017, https://www.bjs.gov/index.cfm?ty=datool &surl=/arrests/index.cfm#.

47. U.S. Department of Health and Human Services, Substance Abuse and Mental Health Services Administration, Center for Behavioral Health Statistics and Quality, *National Survey on Drug Use and Health, 2013*, ICPSR35509-v3 (Ann Arbor, MI: Inter-University Consortium for Political and Social Research [distributor], 2015), https://doi.org/10.3886 /ICPSR35509.v3.

48. One can perform this calculation (the probability of being arrested conditional on selling drugs) directly using the database, but it would be hopelessly biased downward, because people who were arrested and then incarcerated, even briefly, could not have completed the survey. Thus, the survey can capture only people who were arrested and not incarcerated or incarcerated earlier in the year and later freed. It works better as a measure of people who "got away with it."

49. I used a logit regression in STATA to perform this calculation. T-stat on black binary variable is 4.7. Sample size is 6,662 men aged 18 to 30 who were either black or white. If I drop age restrictions, I estimate that black males are 4.5 times more likely to be arrested on drug charges, with a z-statistic of 6.3 (sample size is 18,670). U.S. Department of Health and Human Services, *National Survey on Drug Use and Health, 2013*. I defined common illegal drugs as marijuana, heroin, crack, cocaine, LSD, and meth. Drug sales question asked: "During the past 12 months, how many times have you sold illegal drugs?"

50. Author analysis of raw 2014 data from Stop-and-Frisk Data, https://www.nyclu.org /en/stop-and-frisk-data.

51. Centers for Disease Control and Prevention, National Center for Health Statistics, *Compressed Mortality File 1999–2016* on CDC WONDER Online Database, released December 2017. Data are from the *Compressed Mortality File 1999–2016*, series 20, no. 2V, 2017, http://wonder.cdc.gov/cmf-icd10.html, as compiled from data provided by the 57 vital statistics jurisdictions through the Vital Statistics Cooperative Program. My analysis is of deaths from two major ICD-10 categories: "F10–F19 (Mental and behavioral disorders due to psychoactive substance use)," which include opioids, cocaine, marijuana, tobacco; and "X40–X49 (Accidental poisoning by and exposure to noxious substances)."

52. Federal Bureau of Investigation, *Crime in the United States, 2013*, https://ucr.fbi.gov /crime-in-the-u.s/2013/crime-in-the-u.s.-2013/tables/table-43.

53. United States Department of Health and Human Services, Substance Abuse and Mental Health Services Administration, Center for Behavioral Health Statistics and Quality, *National Survey on Drug Use and Health, 2013*, ICPSR35509-v1 (Ann Arbor, MI: Inter-University Consortium for Political and Social Research [distributor], 2014-11-18), http:// doi.org/10.3886/ICPSR35509.v1.

54. Federal Bureau of Investigation, *Crime in the United States, 2013*.

55. For thorough discussion of this topic, see Michelle Alexander, *The New Jim Crow: Mass Incarceration in the Age of Colorblindness* (New York: New Press, 2010).

56. Jonathan Rothwell, "Drug Offenders in American Prisons: The Critical Distinction between Stock and Flow" (Washington, DC: The Brookings Institution, November 25, 2015).

57. Bruce Western, "The Impact of Incarceration on Wage Mobility and Inequality," *American Sociological Review* 67.4 (2002): 526–46; Isabel V. Sawhill, Scott Winship, and Kerry Searle Grannis, "Pathways to the Middle Class: Balancing Personal and Public Responsibilities," *Issues in Science and Technology* 29.2 (2013): 47–54.

9. UNEQUAL ACCESS TO THE BUYING AND SELLING
OF PROFESSIONAL SERVICES

1. Darryl R. Biggar and Michael Owen Wise, "Competition in Professional Services" (February 3, 2000), OECD, Best Practice Roundtables in Competition Policy No. 27, https://ssrn.com/abstract=318763 or http://dx.doi.org/10.2139/ssrn.318763.

2. Sheilagh Ogilvie, "The Economics of Guilds," *Journal of Economic Perspectives* 28.4 (2014): 169–92.

3. Author analysis of data from OECD.STAT, "Health Care Resources: Remuneration of Health Professionals," https://stats.oecd.org/ (accessed April 3, 2018).

4. My analysis of IPUMS USA 2012–2016 American Community Survey, using the "occ-soc" category "physicians and surgeons"; see Steven Ruggles, Sarah Flood, Ronald Goeken, Josiah Grover, Erin Meyer, Jose Pacas, and Matthew Sobek, IPUMS USA: Version 9.0 [2012–2016 American Community Survey] (Minneapolis, MN: IPUMS, 2019), https://doi.org/10.18128/D010.V9.0.

5. Eurostat data show that 37 percent of doctors in Belgium are general practitioners and that all doctors are compensated at a level 4.5 times that of the average Belgian; physicians, by specialty, http://ec.europa.eu/eurostat/statistics-explained/index.php?title=File:Physicians,_by_speciality,_2015_HLTH17.png (accessed May 30, 2019). The corresponding figure for the United States using IPUMS USA data from 2012–2016 is 4.9, as reported in the text.

6. My analysis of IPUMS USA, 2012–2016 data from the U.S. Census Bureau's American Community Survey.

7. "Is Medical School Worth It Financially?," Best Medical Degrees, http://www.bestmedicaldegrees.com/is-medical-school-worth-it-financially/ (accessed June 4, 2019); "Net Price at For-Profit Institutions by Dependency Status and Income, 2011–12," Trends in Higher Education, https://trends.collegeboard.org/college-pricing/figures-tables/net-price-for-profit-institutions-dependency-status-income-2011-12 (accessed June 4, 2019).

8. Leiyu Shi and Douglas A. Singh, "The Evolution of Health Services in the United States," chap. 3 in *Delivering Health Care in America: A Systems Approach* (Burlington, MA: Jones & Bartlett Learning, 2014).

9. Institute of Medicine, *The Future of Nursing: Leading Change, Advancing Health* (Washington, DC: The National Academies Press, 2011).

10. M. Laurant, D. Reeves, R. Hermens, J. Braspenning, R. Grol, and B. Sibbald, "Substitution of Doctors by Nurses in Primary Care," *Cochrane Database of Systematic Reviews* no. 4 (2004): art. no.: CD001271, doi: 10.1002/14651858.CD001271.pub2.

11. Chris Hafner-Eaton and Laurie K. Pearce, "Birth Choices, the Law, and Medicine: Balancing Individual Freedoms and Protection of the Public's Health," *Journal of Health Politics, Policy and Law* 19.4 (1994): 813–35.

12. Kenneth C. Johnson and Betty-Anne Daviss, "Outcomes of Planned Home Births with Certified Professional Midwives: Large Prospective Study in North America," *BMJ* 330.7505 (2005): 1416.

13. Brian Dulisse and Jerry Cromwell, "No Harm Found When Nurse Anesthetists Work without Supervision by Physicians," *Health Affairs* 29.8 (2010): 1469–75.

14. American Association of Nurse Practitioners, "State Practice Environment," https://www.aanp.org/legislation-regulation/state-legislation/state-practice-environment/66-legislation-regulation/state-practice-environment/1380-state-practice-by-type (accessed September 2017).

15. American College of Nurse-Midwives, State Resource Center, http://www.midwife.org/State-Resource-Center (accessed May 30, 2019); American Association of Nurse Anesthetists, "State Legislative and Regulatory Requirements (50-state summaries)," http://www.aana.com/advocacy/stategovernmentaffairs/Pages/Federal-Supervision-Rule-Opt-Out-Information.aspx (accessed May 30, 2019).

16. Stephen Isaacs and Paul Jellinek, "Accept No Substitute: A Report on Scope of Practice" (The Physicians Foundation, November 2012), 1.

17. Isaacs and Jellinek, "Accept No Substitute," 1.

18. Isaacs and Jellinek, "Accept No Substitute."

19. Isaacs and Jellinek, "Accept No Substitute."

20. Data in this paragraph are from FollowtheMoney.org, https://www.followthemoney.org/ (accessed May 23, 2019).

21. California Legislative Information, SB-323 Nurse Practitioners: Scope of Practice, https://leginfo.legislature.ca.gov/faces/billVotesClient.xhtml?bill_id=201520160SB323 (accessed May 23, 2019); contributions data are from FollowtheMoney.org, https://www.followthemoney.org/ (accessed May 23, 2019).

22. Elizabeth Aguilera, "Nurse Practitioner Autonomy Bill Fails in State Assembly (updated)," June 30, 2015, http://www.scpr.org/news/2015/06/30/52800/nurse-practitioner-autonomy-bill-fails-in-state-as/.

23. These data are from FollowtheMoney.org, which compiles state campaign disclosure records. The funding here applies to 2014 and 2016 campaigns; see https://www.followthemoney.org/ (accessed May 23, 2019).

24. California Medical Association, "Dangerous Bill Putting Patients in Harm's Way Barely Passes Assembly Committee," Press Release, August 13, 2013, http://www.cmanet.org/news/press-detail/?article=dangerous-bill-putting-patients-in-harms-way.

25. The American Medical Association, House of Delegates, 2017, https://www.ama-assn.org/sites/default/files/media-browser/public/hod/i17-refcommb-annotated.pdf (accessed April 13, 2018); see congratulatory press release supporting the resolution against independent nurse practice from the American Society of Anesthesiologists, https://www.asahq.org/advocacy/fda-and-washington-alerts/washington-alerts/2017/11/ama-adopts-asa-led-resolution-opposing-the-onerous-aprn-initiative.

26. The American Medical Association, "Scope of Practice," https://www.ama-assn.org/about/scope-practice (accessed April 13, 2018). See also American Medical Association, "Physician Assistant Scope of Practice," Advocacy Resource Center, https://www.ama-assn.org/sites/ama-assn.org/files/corp/media-browser/public/arc-public/state-law-physician-assistant-scope

-practice.pdf (accessed May 23, 2019); "Independent Practice of Medicine by Advanced Registered Nurses H-35.988," https://policysearch.ama-assn.org/policyfinder/detail/aprn%20compact?uri=%2FAMADoc%2FHOD.xml-0-2995.xml (accessed May 23, 2019).

27. Edgar Walters, "Medical Authority Bills Spark More Doc Fights," *Texas Tribune*, April 21, 2015, https://www.texastribune.org/2015/04/21/doc-fighting-bills-would-change-scope-medical-prac/.

28. "Quality Eye Care Defense Fund," Texas Ophthalmological Foundation, http://www.texaseyes.org/qedf-lobbying-fund (accessed June 4, 2019).

29. The Center for Responsive Politics, Top Spender, https://www.opensecrets.org/lobby/top.php?showYear=2016&indexType=s (accessed September 29, 2017).

30. Ronald Hamowy, "The Early Development of Medical Licensing Laws in the United States," *Journal of Libertarian Studies* 3 (1979): 73–119.

31. Paul J. Feldstein, *Health Associations and the Demand for Legislation: The Political Economy of Health* (Cambridge, MA: Ballinger Publishing, 1977), 59.

32. Christy Ford Chapin, *Ensuring America's Health: The Public Creation of the Corporate Health Care System* (Cambridge: Cambridge University Press, 2015).

33. Christine C. Kushner, *The Feasibility of Health Care Cooperatives in Rural America: Learning from the Past to Prepare for the Future* (Chapel Hill: University of North Carolina Health Services Research Center, 1991), https://www.shepscenter.unc.edu/rural/pubs/report/WP12.pdf.

34. Data on income are from U.S. Bureau of Economic Analysis, National Income and Product Accounts, "Table 2.1. Personal Income and Its Disposition," https://www.bea.gov/ (accessed June 19, 2019). I divided "personal income" by population to calculate average incomes. Data on health insurance premiums for 2018 are reported by the National Conference of State Legislatures, Health Insurance Premiums and Increases, December 4, 2018, http://www.ncsl.org/research/health/health-insurance-premiums.aspx.

35. Kushner, *The Feasibility of Health Care Cooperatives in Rural America*.

36. Ford Chapin, *Ensuring America's Health*.

37. Paul Starr, *The Social Transformation of American Medicine: The Rise of a Sovereign Profession and the Making of a Vast Industry* (New York: Basic Books, 2008).

38. "Indictment of the American Medical Association for Activities in Washington," *New York Times*, December 21, 1938.

39. J. Brosig-Koch, H. Hennig-Schmidt, N. Kairies-Schwarz, and D. Wiesen, "The Effects of Introducing Mixed Payment Systems for Physicians: Experimental Evidence," *Health Economics* 26.2 (2017): 243–62.

40. Ford Chapin, *Ensuring America's Health*.

41. Karen Smiley, *Medical Billing & Coding for Dummies*, 2nd ed. (Hoboken, NJ: Wiley and Sons, 2015).

42. Bureau of Labor Statistics, Occupational Employment Statistics, Occupational Employment and Wages, May 2018, 29-2071: Medical Records and Health Information Technicians, https://www.bls.gov/oes/current/oes292071.htm.

43. Bureau of Labor Statistics, Occupational Employment Statistics, Occupational Employment and Wages, May 2018, 43-3021: Billing and Posting Clerks, https://www.bls.gov/oes/current/oes433021.htm.

44. It should be said that these numbers understate the actual numbers of billing professionals and doctors, because the Occupational Employment Statistics from which they are derived exclude owners of unincorporated businesses, which describes many doctors, and the self-employed, who contract out their services in the case of records keepers (U.S. Bureau of

Labor Statistics, Occupational Employment Statistics, https://www.bls.gov/oes/home.htm [accessed May 30, 2019]). Census data from 2016 show that there are approximately one million physicians and surgeons. The ratio of administrators to physicians is probably still around 1 to 2, but even 1 to 3 would be excessive.

45. For relevant discussion, see Jonathan Rothwell, "No Recovery: An Analysis of Long-term Productivity Decline" (Washington, DC: Gallup Organization, 2017); C. Peterson and R. Burton, "U.S. Health Care Spending: Comparison with Other OECD Countries" (Washington, DC: Congressional Research Service, 2007).

46. D. Morra, S. Nicholson, W. Levinson, D. Gans, T. Hammonds, and L. Casalino, "U.S. Physician Practices versus Canadians: Spending Nearly Four Times as Much Money Interacting with Payers," *Health Affairs* 30.8 (2011): 1443–50; J. Minnot, "What Are the Costs to Physicians of Administrative Complexity in Their Interactions with Payers?" *Findings Brief: Health Care Financing & Organization* 13.2 (2010): 1–3.

47. A. Jiwani, D. Himmelstein, S. Woolhandler, and J. G. Kahn, "Billing and Insurance-Related Administrative Costs in United States' Health Care: Synthesis of Micro-Costing Evidence," *BMC Health Services Research* 14 (2014): 556, https://bmchealthservres.biomedcentral.com/articles/10.1186/s12913-014-0556-7; E. Wikler, P. Basch, and D. Cutler, *Three Strategies for Reducing Health Care Administrative Costs* (Washington, DC: Center for American Progress, 2012).

48. Centers for Medicare and Medicaid Services, 2016 National Health Expenditure Accounts, https://www.cms.gov/Research-Statistics-Data-and-Systems/Statistics-Trends-and-Reports/NationalHealthExpendData/NationalHealthAccountsHistorical.html.

49. M. H. Michal, M. S. Pekarske, M. K. McManus, and R. Van Deuren, "Corporate Practice of Medicine Doctrine: 50 State Survey Summary" (Madison, WI: Center to Advance Palliative Care and National Hospice and Palliative Care Organization, 2006).

50. OECD, "Health Workforce Policies in OECD Countries: Right Jobs, Right Skills, Right Places" (Paris: OECD, 2016), http://www.oecd.org/publications/health-workforce-policies-in-oecd-countries-9789264239517-en.htm.

51. Canadian Medical Protective Association, "Physicians and Nurse Practitioners: Working Collaboratively as Independent Health Professionals," 2014, https://www.cmpa-acpm.ca/en/advice-publications/browse-articles/2014/physicians-and-nurse-practitioners-working-collaboratively-as-independent-health-professionals.

52. Australian Medical Association, "Independent Nurse Practitioners," 2005, https://ama.com.au/system/tdf/documents/AMA_Independent_Nurse_Practitioner_Position_Statement.pdf?file=1&type=node&id=40709; J. Carvel, "Nurses to Get Far-Reaching Prescribing Powers," *Guardian*, November 10, 2005, 4. For further discussion, see S. Elsom, B. Happell, and E. Manias, "Nurse Practitioners and Medical Practice: Opposing Forces or Complementary Contributions?" *Perspectives in Psychiatric Care* 45.1 (2009): 9–16.

53. H. Eckstein, *Pressure Group Politics: The Case of the British Medical Association* (Stanford, CA: Stanford University Press, 1960), 92.

54. N. Ketel, E. Leuven, H. Oosterbeek, and B. Klaauw, "Do Dutch Dentists Extract Monopoly Rents?," *Journal of Health Economics* 63 (2019): 145–58.

55. Morris M. Kleiner and Kyoung Won Park, "Battles among Licensed Occupations: Analyzing Government Regulations on Labor Market Outcomes for Dentists and Hygienists" (Cambridge, MA: NBER Working Paper 16560, 2010).

56. M. Langelier, B. Baker, and T. Continelli, *Development of a New Dental Hygiene Professional Practice Index by State, 2016* (Rensselaer, NY: Oral Health Workforce Research

Center, Center for Health Workforce Studies, School of Public Health, State University of New York, Albany, November 2016).

57. Oral Health Workforce Research Center, "Variation in Dental Hygiene Scope of Practice by State," http://www.oralhealthworkforce.org/resources/variation-in-dental-hygiene -scope-of-practice-by-state/ (accessed May 30, 2019).

58. David A. Nash, Jay W. Freedman, Kavita R. Mathu-Muju, Peter G. Robinson, Julie Satur, Susan Moffat, Rosemary Kardos, et al., "A Review of the Global Literature on Dental Therapists," *Community Dentistry and Oral Epidemiology* 4 2.1 (2014): 1–10.

59. Jay W. Friedman and Kavita R. Mathu-Muju, "Dental Therapists: Improving Access to Oral Health Care for Underserved Children," *American Journal of Public Health* 104.6 (2014): 1005–9; Mary Jordan, "The Unexpected Political Power of Dentists," *Washington Post*, July 1, 2017, https://www.washingtonpost.com/politics/the-unexpected-political-power -of-dentists/2017/07/01/ee946d56-54f3-11e7-a204-ad706461fa4f_story.html?noredirect =on&utm_term=.57acfb330cc9.

60. United States Supreme Court, *North Carolina State Board of Dental Examiners v. Federal Trade Commission*, 2015, https://www.ftc.gov/system/files/documents/cases/150225nc dentalopinion.pdf.

61. For the first set of evidence, see chapter 5. For the advanced analysis, see John Abowd, Francis Kramarz, Paul Lengermann, Kevin McKinney, and Sébastien Roux, "Persistent Inter-Industry Wage Differences: Rent Sharing and Opportunity Costs," *IZA Journal of Labor Economics* 1.1 (2012): 1–25.

62. Luxembourg Income Study (LIS) Database, 2019, http://www.lisdatacenter.org.

63. OECD, "Competition in Professional Services."

64. Iain Paterson, Marcel Fink, and Anthony Ogus, *Economic Impact of Regulation in the Field of Liberal Professions in Different Member States* (Brussels: CEPS, 2003); OECD, "Competitive Restrictions in Legal Professions 2007," Directorate for Financial and Enterprise Affairs Competition Committee, DAF/COMP (2007) 39 (2009), https://www .oecd.org/regreform/sectors/40080343.pdf. "In Finland, non-lawyers could represent clients in court but since 2002 a law degree is required to perform those services" (Stockholm Institute for Scandinavian Law, "Finnish Bar Association," 52, http://www.scandinavianlaw .se/pdf/46-15.pdf. [accessed May 30, 2019]).

65. Paterson, Fink, and Ogus, *Economic Impact of Regulation*.

66. National Conference of Bar Examiners, 2015 Statistics, http://www.ncbex.org /dmsdocument/195 (accessed May 31, 2019).

67. Society of American Law, "Teachers Statement on the Bar Exam, July 2002," *Journal of Legal Education* 52.3 (2002): 446–52.

68. Seth Williams, "Closing Real Estate Deals with an Attorney—When & Where Is It Required?" REtipster, https://retipster.com/real-estate-closing-agents/ (accessed November 2, 2017).

69. *Goldfarb v. Virginia State Bar*, 421 U.S. 773, 788–789, n. 17, 95 S.Ct. 2004, 2013, 44 L.Ed.2d 572 (1975).

70. The American Bar Association, Model Rules of Professional Conduct, 5.4, https:// www.americanbar.org/groups/professional_responsibility/publications/model_rules_of _professional_conduct/rule_5_4_professional_independence_of_a_lawyer.html (accessed May 31, 2019).

71. ABA Commission on the Future of Legal Services, "For Comment: Issues Paper Regarding Alternative Business Structures," April 8, 2016, http://abafuturesreport.com /#download-full-report.

72. ABA Commission on the Future of Legal Services, "For Comment."

73. Gallup, Honesty/Ethics in Professions, December 3–12, 2018, and December 4–11, 2017, http://news.gallup.com/poll/1654/Honesty-Ethics-Professions.aspx. (Item states, "Please tell me how you would rate the honesty and ethical standards of people in these different fields—very high, high, average, low, or very low?")

74. American Bar Association Consortium on Legal Services and the Public, "Legal Needs and Civil Justice: A Survey of Americans," 1994, https://www.americanbar.org/content/dam/aba/administrative/legal_aid_indigent_defendants/downloads/legalneedstudy.authcheckdam.pdf.

75. Washington State Supreme Court Task Force on Civil Equal Justice Funding, "The Washington State Civil Legal Needs Study," 2003, http://www.courts.wa.gov/newsinfo/content/taskforce/civillegalneeds.pdf.

76. Washington State Supreme Court Task Force on Civil Equal Justice Funding, "2015 Washington State Civil Legal Needs Study Update," http://ocla.wa.gov/wp-content/uploads/2015/10/CivilLegalNeedsStudy_October2015_V21_Final10_14_15.pdf.

77. Solicitors Regulation Authority, "Improving Access—Tackling Unmet Legal Needs," June 2017, https://www.sra.org.uk/risk/resources/legal-needs.page#.

78. Lorelei Laird, "Starved of Money for Too Long, Public Defender Offices Are Suing—and Starting to Win," *ABA Journal*, January 2017, http://www.abajournal.com/magazine/article/the_gideon_revolution; "Attorney General Eric Holder Speaks at the American Bar Association's National Summit on Indigent Defense" (Washington, DC: U.S. Department of Justice, February 4, 2012), https://www.justice.gov/opa/speech/attorney-general-eric-holder-speaks-american-bar-association-s-national-summit-indigent. For facts on overburden of case loads, see Donald J. Farole and Lynn Langton, *County-Based and Local Public Defender Offices, 2007* (Washington, DC: U.S. Department of Justice, Office of Justice Programs, Bureau of Justice Statistics, 2010).

79. Limited Practice Officers, https://www.wsba.org/for-legal-professionals/join-the-legal-profession-in-wa/limited-practice-officers (accessed May 31, 2019); Washington Supreme Court, Admission and Practice Rule 12, "Limited Practice Rule for Limited Practice Officers," https://www.courts.wa.gov/court_rules/?fa=court_rules.display&group=ga&set=apr&ruleid=gaapr12 (accessed May 31, 2019); Williams, "Closing Real Estate Deals with an Attorney."

80. Scott A. Smith, Juan Pablo Paredes, Rebecca M. Baker, and Mark Hanku Kim, "Practice of Law Board Resignations," a letter to the Washington State Supreme Court, November 9, 2015, http://www.abajournal.com/files/Letter_to_Supreme_Court_Explaining_Resignations.pdf.

81. Robert Ambrogi, "Washington State Moves around UPL, Using Legal Technicians to Help Close the Justice Gap," *ABA Journal*, January 2015, http://www.abajournal.com/magazine/article/washington_state_moves_around_upl_using_legal_technicians_to_help_close_the.

82. Ambrogi, "Washington State Moves around UPL."

83. Washington State Court Rules, Admission and Practice Rules, Rule 28, Limited Practice Rule for Limited License Legal Technicians, http://www.courts.wa.gov/court_rules/?fa=court_rules.list&group=ga&set=apr (accessed May 31, 2019).

84. U.S. Bureau of Labor Statistics, Occupational Employment Statistics, 2017, https://www.bls.gov/oes/current/oes_42660.htm#23-0000.

85. Smith et al., "Practice of Law Board Resignations"; Victor Li, "Board Members Quit, Blast Washington State Bar in Fight over UPL, Legal Technicians," *ABA Journal*,

November 9, 2015, http://www.abajournal.com/news/article/Board_members_quit_blast _Washington_State_Bar_in_fight_over_UPL.

86. Smith et al., "Practice of Law Board Resignations."

87. Thomas M. Clarke and Rebecca L. Sandefur, "Preliminary Evaluation of the Washington State Limited License Legal Technician Program," March 2017, p. 9, http://www .americanbarfoundation.org/uploads/cms/documents/preliminary_evaluation_of_the _washington_state_limited_license_legal_technician_program_032117.pdf.

88. Washington State Bar Association, Legal Directory, https://www.mywsba.org /LegalDirectory.aspx (accessed April 16, 2018).

89. My analysis of U.S. Bureau of Economic Analysis, table 6.2D, "Compensation of Employees by Industry" and more recent versions of the same table, as well as table 6.5B, "Full-Time Equivalent Employees by Industry," and its more recent time periods, https://www.bea.gov/.

90. My analysis of IPUMS USA 2012–2016 American Community Survey, using all U.S. residents 18 and older and indnaics.

Tax data analyzed by Jon Bakija, Adam Cole, and Bradley T. Heim, "Jobs and Income Growth of Top Earners and the Causes of Changing Income Inequality: Evidence from US Tax Return Data," unpublished manuscript, Williams College, 2012, who also find that those in medical occupations, lawyers, and financial professionals constitute a larger fraction of the top 1 percent of income earners. They find that 15.7 percent of top income earners are medical workers, 13.9 percent are financial professionals and managers, and 8.4 percent are lawyers.

91. This divides the total number of employees (34,400) by total 2016 compensation and benefits: $11.6 billion. Goldman Sachs, 2016 Annual Report, http://www.goldmansachs.com /investor-relations/financials/current/annual-reports/2016-annual-report/annual-report -2016.pdf.

92. Jacob Sonenshine, "Hedge Fund Managers Are Celebrating Big Pay Increases—Here's How Much You Can Expect to Earn Working at One," *Business Insider*, January 31, 2018, http://www.businessinsider.com/hedge-fund-pay-is-going-up-2018-1.

93. Jonathan Marino, "How Goldman Sachs Makes Money on Its Top Traders—After They Quit," *Business Insider*, May 12, 2015.

94. Usha Rodrigues, "Securities Law's Dirty Little Secret," *Fordham Law Review* 81 (2012): 3389–3437.

95. Abowd et al., "Persistent Inter-Industry Wage Differences"; Brink Lindsey and Steven Teles, *The Captured Economy: How the Powerful Enrich Themselves, Slow Down Growth, and Increase Inequality* (Oxford: Oxford University Press, 2017).

96. Randall S. Kroszner and Philip E. Strahan, "What Drives Deregulation? Economics and Politics of the Relaxation of Bank Branching Restrictions," *Quarterly Journal of Economics* 114.4 (1999): 1437–67.

97. Jith Jayaratne and Philip E. Strahan, "The Finance-Growth Nexus: Evidence from Bank Branch Deregulation," *Quarterly Journal of Economics* 111.3 (1996): 639–70; P. E. Strahan and D. C. Wheelock, "The Real Effects of US Banking Deregulation," commentary, *Review—Federal Reserve Bank of St. Louis* 85.4 (2003): 111–28.

98. Vanguard Mutual Funds, https://investor.vanguard.com/mutual-funds/list#/mutual -funds/asset-class/month-end-returns (accessed June 4, 2019).

99. Alan Rappeport, "A Short History of Hedge Funds," *CFO*, March 27, 2007, http://ww2.cfo.com/banking-capital-markets/2007/03/a-short-history-of-hedge-funds/.

100. U.S. Securities and Exchange Commission, "Updated Investor Bulletin: Accredited Investors," Investor.Gov, January 31, 2019, https://www.investor.gov/additional-re sources/news-alerts/alerts-bulletins/updated-investor-bulletin-accredited-investors.

101. Cary Martin Shelby, "Privileged Access to Financial Innovation," *Loyola University Chicago Law Journal* 47 (2015): 315.

102. Alexander J. Davie, "Accredited Investors vs. Qualified Clients vs. Qualified Purchasers: Understanding Investor Qualifications," *Strictly Business*, blog, August 17, 2017, https://www.strictlybusinesslawblog.com/2017/08/17/accredited-investors-vs-qualified -clients-vs-qualified-purchasers/.

103. Shelby, "Privileged Access to Financial Innovation."

104. KPMG International, "The Value of the Hedge Fund Industry to Investors, Markets, and the Broader Economy" (The Center for Hedge Fund Research, Imperial College London, 2012).

105. "What Are the Hedge Fund Marketing Rules?," Deke Digital, https://www.dekedigital .com/marketing/what-are-the-hedge-fund-marketing-rules/ (accessed June 4, 2019).

106. U.S. Securities and Exchange Commission, Division of Investment Management, "Private Funds Statistics First Calendar Quarter 2017," table 15, https://www.sec.gov /divisions/investment/private-funds-statistics/private-funds-statistics-2017-q1.pdf.

107. Nassim Nicholas Taleb, *Skin in the Game: Hidden Asymmetries in Daily Life* (New York: Random House, 2018).

108. U.S. Securities and Exchange Commission, Division of Investment Management, "Private Funds Statistics First Calendar Quarter 2017," table 14.

10. CREATING A JUST SOCIETY

1. Eric Alden Smith, Kim Hill, Frank W. Marlowe, David Nolin, Polly Wiessner, Michael Gurven, Samuel Bowles, et al., "Wealth Transmission and Inequality among Hunter-Gatherers," *Current Anthropology* 51.1 (2010): 19–34.

2. Robert J. Gordon, *The Rise and Fall of American Growth: The US Standard of Living since the Civil War* (Princeton, NJ: Princeton University Press, 2017).

3. Mancur Olson, *The Rise and Decline of Nations: Economic Growth, Stagflation, and Social Rigidities* (New Haven, CT: Yale University Press, 2008).

4. Brink Lindsey and Steven Teles, *The Captured Economy: How the Powerful Enrich Themselves, Slow Down Growth, and Increase Inequality* (New York: Oxford University Press, 2017).

5. Executive Order 13563—Improving Regulation and Regulatory Review, January 8, 2011, https://www.whitehouse.gov/the-press-office/2011/01/18/executive-order-13563 -improving-regulation-and-regulatory-review.

6. Michael Mandel and Diana G. Carew, "Regulatory Improvement Commission: A Politically-Viable Approach to U.S. Regulatory Reform" (Washington, DC: Progressive Policy Institute, 2013); S.708 Regulatory Improvement Act, https://www.congress.gov/bill /114th-congress/senate-bill/708/text?format=txt (accessed May 31, 2019).

7. Kevin R. Kosar, "Is Regulatory Reform a Hopeless Cause?" (Washington, DC: The Brookings Institution, 2015).

8. Ida Tarbell, *The History of the Standard Oil Company* (New York: McClure, Phillips, and Company, 1904), http://www.pagetutor.com/standard/chapter16_part6.html.

9. Federal Trade Commission, Annual Report, "Enforcement," https://www.ftc.gov /reports/annual-highlights-2015/enforcement (accessed May 31, 2019).

10. Beth Redbird, "The New Closed Shop? The Economic and Structural Effects of Occupational Licensure," *American Sociological Review* 82.3 (2017): 600–624.

11. Jonathan Rothwell, "No Recovery: An Analysis of Long-Term U.S. Productivity Decline" (Washington, DC: Gallup, 2016), https://news.gallup.com/reports/198776/no-recovery-analysis-long-term-productivity-decline.aspx.

12. Rana Foroohar, *Makers and Takers: The Rise of Finance and the Fall of American Business* (New York: Crown Books, 2016).

13. Anat Admati and Martin Hellwig, *The Bankers' New Clothes: What's Wrong with Banking and What to Do about It* (Princeton, NJ: Princeton University Press, 2014).

14. Houman B. Shadab, "Fending for Themselves: Creating a US Hedge Fund Market for Retail Investors," *NYU Journal of Legislature and Public Policy* 11 (2007): 251–319.

15. Mark A. Lemley, "Software Patents and the Return of Functional Claiming," Stanford Public Law Working Paper No. 2117302, October 12, 2012, https://ssrn.com/abstract=2117302 or http://dx.doi.org/10.2139/ssrn.2117302.

16. James Bessen and Michael James Meurer, *Patent Failure: How Judges, Bureaucrats, and Lawyers Put Innovators at Risk* (Princeton, NJ: Princeton University Press, 2008).

17. Mustaqeem Siddiqui and S. Vincent Rajkumar, "The High Cost of Cancer Drugs and What We Can Do about It," *Mayo Clinic Proceedings* 87.10 (2012): 935–43; Vincent Rajkumar, "On the High Price of Cancer Drugs," Library of Economics and Liberty, April 9, 2018, http://www.econtalk.org/archives/2018/04/vincent_rajkuma.html.

18. Jonathan T. Rothwell, "The Effects of Racial Segregation on Trust and Volunteering in US Cities," *Urban Studies* 49.10 (2012): 2109–36; Thomas F. Pettigrew and Linda R. Tropp, "A Meta-Analytic Test of Intergroup Contact Theory," *Journal of Personality and Social Psychology* 90.5 (2006): 751–83.

19. Timothy J. Bartik, "From Preschool to Prosperity: The Economic Payoff to Early Childhood Education" (Kalamazoo, MI: W.E. Upjohn Institute for Employment Research, 2014), https://doi.org/10.17848/9780880994835.

20. Jonathan Rothwell, "No Recovery: An Analysis of Long-Term Productivity Decline" (Washington, DC: Gallup 2016), https://news.gallup.com/reports/198776/no-recovery-analysis-long-term-productivity-decline.aspx.

21. OECD, Table D3.2a, "Teachers' Actual Salaries Relative to Earnings of Tertiary-Educated Workers (2015)," in *Education at a Glance 2017: OECD Indicators* (Paris: OECD, 2017), http://dx.doi.org/10.1787/eag-2017-en; OECD, "Indicator D3: How Much Are Teachers Paid?" *Education at a Glance 2014: OECD Indicators* (Paris: OECD, 2014), http://dx.doi.org/10.1787/888933119815 (accessed May 31, 2019); chart D3.1, "Teachers' Salaries Relative to Earnings for Tertiary-Educated Workers Aged 25–64 (2012)."

22. Rothwell, "No Recovery."

23. Jonathan Rothwell, *The Hidden STEM Economy* (Washington, DC: Metropolitan Policy Program at Brookings, 2013), https://www.brookings.edu/research/the-hidden-stem-economy/.

24. Phillip Toner, "Tradespeople and Technicians in Innovation," in *Fostering Enterprise: The Innovation and Skills Nexus—Research Readings*, ed. Penelope Curtin, John Stanwick, and Francesca Beddie (Adelaide: Australian Government, National Center for Vocational Education Research, 2012); Phillip Toner, Tim Turpin, and Richard Woolley, "The Role and Contribution of Tradespeople and Technicians in Australian Research and Development: An Exploratory Study" (Centre for Industry and Innovation Studies, University of Western Sydney, 2011).

25. Virginia Beach City Public Schools, "21st Century Industry Credentials: An Annual Report of School Performance," http://www.vbschools.com/TCE/content/pdfs/WorkplaceReadinessSkills.pdf (accessed May 10, 2018).

26. Mathilde Almlund, Angela Lee Duckworth, James Heckman, and Tim Kautz, "Personality Psychology and Economics," in *Handbook of the Economics of Education* (Elsevier, 2011), 4:1–81; Falk Leichsenring and Sven Rabung, "Effectiveness of Long-Term Psychodynamic Psychotherapy: A Meta-Analysis," *Journal of the American Medical Association* 300.13 (2008): 1551–65.

27. Martin R. West, "Should Non-Cognitive Skills Be Included in School Accountability Systems? Preliminary Evidence from California's CORE Districts," *Evidence Speaks Reports* 1.13 (2016), https://www.brookings.edu/research/should-non-cognitive-skills-be-included-in-school-accountability-systems-preliminary-evidence-from-californias-core-districts/.

APPENDIX

1. World Inequality Database, https://wid.world/ (accessed June 5, 2019).

2. IPUMS USA, https://usa.ipums.org/usa/ (accessed June 5, 2019).

3. Luxembourg Income Study, https://www.lisdatacenter.org/ (accessed June 5, 2019).

4. Thomas Piketty, Emmanuel Saez, and Gabriel Zucman, *Distributional National Accounts: Methods and Estimates for the United States*, no. w22945 (Cambridge, MA: National Bureau of Economic Research, 2016).

5. American Academy of Family Physicians, https://www.udsmapper.org/zcta-crosswalk.cfm (accessed May 25, 2019).

6. Missouri Census Data Center, Geocorr 2014: Geographic Correspondence Engine, http://mcdc.missouri.edu/websas/geocorr14.html (accessed May 25, 2019).

7. Robert C. Feenstra, Robert Inklaar, and Marcel P. Timmer, "The Next Generation of the Penn World Table," *American Economic Review* 105.10 (2015): 3150–82, www.ggdc.net/pwt.

8. Robert Carroll, "Income Mobility and the Persistence of Millionaires, 1999 to 2007," Tax Foundation Special Report No. 180 (Washington, DC, 2010), https://taxfoundation.org/article/income-mobility-and-persistence-millionaires-1999-2007.

9. Life evaluation is measured by the following item on the Gallup World Poll: "Please imagine a ladder, with steps numbered from 0 at the bottom to 10 at the top. The top of the ladder represents the best possible life for you and the bottom of the ladder represents the worst possible life for you. On which step of the ladder would you say you personally feel you stand at this time?" (https://www.gallup.com/analytics/232838/world-poll.aspx [accessed June 5, 2019]).

10. The World Bank, "GDP per Capita, PPP (Current International $)," https://data.worldbank.org/indicator/NY.GDP.PCAP.PP.CD (accessed June 5, 2019).

11. Charles I. Jones, "The Facts of Economic Growth," in *Handbook of Macroeconomics* (Elsevier, 2016), 2: 3–69; Chang-Tai Hsieh, Erik Hurst, Charles I. Jones, and Peter J. Klenow, *The Allocation of Talent and US Economic Growth*, no. w18693 (Cambridge, MA: National Bureau of Economic Research, 2013).

12. For a related argument, see Kevin M. Murphy, Andrei Shleifer, and Robert W. Vishny, "The Allocation of Talent: Implications for Growth," *Quarterly Journal of Economics* 106.2 (1991): 503–30.

·

INDEX

Page numbers in *italics* refer to figures and tables.